T0320494

Bio–Inspired Computing for Information Retrieval Applications

D.P. Acharjya
School of Computing Science and Engineering, VIT University, India

Anirban Mitra
Vignan Institute of Technology and Management, India

A volume in the Advances in Knowledge Acquisition, Transfer, and Management (AKATM) Book Series

www.igi-global.com

Published in the United States of America by
    IGI Global
    Information Science Reference (an imprint of IGI Global)
    701 E. Chocolate Avenue
    Hershey PA 17033
    Tel: 717-533-8845
    Fax: 717-533-8661
    E-mail: cust@igi-global.com
    Web site: http://www.igi-global.com

Copyright © 2017 by IGI Global. All rights reserved. No part of this publication may be reproduced, stored or distributed in any form or by any means, electronic or mechanical, including photocopying, without written permission from the publisher.
Product or company names used in this set are for identification purposes only. Inclusion of the names of the products or companies does not indicate a claim of ownership by IGI Global of the trademark or registered trademark.

Library of Congress Cataloging-in-Publication Data

Names: Acharjya, D. P., 1969- editor. | Mitra, Anirban, 1979- editor.
Title: Bio-inspired computing for information retrieval applications / D.P.
  Acharjya and Anirban Mitra, editors.
Description: Hershey, PA : Information Science Reference, [2017] | Includes
  bibliographical references and index.
Identifiers: LCCN 2017000184| ISBN 9781522523758 (hardcover) | ISBN
  9781522523765 (ebook)
Subjects: LCSH: Natural computation. | Information storage and retrieval
  systems. | Querying (Computer science) | Database searching.
Classification: LCC QA76.9.N37 B56 2017 | DDC 005.74--dc23 LC record available at https://
lccn.loc.gov/2017000184

This book is published in the IGI Global book series Advances in Knowledge Acquisition, Transfer, and Management (AKATM) (ISSN: 2326-7607; eISSN: 2326-7615)

British Cataloguing in Publication Data
A Cataloguing in Publication record for this book is available from the British Library.

All work contributed to this book is new, previously-unpublished material. The views expressed in this book are those of the authors, but not necessarily of the publisher.

Advances in Knowledge Acquisition, Transfer, and Management (AKATM) Book Series

ISSN:2326-7607
EISSN:2326-7615

MISSION

Organizations and businesses continue to utilize knowledge management practices in order to streamline processes and procedures. The emergence of web technologies has provided new methods of information usage and knowledge sharing.

The **Advances in Knowledge Acquisition, Transfer, and Management (AKATM) Book Series** brings together research on emerging technologies and their effect on information systems as well as the knowledge society. **AKATM** will provide researchers, students, practitioners, and industry leaders with research highlights surrounding the knowledge management discipline, including technology support issues and knowledge representation.

COVERAGE

- Cognitive Theories
- Cultural Impacts
- Information and Communication Systems
- Knowledge acquisition and transfer processes
- Knowledge management strategy
- Knowledge Sharing
- Organizational Learning
- Organizational Memory
- Small and Medium Enterprises
- Virtual Communities

IGI Global is currently accepting manuscripts for publication within this series. To submit a proposal for a volume in this series, please contact our Acquisition Editors at Acquisitions@igi-global.com or visit: http://www.igi-global.com/publish/.

The Advances in Knowledge Acquisition, Transfer, and Management (AKATM) Book Series (ISSN 2326-7607) is published by IGI Global, 701 E. Chocolate Avenue, Hershey, PA 17033-1240, USA, www.igi-global.com. This series is composed of titles available for purchase individually; each title is edited to be contextually exclusive from any other title within the series. For pricing and ordering information please visit http://www.igi-global.com/book-series/advances-knowledge-acquisition-transfer-management/37159. Postmaster: Send all address changes to above address. Copyright © 2017 IGI Global. All rights, including translation in other languages reserved by the publisher. No part of this series may be reproduced or used in any form or by any means – graphics, electronic, or mechanical, including photocopying, recording, taping, or information and retrieval systems – without written permission from the publisher, except for non commercial, educational use, including classroom teaching purposes. The views expressed in this series are those of the authors, but not necessarily of IGI Global.

Titles in this Series

For a list of additional titles in this series, please visit: www.igi-global.com

Managing Knowledge Resources and Records in Modern Organizations
Priti Jain (University of Botswana, Botswana) and Nathan Mnjama (University of Botswana, Botswana)
Business Science Reference • copyright 2017 • 280pp • H/C (ISBN: 9781522519652) • US $185.00 (our price)

Analyzing the Role of Citizen Science in Modern Research
Luigi Ceccaroni (1000001 Labs, Spain) and Jaume Piera (ICM-CSIC, Spain)
Information Science Reference • copyright 2017 • 355pp • H/C (ISBN: 9781522509622) • US $185.00 (our price)

Scholarly Communication and the Publish or Perish Pressures of Academia
Achala Munigal (Osmania University, India)
Information Science Reference • copyright 2017 • 375pp • H/C (ISBN: 9781522516972) • US $190.00 (our price)

Open Source Solutions for Knowledge Management and Technological Ecosystems
Francisco J. Garcia-Peñalvo (University of Salamanca, Spain) and Alicia García-Holgado (University of Salamanca, Spain)
Business Science Reference • copyright 2017 • 297pp • H/C (ISBN: 9781522509059) • US $195.00 (our price)

Handbook of Research on Social, Cultural, and Educational Considerations of Indigenous Knowledge in Developing Countries
Patrick Ngulube (University of South Africa, South Africa)
Information Science Reference • copyright 2017 • 462pp • H/C (ISBN: 9781522508380) • US $265.00 (our price)

Research 2.0 and the Impact of Digital Technologies on Scholarly Inquiry
Antonella Esposito (University of Milan, Italy)
Information Science Reference • copyright 2017 • 343pp • H/C (ISBN: 9781522508304) • US $185.00 (our price)

Handbook of Research on Theoretical Perspectives on Indigenous Knowledge Systems in Developing Countries
Patrick Ngulube (University of South Africa, South Africa)
Information Science Reference • copyright 2017 • 516pp • H/C (ISBN: 9781522508335) • US $275.00 (our price)

www.igi-global.com

701 E. Chocolate Ave., Hershey, PA 17033
Order online at www.igi-global.com or call 717-533-8845 x100
To place a standing order for titles released in this series,
contact: cust@igi-global.com
Mon-Fri 8:00 am - 5:00 pm (est) or fax 24 hours a day 717-533-8661

Dedicated to:

My beloved children Aditya Acharjya and Aditi Acharjya
D. P. Acharjya

My beloved Parents Amitava Mitra and Anushila Mitra
Anirban Mitra

Editorial Advisory Board

Manjaiah D. H., *Mangalore University, India*
Satchidananda Dehuri, *Fakir Mohan University, India*
X. Z. Gao, *Aalto University, Finland*
Manish R. Joshi, *North Maharashtra University, India*
Harleen Kaur, *Hamdard University, India*
Analava Mitra, *IIT Kharagpur, India*
Anjali Mohapatra, *IIIT Bhubaneswar, India*
Florentina Anica Pintea, *Tibiscus University, Romania*
Utpal Roy, *Visva-Bharati University, India*
Bibhudatta Sahoo, *National Institute of Technology Rourkela, India*
B. Srinivasan, *Monash University – Clayton, Australia*
Noor Zaman, *King Faisal University, Saudi Arabia*

Table of Contents

Preface.. xvi

Acknowledgment xxii

Section 1
Evolutionary Computation in Information Retrieval

Chapter 1

An Innovative Multi-Stage Multi-Dimensional Multiple-Inhomogeneous
Melody Search Algorithm: Symphony Orchestra Search Algorithm (SOSA) 1
Mohammad Kiani-Moghaddam, Shahid Beheshti University, Iran
Mojtaba Shivaie, Sirjan University of Technology, Iran

Chapter 2

Performance Analysis of Classifiers on Filter-Based Feature Selection
Approaches on Microarray Data.. 41
Arunkumar Chinnaswamy, Amrita Vishwa Vidyapeetham University,
Coimbatore Campus, India
Ramakrishnan Srinivasan, Dr. Mahalingam College of Engineering and
Technology, India

Chapter 3

Bio-Inspired Algorithms for Text Summarization: A Review 71
Rasmita Rautray, Siksha 'O' Anusandhan University, India
Rakesh Chandra Balabantaray, IIIT Bhubaneswar, India

Chapter 4

Issues and Challenges in Web Crawling for Information Extraction 93
Subrata Paul, Vignan Institute of Technology and Management, India
Anirban Mitra, Vignan Institute of Technology and Management, India
Swagata Dey, MIPS, MITS, Rayagada, India

Section 2
Bio- and Nature-Inspired Computing and Information Retrieval

Chapter 5
Swarm-Based Clustering for Gene Expression Data 123
P. K. Nizar Banu, B. S. Abdur Rahman University, India
S. Andrews Samraj, Mahendra Engineering College, India

Chapter 6
Significance of Biologically Inspired Optimization Techniques in Real-Time
Applications 150
Sushruta Mishra, C. V. Raman College of Engineering, India
Brojo Kishore Mishra, C. V. Raman College of Engineering, India
Hrudaya Kumar Tripathy, KIIT University, India

Chapter 7
Classification of Faults in Power Transmission Systems Using Modern
Techniques: An Overview 181
Avagaddi Prasad, VIT University, India
J. Belwin Edward, VIT University, India
K. Ravi, VIT University, India

Chapter 8
Generating Efficient Techniques for Information Extraction and Processing
Using Cellular Automata 204
Subrata Paul, Vignan Institute of Technology and Management, India
Anirban Mitra, Vignan Institute of Technology and Management, India

Section 3
Human-Centric and Behavior-Based Computing

Chapter 9
A Novel Hybrid Genetic Algorithm for Unconstrained and Constrained
Function Optimization 230
Rajashree Mishra, KIIT University, India
Kedar Nath Das, NIT Silchar, India

Chapter 10
Gene Expression Programming 269
Baddrud Zaman Laskar, NIT Silchar, India
Swanirbhar Majumder, NERIST, India

Chapter 11
Bio-Inspired Techniques in Rehabilitation Engineering for Control of
Assistive Devices 293
    Geethanjali Purushothaman, VIT University, India

Chapter 12
Bioinspired Algorithms in Solving Three-Dimensional Protein Structure
Prediction Problems 316
    Raghunath Satpathy, MITS Engineering College, India

Compilation of References 338

About the Contributors 379

Index 386

Detailed Table of Contents

Preface xvi

Acknowledgment xxii

Section 1
Evolutionary Computation in Information Retrieval

Chapter 1

An Innovative Multi-Stage Multi-Dimensional Multiple-Inhomogeneous
Melody Search Algorithm: Symphony Orchestra Search Algorithm (SOSA) 1
> *Mohammad Kiani-Moghaddam, Shahid Beheshti University, Iran*
> *Mojtaba Shivaie, Sirjan University of Technology, Iran*

During the past decades, the state-of-the-art, as far as optimization techniques are concerned, is focused on algorithms inspired by physical phenomena, such as the genetic algorithms. Though these algorithms are quite useful in solving complex mathematical problems, an innovative strategy to enhance performance of the music-inspired algorithms is presented in Chapter 1. This strategy uses multiple-inhomogeneous music players and three different well-organized stages for improvisation. This chapter proposes an innovative symphony orchestra search algorithm (SOSA) to solve large-scale non-linear non-convex optimization problems. The strength of the newly proposed algorithm enhances its superiority in comparison with other music-inspired algorithms. The performance of the algorithm is analyzed with network expansion planning (NEP) problem.

Chapter 2

Performance Analysis of Classifiers on Filter-Based Feature Selection
Approaches on Microarray Data 41
> *Arunkumar Chinnaswamy, Amrita Vishwa Vidyapeetham University,*
> *Coimbatore Campus, India*
> *Ramakrishnan Srinivasan, Dr. Mahalingam College of Engineering and*
> *Technology, India*

Machine learning is an artificial intelligence technique that provides computers with the ability to learn without being explicitly programmed. It focuses on the development of computer programs that can change when exposed to new data. Chapter 2 throws light on feature selection in machine learning. This chapter discusses the filter based feature selection methods such as information gain and correlation coefficient. After feature selection, the selected genes are subjected to various classification problems such as Naïve Bayes, Bagging, Random Forest, J48 and Decision Stump. Experimental results show that the filter based approaches reduce the number of gene expression levels effectively and thereby has a reduced feature subset that produces higher classification accuracy compared to other classification techniques.

Chapter 3

Bio-Inspired Algorithms for Text Summarization: A Review............................71
Rasmita Rautray, Siksha 'O' Anusandhan University, India
Rakesh Chandra Balabantaray, IIIT Bhubaneswar, India

Bio-inspired computing is loosely knits together subfields related to the topics of connectionism, social behaviour and emergence. Briefly it is the use of computers to model the living phenomena, and simultaneously study the life to improve the usage of computers. Bio-inspired algorithms have gained a significant popularity to handle hard real world and complex optimization problem. The scope and growth of Bio Inspired algorithms explore new application areas and computing opportunities. Chapter 3 presents a review to bring a better understanding and to motivate the research on bio-inspired algorithms based text summarization.

Chapter 4

Issues and Challenges in Web Crawling for Information Extraction..................93
Subrata Paul, Vignan Institute of Technology and Management, India
Anirban Mitra, Vignan Institute of Technology and Management, India
Swagata Dey, MIPS, MITS, Rayagada, India

Information retrieval is the tracing and recovery of specific information from stored data. Web information retrieval is a challenging area of resent research as enormous data are being collected, gathered, and generated every day. Computational biology and bio inspired techniques are part of a larger revolution that is increasing the processing, storage and retrieving of data in major way. This larger revolution is being driven by the generation and use of information in all forms and in enormous quantities and requires the development of intelligent systems for gathering, storing and accessing information. Chapter 4 describes the concepts, design and implementation of a distributed web crawler that runs on a network of workstations and has been used for web information extraction. It needs to scale several hundred pages per second, is resilient against system crashes and other events, and is capable to adapt various crawling applications.

Section 2
Bio- and Nature-Inspired Computing and Information Retrieval

Chapter 5

Swarm-Based Clustering for Gene Expression Data 123
P. K. Nizar Banu, B. S. Abdur Rahman University, India
S. Andrews Samraj, Mahendra Engineering College, India

Clustering is one of the most important techniques, which group genes of similar expression pattern into a small number of meaningful homogeneous groups or clusters. Gene expression data has certain special characteristics and is a challenging research problem. There are many applications for clustering gene expression data. Hard clustering allows a gene to get placed in exactly one cluster and converges in local optima. Soft clustering approach allows gene to get placed in all the clusters with some membership values. As the hard clustering approach converges in local optimum, an evolutionary computation technique like swarm clustering is required to find the global optimum solution. Chapter 5 studies swarm clustering techniques and evaluation measures for clustering gene expression data.

Chapter 6

Significance of Biologically Inspired Optimization Techniques in Real-Time
Applications 150
Sushruta Mishra, C. V. Raman College of Engineering, India
Brojo Kishore Mishra, C. V. Raman College of Engineering, India
Hrudaya Kumar Tripathy, KIIT University, India

The techniques inspired from the nature based evolution and aggregated nature of social colonies have been promising and shown excellence in handling complicated optimization problems thereby gaining huge popularity recently. These methodologies can be used as an effective problem solving tool thereby acting as an optimizing agent. The recent advances in swarm optimization, evolutionary methods and its applications are discussed in Chapter 6.

Chapter 7

Classification of Faults in Power Transmission Systems Using Modern
Techniques: An Overview 181
Avagaddi Prasad, VIT University, India
J. Belwin Edward, VIT University, India
K. Ravi, VIT University, India

Power system constitutes a major part of the electrical system relating in the present world. Deficiency in power system causes a ton of inconvenience for the maintenance of the system. So transmission system needs a proper protection scheme to ensure continuous power supply to the consumers. The countless extent of power systems and applications requires the improvement in suitable techniques for the fault classification in power transmission systems. This Chapter 7 analyzes the technical literature pertaining to classification in connection with fault classification in power transmission system.

Chapter 8

Generating Efficient Techniques for Information Extraction and Processing
Using Cellular Automata 204

Subrata Paul, Vignan Institute of Technology and Management, India
Anirban Mitra, Vignan Institute of Technology and Management, India

Cellular automaton has proved to be very efficient in carrying out arbitrary information processing. A significant application lies in unifying the information processing. But, in this case the structures used in conventional computer languages are largely inappropriate. The definite organization of computer memory into named areas, stacks, and so on, is not suitable for cellular automata in which processing elements are not distinguished from memory elements. Rather it can be assumed that the data could be represented by an object like a graph, on which transformations can be performed in parallel. Fundamentals of cellular automata and its applications in information processing are discussed in Chapter 8.

Section 3
Human-Centric and Behavior-Based Computing

Chapter 9

A Novel Hybrid Genetic Algorithm for Unconstrained and Constrained
Function Optimization 230

Rajashree Mishra, KIIT University, India
Kedar Nath Das, NIT Silchar, India

During the past decade academic and industrial communities are highly interested in evolutionary techniques for solving optimization problems. Genetic Algorithm (GA) has proved its robustness in solving all most all types of optimization problems. To improve the performance of GA, several modifications have already been done within GA. Recently GA has been hybridized with many other nature-inspired algorithms. As such Bacterial Foraging Optimization (BFO) is popular bio inspired algorithm based on the foraging behavior of E. coli bacteria. Many researchers took active interest in hybridizing GA with BFO. Motivated by such popular hybridization of GA, an attempt has been made in this chapter to hybridize GA with BFO in a novel fashion. The Chemo-taxis step of BFO plays a major role in BFO. So an attempt has been made to hybridize Chemo-tactic step with GA cycle and the algorithm is named as Chemo-inspired Genetic Algorithm (CGA). It has been applied on benchmark functions and real life application problem to prove its efficacy.

Chapter 10

Gene Expression Programming 269

Baddrud Zaman Laskar, NIT Silchar, India
Swanirbhar Majumder, NERIST, India

Gene expression programming is a descendant of genetic algorithm and genetic programming. The advantage is that it takes both the optimization and search technique based on genetics and natural selection. It is gaining popularity because it has to some extent eradicated the limitations of both while keeping the advantages. It is still a new technique not much explored. Chapter 10 discusses elaborately on GEP. In addition, it also discuss various research work done in different fields using GEP as a tool followed up by GEP architectures.

Chapter 11

Bio-Inspired Techniques in Rehabilitation Engineering for Control of
Assistive Devices 293

Geethanjali Purushothaman, VIT University, India

The intelligent control of assistive devices is possible from bio-signals to find the user's intention. The goal of the user intention recognition system is to develop computational methods for decoding the acquired bio-signal data. Pattern recognition system is one of the methods of accomplishing the objective. Bio-inspired techniques in higher level control of assistive device are in progress. Most literatures, demonstrates the application using signals and not much definite study describes the various bio-inspiring computation involved to develop the control of assistive devices in real-time. This Chapter 11 presents various bio-inspiring techniques used in interfacing devices for identification of information from the user intends.

Chapter 12

Bioinspired Algorithms in Solving Three-Dimensional Protein Structure
Prediction Problems 316

Raghunath Satpathy, MITS Engineering College, India

Proteins play a vital molecular role in all living organisms and it is difficult to predict the protein structure. The 3D structure prediction of proteins is very much important in biology and this leads to the discovery of different useful drugs, enzymes, and currently this is considered as an important research domain. The prediction of proteins is related to identification of its tertiary structure. From the computational point of view, different models have been developed along with certain efficient optimization methods to predict the protein structure. Chapter 12 basically discusses the key features of recently developed different types of bio-inspired computational algorithms, applied in protein structure prediction problems.

Compilation of References 338

About the Contributors 379

Index 386

Preface

Biologically-inspired computing is an interdisciplinary field that formalizes processes observed in living systems to design computational methods and process for solving complex problems, or simply to compute artificial systems with more natural traits. Bio inspired computation is the branch of artificial intelligence or computational intelligence that uses computational models of biological, natural or evolutionary processes as key elements in the design and implementation of computer-based problem solving system with having strong learning and adaptation process. It gets idea and inspiration from natural evolution and adaptation. Currently techniques evolved from biologically inspired process are applied to a variety of problems, ranging from scientific research to industry and business.

Bio-inspired computing is devoted to tackling and solving complex, inconsistent and uncertain problems using computational methods and is modeled as per the design principles encountered in the nature. The study on bio inspired computing provides informatics tools with enhanced robustness, scalability, flexibility and which can act, react and interact more effectively with humans. It is a multi-disciplinary field strongly based on computer science, informatics, cognitive science, computational intelligence, biology and robotics. In addition, knowledge acquisition and representation, intelligent computing, knowledge discovery in databases, data (graph, opinion and sentiment) mining are the fields that have evolved into an importance and active area of research because of the challenges and can be associated with Bio-inspired computing for not only solving but also discovering intelligent, flexible and learning process to obtain solutions for the real time problems. Applications of Bio-inspired computing are rapidly growing interdisciplinary field which merges together with database management, probability theory, statistics, intelligent computing and many other related areas. It involves integration of technologies, in order to solve complex and uncertain problems normally requiring a high level of human expertise. The basic objective of all these is to extract useful knowledge, rules and information to derive concepts and processes which will able to handle complex problems and especially when executed to satisfy specific personal or organizational knowledge management requirements.

Bio-inspired computing, nature inspired computing, human centric computing; cellular automata, DNA and membrane computing are active areas of current research for their potential application to many real life problems. Therefore, it is challenging for human beings in analyzing and transforming problems containing uncertainties, and inconsistency. It is very difficult to analyze, optimize and extract knowledge from a universe due to limitation of computing resources to solve problems dealing with uncertainty. Therefore, it is an active area of current research in computer science, information technology, and management. The objective of this edited book is to provide the researchers of computer science, information technology, and management the recent advances in the fields of Bio-inspired computing in particular with data analysis and information retrieval. To achieve these objectives, theoretical advances, concepts and its applications to real life problems will be stressed upon. This has been done to make the edited book more flexible and to stimulate further research interest in topics. It is expected that besides providing up to date knowledge in the field this edited volume will provide a launch pad for future research.

Data analysis is of prime importance in the context of computing paradigms. In addition, analyzing uncertainties and inconsistency present in data is of challenging. Additionally, the complexities involved in the applications often combine aspects of high-performance or supercomputing, parallel and grid computing and distributed computing to achieve intelligent, adaptable, learnable and flexible solutions. The key to realizing the benefits of Bio-inspired computing is the real life applications and it leads to modern computing environments that help different organizations and other research areas.

Many of the researchers in different organizations across the globe have been doing research in Bio-Inspired Computing for Information Retrieval Applications. To keep abreast with this development, it is an effort to bring the recent advances in Bio-Inspired Computing for Information Retrieval Applications and its emerging applications in a cohesive manner. The main objective is to bring most of the major developments in the above mentioned area in a precise manner, so that it can serve as a handbook for many researchers. Also, many of the universities have introduced this topic as a course at the postgraduate level. We trust and hope that this book will help the researchers, who have interest in Bio-Inspired Computing for Information Retrieval Applications, to keep insight into recent advances and their importance in real-life applications.

This book comprises of three sections. First section of the edited book stressed upon topics related to Evolutionary Computation in Information Retrieval. Second section covers topics under Bio and Nature Inspired Computing and Information Retrieval. Third section focuses on Human Centric and Behavior Based Computing.

It is aimed that the theoretical concepts and real life problems to be covered in this edited volume will facilitate researchers to understand most of the recent trends of Bio-inspired computing in information retrieval to pursue further research. This volume can also be used as reference by the readers who are interested to enhance their knowledge in these fields of research. In addition, this edited book aims to provide state-of-the-art report on relevant recent advances, its theoretical aspects and applications in solving real life problems.

During the past decades the state-of-the-art, as far as optimization techniques are concerned, is focused on algorithms inspired by physical phenomena, such as the genetic algorithms. Though these algorithms are quite useful in solving complex mathematical problems, an innovative strategy to enhance performance of the music-inspired algorithms is presented in Chapter 1. This strategy uses multiple-inhomogeneous music players and three different well-organized stages for improvisation. This chapter proposes an innovative symphony orchestra search algorithm (SOSA) to solve large-scale non-linear non-convex optimization problems. The strength of the newly proposed algorithm enhances its superiority in comparison with other music-inspired algorithms. The performance of the algorithm is analyzed with network expansion planning (NEP) problem.

Machine learning is an artificial intelligence technique that provides computers with the ability to learn without being explicitly programmed. It focuses on the development of computer programs that can change when exposed to new data. Chapter 2 troughs light on feature selection in machine learning. This chapter discusses the filter based feature selection methods such as information gain and correlation coefficient. Since after feature selection, the selected genes are subjected to various classification problems such as Naïve Bayes, Bagging, Random Forest, J48 and Decision Stump. Experimental results show that the filter based approaches reduce the number of gene expression levels effectively and thereby has a reduced feature subset that produces higher classification accuracy compared to other classification techniques.

Bio-inspired computing is loosely knits together subfields related to the topics of connectionism, social behaviour and emergence. Briefly it is the use of computers to model the living phenomena, and simultaneously study the life to improve the usage of computers. Bio-inspired algorithms have gained a significant popularity to handle hard real world and complex optimization problem. The scope and growth of Bio Inspired algorithms explore new application areas and computing opportunities. Chapter 3 presents a review to bring a better understanding and to motivate the research on bio-inspired algorithms based text summarization.

Information retrieval is the tracing and recovery of specific information from stored data. Web information retrieval is a challenging area of resent research as enormous data are being collected, gathered, and generated every day. Computational biology and bio inspired techniques are part of a larger revolution that is increasing the processing, storage and retrieving of data in major way. This larger revolution is being driven by the generation and use of information in all forms and in enormous quantities and requires the development of intelligent systems for gathering, storing and accessing information. Chapter 4 describes the concepts, design and implementation of a distributed web crawler that runs on a network of workstations and has been used for web information extraction. It needs to scale several hundred pages per second, is resilient against system crashes and other events, and is capable to adapt various crawling applications.

Clustering is one of the most important techniques, which group genes of similar expression pattern into a small number of meaningful homogeneous groups or clusters. Gene expression data has certain special characteristics and is a challenging research problem. There are many applications for clustering gene expression data. Hard clustering allows a gene to get placed in exactly one cluster and converges in local optima. Soft clustering approach allows gene to get placed in all the clusters with some membership values. As the hard clustering approach converges in local optimum, an evolutionary computation technique like swarm clustering is required to find the global optimum solution. Chapter 5 studies swarm clustering techniques and evaluation measures for clustering gene expression data.

The techniques inspired from the nature based evolution and aggregated nature of social colonies have been promising and shown excellence in handling complicated optimization problems thereby gaining huge popularity recently. These methodologies can be used as an effective problem solving tool thereby acting as an optimizing agent. The recent advances in swarm optimization, evolutionary methods and its applications are discussed in Chapter 6.

Power system constitutes a major part of the electrical system relating in the present world. Deficiency in power system causes a ton of inconvenience for the maintenance of the system. So transmission system needs a proper protection scheme to ensure continuous power supply to the consumers. The countless extent of power systems and applications requires the improvement in suitable techniques for the fault classification in power transmission systems. This Chapter 7 analyzes the technical literature pertaining to classification in connection with fault classification in power transmission system.

Chapter 8

Cellular automaton has proved to be very efficient in carrying out arbitrary information processing. A significant application lies in unifying the information processing. But, in this case the structures used in conventional computer languages are largely inappropriate. The definite organization of computer memory into named areas, stacks, and so on, is not suitable for cellular automata in which processing elements are not distinguished from memory elements. Rather it can be assumed that the data could be represented by an object like a graph, on which transformations can be performed in parallel. Fundamentals of cellular automata and its applications in information processing are discussed in Chapter 8.

Genetic algorithm has proved its robustness in solving all most all types of optimization problems. Several modifications have already been done within genetic algorithm to improve its efficiency. It also has been hybridized with many other nature-inspired algorithms. Many researchers took active interest in hybridizing it with bacterial foraging optimization. Motivated by such popular hybridization of GA, an attempt has been made to hybridize genetic algorithm with bacterial foraging optimization in a novel fashion in Chapter 9. An attempt has been made to hybridize chemo-tactic step with genetic algorithm cycle in this chapter. The proposed algorithm has been applied on benchmark functions to prove its efficacy.

Gene expression programming is a descendant of genetic algorithm and genetic programming. The advantage is that it takes both the optimization and search technique based on genetics and natural selection. It is gaining popularity because it has to some extent eradicated the limitations of both while keeping the advantages. It is still a new technique not much explored. Chapter 10 discusses elaborately on GEP. In addition, it also discuss various research work done in different fields using GEP as a tool followed up by GEP architectures.

The intelligent control of assistive devices is possible from bio-signals to find the user's intention. The goal of the user intention recognition system is to develop computational methods for decoding the acquired bio-signal data. Pattern recognition system is one of the methods of accomplishing the objective. Bio-inspired techniques in higher level control of assistive device are in progress. Most literatures, demonstrates the application using signals and not much definite study describes the various bio-inspiring computation involved to develop the control of assistive devices in real-time. This Chapter 11 presents various bio-inspiring techniques used in interfacing devices for identification of information from the user intends.

Proteins play a vital molecular role in all living organisms and it is difficult to predict the protein structure. The 3D structure prediction of proteins is very much important in biology and this leads to the discovery of different useful drugs, enzymes, and currently this is considered as an important research domain. The prediction of proteins is related to identification of its tertiary structure. From the computational point of view, different models have been developed along with certain efficient optimization methods to predict the protein structure. Chapter 12 basically discusses the key features of recently developed different types of bio-inspired computational algorithms, applied in protein structure prediction problems.

We continued our effort to keep the book reader-friendly. By a problem solving approach, we mean that researchers learn the material through real life examples that provide the motivation behind the concepts and its relation to the real world problems. At the same time, readers must discover a solution for the non-trivial aspect of the solution. We trust and hope that the book will help the readers to further carryout their research in different directions.

D.P. Acharjya
School of Computing Science and Engineering, VIT University, India

Anirban Mitra
Vignan Institute of Technology and Management, India

Acknowledgment

It is with great sense of satisfaction that we present our Book entitled "Bio-Inspired Computing for Information Retrieval Applications" and wish to express our views to all those who helped us both direct and indirect way to complete this work. First of all we would like to thank the authors those who have contributed to this edited book. We acknowledge, with sincere gratitude the kindness of the School of Computing Science and Engineering, VIT University, India and VITAM, Berhampur, India to provide an opportunity to carry out this research work. In addition, we are also thankful to VIT University, India and VITAM India for providing facilities to complete this project.

While writing, contributors have referred several books and journals; we take this opportunity to thank all those authors and publishers. We are extremely thankful to the editorial board, reviewers for their support during the process of evaluation. At last but not the least, we thank the production team of IGI Global, USA for encouraging us and extending their full cooperation and help in timely completion of this edited book.

D.P. Acharjya
School of Computing Science and Engineering, VIT University, India

Anirban Mitra
Vignan Institute of Technology and Management, India

Section 1
Evolutionary Computation in Information Retrieval

Chapter 1
An Innovative Multi-Stage Multi-Dimensional Multiple-Inhomogeneous Melody Search Algorithm:
Symphony Orchestra Search Algorithm (SOSA)

Mohammad Kiani-Moghaddam
Shahid Beheshti University, Iran

Mojtaba Shivaie
Sirjan University of Technology, Iran

ABSTRACT

In this book chapter, the authors present an innovative strategy to enhance performance of the music-inspired algorithms. In this strategy, by using multiple-inhomogeneous music players and three different well-organized stages for improvisation, an innovative symphony orchestra search algorithm (SOSA) is proposed to solve large-scale non-linear non-convex optimization problems. Using multiple-inhomogeneous music players with different tastes, ideas, experiences can conduct players to choose better pitches, and increase the probability of playing a better melody. The strength of the newly proposed algorithm can enhance its superiority in comparison with other music-inspired algorithms, when feasible area of the solution space, and or dimensions of the optimization problem increases. Network expansion planning (NEP) problem has been employed to evaluate the performance of the newly proposed SOSA, compared with other existing optimization algorithms. The NEP problem is a large-scale non-convex optimization problem having a non-linear, mixed-integer nature.

DOI: 10.4018/978-1-5225-2375-8.ch001

Copyright ©2017, IGI Global. Copying or distributing in print or electronic forms without written permission of IGI Global is prohibited.

INTRODUCTION

Background and Motivation

The most recently, many meta-heuristic optimization techniques that are conceptually different from the traditional mathematical programming techniques have been developed in order to solve the large-scale, mixed-integer, non-linear and non-convex optimization problems (Lee & El-Sharkawi, 2008). This is because of the superiority of the non-traditional meta-heuristic optimization techniques in comparison with traditional mathematical programming techniques, when feasible area of the solution space and or dimensions of the optimization problem increases (Lee & El-Sharkawi, 2008). The non-traditional meta-heuristic optimization techniques have been inspired by certain attributes and behavior of biological, swarm of fauna, and neurobiological systems. The most popular meta-heuristic algorithms can be classified into genetic algorithm (GA) (Holland, 1975), particle swarm optimization (PSO) (Kennedy & Eberhart), simulated annealing (SA) (Kirkpatrick, Gelatt & Vecchi, 1983), Tabu search (TS) (Glover, 1977), ant colony optimization (ACO) (Dorigo, Maniezzo & Colorni, 1996), artificial bee colony (ABC) (Karaboga, 2005), artificial fish-swarm (AFS) (Li, Shao & Qian, 2002), bacterial foraging optimization (BFO) (Passino, 2002), bat algorithm (BA) (Yang, 2010), cuckoo search (CS) (Yang & Deb, 2009), firefly algorithm (FA) (Yang, 2009), etc. As further elucidation, the details of these algorithms are tabulated in Table 1. These studies into the meta-heuristic optimization techniques show that most of aforementioned algorithms are employed only for solving a specific class of convex and non-convex optimization problems. This is because of the fact that the performance of these meta-heuristic algorithms depend on a confined solution space. In other word, in every new generation, a new set of vectors is produced by using randomized selection and improved operators from the limited set of vectors. Therefore, these meta-heuristic algorithms cannot maintain their proper performance by increasing the irregular dimensions of real-world large-scale optimization problems.

As a result, researchers and engineers in different area of sciences are enthusiastic to use innovative alternatives in the optimization techniques, to improve the performance and efficiency of solving the real-word large-scale optimization problems.

Literature Review and Contributions

In the evolutionary computation literature, in the broadest sense, the optimization techniques can be classified into traditional (i.e., direct methods, gradient methods, linear programming methods, interior point methods), and non-traditional (i.e., swarm intelligence based algorithms, bio-inspired algorithms, physics and chemistry based algorithms) optimization techniques. Most of the real-world optimization problems involve complexities like discrete, continuous or mixed decision-making variables, multiple conflicting objective functions, non-linearity, discontinuity, etc. The feasible area of the solution space and/or dimensions of the optimization problem may be so large that the global optimum cannot be found in reasonable time. The traditional optimization techniques may not be efficient to solve such problems. Hence, various non-traditional meta-heuristic optimization techniques (see Table 1) can be used in such situations (Lee & El-Sharkawi, 2008). The performance of the non-traditional meta-heuristic algorithms can be affected by increasing the search space and also dimension of the optimization problem.

On the other hand, these optimization algorithms have some disadvantages, such as: require to initial value settings of the decision-making variables, require to derivative information, and lack of use of all stored solution vectors in the memory to produce new solution vector, etc. (Lee & El-Sharkawi, 2008). In order to modify these disadvantages, many efforts have been accomplished during the last decade, such as: (Geem, 2001; Mahdavi, 2007; Omran, 2008; Wang, 2010; Pan, 2010a; Pan, 2010b; Zou, 2010; Ashrafi, 2011). In a study by Geem, Kim, and Loganathan (2001), a new population-based meta-heuristic optimization algorithm is developed, named harmony search algorithm (HSA). The original HSA is inspired based on the music-improvisation process, which music player improvises its music instrument pitches step-by-step to obtain the best substitution of pitch in harmony. In addition, there are several technical publications in the area of improving performance of original

Table 1. A list of the most popular meta-heuristic algorithms

No.	Refs.	Algorithms	Inspired idea
1	(Holland, 1975)	GA	Natural evolution
2	(Kennedy & Eberhart)	PSO	Swarm behavior of birds
3	(Kirkpatrick, Gelatt & Vecchi, 1983)	SA	Simulated annealing
4	(Glover, 1977)	TS	Tabu routes (solutions)
5	(Dorigo, Maniezzo & Colorni, 1996)	ACO	Swarm behavior of ants
6	(Karaboga, 2005)	ABC	Swarm behavior of bees
7	(Li, Shao & Qian, 2002)	AFS	Swarm behavior of fishes
8	(Passino, 2002)	BFO	Bacterial foraging
9	(Yang, 2010)	BA	Sound system of bats
10	(Yang & Deb, 2009)	CS	Behavior of cuckoo for flyblow
11	(Yang, 2009)	FA	Fireflies shine

HSA (Mahdavi, 2007; Omran, 2008; Wang, 2010; Pan, 2010a; Pan, 2010b; Zou, 2010; Ashrafi, 2011). In a study by Mahdavi, Fesanghary, and Damangir (2007), the improved harmony search algorithm (IHSA) is reported by updating the value of bandwidth (BW) and pitch adjustment rate (PAR) parameters in each generation to overcome the drawbacks associated with fixed values of these parameters in the original HSA. In another study (Omran, Mahdavi & Damangir, 2008), a global-best harmony search algorithm (GHSA) is given by borrowing the main concepts of swarm intelligence of the PSO algorithm to modify pitch adjustment rule. In the pitch adjustment rule, the value of each new decision-making variable is generated by using a random decision-making variable amongst any one of the decision-making variables of the best harmony vector stored in the harmony memory (HM). In a study by Wang and Huang (2010), a new variant of original HSA called self-adaptive harmony search algorithm (SAHSA) is proposed by dynamically updating the value of the harmony memory consideration rate (HMCR), PAR and BW parameters according to a learning mechanism. Furthermore, the SAHSA employs the low-discrepancy sequences for initializing of the HM instead of using the pseudo-random number generator. In a study (Pan, Suganthan, Tasgetiren & Liang, 2010a), another new variant of original HSA called self-adaptive global-best harmony search algorithm (SGHSA) is addressed by using the concept of the GHSA. The difference between the GHSA and the SGHSA appears in the memory consideration and pitch adjustment rules. In accordance with the modified pitch adjustment rule in the SGHSA, the value of each new decision-making variable is generated by using a corresponding decision-making variables of the best harmony vector stored in the HM; while, in the GHSA, this value is generated by using a random decision-making variable amongst any one of the decision-making variables of the best harmony vector stored in the HM. In another study (Pan, Suganthan, Liang & Tasgetiren, 2010b), a local-best harmony search algorithm with dynamic subpopulations (DLHSA) is described by inspiring the PSO algorithm. In the DLHSA, the HM is dynamically divided into many sub-HMs, and new harmony vectors are individually improvised for the small-sized sub-HMs. In a study (Zou, Gao, Wu & Li, 2010), a new variant of the original HSA named novel global harmony search algorithm (NGHSA) is represented by replacing the PAR, BW and HMCR parameters in the original HSA with new two important operations: i) position updating, and ii) genetic mutation. On the other hand, a novel enhanced version of the original HSA, denoted by melody search algorithm (MSA), is reported on the basis of the improvisation of melodies in the music process in (Ashrafi & Dariane, 2011). The MSA is inspired by borrowing the main concepts of the HSA; however, the MSA is completely different in structure. The HSA uses a single HM; while, the MSA employs several memories, called player memory (PM) to obtain the best substitution of pitch in a melody. As further explanation, all improvements of the original HSA are classified into three classes, as follows:

- The first class improves the original HSA in terms of parameters setting, such as: IHSA (Mahdavi, Fesanghary & Damangir, 2007), GHSA (Omran, Mahdavi & Damangir, 2008), DHSA (Chakraborty, Roy, Das, Jain & Abraham, 2009), SHPSOS (Zhao, Liu, Zhang & Wang, 2015), SAMOHSA (Dai, Yuan & Zhang, 2015), I-ITHSA (Turgut, Turgut & Coban, 2014), EHSA (Maheri & Narimani, 2014), IGHSA (Xiang, An, Li, He & Zhang, 2014), GDHSA (Khalili, Kharrat, Salahshoor & Haghighat-Sefat, 2014), LAHSA (Enayatifar, Yousefi, Abdullah & Darus, 2013), ITHSA (Yadav, Kumar, Panda & Chang, 2012), HSA-variant (Wang, 2010; Mukhopadhyay, 2008; Hasancebi, 2009; Saka, 2009; Degertekin, 2008; Kattan, 2010; Geem, 2005; Al-Betar, 2010a; Geem, 2006; Amaya, 2015; Zhang, 2015; Contreras, 2014), etc.

- The second class improves the original HSA with respect to hybridizing of the components of the HSA with other meta-heuristic algorithms. This class is also classified into two sub-classes, as follows:
  - The first sub-class is the incorporation of other meta-heuristic algorithms with the HSA: HSA+PSO+GA (Zou, Gao, Wu & Li, 2010), HSA+SA (Taherinejad, 2009), HSA+PSO (Omran, Mahdavi & Damangir, 2008), (Zhao, 2015; Geem, 2009), HSA+DPSO (Santos-Coelho & De-Andrade-Bernert, 2009), HSA+GA (Al-Betar, Khader & Nadi, 2010b), HSA+CSA (Wang, Gao & Ovaska, 2009), HSA+GA+SA+IAS (Lee & Zomaya, 2009), HSA+SQP (Fesanghary, Mahdavi, Minary-Jolandan & Alizade, 2008), HSA+FCM (Alia, 2009a; Alia, 2009b; Alia, 2010), HSA+k-means (Forsati, 2008; Mahdavi, 2008), HSA+Solver (Ayvaz, Kayhan, Ceylan & Gurarslan, 2009), HSA+NM-SA (Jang, Kang & Lee, 2008), HSA+Taguchi (Yildiz, 2008; Yildiz, 2010), HSA+DE (Gao, 2008; Gao, 2009), HSA+EA (Hassan, Doush, Maghayreh, Alkhateeb & Hamdan, 2014), HSA+QC (Layeb, 2013), IHSA+FCM (Malaki, Pourbagheri & Abolhassani, 2008), etc.
  - The second sub-class is the incorporation of the original HSA with other meta-heuristic algorithms: PSO+HSA (Li, Mitianoudis & Stathaki, 2007), PSOPC+ACO+HSA (Kaveh & Talatahari, 2009), GA+Simplex+TS+HSA (Qinghua, Shida & Youlin, 2006), GA+HSA (Li, 2008; Nadi, 2010), LDA+HSA (Moeinzadeh, Asgarian, Zanjani, Rezaee & Seidi, 2009), COA+HSA (Yuan, Zhao, Yang & Wang, 2014), etc.

- The third class inspires by the main concepts of the HSA and provides a new computational structure. In other words, the existing algorithms in this class are considered as new music inspired algorithms (e.g., MSA (Ashrafi, 2011; Ashrafi, 2013)).

In general, the music-inspired optimization algorithms compared with other meta-heuristic optimization algorithms (see Table 1) have several considerable advantages, such as:

- Improvising a new solution vector by considering entire the existing solution vectors in the HM; while, new solution vectors in other meta-heuristic optimization algorithms produce based on randomized selection and improved operators from the limited set of vectors;
- Having fewer mathematical requirements, and not required to the initial settings of value of the decision-making variables; and finally,
- Considering each decision-making variable in a solution vector independently of one another.

These features can increase the flexibility and robustness of music-inspired optimization algorithms; and therefore, can enhance possibility of generating better solution vectors.

This book chapter, then, focused on presenting a new music-inspired algorithm, called symphony orchestra search algorithm (SOSA), to enhance performance of the music-inspired algorithms. In this book chapter, by using multiple-inhomogeneous music players and three different well-organized stages for improvisation, an innovative SOSA is proposed to solve large-scale non-convex non-linear mixed-integer optimization problems. The strength of the newly proposed algorithm can enhance its superiority in comparison with other optimization algorithms, when feasible area of the solution space, and or dimensions of the optimization problem increases. Moreover, a multi-objective network expansion planning (NEP) problem is considered to evaluate the efficiency the newly proposed SOSA. In this problem, simultaneous optimization of investment cost, congestion cost, users' benefit and expected customer interruption cost are considered; while, satisfying system adequacy and static security. Also, the performance of the proposed SOSA is compared with the MSA, HSA and non-dominated sorting genetic algorithm-II (NSGA-II).

The rest of this book chapter is organized, as follows: Section 2 provides an overview of the music-inspired optimization algorithms. The newly proposed SOSA is described in Section 3. Section 4 provides the application of the music-inspired algorithms to solve network planning problem. Finally, Section 5 is devoted to concluding remarks.

THE MUSIC-INSPIRED OPTIMIZATION ALGORITHMS: FROM PAST TO PRESENT

Harmony Search Algorithm

As previously mentioned, the HSA is a population-based meta-heuristic optimization algorithm (Geem, Kim & Loganathan, 2001), which inspired by music phenomenon. The main steps of the HSA are classified as follows: 1) initialize of the optimization problem and the HSA parameters, i.e., input data, 2) initialize the HM, 3) improvise a new harmony vector, 4) update the HM, and 5) check the stopping criterion and repeat third and fourth steps. In addition, the HSA parameters and their abbreviation are tabulated in Table 2. In step 2, the HM matrix is randomly filled by considering HMS and by initialing harmony vectors according to the equations (1)-(3). It is worth noting that the equations (2)-(3) are considered for continuous and discrete decision-making variables, respectively.

$$HM = \begin{bmatrix} x_{(1)}^{(1)} & x_{(1)}^{(2)} & \cdots & x_{(1)}^{(N)} \\ x_{(2)}^{(1)} & x_{(2)}^{(2)} & \cdots & x_{(2)}^{(N)} \\ \vdots & \vdots & \cdots & \vdots \\ x_{(HMS)}^{(1)} & x_{(HMS)}^{(2)} & \cdots & x_{(HMS)}^{(N)} \end{bmatrix} \tag{1}$$

$$x_{(j)}^{(n)} = LB^{(n)} + rand(0,1) \times (UB^{(n)} - LB^{(n)}); \forall n \in N, \forall j \in HMS \tag{2}$$

$$x_{(j)}^{(n)} = x^{(n)}(l); \forall n \in N, \forall j \in HMS, \forall l = rand(\{1,2,...,U\}) \tag{3}$$

In step 3, a new harmony vector, $X_{new} = \left(x_{new}^{(1)}, x_{new}^{(2)}, ..., x_{new}^{(N)} \right)$, is created based on three improvisation rules: 1) memory consideration, 2) pitch adjustment, and 3) random selection. The implementation of the improvisation procedure for discrete and continuous decision-making variables in the HSA is expressed in Table 3 (Omran, 2008; Geem, 2009; Lee, 2005; Shivaie, 2014; Shivaie, 2013a). In step 4, by calculating the values of the objective functions, new improvised harmony vector is compared with existing harmony vectors in the HM. In this case, if new harmony vector is better than the worst harmony vector, it replaces the old one in the HM and the existing worst harmony vector discards from the HM. In step 5, third and fourth steps are iterated till stopping criterion of the HSA, namely, NI, is satisfied.

Melody Search Algorithm

The MSA is inspired by borrowing the main concepts of the HSA; however, the MSA is completely different in structure. The HSA employs an individual HM; while, the MSA uses multiple memories, called PM. Multiple PMs are organized a melody memory (MM). Therefore, the MSA is an enhanced version of the HSA. The optimization process of the MSA is classified in three steps for every specific optimization problem, as follows (Ashrafi & Dariane, 2013):

Step 1: Initialize the optimization problem and the MSA parameters, i.e., input data.
Step 2: Single improvisation procedure:

    Sub-step 2.1: Define initial all $PM_{(i)}$.

    Sub-step 2.2: Improvise a new melody for each PM.

    Sub-step 2.3: Update all $PM_{(i)}$.

    Sub-step 2.4: Iterate internal steps 2.2 and 2.3 till stopping criterion in the second step, i.e., NII, is satisfied.

Step 3: Group improvisation procedure:

    Sub-step 3.1: Improvise a new melody for each PM based on new feasible area of pitches.

    Sub-step 3.2: Update all $PM_{(i)}$.

    Sub-step 3.3: Find the new feasible areas of upper and lower of pitches for subsequent improvisation (just for randomization).

    Sub-Step 3.4: Iterate internal steps 3.1, 3.2 and 3.3 till stopping criterion in the third step, i.e., NI, is satisfied.

Table 2. The HSA parameters and their abbreviation

No.	HSA parameters	Abbreviation	Parameter range
1	Distance bandwidth	BW	$BW \in \mathrm{R}^{(N)} > 0$
2	Harmony memory	HM	—
3	Harmony memoryconsidering rate	HMCR	$0 \leq HMCR \leq 1$
4	Harmony memory size	HMS	$HMS \geq 1$
5	Maximum number of iteration	NI	$NI \geq 1$
6	Number of decision-making variables	N	$N \geq 1$
7	Pitch adjusting rate	PAR	$0 \leq PAR \leq 1$

Table 3. The implementation of the improvisation procedure for discrete and continuous decision-making variables in the HSA

Input: N, HMCR, PAR, BW, U, $UB^{(n)}$, $LB^{(n)}$,
1:   **for** each decision-making variable: $n \in \left[1, 2, \ldots, N\right]$ **do**
2:   **if** *rand* (0,1) ≤ HMCR **then (harmony memory consideration rate)**
3: $X_{new}^{(n)} = X_{(j)}^{(n)}; \ \forall j = rand\left(\left\{1, 2, \ldots, HMS\right\}\right)$
4:   **if** *rand* (0,1) ≤ PAR **then (pitch adjustment rate)**
5: $X_{new}^{(n)} = X_{old}^{(n)}\left(u \pm m\right); \ \forall m = rand\left(\left\{\ldots, -2, -1, 1, 2, \ldots\right\}\right)$; for discrete decision-making variables
6: $X_{new}^{(n)} = X_{old}^{(n)} \pm rand\left(0,1\right).BW$; for continuous decision-making variables
7:   **end if**
8:   **else if (random selection)**
9: $X_{new}^{(n)} = X^{(n)}\left(l\right); \ \forall l = rand\left(\left\{1, 2, \ldots, U\right\}\right)$; for discrete decision-making variables
10: $X_{new}^{(n)} = LB^{(n)} \pm rand\left(0,1\right).\left(UB^{(n)} - LB^{(n)}\right)$; for continuous decision-making variables
11:   **end if**
12:   **end for**
Output: X_{new} (new harmony vector)

In the step 1, the optimization problem is defined initially as minimize {$f(x)$ | $x \in X$} subject to constraints, which "X" is the set of the possible range of the decision variables and "x" is the set of decision-making variables. In addition, the MSA parameters which can alter in any optimization problem are classified in Table 4. In the step 2, seeking for the well-designed configurations of pitches is separately performed by each music player. In the sub-step 2.1, all $PM_{(i)}$ matrixes are randomly generated by initial melodies and the MM structure is also organized by multiple $PM_{(i)}$ according to the equations (4)-(6).

Table 4. The MSA parameters and their abbreviation

No.	MSA parameters	Abbreviation	Parameter range
1	Distance bandwidth	BW	$BW \in R^{(N)}{}_{>0}$
2	Melody memory	MM	—
3	Maximum number of iteration for second step	NII	NII$\geq$1
4	Maximum number of iteration for third step	NI	NI$\geq$1
5	Number of decision-making variables	N	N$\geq$1
6	Player memory number	PMN	PMN$\geq$1
7	Player memory considering rate	PMCR	0$\leq$PMCR$\leq$1
8	Player memory size	PMS	PMS$\geq$1
9	Pitch adjusting rate	PAR	0$\leq$PAR$\leq$1

$$\text{MM} = \begin{bmatrix} \text{PM}_{(1)} & \cdots & \text{PM}_{(i)} & \cdots & \text{PM}_{(PMN)} \end{bmatrix}^{\square} ; \forall i \in PMN \tag{4}$$

$$PM_{(i)} = \begin{bmatrix} x^{(1)}_{(i),(1)} & x^{(2)}_{(i),(1)} & \cdots & x^{(N)}_{(i),(1)} \\ x^{(1)}_{(i),(2)} & x^{(2)}_{(i),(2)} & \cdots & x^{(N)}_{(i),(2)} \\ \vdots & \vdots & \vdots & \vdots \\ x^{(1)}_{(i),(PMS)} & x^{(2)}_{(i),(PMS)} & \cdots & x^{(N)}_{(i),(PMS)} \end{bmatrix} ; \forall i \in PMN \tag{5}$$

$$x^{(n)}_{(i),(j)} = LB^{(n)} + rand(0,1).(UB^{(n)} - LB^{(n)}); \forall n \in N, \forall i \in PMN, \forall j \in PMS \tag{6}$$

In the sub-step 2.2, a new melody vector is improvised for each PM by an alternative improvisation procedure (AIP) (Ashrafi & Dariane, 2013). The implementation of the improvisation procedure for continuous decision-making variables in the MSA is represented in Table 5. In the sub-step 2.3, by calculating the values of the objective functions, new melody vector of melody player i, $X_{(i),\text{new}} = \left(x^{(1)}_{(i),\text{new}}, x^{(2)}_{(i),\text{new}}, \ldots, x^{(N)}_{(i),\text{new}} \right)$, is compared with existing melody vectors in $PM_{(i)}$. In this case, if new melody vector is better than the worst melody vector, it replaces the old one in the $PM_{(i)}$ and the existing worst melody discards from the

$PM_{(i)}$. In the sub-step 2.4, internal steps 2.2 and 2.3 are iterated till stopping criterion in the second step, i.e., NII, is satisfied. In the step 3, seeking for the well-designed configurations of pitches are accomplished by an interaction-based process among the music players; whereas, feasible areas of pitches are updated. In the sub-step 3.1, similar to internal step 2.2, the AIP is applied to improvise a new melody vector from each PM in accordance with the feasible areas of pitches. In the sub-step 3.2, the all $PM_{(i)}$ are updated similar to performed process in internal step 2.3. In the sub-step 3.3, by storing well-designed melody variables of each PM, new feasible areas of pitches can be determined for the subsequent improvisation (just for randomization). Hence, the main difference between the HSA and MSA can be clearly observed in here. This procedure is addressed in Table 6. In the final internal step, internal steps 3.1, 3.2 and 3.3 are iterated till stopping criterion in the third step, i.e., NI, is satisfied.

THE NEWLY PROPOSED ALGORITHM: SYMPHONY ORCHESTRA SEARCH ALGORITHM

In the music phenomenon, harmony is the utilization of concurrent pitches or chords, and is mostly implied to the vertical characteristic of the music phenomenon. In other words, a harmony refers to how to build chords and its arrangement. However, a melody generally refers to a number of musical sounds, which one heard and followed by another one, and is mostly implied to the horizontal characteristic of the music phenomenon. Also, in the music phenomenon, a symphony orchestra refers to a set of musicians with different music instruments, which perform a musical piece with one another. In other words, a symphony orchestra is organized by multiple groups of musicians with different music instruments, tastes, ideas and experiences. As stated earlier, the HSA has been organized by a homogeneous music player with a single improvisation procedure. In other words, the HSA is like a music player that plays a song with a music instrument (e.g., guitar, piano, violin, contrabass, trumpet or other item). In the HSA, music players improvise its music instrument pitches step-by-step in order to obtain the best substitution of pitch in harmony. Therefore, the HSA is labeled as a single-stage single-dimensional single-homogeneous algorithm. The MSA has been established by homogeneous music players with two-stage improvisation: single and group improvisation. In other words, the MSA is similar to a group of music players which all music players have a same music instrument, namely, all music players are players of guitar or other items. As a result, the MSA are labeled as a two-stage multi-dimensional homogeneous music players algorithm. In the single improvisation, each music player existing in group of music players can

Table 5. The implementation of the improvisation procedure for discrete and continuous decision-making variables in the MSA

Input: N, PMN, PMS, PMCR, BW_{min}, BW_{max}, PAR_{min}, PAR_{max}, $UB^{(n)}$, $LB^{(n)}$,	
1:	**for** each melody player: $i \in \left[1, 2, \ldots, PMN\right]$ **do**
2:	**for** each decision-making variable: $n \in \left[1, 2, \ldots, N\right]$ **do**
3:	**if** *rand* $(0,1) \leq$ PMCR **then (player memory consideration rate)**
4:	**if** *iteration counter* = odd
5:	$X_{(i),\text{new}}^{(n)} = X_{(i),(j)}^{(n)} \pm rand\left(0,1\right).BW_{(gn)}; \; \forall j = rand\left(\left\{1, 2, \ldots, PMS\right\}\right)$
6:	**else**
7:	$X_{(i),\text{new}}^{(n)} = X_{(i),(j)}^{(h)} \pm rand\left(0,1\right).BW_{(gn)};$ $\forall j = rand\left(\left\{1, 2, \ldots, PMS\right\}\right), \; \forall h = rand\left(\left\{1, 2, \ldots, N\right\}\right)$
8:	**end if**
9:	**if** *rand* $(0,1) \leq PAR_{(gn)}$ **then (pitch adjustment rate)**
10:	$X_{(i),\text{new}}^{(n)} = X_{(i),(best)}^{(n)};$ where the *"best"* subscript stands for the best melody vector in any certain $PM_{(i)}$
11:	**end if**
12:	**end if**
13:	**else (random selection)**
14:	$X_{(i),\text{new}}^{(n)} = LB^{(n)} \pm rand\left(0,1\right).\left(UB^{(n)} - LB^{(n)}\right);$
15:	**end if**
16:	**end for**
17:	**end for**
Output: $X_{(i),\text{new}}$ (new melody vector)	

Table 6. The implementation procedure to find the feasible areas of pitches in the MSA

Input:	$X_{(i),(best)}^{(n)}$; $\forall i = 1, 2, \dots, PMN$, $\quad \forall n = 1, 2, \dots, N$
1:	**for** each decision-making variable: $n \in \left[1, 2, \dots, N\right]$ **do**
2:	$LB^{(n)} = \min\left(X_{(i),(best)}^{(n)}\right)$; $\forall i = 1, 2, \dots, PMN$
3:	$UB^{(n)} = \max\left(X_{(i),(best)}^{(n)}\right)$; $\forall i = 1, 2, \dots, PMN$
4:	**end for**
Output:	$LB^{(n)}$, $UB^{(n)}$ (lower and upper bounds of all decision-making variables, respectively).

individually improvise its melody. In the group improvisation, however, each music player can improvise its melody by considering process of music performance, and interactive relationship among the members of a music group.

In this book chapter, the authors' aim is to inspire more research to attain better insight into efficient music-inspired algorithms and solve large-scale real-world optimization problems. Therefore, in this book chapter, with a new point of view, an innovative SOSA is developed to enhance the efficiency of the music-inspired algorithms. The newly proposed SOSA has been organized by multiple-music players with different music instruments, such as: players of clarinet, players of violin, players of violoncello, players of panpipe, etc. In addition, this new algorithm employs three different well-organized stages for optimization: 1) single improvisation stage, 2) group improvisation stage with multiple-homogeneous music players, and 3) group improvisation stage with multiple-inhomogeneous music players. As a result, the SOSA is labeled as a multi-stage, multi-dimensional multiple-inhomogeneous music players algorithm. Table 7 shows an analogy between attributes of the HSA, the MSA, and the newly proposed SOSA. The differences among the structures of harmony, melody and symphony orchestra in music phenomenon are depicted in Figure 1. Also, Figure 2 illustrates an analogy among the proposed structure of the SOSA and structures of the HSA and the MSA.

As can be seen from Figure 2, the proposed SOSA is similar to a symphony orchestra, which is organized by multiple-inhomogeneous music players; while, each group of music players has a different music instrument (e.g., group of music players of guitar, group of music players of violin, group of music players of vio-

Table 7. Attributes of the HSA, the MSA, and the Newly Proposed SOSA

Music-inspired algorithms	Attributes
HSA	• Single stage: It has only a single improvisation procedure. • Single dimensional: It has only a single music player. • Single homogeneous music player: It has been organized by one kind of music player, such as: only player of guitar, etc.
MSA	• Two-Stage: It has two different improvisation procedures, such as: single improvisation and group improvisation procedures with homogeneous music players. • Multi-Dimensional: It has multiple music players. • Homogeneous Music Players: It has been organized by only one group of music players, such as: only group of players of guitar, etc.
SOSA	• Multi-Stage: It has three different improvisation procedures, such as: single improvisation, group improvisation with multiple-homogeneous music players, and group improvisation procedures with multiple-inhomogeneous music players. • Multi-Dimensional: It has multiple music players. • Multiple-Inhomogeneous Music Players: It has been organized by different music players groups with different musical instruments, such as: group of players of guitar, and or violin, violoncello, panpipe, etc.

Figure 1. The concepts of the harmony and the melody and also the symphony orchestra in music phenomenon

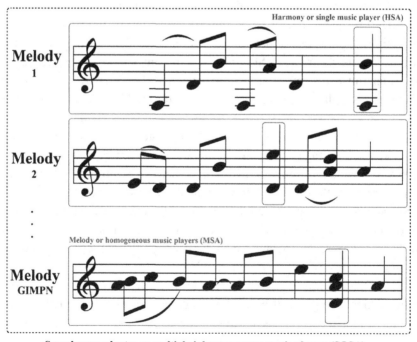

Symphony orchestra or multiple-inhomogeneous music players (SOSA)

Figure 2. The proposed structure of the SOSA

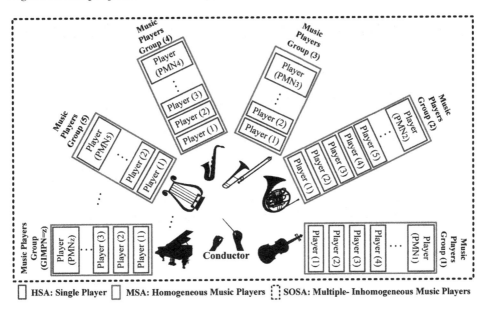

☐ HSA: Single Player ☐ MSA: Homogeneous Music Players ⸨ SOSA: Multiple- Inhomogeneous Music Players

loncello, etc.). Although the SOSA has been inspired from fundamental concepts of the HSA and MSA; however, this new algorithm is completely different in structure. The HSA and MSA employ an individual HM, and MM, respectively. Each MM also organizes by multiple HM. However, the proposed SOSA uses multiple MM in symphony orchestra memory (SOM). In the proposed structure of the SOSA, the group improvisation with homogeneous music players is accomplished by interacting music players existing in each MM with each other similar to the performance of musicians in a specific music group. In the group improvisation with multiple-inhomogeneous music players, music players existing in symphony orchestra interact to each other like the performance of different music players in the symphony orchestra. The proposed SOM structure has been compared to the HM and the MM structures, as shown in Figure 3.

Computational Stages of the Newly Proposed SOSA

The computational stages of the newly proposed SOSA consist of three different stages. In the first computational stage, each music player existing in symphony orchestra can individually improvise its melody without taking type and effect of other musicians into account. In the second computational stage, all homogeneous music players existing in group m of music players (i.e., an analogous group of music players in the orchestra symphony) have a group performance, and improvise their

Figure 3. The structures of the HM, MM and SOM

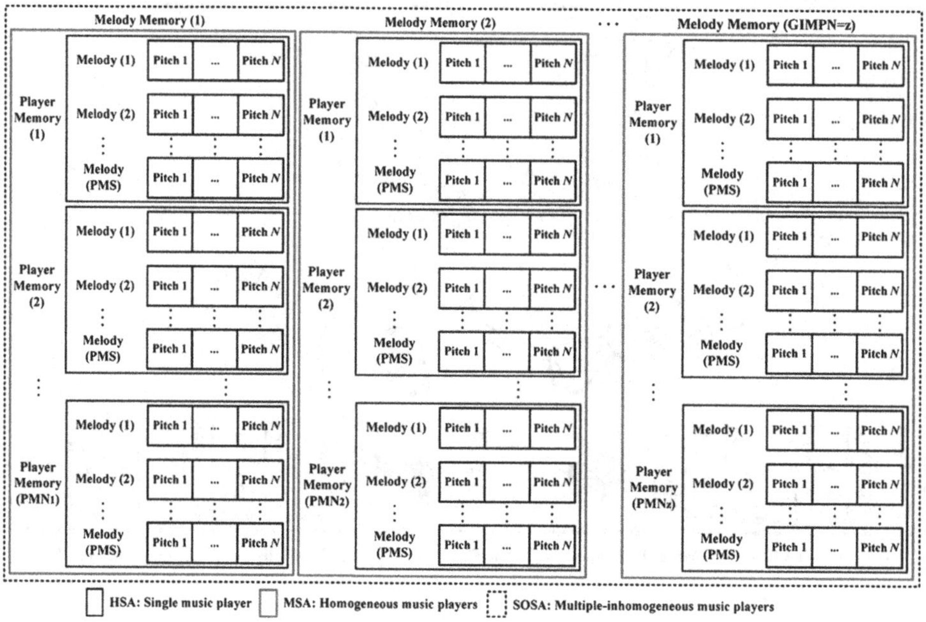

melodies by imitating the interactive relationship among members of respective music players group. In the third computational stage, all inhomogeneous music players (i.e., multiple heterologous music players groups in the orchestra symphony) have a symphonious performance in the symphony orchestra, and improvise their melodies by considering effects of all musicians existing in the symphony orchestra. The optimization process of the newly proposed SOSA is represented with a flowchart in Figure 4.

This process is classified in four stages for every considered optimization problem, as follows:

Stage 1: Initialize the optimization problem and choose the SOSA parameters.

Stage 2: Single improvisation stage:

  Sub-stage 2.1: Initialize the memory of all music players existing in the symphony orchestra ($PM_{(i)}^{(m)}$).

  Sub-stage 2.2: Improvise a new melody by each music player existing in the symphony orchestra, individually.

  Sub-stage 2.3: Update all ($PM_{(i)}^{(m)}$).

  Sub-stage 2.4: Iterate internal stages 2.2 and 2.3 till stopping criterion in the second stage, i.e., NIII, is satisfied.

Figure 4. Optimization procedure of the newly proposed SOSA

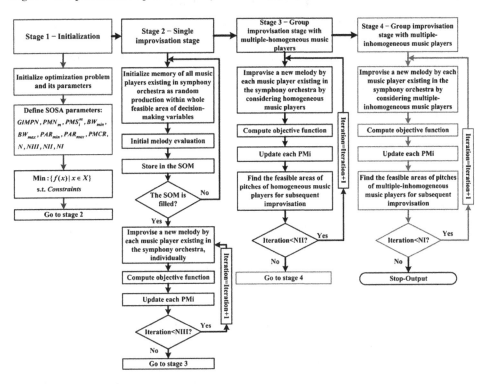

Stage 3: Group improvisation stage with multiple-homogeneous music players:

> **Sub-stage 3.1:** Improvise a new melody by each music player existing in the symphony orchestra by considering homogeneous music players.
>
> Sub-stage 3.2: Update all ($PM_{(i)}^{(m)}$).
>
> **Sub-stage 3.3:** Find the feasible areas of pitches of homogeneous music players for subsequent improvisation (only for randomization).
>
> **Sub-stage 3.4:** Iterate internal stages 3.1, 3.2 and 3.3 till stopping criterion in the third stage, i.e., *NII*, is satisfied.

Stage 4: Group improvisation stage with multiple-inhomogeneous music players:

> **Sub-stage 4.1:** Improvise a new melody by each music player existing in the symphony orchestra by considering multiple-inhomogeneous music players.
>
> **Sub-stage 4.2:** Update all ($PM_{(i)}^{(m)}$).
>
> **Sub-stage 4.3:** Find the feasible areas of pitches of multiple-inhomogeneous music players for subsequent improvisation (only for randomization).
>
> **Sub-stage 4.4:** Iterate internal stages 4.1, 4.2 and 4.3 till stopping criterion in the fourth stage, i.e., NI, is satisfied.

17

Stage 1: Initialize the Optimization Problem and Algorithm Parameters

In the first stage of SOSA, the optimization problem is defined, as follows:

$$\text{Minimize (or Maximize)} : f(x)$$
$$s.t. : x^{(n)} \in X^{(n)}; \forall n \in N$$
$$g_{(a)}(x) \geq 0; \forall a \in A \tag{7}$$
$$h_{(b)}(x) = 0; \forall b \in B$$

In the equation (7), $f(x)$ is objective function, $x^{(n)}$ is decision-making variable n, N is the number of pitches of melody vector or decision-making variables, $X^{(n)}$ is feasible areas for value of decision-making variable n, which is equal to $X^{(n)} = \left\{ x^{(n)}(1), x^{(n)}(2), ..., x^{(n)}(U), \right\}$ for discrete decision-making variables, or is equal to $UB^{(n)} \leq X^{(n)} \leq LB^{(n)}$ for continuous decision-making variables. U is the number of values of discrete decision-making variables. $UB^{(n)}$ and $LB^{(n)}$ are the upper and the lower bound for decision-making variable n, respectively. Also, $g(x)$ and $h(x)$ are the set of the inequality and quality constraint, respectively. In this stage, the SOSA parameters are categorized in Table 8. In the proposed structure, the SOM is organized as a memory location that all of improvised melody vectors are stored in it by musicians existing in the symphony orchestra.

Stage 2: Single Improvisation Stage

In this stage, searching for a well-designed configuration of pitches in the proposed SOSA is individually performed by each music player. In the initial sub-stage of the stage 2, memory of music players are randomly generated in the feasible area of decision-making variables by initial melodies according to the size of the music player memories. As stated hitherto, the SOM structure is organized by multiple MM ($MM_{(m)}$), and each MM is formed by multiple players' memories ($PM_{(i)}^{(m)}$), as follows:

$$SOM = \left[MM_{(1)}, MM_{(2)}, ..., MM_{(m)}, ...MM_{(GIMPN)} \right]; \forall m \in GIMPN \tag{8}$$

$$MM_{(m)} = \left[PM_{(1)}^{(m)}, PM_{(2)}^{(m)}, ..., PM_{(i)}^{(m)}, ..., PM_{(PMN_{(m)})}^{(m)} \right]^{\square}; \forall m \in GIMPN, \forall i \in PMN_{(m)} \tag{9}$$

Table 8. The newly proposed SOSA parameters

No.	SOSA parameters	Abbreviation	Parameter range
1	Bandwidth	BW	$BW \in \boldsymbol{R}^{(N)}_{>0}$
2	Maximum number of iterations for second stage	NIII	$NIII \geq 1$
3	Maximum number of iterations for third stage	NII	$NII \geq 1$
4	Maximum number of iterations for fourth stage	NI	$NI \geq 1$
5	Number of groups of the inhomogeneous music players	GIMPN	$GIMPN \geq 1$
6	Number of player memories of group m	$\boldsymbol{PMN}_{(m)}$	$\boldsymbol{PMN}_{(m)} \geq 1$
7	Number of decision-making variables	N	$N \geq 1$
8	Player memory considering rate	PMCR	$0 \leq PMCR \leq 1$
9	Pitch adjusting rate	PAR	$0 \leq PAR \leq 1$
10	Player memory size of player i in the music players group m	$\boldsymbol{PMS}^{(m)}_{(i)}$	$\boldsymbol{PMS}^{(m)}_{(i)} \geq 1$
11	Symphony orchestra memory	SOM	---

$$PM^{(m)}_{(i)} = \begin{bmatrix} x^{(1)}_{(m),(i),(1)} & x^{(2)}_{(m),(i),(1)} & \cdots & x^{(n)}_{(m),(i),(1)} & \cdots & x^{(N)}_{(m),(i),(1)} & | & Fit^{(1)}_{(m),(i)} \\ x^{(1)}_{(m),(i),(2)} & x^{(2)}_{(m),(i),(2)} & \cdots & x^{(n)}_{(m),(i),(2)} & \cdots & x^{(N)}_{(m),(i),(2)} & | & Fit^{(2)}_{(m),(i)} \\ \vdots & \vdots & \vdots & \vdots & \vdots & \vdots & | & \vdots \\ x^{(1)}_{(m),(i),(j)} & x^{(2)}_{(m),(i),(j)} & \cdots & x^{(n)}_{(m),(i),(j)} & \cdots & x^{(N)}_{(m),(i),(j)} & | & Fit^{(j)}_{(m),(i)} \\ \vdots & \vdots & \vdots & \vdots & \vdots & \vdots & | & \vdots \\ x^{(1)}_{(m),(i),(PMS^{(m)}_{(i)})} & x^{(2)}_{(m),(i),(PMS^{(m)}_{(i)})} & \cdots & x^{(n)}_{(m),(i),(PMS^{(m)}_{(i)})} & \cdots & x^{(N)}_{(m),(i),(PMS^{(m)}_{(i)})} & | & Fit^{(PMS^{(m)}_{(i)})}_{(m),(i)} \end{bmatrix}$$

$$; \forall m \in GIMPN, \forall i \in PMN_{(m)}, \forall j \in PMS^{(m)}_{(i)}, \forall n \in N \tag{10}$$

$$x^{(n)}_{(m),(i),(j)} = LB^{(n)}_{(m)} + rand(0,1).(UB^{(n)}_{(m)} - LB^{(n)}_{(m)}); \forall m \in GIMPN, \forall i \in PMN_{(m)}, \forall j \in PMS^{(m)}_{(i)}, \forall n \in N \tag{11}$$

$$x^{(n)}_{(m),(i),(j)} = X^{(n)}(l); \forall m \in GIMPN, \forall i \in PMN_{(m)}, \forall j \in PMS^{(m)}_{(i)}, \forall n \in N, \forall l = rand(\{1,2,...,U\}) \tag{12}$$

It is worth noting that the equations (11)-(12) are considered for continuous and discrete decision-making variables, respectively.

In here, the main differences between the proposed SOSA and other music-inspired algorithms are illustrated, as follows:

- The HSA and MSA have a single HM and single MM, respectively. A MM is established by multiple HM. The SOSA, however, has multiple MM (see equation (8)).
- In the proposed SOSA, the number of music players existing in each group of music players is considered to be different from other groups of music players. In other words, the number of music players (i.e., $PMN_{(m)}$) depends on index of groups of musicians; while, the HSA and the MSA are organized by only a music player and by only a group of musicians, respectively.
- In the proposed SOSA, the size of memory of each music player existing in the symphony orchestra is considered to be different from other music players. In simpler terms, the size of memory of each music player (i.e., $PMS_{(i)}^{(m)}$) depends on index of music players groups and index of music players in group m.
- In the proposed SOSA, the feasible areas of pitches or upper and lower bound of decision-making variable n (i.e., $UB_{(m)}^{(n)}$, $LB_{(m)}^{(n)}$) depend on index of groups of musicians. In the single improvisation stage, the upper and lower bound of decision-making variables for all music players groups are considered to be equal to the upper and lower bound of optimization problem. However, the new feasible areas can be determined both in the group improvisation stage with multiple-homogeneous music players, and in group improvisation stage with multiple-inhomogeneous music players.

As a result, these considerable features of the proposed SOSA can increase the diversity of solutions, improve the convergence speed of the algorithm; and finally, avoid of trapping in a local optimum point. In the sub-stage 2.2, each music player in the symphony orchestra improvises individually a new melody vector by considering its music instrument. In here, the authors present a well-founded improvisation procedure to generate a new melody vector based on the improvisation rules: 1) memory consideration, 2) pitch adjustment, and 3) random selection. In the sub-stage 2.3, by calculating the values of the objective functions, new improvised melody vectors by music player i in group m are compared with existing melody vectors in the memory. In this case, if new melody vector is better than the worst melody vector, it replaces the old one in the $PM_{(i)}^{(m)}$ and the existing worst melody discards from the $PM_{(i)}^{(m)}$. In the sub-stage 2.4, internal stages 2.2 and 2.3 are iterated till stopping criterion in the second stage, i.e., NIII, is satisfied.

Stage 3: Group Improvisation Stage with Multiple-Homogeneous Music Players

In this stage, to obtain well-designed configurations of pitches, music players of group m play their music instruments independently of other groups by considering interactive relationship among members of group. In the sub-stage 3.1, each music player in the symphony orchestra improvises a new melody vector according to interactive relationship among members of its group, and learning from the best music player associated with its group. In the sub-stage 3.2, the memory of music players in the symphony orchestra is updated based on performed procedure in sub-stage 2.3. In the sub-stage 3.3, the best melody is selected from entire music players of group m. Also, new feasible areas of pitches related to each decision-making variable in group m are determined for the next improvisation procedure. The implementation of this procedure has been expressed in Table 9. In the sub-stage 3.4, internal stages 3.1, 3.2 and 3.3 are iterated till stopping criterion in the stage 3, i.e., NII, is satisfied.

Stage 4: Group Improvisation Stage with Multiple-Inhomogeneous Music Players

In this stage, each music player existing in the symphony orchestra improvises its melody by considering different experiences, tastes and ideas of music players (i.e., music players with different music instruments), and taking the best music player of the symphony orchestra into account. Different melodies existing in the symphony orchestra and interactive relationship among all members of symphony orchestra can effectively conduct musician to choice better pitches, and increase the probability of playing a better melody. In this sub-stage 4.1, each music player in the symphony orchestra improvises a new melody vector by using the proposed improvisation procedure according to interactive relationship among members of the symphony orchestra, and learning from the best music player existing in the symphony orchestra. In the sub-stage 4.2, the memory of music players in the symphony orchestra is updated based on performed procedure in sub-stage 2.3. In the sub-stage 4.3, the best melody of each group of music players is chosen; and then, new feasible areas of pitches associated with each decision-making variable in the symphony orchestra is determined for the subsequent improvisation procedure. The implementation of this procedure has been represented in Table 10. In the sub-stage

Table 9. The implementation procedure to find the feasible areas of pitches for homogeneous music players in the SOSA

Input: $X^{(n)}_{(m),(i),(best)}$; $\forall m = 1, 2, \ldots, GIMPN, \ \forall i = 1, 2, \ldots, PMN_{(m)}, \ \ \forall n = 1, 2, \ldots, N$	
1:	**for** each music players group: $m \in \left[1, 2, \ldots, GIMPN\right]$ **do**
2:	**for** each decision-making variable: $n \in \left[1, 2, \ldots, N\right]$ **do**
3:	$LB^{(n)}_{(m)} = \min\left(X^{(n)}_{(m),(i),(best)}\right); \forall i = 1, 2, \ldots, PMN_{(m)}$
4:	$UB^{(n)}_{(m)} = \max\left(X^{(n)}_{(m),(i),(best)}\right); \forall i = 1, 2, \ldots, PMN_{(m)}$
5:	**end for**
6:	**end for**
Output: $LB^{(n)}_{(m)}$, $UB^{(n)}_{(m)}$ (lower and upper bounds of decision-making variable n for music players group m, respectively).	

4.4, internal stages 4.1, 4.2 and 4.3 are iterated till stopping criterion in the stage 4, i.e., NI, is satisfied.

The New Improvisation Procedure for the Proposed SOSA

In the newly proposed SOSA, a new improvisation procedure is employed to generate new melody vectors based on the main concepts of improvisation rules: 1) memory consideration, 2) pitch adjustment, and 3) random selection. In the memory consideration, two different rules are frequently implemented for continuous and discrete decision-making variables. For continuous decision-making variables, each rule organizes a linear combination of a selected variable from current music player memory, and a proportion of bandwidth. For discrete decision-making variables, however, each rule forms a selected variable from current music player memory. In the first rule, the value of each new decision-making variable (i.e., $X^{(n)}_{(m),(i),\text{new}}$, decision-making variable n in music player memory i in music players group m) is generated by using a corresponding decision-making variable of the respective music player memory (i.e.,

$X^{(n)}_{(m),(i),(j)}; \forall m = 1, ..., GIMPN, \forall i = 1, ..., PMN_{(m)}, \forall n = 1, ..., N, \forall j = rand(\{1, 2, ..., PMS^{(m)}_{(i)}\})$

In the second rule, the value of each new decision-making variable is generated by using a random decision-making variable amongst any one of the decision-making variables of the respective music player memory. The first rule enhances the convergence rate of the proposed optimization algorithm; while, the second rule increases the diversity of the generated solutions. Another important difference between the proposed SOSA and the MSA has been appeared in pitch adjustment rule. In the MSA, the pitch adjustment rule is similar to the single improvisation procedure and group improvisation procedure.

Table 10. The implementation procedure to find the feasible areas of pitches for inhomogeneous music players in the SOSA

Input: $X^{(n)}_{(m),(best),(best)}$; $\forall m = 1, 2, ..., GIMPN, \forall i = 1, 2, ..., PMN_{(m)}, \forall n = 1, 2, ..., N$	
1:	**for** each decision-making variable: $n \in [1, 2, ..., N]$ **do**
2:	$LB^{(n)} = \min\left(X^{(n)}_{(m),(best),(best)}\right); \forall m = 1, 2, ..., GIMPN$
3:	$UB^{(n)} = \max\left(X^{(n)}_{(m),(best),(best)}\right); \forall m = 1, 2, ..., GIMPN$
4:	**end for**
5:	**for** each music players group: $m \in [1, 2, ..., GIMPN]$ **do**
6:	$LB^{(n)}_{(m)} = LB^{(n)}; \forall n = 1, 2, ..., N$
7:	$UB^{(n)}_{(m)} = UB^{(n)}; \forall n = 1, 2, ..., N$
8:	**end for**
Output: $LB^{(n)}_{(m)}, UB^{(n)}_{(m)}$ (lower and upper bounds of decision-making variable n for music players group m, respectively).	

In the proposed SOSA, however, this rule is considered to be different in single improvisation, group improvisation with multiple-homogeneous music players, and group improvisation with multiple-inhomogeneous music players stages. In the pitch adjustment rule in single improvisation, the value of each new decision-making variable is generated by using a corresponding decision-making variable of the best melody vector stored in the respective music player memory (i.e., $X_{(m),(i),(best)}^{(n)}$; $\forall m = 1,...,GIMPN$, $\forall i = 1,...,PMN_{(m)}$, $\forall n = 1,...,N$). This value in group improvisation with multiple-homogeneous music players is generated by using a corresponding decision-making variable of the best melody vector stored in the memory of the best music player existing in the respective group of music players (i.e., $X_{(m),(best),(best)}^{(n)}$; $\forall m = 1,...,GIMPN$, $\forall n = 1,...,N$). Finally, this value in group improvisation with multiple-inhomogeneous music players is produced by using a corresponding decision-making variable of the best melody vector stored in the memory of the best music player existing in the best group of music players (i.e., $X_{(best),(best),(best)}^{(n)}$; $\forall n = 1,...,N$). In other words, each music player follows the best melody stored in its memory in single improvisation. However, in group improvisation with multiple-homogeneous music players, each music player follows the best melody stored in the memory of the best music player of its group. For the reason, in group improvisation multiple-inhomogeneous music players, each music player follows the best melody stored in the memory of the best music player of the symphony orchestra. In random selection rule, the value of each new decision-making variable for continuous decision-making variables is randomly generated by considering feasible areas of each decision-making variable. This value is randomly selected from the set of all candidate discrete values, namely, $\left\{ x^{(n)}(1), x^{(n)}(2),..., x^{(n)}(U) \right\}$, for discrete decision-making variables. The implementation of the improvisation procedure for continuous and discrete decision-making variables in the SOSA is represented in Table 11. To improve performance of the proposed SOSA and avoid getting trapped in local minimum, dynamic relationships of PAR and BW parameters is chosen in here. The PAR and BW parameters are dynamically updated by increasing the generation number according to the following equations.

$$PAR_{(gn)} = PAR_{min} + \frac{\left(PAR_{max} - PAR_{min} \right)}{NI}.(gn) \tag{13}$$

$$BW_{(gn)} = BW_{max} \times \exp^{\left(\frac{Ln\left(BW_{min} / BW_{max} \right)}{NI}.(gn) \right)} \tag{14}$$

Table 11. The implementation of the improvisation procedure for discrete and continuous decision-making variables in the SOSA

Input: N, GIMPN, $PMN_{(m)}$, $PMS_{(i)}^{(m)}$, PMCR, BW_{min}, BW_{max}, PAR_{min}, PAR_{max}, U, $UB^{(n)}$, $LB^{(n)}$	
1:	**for** each music players group: $m \in \left[1, 2, \ldots, GIMPN\right]$ **do**
2:	**for** each music player in music players group *m*: $i \in \left[1, 2, \ldots, PMN_{(m)}\right]$ **do**
3:	**for** each decision-making variable: $n \in \left[1, 2, \ldots, N\right]$ **do**
4:	**if** *rand* $(0,1) \le$ PMCR **then (player memory considering rate)**
5:	**if** *iteration counter* == odd
6:	$X_{(m),(i),\text{new}}^{(n)} = X_{(m),(i),(j)}^{(n)} \pm rand\left(0,1\right).BW_{(gn)}$; $\forall\, j = rand\left(\left\{1, 2, \ldots, PMS_{(i)}^{(m)}\right\}\right)$; for continuous decision-making variables.
7:	$X_{(m),(i),\text{new}}^{(n)} = X_{(m),(i),(j)}^{(n)}$; $\forall\, j = rand\left(\left\{1, 2, \ldots, PMS_{(i)}^{(m)}\right\}\right)$; for discrete decision-making variables.
8:	**else**
9:	$X_{(m),(i),\text{new}}^{(n)} = X_{(m),(i),(j)}^{(h)} \pm rand\left(0,1\right).BW_{(gn)}$; $\forall\, j = rand\left(\left\{1, 2, \ldots, PMS_{(i)}^{(m)}\right\}\right)$, $\forall\, h = rand\left(\left\{1, 2, \ldots, N\right\}\right)$; for continuous decision-making variables.
10:	$X_{(m),(i),\text{new}}^{(n)} = X_{(m),(i),(j)}^{(h)}$; $\forall\, j = rand\left(\left\{1, 2, \ldots, PMS_{(i)}^{(m)}\right\}\right)$, $\forall\, h = rand\left(\left\{1, 2, \ldots, N\right\}\right)$; for discrete decision-making variables.
11:	**end if**
12:	**if** *rand* $(0,1) \le PAR_{(gn)}$ **then (pitch adjusting rate)**
13:	**switch** 1

continued on following page

Table 11. Continued

14:	**Case** Iteration counter $\leq$ NIII **then**
15:	$X^{(n)}_{(m),(i),\text{new}} = X^{(n)}_{(m),(i),(best)}$; for continuous and discrete decision-making variables.
16:	**Case** Iteration counter > NIII && Iteration counter $\leq$ NII **then**
17:	$X^{(n)}_{(m),(i),\text{new}} = X^{(n)}_{(m),(best),(best)}$; for continuous and discrete decision-making variables.
18:	**Case** Iteration counter > NII && Iteration counter $\leq$ NI **then**
19:	$X^{(n)}_{(m),(i),\text{new}} = X^{(n)}_{(best),(best),(best)}$; for continuous and discrete decision-making variables.
20:	**end switch**
21:	**end if**
22:	**else (random selection)**
23:	$X^{(n)}_{(m),(i),\text{new}} = LB^{(n)}_{(m)} \pm rand\left(0,1\right).\left(UB^{(n)}_{(m)} - LB^{(n)}_{(m)}\right)$; for continuous decision-making variables.
24:	$X^{(n)}_{(m),(i),\text{new}} = X^{(n)}_{(m),(i)}\left(l\right)$; $\forall l = rand\left(\{1,2,...,U\}\right)$; for discrete decision-making variables.
25:	**end if**
26:	**end for**
27:	**end for**
28:	**end for**
Output:	$X^{(n)}_{(m),(i),\text{new}}$ (new melody vector)

In equation (13), $PAR_{(gn)}$ is the pitch adjustment rate in generation *gn*. PAR_{min} and PAR_{max} are the minimum and maximum pitch adjustment rates, respectively. In equation (14), $BW_{(gn)}$ is the distance bandwidth in generation *gn*. Also, BW_{min} and BW_{max} are the minimum and maximum bandwidths, respectively.

APPLICATION OF THE MUSIC-INSPIRED ALGORITHMS TO SOLVE NETWORK PLANNING

In order to evaluate the performance of the newly proposed SOSA, compared with other existing optimization problems, the authors consider a multi-objective NEP problem. To do so, the NEP problem is decomposed into a long-term planning master problem and a short-term operating slave problem. In the slave problem, network operating is carried out by maximizing social welfare function under a pool-based competitive market.

$$\text{Max.:}\ SWF = \sum_{j=1}^{J} \frac{1}{2} \delta_{(j)} d_{(j)}^2 + \sigma_{(j)} d_{(j)} + \zeta_{(j)} - \sum_{i=1}^{I} \frac{1}{2} \alpha_{(i)} g_{(i)}^2 + \beta_{(i)} d_{(i)} + \psi_{(i)}; \forall j \in J, \forall i \in I \tag{15}$$

This function is formed by the total benefit function minus the total apparent generation cost which is presented, as follow (Shivaie, Sepasian & Sheikh-El-Eslami, 2013b):

Subject to:

$$\sum_{j=1}^{J} d_{(j)} - \sum_{i=1}^{I} g_{(i)} = 0; \forall j \in J, \forall i \in I \tag{16}$$

$$\underline{g}_{(i)} \leq g_{(i)} \leq \overline{g}_{(i)}; \forall i \in I \tag{17}$$

$$\underline{d}_{(j)} \leq d_{(j)} \leq \overline{d}_{(j)}; \forall j \in J \tag{18}$$

$$-\underline{f}_{(l)} \leq f_{(l)} \leq \overline{f}_{(l)}; \forall l \in L \tag{19}$$

Equation (16) indicates the balance between generation and consumption. Equations (17)-(19) show limitations which are associated with generation, consumption, and the lines flow, respectively. Also, in equation (19), $f_{(l)}\left(g_{(i)}, d_{(j)}\right)$ is a function of generation and consumption. By solving operation problem (15)–(19), Locational Marginal Prices (LMPs) will be determined for all users. It is worth noting that the offer price of producers and bid price of consumers can be found in (Shivaie, Sepasian & Sheikh-El-Eslami, 2013b). On the other hand, in the planning master problem, investment cost index (ICI), total congestion cost index (TCCI), users'

benefit index (UBI) and expected customer interruption cost (ECOST) are taken into consideration as four objective functions in the optimization process, as follows:
Min.:

$$\mathbf{OF}_1 : ICI_{(m)} = \sum_{(s,r)\in\Omega} [CL_{(s),(r)} . \eta_{(s),(r)}] \times \frac{\nu(1+\nu)^T}{(1+\nu)^T - 1} \tag{20}$$

$$\mathbf{OF}_2 : TCCI_{(m)} = \sum_{p\in P} \Delta t_{(p)} . \left(\sum_{(s,r)\in\Omega} (lmp_r - lmp_s) . f_{sr} \right) \tag{21}$$

$$\mathbf{OF}_3 : ECCI_{(m)} = \sum_{e\in E} LCC_{(e)} \times sp_{(e)} \tag{22}$$

Max.:

$$\mathbf{OF}_4 : UBI_{(m)} = \sum_{p\in P} \Delta t_{(p)} . \Delta_m SWF \tag{23}$$

Subject to constraints (16)-(19) and also:

$$S^T F + G - D = 0 \tag{24}$$

$$f_{(s),(r)} - \gamma_{(s),(r)}(\eta^0_{(s),(r)} + \eta_{(s),(r)})(\theta_{(s)} - \theta_{(r)}) = 0; \forall (s,r) \in \Omega \tag{25}$$

$$\left| f_{(s),(r)} \right| \le (\eta^0_{(s),(r)} + \eta_{(s),(r)}) \overline{f}_{(s),(r)}; \forall (s,r) \in \Omega \tag{26}$$

$$0 \le \eta_{(s),(r)} \le \overline{\eta}_{(s),(r)} ; \eta_{(s),(r)} \ is \ integer \ variable, \forall (s,r) \in \Omega \tag{27}$$

$$Y_{(s),(r)} = -(y^0_{(s),(r)} + \eta_{(s),(r)} \tau_{(s),(r)}) ; s \ne r, \forall (s,r) \in \Omega \tag{28}$$

$$Y_{(s),(s)} = y_{s0} + \sum_{r\in s}(y^0_{(s),(r)} + \eta_{(s),(r)} \tau_{(s),(r)}) ; s \ne r, \forall (s,r) \in \Omega \tag{29}$$

Equations (24)-(25) are load flow relationships, and equation (26) points to the power flow limitations. Equation (27) requires transmission line expansion within the bounds of maximum line addition. Equations (28)-(29) simply update the network admittance matrix with expansion. The mathematical symbols, used throughout this section of the book chapter, are specified in (Shivaie, Sepasian & Sheikh-El-Eslami, 2013b).

Case Study and Simulation Results

In this section, the proposed multi-objective NEP problem was implemented in the Matlab environment using a Core i5 CPU clocking at 2.20 GHz and 6 GB RAM, and was implemented in the large-scale Iranian 400-kV transmission network, which shown in Figure 5. Network data and details of this test system can be found in (Shivaie & Ameli, 2016). Also, the required data for the NEP problem can be found in (Shivaie, Sepasian & Sheikh-El-Eslami, 2013b). The proposed multi-objective NEP problem has been performed by using the newly proposed SOSA, MSA, HSA, and NSGA-II. The newly proposed SOSA parameters adjustments have been given in Table 12. Also, the parameters adjustments of the MSA, HSA, and NSGA-II can be found in (Shivaie, 2016; Shivaie 2014; Shivaie, 2013a). After obtaining of non-dominated set, it is favorable to determine a flexible and realistic solution, which

Figure 5. Large-scale Iranian 400-kV transmission network

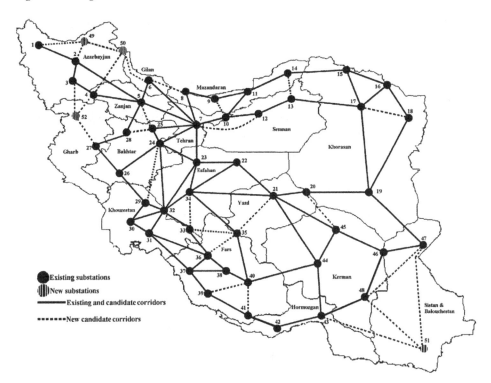

Table 12. Parameters adjustments of the newly proposed SOSA

No.	SOSA parameters	Values	No.	SOSA parameters	Values
1	*GIMPN*	4	7	BW_{min}	0.4
2	$PMN_{(m)}$	10	8	BW_{max}	0.9
3	$PMS_{(i)}^{(m)}$	250	9	NIII	400
4	HMCR	0.85	10	NII	600
5	PAR_{min}	0.2	11	NI	800
6	PAR_{max}	2	12	---	---

shows a compromise between different objectives. While, many methods have been employed to select a trade-off solution among a set of solutions, the fuzzy satisfying method (FSM) has been used in this book chapter due to its simplicity and similarity to human reasoning.

The fuzzy sets are defined by membership functions, which show the degree of membership in a fuzzy set using values from 0 to 1. In the FSM, there are many types of membership functions. In here, the linear type has been employed for all objectives. After definition of the membership function for each objective, the final solution is selected by the min-max formulation (conservative approach). Detailed description of this approach can be found in (Shivaie 2014; Shivaie, 2013a; Shivaie, 2013b). The calculated values of the multi-objective NEP problem by proposed optimization algorithms have been given in Table 13. As the results show, the multi-objective NEP problem by the SOSA leads to more efficient results than other optimization algorithms. Moreover, an Index of Cost Saving (ICS) is defined and implemented to more clearly assess the performance of the used optimization algorithms, as follows (Shivaie & Ameli, 2016):

$$ICS_{(a,b)} = \begin{cases} 1 - \dfrac{V_{(a)}^{OF}}{V_{(b)}^{OF}} & ; for \text{ minimization} \\ \dfrac{V_{(a)}^{OF}}{V_{(b)}^{OF}} - 1 & ; for \text{ maximization} \end{cases} \tag{30}$$

In other words, the ICS indicates the cost saving observed from the performance of each optimization algorithm, compared with the other optimization algorithms.

It is worth noting that in equation (30), $V_{(a)}^{OF}$ and $V_{(b)}^{OF}$ are the obtained values of objective functions by the optimization algorithms a and b, respectively. The ICS for the used optimization algorithms is tabulated in Table 14. As the results show, the performance of the newly proposed SOSA is more efficient than other optimization algorithms. For example, the ICS for investment cost by the newly proposed SOSA is 13.092%, 31.507% and 34.320% better than that by the MSA, original

Table 13. The NEP problem objectives by used optimization algorithms

No.	NEP problem indices	Calculated values of the NEP indices			
		SOSA	MSA	HSA	NSGA-II
1	Investment cost index (m$)	115.068	132.403	168.001	175.197
2	Total congestion cost index (m$)	13.807	16.681	18.912	19.005
3	Users' benefit index (m$)	382.361	294.548	259.230	246.219
4	Expected customer interruption cost index(k$/h)	85.744	89.735	97.261	99.337

Table 14. The ICS by using SOSA, MSA, HSA, and NSGA-II for different indices

No.	The NEP indices	Optimization algorithms	Optimization algorithms			
			SOSA	MSA	HSA	NSGA-II
1	ICS for investment cost index (%)	SOSA	0	13.092	31.507	34.320
		MSA	-15.065	0	21.189	24.426
		HSA	-46.001	-26.886	0	4.107
		NSGA-II	-52.255	-32.321	-4.283	0
2	ICS for total congestion cost index (%)	SOSA	0	17.229	26.993	27.350
		MSA	-20.815	0	11.796	12.228
		HSA	-36.973	-13.374	0	0.489
		NSGA-II	-37.647	-13.932	-0.491	0
3	ICS for users' benefit index (%)	SOSA	0	29.812	47.498	55.293
		MSA	-22.965	0	13.624	19.628
		HSA	-32.202	-11.990	0	5.284
		NSGA-II	-35.605	-16.407	-5.019	0
4	ICS for expected customer interruption cost index (%)	SOSA	0	4.447	11.841	13.683
		MSA	-4.654	0	7.737	9.666
		HSA	-13.431	-8.386	0	2.089
		NSGA-II	-15.853	-10.700	-2.134	0

Figure 6. Convergence characteristics of the proposed optimization algorithms

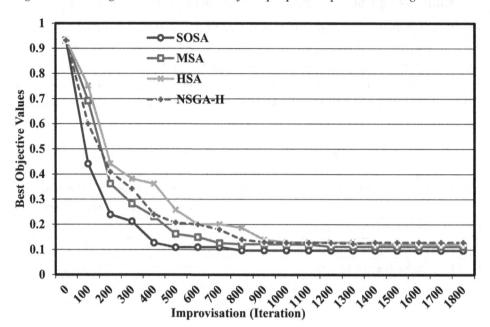

HSA, and NSGA-II, respectively. Furthermore, the convergence characteristic of the newly proposed SOSA is presented in Figure 6, and compared with convergence characteristics of the MSA, HSA, and NSGA-II. Looking at Figure 6, it can be observed that for real-word large-scale NEP problem proposed SOSA algorithm shows better convergence characteristic.

CONCLUSION

In this book chapter, the authors were presented an innovative strategy to enhance performance of the music-inspired optimization algorithms. In this strategy, by using multiple-inhomogeneous music players and three different well-organized stages for improvisation, an innovative symphony orchestra search algorithm (SOSA) was proposed to solve large-scale mixed-integer non-linear non-convex optimization problems with reasonable accuracy and convergence. Single improvisation stage, group improvisation stage with multiple-homogeneous music players, and group improvisation stage with multiple-inhomogeneous music players were considered as three different stages for improvisation in the SOSA. As a result, the SOSA was labeled as a multi-stage, multi-dimensional multiple-inhomogeneous music players optimization algorithm. Employing multiple-inhomogeneous music players in the proposed strategy with different tastes, ideas, experiences under interactive relationships among homogeneous and inhomogeneous music players can effectively conduct players to select better pitches, and increase the probability of playing a better melody. The newly proposed SOSA was successfully implemented on a large-scale non-convex optimization problem having non-linear mixed-integer nature, called the NEP problem, and tested on a real-world network. In addition, to demonstrate the efficiency and capability of the proposed SOSA, the performance of the proposed SOSA has been compared with the MSA, the HSA, and the NSGA-II. The obtained results from case study show that the newly proposed SOSA were more economical and effective than the calculated results from the MSA, the HSA, and the NSGA-II. As a result, the SOSA may be an appropriate algorithm for finding an optimal solution with higher accuracy and speed in comparison to other algorithms.

REFERENCES

Al-Betar, M., Khader, A., & Liao, I. (2010a). A harmony search with multi-pitch adjusting rate for the university course timetabling. In Z. W. Geem (Ed.), *Recent Advances in Harmony Search Algorithm* (pp. 147–161). Springer. doi:10.1007/978-3-642-04317-8_13

Al-Betar, M. A., Khader, A. T., & Nadi, F. (2010b). Selection mechanisms in memory consideration for examination timetabling with harmony search. *12th Annual Conference on Genetic and Evolutionary Computation,* 1203-1210.

Alia, O. M., Mandava, R., & Aziz, M. E. (2010). A hybrid harmony search algorithm to mri brain segmentation. *The 9th IEEE International Conference on Cognitive Informatics,* 712-719.

Alia, O. M., Mandava, R., Ramachandram, D., & Aziz, M. E. (2009a). A novel image segmentation algorithm based on harmony fuzzy search algorithm. *International Conference of Soft Computing and Pattern Recognition*, 335-340. doi:10.1109/SoCPaR.2009.73

Alia, O. M., Mandava, R., Ramachandram, D., & Aziz, M. E. (2009b). Dynamic fuzzy clustering using harmony search with application to image segmentation. *International Symposium on Signal Processing and Information Technology*, 538-543. doi:10.1109/ISSPIT.2009.5407590

Amaya, I., Cruz, J., & Correa, R. (2015). Harmony search algorithm: A variant with self-regulated fretwidth. *Applied Mathematics and Computation, 266*, 1127–1152. doi:10.1016/j.amc.2015.06.040

Ashrafi, S. M., & Dariane, A. B. (2011). A novel and effective algorithm for numerical optimization: melody search algorithm. *International Conference on Hybrid Intelligent Systems*, 109-114.

Ashrafi, S. M., & Dariane, A. B. (2013). Performance evaluation of an improved harmony search algorithm for numerical optimization: Melody search (MS). *Engineering Applications of Artificial Intelligence, 26*(4), 1301–1321. doi:10.1016/j. engappai.2012.08.005

Ayvaz, M. T., Kayhan, A. H., Ceylan, H., & Gurarslan, G. (2009). Hybridizing the harmony search algorithm with a spreadsheet solver for solving continuous engineering optimization problems. *Engineering Optimization, 41*(12), 1119–1144. doi:10.1080/03052150902926835

Chakraborty, P., Roy, G. G., Das, S., Jain, D., & Abraham, A. (2009). An improved harmony search algorithm with differential mutation operator. *Fundamenta Informaticae, 95*(4), 401–426.

Contreras, J., Amaya, I. A., & Correa, R. (2014). An improved variant of the conventional harmony search algorithm. *Applied Mathematics and Computation, 227*(4), 821–830. doi:10.1016/j.amc.2013.11.050

Dai, X., Yuan, X., & Zhang, Z. (2015). A self-adaptive multi-objective harmony search algorithm based on harmony memory variance. *Applied Soft Computing, 35*, 541–557. doi:10.1016/j.asoc.2015.06.027

Degertekin, S. (2008). Optimal design of steel frames using harmony search algorithm. *Structural and Multidisciplinary Optimization, 36*(4), 393–401. doi:10.1007/s00158-007-0177-4

Dorigo, M., Maniezzo, V., & Colorni, A. (1996). Ant system: Optimization by a colony of cooperating agents. *IEEE Transactions on Systems, Man, and Cybernetics, 26*(1), 29–41. doi:10.1109/3477.484436 PMID:18263004

Enayatifar, R., Yousefi, M., Abdullah, A. H., & Darus, A. N. (2013). LAHS: A novel harmony search algorithm based on learning automata. *Numerical Simulation, 18*(12), 3481–3497. doi:10.1016/j.cnsns.2013.04.028

Fesanghary, M., Mahdavi, M., Minary-Jolandan, M., & Alizade, Y., (2008). Hybridizing harmony search algorithm with sequential quadratic programming for engineering optimization problems. *Computer Methods in Applied Mechanics and Engineering, 197*(33-40), 3080-3091.

Forsati, R., Mahdavi, M., Kangavari, M., & Safarkhani, B. (2008). Web page clustering using harmony search optimization.*Canadian Conference on Electrical and Computer Engineering*, 1601-1604. doi:10.1109/CCECE.2008.4564812

Gao, X. Z., Wang, X., & Ovaska, S. J. (2008). Modified harmony search methods for uni-modal and multi-modal optimization.*8th International Conference on Hybrid Intelligent Systems*, 65-72. doi:10.1109/HIS.2008.20

Gao, X. Z., Wang, X., & Ovaska, S. J. (2009). Uni-modal and multi-modal optimization using modified harmony search methods. *International Journal of Innovative Computing, Information, & Control*, 5(10), 2985–2996.

Geem, Z. W. (2006). Improved harmony search from ensemble of music players. In B. Gabrys, R. J. Howlet, & L. C. Jain (Eds.), Knowledge-Based Intelligent Information and Engineering Systems (pp. 86-93). Bournemouth, UK: Springer. doi:10.1007/11892960_11

Geem, Z. W. (2009). Particle-swarm harmony search for water network design. *Engineering Optimization*, 41(4), 297–311. doi:10.1080/03052150802449227

Geem, Z. W., Kim, G. H., & Loganathan, G. V. (2001). A new heuristic optimization algorithm: Harmony search. *Simulation*, 76(2), 60–68. doi:10.1177/003754970107600201

Geem, Z. W., Tseng, C. L., & Park, Y. (2005). Harmony search for generalized orienteering problem: best touring in china. In L. Wang, K. Chen, & Y. S. Ong (Eds.), Advances in Natural Computation (pp. 741-750). Changsha: Springer. doi:10.1007/11539902_91

Glover, F. (1977). Heuristic for integer using surrogate constraint. *Decision Sciences*, 8(1), 156–166. doi:10.1111/j.1540-5915.1977.tb01074.x

Hasancebi, O., Erdal, F., & Saka, M. P. (2009). An adaptive harmony search method for structural optimization. *Journal of Structural Engineering*, 136(4), 419–431. doi:10.1061/(ASCE)ST.1943-541X.0000128

Hassan, B. H. F., Doush, I. A., Maghayreh, E. I. A., Alkhateeb, F., & Hamdan, M. (2014). Hybridizing harmony search algorithm with different mutation operators for continuous problems. *Applied Mathematics and Computation*, 232, 1166–1182. doi:10.1016/j.amc.2013.12.139

Holland, J. H. (1975). *Adaptation in natural and artificial systems*. Ann Arbor, MI: University of Michigan Press.

Jang, W. S., Kang, H. I., & Lee, B. H. (2008). Hybrid simplex-harmony search method for optimization problems.*IEEE Congress on Evolutionary Computation*, 4157-4164. doi:10.1109/CEC.2008.4631365

Karaboga, D. (2005). *An idea based on honey bee swarm for numerical optimization.* Technical Report-TR06. Available at http://mf.erciyes.edu.tr/abc/pub/tr06_2005.pdf

Kattan, A., Abdullah, R., & Salam, R. A. (2010). Harmony search based supervised training of artificial neural network.*International Conference on Intelligent Systems, Modeling and Simulation*, 105-110. doi:10.1109/ISMS.2010.31

Kaveh, A., & Talatahari, S. (2009). Particle swarm optimizer, ant colony strategy and harmony search scheme hybridized for optimization of truss structures. *Computers & Structures*, *87*(5-6), 267–283. doi:10.1016/j.compstruc.2009.01.003

Kennedy, J., & Eberhart, R. C. (1995). Particle swarm optimization.*Proceeding of IEEE International Conference on Neural Networks*, 1942-1948. doi:10.1109/ICNN.1995.488968

Khalili, M., Kharrat, R., Salahshoor, K., & Haghighat-Sefat, M. (2014). Global dynamic harmony search algorithm: GDHS. *Applied Mathematics and Computation*, *228*, 195–219. doi:10.1016/j.amc.2013.11.058

Kirkpatrick, S., Gelatt, C. D., & Vecchi, M. P. (1983). Optimization by simulated annealing. *Science*, *220*(4598), 671–680. doi:10.1126/science.220.4598.671 PMID:17813860

Layeb, A. (2013). A hybrid quantum inspired harmony search algorithm for 01 optimization problems. *Journal of Computational and Applied Mathematics*, *253*, 14–25. doi:10.1016/j.cam.2013.04.004

Lee, K. S., Geem, Z. W., Lee, S. H., & Bae, K. W. (2005). The harmony search heuristic algorithm for discrete structure optimization. *Engineering Optimization*, *37*(7), 663–684. doi:10.1080/03052150500211895

Lee, K. Y., & El-Sharkawi, M. A. (Eds.). (2008). *Modern heuristic optimization techniques*. Hoboken, NJ: John Wiley & Sons. doi:10.1002/9780470225868

Lee, Y. C., & Zomaya, A. Y. (2009). Fusion of clonal selection algorithm and harmony search method in optimization of fuzzy classification systems.*IEEE International Symposium on Parallel and Distributed Processing*, 1-8.

Li, M. J., Ng, M. K., Cheung, Y. M., & Huang, J. Z. (2008). Agglomerative fuzzy k-means clustering algorithm with selection of number of clusters. *IEEE Transactions on Knowledge and Data Engineering*, *20*(11), 1519–1534. doi:10.1109/TKDE.2008.88

Li, Q., Mitianoudis, N., & Stathaki, T. (2007). Spatial kernel k-harmonic means clustering for multi-spectral image segmentation. *Image Process IET*, *1*(2), 156–167. doi:10.1049/iet-ipr:20050320

Li, X. L., Shao, Z. J., & Qian, J. X. (2002). Optimization method based on autonomous animates: Fish-swarm algorithm. *System Engineering Theory and Practice*, *22*(11), 32–38.

Mahdavi, M., Chehreghani, M. H., Abolhassani, H., & Forsati, R. (2008). Novel meta-heuristic algorithms for clustering web documents. *Applied Mathematics and Computation*, *201*(1-2), 441–451. doi:10.1016/j.amc.2007.12.058

Mahdavi, M., Fesanghary, M., & Damangir, E. (2007). An improved harmony search algorithm for solving optimization problems. *Applied Mathematics and Computation*, *188*(2), 1567–1579. doi:10.1016/j.amc.2006.11.033

Maheri, M. R., & Narimani, M. M. (2014). An enhanced harmony search algorithm for optimum design of side sway steel frames. *Computers & Structures*, *136*(4), 78–89. doi:10.1016/j.compstruc.2014.02.001

Malaki, M., Pourbagheri, J. A., & Abolhassani, H. (2008). *A combinatory approach to fuzzy clustering with harmony search and its applications to space shuttle data.* SCIS & ISIS.

Moeinzadeh, H., Asgarian, E., Zanjani, M., Rezaee, A., & Seidi, M. (2009). Combination of harmony search and linear discriminate analysis to improve classification.*Third Asia International Conference on Modeling & Simulation*, 131-135. doi:10.1109/AMS.2009.125

Mukhopadhyay, A., Roy, A., Das, S., & Abraham, A. (2008). Population-variant and explorative power of harmony search: An analysis.*Third International Conference on Digital Information Management*.

Nadi, F., Khader, A. T., & Al-Betar, M. A. (2010). Adaptive genetic algorithm using harmony search.*12th Annual Conference on Genetic and Evolutionary Computation*, 819-820.

Omran, M. G. H., Mahdavi, M., & Damangir, E. (2008). Global best harmony search. *Applied Mathematics and Computation, 198*(2), 643–656. doi:10.1016/j.amc.2007.09.004

Pan, Q. K., Suganthan, P. N., Liang, J. J., & Tasgetiren, M. F. (2010b). A local-best harmony search algorithm with dynamic sub-populations. *Engineering Optimization, 42*(2), 101–117. doi:10.1080/03052150903104366

Pan, Q. K., Suganthan, P. N., Tasgetiren, M. F., & Liang, J. J. (2010a). A self-adaptive global best harmony search algorithm for continuous optimization problems. *Applied Mathematics and Computation, 216*(3), 830–848. doi:10.1016/j.amc.2010.01.088

Passino, K. M. (2002). Biomimicry of bacterial foraging for distributed optimization and control. *IEEE Control Systems, 22*(3), 52–67. doi:10.1109/MCS.2002.1004010

Qinghua, L., Shida, Y., & Youlin, R. (2006). A hybrid algorithm for optimizing multi-modal functions. *Wuhan University Journal of Natural Sciences, 11*(3), 551–554. doi:10.1007/BF02836663

Saka, M. P., & Hasancebi, O. (2009). Adaptive harmony search algorithm for design code optimization of steel structure. *Harmony Search Algorithms for Structural Design Optimization, 239*, 79–120. doi:10.1007/978-3-642-03450-3_3

Santos-Coelho, L. D., & De-Andrade-Bernert, D. L. (2009). An improve harmony search algorithm for synchronization of discrete-time chaotic systems. *Chaos, Solitons, and Fractals, 41*(5), 2526–2532. doi:10.1016/j.chaos.2008.09.028

Shivaie, M., & Ameli, M.-T. (2016). Strategic multiyear transmission expansion planning under severe uncertainties by a combination of melody search algorithm and Powell heuristic method. *Energy, 115*, 338–352. doi:10.1016/j.energy.2016.08.100

Shivaie, M., Salemnia, A., & Ameli, M.-T. (2013a). Optimal multi-objective placement and sizing of passive and active power filters by a fuzzy-improved harmony search algorithm. *International Transaction on Electrical Energy System, 25*(3), 520–546. doi:10.1002/etep.1863

Shivaie, M., Salemnia, A., & Ameli, M.-T. (2014). A multi-objective approach to optimal placement and sizing of multiple active power filters using a music-inspired algorithm. *Applied Soft Computing, 22*, 189–204. doi:10.1016/j.asoc.2014.05.011

Shivaie, M., Salemnia, A., & Sheikh-El-Eslami, M. K. (2013b). Multi-objective transmission expansion planning based on reliability and market considering phase shifter transformers by fuzzy-genetic algorithm. *International Transaction on Electrical Energy System, 23*(8), 1468–1489. doi:10.1002/etep.1672

Taherinejad, N. (2009). Highly reliable harmony search algorithm. *European Conference on Circuit Theory and Design*, 818-822. doi:10.1109/ECCTD.2009.5275109

Turgut, O. E., Turgut, M. S., & Coban, M. T. (2014). Design and economic investigation of shell and tube heat exchangers using improved intelligent tuned harmony search algorithm. *Ain Shams Engineering Journal, 5*(4), 1215–1231. doi:10.1016/j.asej.2014.05.007

Wang, C. M., & Huang, Y. F. (2010). Self-adaptive harmony search algorithm for optimization. *Expert Systems with Applications, 37*(4), 2826–2837. doi:10.1016/j.eswa.2009.09.008

Wang, X., Gao, X. Z., & Ovaska, S. J. (2009). Fusion of clonal selection algorithm and harmony search method in optimization of fuzzy classification systems. *International Journal of Bio-inspired Computation, 1*(1), 80–88. doi:10.1504/IJBIC.2009.022776

Xiang, W., An, M., Li, Y., He, R., & Zhang, J. (2014). An improved global-best harmony search algorithm for faster optimization. *Expert Systems with Applications, 41*(13), 5788–5803. doi:10.1016/j.eswa.2014.03.016

Yadav, P., Kumar, R., Panda, S. K., & Chang, C. S. (2012). An intelligent tuned harmony search algorithm for optimization. *Information Science, 196*, 47–72. doi:10.1016/j.ins.2011.12.035

Yang, X. S. (2009). Firefly algorithm for multimodal optimization. *Stochastic Algorithm: Foundations and Applications, 5792*, 169–178. doi:10.1007/978-3-642-04944-6_14

Yang, X. S. (2010). A new metaheuristic bat-inspired algorithm. *Nature Inspired Cooperative Strategies for Optimization, 284*, 65–74. doi:10.1007/978-3-642-12538-6_6

Yang, X. S., & Deb, S. (2009). Cuckoo search via levy flights. *World Congress on Nature & Biologically Inspired Computing*, 210-214. doi:10.1109/NABIC.2009.5393690

Yildiz, A. R. (2008). Hybrid taguchi-harmony search algorithm for solving engineering optimization problems. *Journal of Industrial Engineering: Theory. Applications and Practice, 15*(3), 286–293.

Yildiz, A. R., & Ozturk, F. (2010). Hybrid taguchi-harmony search approach for shape optimization. In Z. W. Geem (Ed.), *Recent Advances In Harmony Search Algorithm* (pp. 89–98). Springer. doi:10.1007/978-3-642-04317-8_8

Yuan, X., Zhao, J., Yang, Y., & Wang, Y. (2014). Hybrid parallel chaos optimization algorithm with harmony search algorithm. *Applied Soft Computing, 17*, 12–22. doi:10.1016/j.asoc.2013.12.016

Zhang, B., Pan, Q. K., Zhang, X. L., & Duan, P. Y. (2015). An effective hybrid harmony search-based algorithm for solving multidimensional knapsack problems. *Applied Soft Computing*, *29*, 288–297. doi:10.1016/j.asoc.2015.01.022

Zhao, F., Liu, Y., Zhang, C., & Wang, J. (2015). A self-adaptive harmony PSO search algorithm and its performance analysis. *Expert Systems with Applications*, *42*(21), 7436–7455. doi:10.1016/j.eswa.2015.05.035

Zou, D., Gao, L., Wu, J., & Li, S. (2010). Novel global harmony search algorithm for unconstrained problems. *Neurocomputing*, *37*(16-18), 3308–3318. doi:10.1016/j. neucom.2010.07.010

Chapter 2
Performance Analysis of Classifiers on Filter–Based Feature Selection Approaches on Microarray Data

Arunkumar Chinnaswamy
Amrita Vishwa Vidyapeetham University, Coimbatore, Campus, India

Ramakrishnan Srinivasan
Dr. Mahalingam College of Engineering and Technology, India

ABSTRACT

The process of Feature selection in machine learning involves the reduction in the number of features (genes) and similar activities that results in an acceptable level of classification accuracy. This paper discusses the filter based feature selection methods such as Information Gain and Correlation coefficient. After the process of feature selection is performed, the selected genes are subjected to five classification problems such as Naïve Bayes, Bagging, Random Forest, J48 and Decision Stump. The same experiment is performed on the raw data as well. Experimental results show that the filter based approaches reduce the number of gene expression levels effectively and thereby has a reduced feature subset that produces higher classification accuracy compared to the same experiment performed on the raw data. Also Correlation Based Feature Selection uses very fewer genes and produces higher accuracy compared to Information Gain based Feature Selection approach.

DOI: 10.4018/978-1-5225-2375-8.ch002

Copyright ©2017, IGI Global. Copying or distributing in print or electronic forms without written permission of IGI Global is prohibited.

1. INTRODUCTION

Statistical analysis of differentially expressed genes helps to assign them to different classes. This process enhances the basic understanding of the biological processes in the system. The activity of thousands of genes could be investigated simultaneously using the concept of microarray gene expression technology. Gene expression profiles are used to predict the relative abundance and presence of mRNA in the genes. The results obtained using suitable discriminant analysis represent the state of the cell that serves as a tool for the diagnosis, prediction and treatment of diseases. The hybridization process is used for generating DNA microarray samples. This process can be done in two ways. In the first method, during the process of hybridization, the messenger RNA (mRNA) taken from sample tissues or from the blood stream is converted to cDNA if it uses spotted arrays. RNA profiles may be noisy and might be unequally sampled over time. The second method involves the use of Affymetrix chips that hybridizes the oligonucleotides on the surface of the chip array. The simultaneous measurement and monitoring of thousands of genes using a single experiment is made possible by using DNA microarray technology (Li Yeh Chuang, Kuo-Chuan Wu, & Cheng-Hong Yang, 2008). The production of proteins in a gene signifies the gene expression level that aids in identifying the membership of the different classes. The presence of a wide variety of gene expression problems helps in advancement in the field of clinical medicine using results produced by several microarray experiments. Microarray data finds its application in the areas of cancer classification, disease diagnosis, prediction and treatment and most importantly in the area of gene identification that would be used in drug development at later stages. This has been a recent advancement in the area of clinical research. Microarray cancer data is combined with statistical techniques to analyze the gene expression patterns to identify potential bio markers for the diagnosis and treatment of different types of cancer (Arunkumar C & Ramakrishnan S, 2014).

The most common challenge in bioinformatics is the process of selecting relevant and non redundant genes from the dataset. Complex biological problems can only be solved by predicting and classifying the genes in the most efficient way. Feature Selection and Classification are considered to be the two key tasks in microarray gene expression analysis. The process of classification purely depends on Feature selection as the fewer gene subsets will contribute to adequate increase in classifier accuracy. Identification of a subset of differentially expressed genes is the main goal of feature selection. This identified subset would exhibit strong correlation between different classes and this helps to distinguish features between these classes. Another important measure is to avoid overfitting and build faster and cost effective models. During the process of feature selection there might be situations wherein a weakly ranked gene might perform well and a critical gene might be left out during the process of classification. The problem of classification is time consuming because of the fact that the sample size is very small and the dimensionality of the data is very large. The process of feature selection performed before classification reduces the running time and also increases the accuracy of prediction. Lot of research is carried out in predicting the essential features before the classification process and therefore increases the accuracy of prediction. In general, two key aspects govern the process of gene (feature) selection. They are functionally similar and closely related genes and the second is to find the smallest subset of genes that can provide meaningful diagnostic information for disease prediction and treatment without reduction in accuracy (Li Yeh Chuang et al., 2008). The process of disease diagnosis and treatment requires the use of only a small subset of genes and this subset helps in increasing the predictive accuracy. The predictive accuracy could be increased and incomprehensibility could be avoided by choosing the best feature selection method. The primary goal of classification is to build an efficient model that would identify differentially expressed genes and it could further be used to identify the classes in unknown samples. In this study, we used two filter based approaches to perform feature selection. They are easy to use, simple and computationally efficient (Cheng San Yang, Cheng-San Yang, Li-Yeh Chuang, Chao-Hsuan Ke, & Cheng-Hong Yang 2008).

2. RELATED METHODS

Supervised methods are used majorly for class comparison and prediction in microarray gene expression data. The difference between known classes is obtained using class comparison. Diagnosis of a tumor sample and assigning it to a class is done using class prediction. It builds a predictor model which deploys a multivariate function whose gene expression levels vary for different classes of tumors under study. The genes identified in class comparison are used by the predictor model for assignment into different classes. The major drawback of this model is overfitting (Ainhoa Perez Diez, Andrey Morgun, & Natalia Shulzhenko, 2007). The classifier produces higher accuracy level when deployed on the feature set on which it was built but might perform at a lower rate when tested on independent samples. Hence it becomes absolutely essential to validate the gene predictor. It is ideal to train the classifier using a training set and perform testing using an independent test set. The accuracy of the gene predictor might decrease because of the inclusion of a few misclassified samples. This could be because of neither sensitive nor specific diagnostic tests carried out to classify the samples in apriori fashion. Hence microarray gene expression data can be considered as the 'gold standard' for analyzing the gene information and performing the classification of diseases (Martinez-Glez V, Franco-Hernandez C, Rey JA, & 2008).

There are three different categories of Feature Selection. They are Supervised, Unsupervised and semi-supervised. Also Feature subset selection methods in machine learning algorithms can be classified into four types namely filter approach, wrapper approach, embedded approach and hybrid approach. There are several methods available in literature to perform the process of Feature Selection namely Filter Approaches that do not require a learning algorithm for a predictive model, Wrapper Approaches that are tailor-made for a particular classifier, regularized least squares, branch and bound algorithms and Support Vector Machines. The Filter approach is independent of the learning algorithm and hence it is easy to implement and performs faster computation. Once the feature selection is done, it can be used as input to the different classifiers. Wrapper approaches are computationally intensive as it needs to evaluate each of the features to perform the classification. Various feature ranking and feature selection techniques have been proposed such as Correlation-based Feature Selection (CFS), Principal Component Analysis (PCA), Gain Ratio (GR) attribute evaluation, Chi-square Feature Evaluation, Fast Correlation-based Feature selection (FCBF), Information gain, Euclidean distance, t-test and Markov blanket filter (Seetharam L, Venkata Subba Reddy P, & Laxmi B.Rananavare, 2011). Some of the above filter methods do not perform feature selection. Instead they perform feature ranking and hence they need to be combined with suitable search methods to estimate the number of attributes required for classification. Such filters are often used with forward selection, which considers only additions to the feature subset, backward elimination, bi-directional search, best-first search, genetic search and other methods (Shahram Golzari, Shyamala Doraisamy, Md Nasir B. Sulaiman, Nur Izura Udzir, & Noris Mohd. Norowi, 2008).

The four diseases analyzed are ALL/AML, Lung Cancer, Prostate Cancer and Ovarian Cancer. These four diseases fall under the category of binary class problems. The different modalities used for diagnosis of these diseases are given as under in Table 1:

Table 1. Description of the Modalities used for Cancer Diagnosis

Name of the Disease	Modalities used for Diagnosis
ALL/AML	Blood Test, Bone Marrow Test(Aspiration and Biopsy), Lumbar Puncture, Microarray Analysis
LUNG CANCER	Biopsy, Sputum cytology, Imaging tests(X-Ray/CT), Microarray Analysis
PROSTATE CANCER	Digital Rectal Exam, Prostate specific antigen test, Ultrasound, Prostate Biopsy, Microarray Analysis
OVARIAN CANCER	Biopsy, Ultrasound, CT, Barium Enema X-ray, PET Scan, Microarray Analysis

Microarray Analysis and Biopsy are the two methods that exist in common among the different types of cancer. There are certain complications that might arise after biopsy that includes hemorrhage, infection, puncture damage to nearby organs and skin numbness around the biopsy site. In addition to the above complications post biopsy, some issues that exist are the biopsy is performed from a small local site whereas the cancerous tissue might be present elsewhere. This might not produce the desired result.

In the first step, the classifiers are applied on raw dataset. The accuracy of the classifiers is analyzed. The sequence of steps followed in Method 1 is depicted in Figure 1 and marked as A1, A2 and A3. In the second step, filter based approaches are used for feature selection and then the classifiers are applied. The sequence of steps followed in Method 2 is depicted in Figure 1 and marked as B1, B2, B3 and B4.

Experimental results proved that the classifier accuracy is greatly improved after the feature selection is performed on the dataset.

2.1 Information Gain

The traditional filter based approach called as Information Gain (IG) assigns a weight value to each gene in the dataset. After this process, genes with higher values for their weights are chosen to represent the candidate set that could be used for classification (Cheng-San Yang, Li-Yeh Chuang, Jung-Chike Li, & Cheng-Hong Yang, 2008). The concept of decision tree classifiers is used for Feature Selection using Information gain that exhibits good classification performance (Martin-Valdivia M T, Diaz-Galiano M C, Montejo-Raez A, & Urena-Lopez L A, 2008). Information Gain based feature selection focuses on selecting the key features that reveal maximum information about a particular class or a group of classes. Considering an ideal scenario, these features will be present in a single class as these features would be highly discriminative (Mukras R, Wiratunga N, Lothian R, Chakraborti S, & Harper D, 2007). The concept of entropy is the key to Information Gain as it provides a suitable measure for the same. It gives a measure of the reduction in the

Figure 1. Steps followed using Method 1(A1, A2, A3) and Method 2(B1, B2, B3, B4)

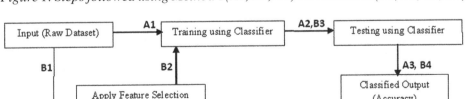

entropy value after finding the values of specific attributes. Therefore, Information Gain value indicates the amount of information that would be contributed by a specific attribute in the dataset (Martin Valdivia et al., 2008). Each feature in the dataset produces an Information Gain value that would be used to select or discard a particular feature (gene). Hence it becomes necessary to define a suitable threshold value. The feature selection process is done if the IG value is higher than the defined threshold. Information Gain is calculated using equation 1 as

$$Gain(S,A) = Entropy(S) - sum(|S_v|/|S|) * Entropy(S_v))$$ (1)

Where S is a sample of training examples, Gain(S, A) is the expected reduction in entropy due to sorting S on attribute A, S_v is the set of training instances remaining from S after restricting to those for which attribute A has value v.

Let *S* be the set of *n* instances and *C* be the set of k classes. $P(C_i, S)$ represents the fraction of the example in *S* that has class C_i. Then, the expected information from this class membership is given by equation 2 as

$$Info(S) = -\sum P(C_i,S) * log(P(C_i,S))$$ (2)

If a particular attribute *A* has *v* distinct values, the expected information is obtained by the decision tree in which *A* is the root, and the weighted sum of expected information of the subsets of *A* is based on the distinct values. Let S_i be the set of instances and A_i the value of attribute *A* as in equation 3 as

$$InfoA(S) = -\sum(S_i/S) * Info(S_i)$$ (3)

Then, the difference between *Info(S)* and *InfoA(S)* provides the information gained by partitioning *S* according to the test *A* as in equation 4 as

$$Gain(A) = Info(S) - InfoA(S)$$ (4)

Information gain values of individual attributes are found out using WEKA (machine learning software in java). Attributes having non-zero information gain are selected and fed to the different classifier algorithms and the results are analyzed (Cheng-Huei Yang, Li-Yeh Chuang, & Cheng-Hong Yang, 2010).

2.2 Correlation Coefficient

Correlation based heuristic evaluation function is used to rank the subset of genes in Correlation based feature selection by computing its coefficients. A subset of attributes is evaluated by considering the identification ability of each attribute. It overcomes the disadvantage of univariate filter approaches that does not take into account the interaction between features (Mark.A.Hall, 1999; Cosmin Lazar et al., 2012). The identification ability of each of the attributes is used to evaluate a subset of attributes. The correlation that exists among the different genes in the dataset could be identified using a multivariate approach in an effective manner. Pearsons correlation coefficient is very sensitive to the presence of outliers and noise (Li M. Fu & Eun Seog Youn, 2003; Joaquim F. Pinto da Costa, Hugo Alonso, & Lui's Roque, 2011). The relationship between genes can be measured by the process of correlation (Cheng-San Yang, Li-Yeh Chuang, Chao-Hsuan Ke, & Cheng-Hong Yang, 2008). The linear relationship between two variables is depicted by using the most common measure of correlation in statistics called the Pearson Product Moment Correlation. Formula for calculating Pearson correlation between features x_i and y_i is given in equation 5 as

$$Correlation = \sum(x_i\text{-}mean(x_i))*(y_i\text{-}mean(y_i)/n*\sigma(x_i)*\sigma(y_i)) \qquad (5)$$

Pearson correlation coefficient between attributes is found out. Genes that possess low inter-correlation are selected (Arunkumar C & Ramakrishnan S, 2014; Ammu Prasanna Kumar & Preeja Valsala, 2013). The WEKA tool is used to implement CFS for selecting a subset of attribute gene information from a larger dataset. The selected genes were used to study the different types of cancer. The attributes exhibit high correlation if the value of correlation coefficient lies between 0.5 and 1 and is said to be less correlated if its value lies between 0.3 and 0.5 (Arunkumar C & Ramakrishnan S, 2015).

2.3 Naive Bayes Classifier

A Naive Bayes classifier is a simple probabilistic classifier that follows the independent feature model. This model uses the Bayes theorem as a basis that employs strong independent assumptions. It is also one of the oldest classifiers that use the Bayes rule for classification (Pradipta Maji, 2012). In simple terms, a naive Bayes classifier works on the concept of total independence. It means that the presence of a candidate gene in a subset is unrelated to the presence of any other gene and vice-versa (Kumaravel A & Aarthi A, 2013). For example, consider the classification problem of different types of tumors. A tumor could be identified based on certain gene expression levels or features and tests. This classifier assumes that the presence of each gene contributes independently to the identification of the tumor class even if these feature genes are dependent among themselves or on other feature subsets. An important part of this algorithm is that it is independent of the features and produces excellent results (Qinbao Song, Jingjie Ni, & Guangtao Wang, 2013).

In a supervised learning environment, the naive bayes classifier could be trained very efficiently. This requires knowledge of the nature of the probability model. Many practical applications involve the usage of the Maximum likelihood method. In such cases, the model could work perfectly without using any of the Bayesian methods or the concept of Bayesian probability. Naive Bayes classifiers are most suitable for complex real world problems. This has been true even though the classifier has a naïve design and all assumptions made are over simplified. Even though the analysis of the Bayesian classification problems in 2004 showed some unreasonable efficacy, this classifier outperforms more current approaches like trees and random forests. The requirement of fewer feature samples during the training phase is the major advantage of this Classifier. The mean and variance is computed using this small sample of data during classification. It does not require the calculation of the entire covariance matrix. Since it uses independent variables, the variances of the variables of each class only need to be computed (Shadab Adam Pattekari & Asma Parveen, 2012; Acharjya D P, Debasrita Roy & Rahaman A, 2012).

2.4 Bagging

Bagging is also called bootstrap aggregation. This ensemble method randomly redistributes the training set to create individuals for training each classifier. The training set of the classifier is generated by randomly drawing 'M' samples with replacement from a total sample size of 'N'. In certain cases, some samples may be repeated while others may be left out. The individual classifiers in the ensemble are generated by random sampling of the training set. The Bagging method is very effective on Decision Trees and Neural networks which are considered as unstable learning algorithms. Minor changes in the training set results in major changes in the classifier accuracy. Bootstrap is completely automatic process. No theoretical calculations are required for the Bootstrap process. It is not based on asymptotic results (Gulshan Kumar & Krishan Kumar, 2012; Govindarajan M & Chandrasekaran R M, 2011).

2.5 Random Forest

Many classification trees are grown by random forests. The input vectors are placed under each of the trees in a forest in order to classify a new object. The process of 'voting' is carried out for the purpose of classification. The classification with the maximum number of votes among existent trees in a forest is chosen. The strength of individual tree and the correlation greatly influence the forest error rate. Increase in strength decreases the error rate whereas increase in correlation increases the error rate. A strong classifier is obtained only if the error rate is less. Two data objects are generated by random forests. Whenever sampling is done with replacement on the training set for the current tree, 33% of the cases would be left out of the sample. An unbiased estimate of the classification error could be obtained by using OOB as and when trees are added to the forest. During the process of tree building, the entire data is run down the tree in order to compute the proximity values for each pair. The value of proximity can be incremented by one if two pairs occupy the same terminal node. Normalization is done on all proximity values by dividing by the number of trees after the entire run is completed. The main uses of proximities are for replacing missing data, illumination of low dimensional views of data and location of outliers. Random forest is sensitive to 'm', the only adjustable parameter. Increase or decrease in the value of 'm' will increase the correlation or decrease the strength. Hence an optimal value for 'm' needs to be found which is possible by using the OOB (out-of-bag) error rate (Florin Leon, Catalin Lisa, & Silvia Curteanu, 2010). The working of the Random Forest Classifier is depicted by means of a flowchart as in Figure 2

Some of the features of Random Forest include highest accuracy among the available algorithms, efficient execution in large datasets, ability to handle thousands of variables without variable deletion, ability to highlight the important variables in a classification, generation of an internal unbiased estimate of the generalization error as the forest building progresses, error balancing in unbalanced datasets, implementation of effective methods to populate the missing data and maintaining the accuracy at the same time, detecting variable interactions, computation of proximity between pairs of cases that can be used in clustering, computation of prototypes that provide information about the relation between variables, the ability to apply this technique to label the unsupervised data and to detect the presence of outliers (Jian-Hua Huang, Rui-Hua He, Lun-Zhao Yi, Hua-Lin Xie, Dong-sheng Cao, & Yi-Zeng Liang, 2013).

2.6 J48

J48 classifier is the most useful, simple, predictive C4.5 binary decision tree for classification based on decision trees or rules. This algorithm involves the process of building a tree and then applying it to each tuple in the database. This results in the classification of that tuple. All missing values are ignored by this algorithm. It divides the data into ranges based on the gene expression values that are available in the training sample. It predicts the target value of a new sample with knowledge of the available data. The attribute value that needs to be predicted is called a dependent variable since its value is determined by the other attributes. All attributes that help

Figure 2. Flowchart for Random Forest Classifier

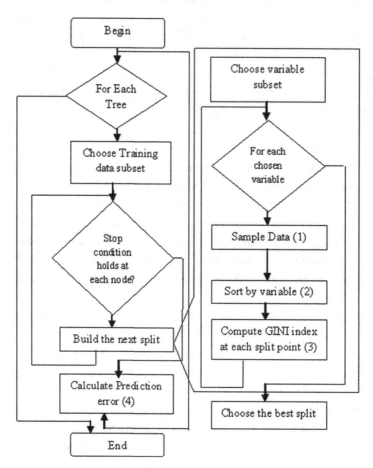

in predicting the value of a dependent variable is called an independent variable specific to a particular dataset. The decision tree is divided into internal nodes, branches and terminal nodes. Internal nodes represent the different gene expression values, the branches indicate the possible values of the genes in the observed samples and the terminal nodes represent the final classified output (dependent variable). This classifier adopts a simple approach for classification. This algorithm works on the basic concept of Information Gain. Whenever a new feature is encountered, it first creates a decision tree based on available data from the training samples. This is done by choosing the feature with the highest information gain. Whenever the values are unambiguous the branch is terminated and the target value obtained is assigned. Else attributes that possess high values for information gain are searched. The algorithm terminates if attributes are exhausted or a combination of attributes is determined. In the worst case, if all attributes are exhausted or an unambiguous result is not found, a target value for the branch is assigned which would be the value that a majority of the features in that branch possess (Suneetha Manne & Sameen Fatima, 2011; Bhagya Shree S R & Sheshadri, H.S, 2014; Nikhil Sanyog Choudhary, Himanshu Yadav, & Anurag Jain, 2015).

2.7 Decision Stump

A one level decision tree makes up a decision stump also called a 1-rule. It derives this name as it makes a decision based on a single feature. This machine learning model consists of one root also called the internal node which is connected immediately to its leaves or terminal nodes. Several variants exist based on the type of the input feature. For nominal features, one may build a stump which contains a leaf for each possible feature value or a stump with the two leaves, one of which corresponds to some chosen category, and the other leaf to all the other categories. For binary features these two schemes are identical. A missing value may be treated as yet another category. The stump consists of two leaves in the case of continuous features. One leaf might correspond to a feature value above the threshold and the other below the threshold. However, rarely, multiple thresholds may be chosen and the stump therefore contains three or more leaves. Bagging and boosting ensemble uses decision stumps as a base or weak learner (Mohammad Massinaei, Sedaghati M R, & Rezvani R, 2014). The algorithm for decision stump classifier is depicted below:

Given: $(x_1, y_1), \ldots, (x_m, y_m); x_i \, \varepsilon \, X, \, y_i \, \varepsilon \, \{-1, 1\}$
Initialize weights $D_1(i) = 1/m$
For $t=1, \ldots, T$:

1. *(Call WeakLearn), which returns the weak classifier $h_t: X \to \{-1, 1\}$ with minimum error w.r.t Distribution D_t;*
2. *Choose $\alpha_t \, \varepsilon \, R$*
3. *Update $D_{t+1}(i) = D_t(i)exp(-\alpha_t y_i h_t(xi)) / Z_t$ where Z_t is a normalization factor chosen so that D_{t+1} is a distribution*
4. *Output the strong classifier $H(x) = sign(\sum \alpha_t h_t(x))$*

3. DATASET DESCRIPTION

This chapter uses four binary category cancer-related human gene expression data sets, which are downloaded from Kent ridge biomedical repository to evaluate the performance of the proposed method. This database is considered as the benchmark

Table 2. Description of the Dataset used for the study

Dataset Name	Number of Genes in Raw Dataset
ALL/AML	7,129
Lung Cancer	12,533
Ovarian Cancer	15,154
Prostate Cancer	12,600

dataset for microarray data. This dataset is being used as the 'gold standard' for microarray data as it is being used extensively in most of the papers listed below. This dataset is also used in *"Science and Nature Journals" and "IEEE Transactions"* which are one of the most reputed and high impact journals in the world. Some of the papers that make use of this dataset are (Sheng Liu et al., 2012; Yukyee Leung & Yeungsam Hung, 2010; Guoli Ji, Zijiang Yang, & Wenjie You, 2011). The data format is shown in Table 2; it includes the data set name, the number of genes, number of training and testing samples.

Acute lymphoblastic leukemia, also known as acute lymphocytic leukemia or acute lymphoid leukemia (ALL), is an acute form of leukemia, or cancer of the white blood cells, characterized by the overproduction and accumulation of cancerous, immature white blood cells, known as lymphoblast. Acute myeloid leukemia (AML), also known as acute myelogenous leukemia or acute nonlymphocytic leukemia (ANLL), is a cancer of the myeloid line of blood cells, characterized by the rapid growth of abnormal white blood cells that accumulate in the bone marrow and interfere with the production of normal blood cells. The dataset consists of 72 samples out of which 47 are ALL and 25 are AML.

Lung cancer, also known as carcinoma of the lung or pulmonary carcinoma, is a malignant lung tumor characterized by uncontrolled cell growth in tissues of the lung. If left untreated, this growth can spread beyond the lung by process of metastasis into nearby tissue or other parts of the body. Most cancers that start in the lung, known as primary lung cancers, are carcinomas that derive from epithelial cells. The dataset consists of 181 tissue samples out of which 150 belong to ADCA and 31 are MPM.

Ovarian cancer is a type of cancer that begins in the ovaries. This develops in women who have higher risk of development due to family or personal history. The dataset consists of 253 samples out of which 162 are ovarian cancer and 91 are controls (normal).

Prostate cancer, also known as carcinoma of the prostate, is the development of cancer in the prostate, a gland in the male reproductive system. Most prostate cancers are slow growing; however, some grow relatively quickly. The cancer cells may spread from the prostate to other parts of the body, particularly the bones and lymph nodes. The dataset consists of 136 samples out of which 77 are tumor samples and 59 are non-tumor (normal) samples.

4. EXPERIMENTAL RESULTS

The performance of the proposed method is evaluated by using selected feature gene subsets from microarray cancer gene expression data using five different classifiers. The entire dataset is used for the purpose of training and testing by using 10-fold cross validation strategy.

This study tested and compared the information gain based filter feature selection method's performance on the classification of four binary-class cancer microarray expression data sets. This performance is evaluated against correlation based filter. After feature selection, the selected feature subsets are evaluated using five different classifiers using a 10-fold cross validation technique. The number of features (genes) selected by different feature selection methods are tabulated in Table 3

With reference to Table 3 above, in the case of the ALL/AML dataset with 7129 genes in the raw dataset, correlation based filter method selects 1.14% (81 genes) of the total genes and produces an accuracy of 100% in majority of the cases. In the case of Lung Cancer dataset, it selects 1.28% (160 genes) from the raw dataset and produces a classifier accuracy of 95-100%. In the case of Ovarian Cancer dataset, it selects 0.23% (35 genes) from the raw dataset and produces a classifier accuracy of 96-100%. In the case of Prostate Cancer dataset, it selects 0.6% (75 genes) from the raw dataset and produces a classifier accuracy of 85-100% with the exception of Naïve Bayes classifier that produces 63.97% which is higher than Information Gain based feature selection approach.

In order to evaluate the performance of the classifier, the following parameters are used namely Accuracy, Precision, Recall, F-Measure and Region of Character-istic (ROC) Area. In order to compute the above parameters, it is essential to define certain terminologies namely:

Table 3. Number of Genes selected by Filter Based Methods

Dataset	Raw Dataset	Information Gain	Correlation Coefficient
ALL/AML	7,129	1025	81
Lung Cancer	12,533	4981	160
Ovarian Cancer	15,154	6237	35
Prostate Cancer	12,600	2657	75

- True Positive(t_p) – equivalent with hit
- True Negative(t_n) – Correct rejection
- False Positive(f_p) – False Alarm
- False Negative(f_n) – Miss

The true positive, true negative, false positive and false negative could be computed easily by observing the confusion matrix. The sample confusion matrix is shown in the Figure 3.

The formulae used to compute the Accuracy of the classifier is given in equation 6 as

$$\text{Accuracy} = (t_p + t_n) / (t_p + t_n + f_p + f_n) \tag{6}$$

The denominator value in Eq 2 is called the total population size. The comparative chart representing the classifier accuracy for the raw dataset, information gain and correlation coefficient feature selection is depicted in Figure 4, Figure 5, Figure 6 and Figure 7 as below

Precision and Recall are the two basic parameters used for evaluation in search strategies and based on understanding and measure of relevance. Precision also called the positive predictive value is the fraction of the retrieved instances that are relevant. Recall also called as sensitivity is the fraction of relevant instances that are retrieved.

The formulae used to compute the Precision is given in equation 7 as

$$\text{Precision} = t_p / (t_p + f_p) \tag{7}$$

Figure 3. Sample Confusion Matrix

```
=== Confusion Matrix ===


    a  b    <-- classified as
   41  6 |   a = ALL
    6 19 |   b = AML
```

Figure 4. Accuracy for the raw dataset, information gain and correlation coefficient feature selection

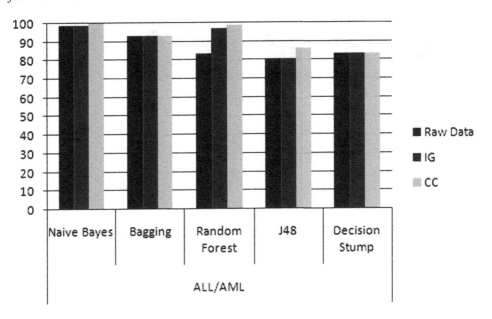

Figure 5. Accuracy for the raw dataset, information gain and correlation coefficient feature selection

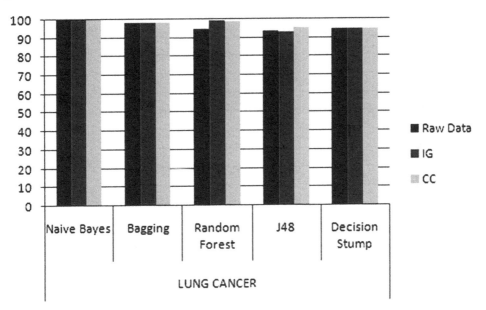

Figure 6. Accuracy for the raw dataset, information gain and correlation coefficient feature selection

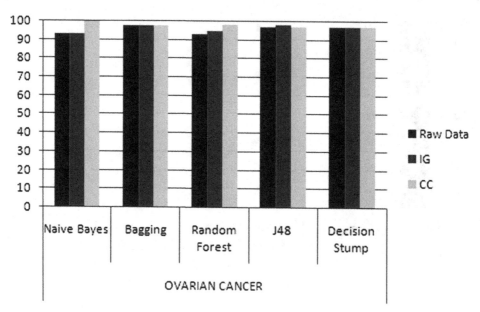

Figure 7. Accuracy for the raw dataset, information gain and correlation coefficient feature selection

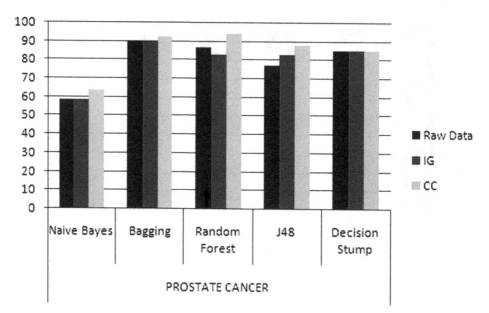

Figure 8. Sample Confusion Matrix for computing Precision and Recall

```
=== Confusion Matrix ===


 a  b   <-- classified as
29 48 |  a = Tumor
 1 58 |  b = Normal
```

The formulae used to compute the Recall also called Sensitivity is given in equation 8 as

$$Recall = t_p/(t_p+f_n) \tag{8}$$

The Precision and Recall could be easily computed from the confusion matrix. Consider a resultant sample confusion matrix for the Prostate cancer dataset obtained by applying the correlation based filter on a naïve bayes classifier as given below in Figure 8 below:

The row total of the above confusion matrix in Figure 7 is R1 – 77 and R2 - 59. Similarly, the column total of the above confusion matrix is C1 – 30 and C2 – 106.

The Precision for Label a is computed using the formula in equation 9 as

$$Precision \text{ (for label A)} = TP\_a/(TP\_a+FP\_a) \tag{9}$$

where TP stands for True Positive and FP stands for True Negative.

Precision (for label A) = 29/R1 (77) = 0.376

Precision (for label B) = 58/R2 (59) = 0.983

After the Precision values are computed for each label, the average value is computed and is found to be 0.679. The precision values are computed for the four datasets and tabulated in Tables 4-7

The Recall for Label a is computed using the formula in equation 10 as

$$Recall \text{ (for label A)} = TP\_a/(TP\_a+FN\_a) \tag{10}$$

where TP stands for True Positive and FN stands for False Negative.

Table 4. Precision for ALL/AML Dataset

ALL/AML - PRECISION			
Classifier	**Information Gain**	**Correlation Coefficient**	**Class**
Naive Bayes	0.979	1.000	ALL
	1.000	1.000	AML
	0.986	1.000	Weighted Average
Bagging	0.938	0.938	ALL
	0.917	0.917	AML
	0.930	0.930	Weighted Average
Random Forest	0.959	1.000	ALL
	1.000	0.962	AML
	0.973	0.987	Weighted Average
J48	0.851	0.894	ALL
	0.720	0.800	AML
	0.806	0.861	Weighted Average
Decision Stump	0.872	0.872	ALL
	0.760	0.760	AML
	0.833	0.833	Weighted Average

Table 5. Precision for Lung Cancer Dataset

LUNG CANCER - PRECISION			
Classifier	**Information Gain**	**Correlation Coefficient**	**Class**
Naive Bayes	1.000	1.000	ADCA
	1.000	1.000	Mesothelioma
	1.000	1.000	Weighted Average
Bagging	0.987	0.987	ADCA
	0.967	0.967	Mesothelioma
	0.983	0.983	Weighted Average
Random Forest	0.993	0.987	ADCA
	1.000	1.000	Mesothelioma
	0.995	0.989	Weighted Average
J48	0.948	0.973	ADCA
	0.852	0.871	Mesothelioma
	0.932	0.956	Weighted Average
Decision Stump	0.955	0.955	ADCA
	0.923	0.923	Mesothelioma
	0.949	0.949	Weighted Average

Table 6. Precision for Ovarian Cancer Dataset

OVARIAN CANCER - PRECISION			
Classifier	**Information Gain**	**Correlation Coefficient**	**Class**
Naive Bayes	0.962	1.000	Cancer
	0.885	1.000	Normal
	0.934	1.000	Weighted Average
Bagging	0.976	0.976	Cancer
	0.978	0.978	Normal
	0.976	0.976	Weighted Average
Random Forest	0.926	0.976	Cancer
	1.000	1.000	Normal
	0.952	0.985	Weighted Average
J48	0.994	0.975	Cancer
	0.957	0.956	Normal
	0.981	0.968	Weighted Average
Decision Stump	0.975	0.975	Cancer
	0.967	0.967	Normal
	0.972	0.972	Weighted Average

Table 7. Precision for Prostate Cancer Dataset

PROSTATE CANCER - PRECISION			
Classifier	**Information Gain**	**Correlation Coefficient**	**Class**
Naive Bayes	0.862	0.967	Tumor
	0.514	0.547	Normal
	0.711	0.785	Weighted Average
Bagging	0.910	0.935	Tumor
	0.897	0.915	Normal
	0.904	0.926	Weighted Average
Random Forest	0.814	0.948	Tumor
	0.860	0.932	Normal
	0.834	0.941	Weighted Average
J48	0.865	0.918	Tumor
	0.790	0.841	Normal
	0.833	0.885	Weighted Average
Decision Stump	0.806	0.806	Tumor
	0.953	0.953	Normal
	0.870	0.870	Weighted Average

Recall (for label A) = 29/C1 (30) = 0.967

Recall (for label B) = 58/C2 (106) = 0.547

After the Recall values are computed for each label, the average value is computed and is found to be 0.757. The recall values are computed for the four datasets and tabulated in Tables 8-11

The F-Score is the harmonic mean of Precision and Sensitivity. In other words, F-Score or F-Measure in statistics is a measure of test's accuracy. It is computed using the formula in equation 11 as

F-score = 2*(Precision*Recall)/(Precision+Recall)   (11)

The F-Measure values are computed for the four datasets and tabulated in Tables 12-15

The Receiver Operating Characteristic (ROC) curve can be plotted for each of the datasets considering the False Positive Rate (FPR) along the X-Axis and True Positive Rate (TPR) along the Y-axis of the graph. The ROC plots for the three

Table 8. Recall for ALL/AML Dataset

ALL/AML - RECALL			
Classifier	**Information Gain**	**Correlation Coefficient**	**Class**
Naive Bayes	1.000	1.000	ALL
	0.960	1.000	AML
	0.986	1.000	Weighted Average
Bagging	0.957	0.957	ALL
	0.880	0.880	AML
	0.931	0.931	Weighted Average
Random Forest	1.000	0.979	ALL
	0.920	1.000	AML
	0.972	0.986	Weighted Average
J48	0.851	0.894	ALL
	0.720	0.800	AML
	0.806	0.861	Weighted Average
Decision Stump	0.872	0.872	ALL
	0.760	0.760	AML
	0.833	0.833	Weighted Average

Table 9. Recall for Lung Cancer Dataset

LUNG CANCER - RECALL			
Classifier	**Information Gain**	**Correlation Coefficient**	**Class**
Naive Bayes	1.000	1.000	ADCA
	1.000	1.000	Mesothelioma
	1.000	1.000	Weighted Average
Bagging	0.993	0.993	ADCA
	0.935	0.935	Mesothelioma
	0.983	0.983	Weighted Average
Random Forest	1.000	1.000	ADCA
	0.968	0.935	Mesothelioma
	0.994	0.989	Weighted Average
J48	0.973	0.973	ADCA
	0.742	0.871	Mesothelioma
	0.934	0.956	Weighted Average
Decision Stump	0.987	0.987	ADCA
	0.774	0.774	Mesothelioma
	0.950	0.950	Weighted Average

Table 10. Recall for Ovarian Cancer Dataset

OVARIAN CANCER – RECALL			
Classifier	**Information Gain**	**Correlation Coefficient**	**Class**
Naive Bayes	0.932	1.000	Cancer
	0.934	1.000	Normal
	0.933	1.000	Weighted Average
Bagging	0.988	0.988	Cancer
	0.956	0.956	Normal
	0.976	0.976	Weighted Average
Random Forest	1.000	1.000	Cancer
	0.857	0.956	Normal
	0.949	0.984	Weighted Average
J48	0.975	0.975	Cancer
	0.989	0.956	Normal
	0.980	0.968	Weighted Average
Decision Stump	0.981	0.981	Cancer
	0.956	0.956	Normal
	0.972	0.972	Weighted Average

Table 11. Recall for Prostate Cancer Dataset

PROSTATE CANCER – RECALL			
Classifier	**Information Gain**	**Correlation Coefficient**	**Class**
Naive Bayes	0.325	0.377	Tumor
	0.932	0.983	Normal
	0.588	0.640	Weighted Average
Bagging	0.922	0.935	Tumor
	0.881	0.915	Normal
	0.904	0.926	Weighted Average
Random Forest	0.909	0.948	Tumor
	0.729	0.932	Normal
	0.831	0.941	Weighted Average
J48	0.831	0.870	Tumor
	0.831	0.898	Normal
	0.831	0.882	Weighted Average
Decision Stump	0.974	0.974	Tumor
	0.695	0.695	Normal
	0.853	0.853	Weighted Average

Table 12. F-Measure for ALL/AML Dataset

ALL/AML - F-MEASURE			
Classifier	**Information Gain**	**Correlation Coefficient**	**Class**
Naive Bayes	0.989	1.000	ALL
	0.980	1.000	AML
	0.986	1.000	Weighted Average
Bagging	0.947	0.947	ALL
	0.898	0.898	AML
	0.930	0.930	Weighted Average
Random Forest	0.979	0.989	ALL
	0.958	0.980	AML
	0.972	0.986	Weighted Average
J48	0.851	0.894	ALL
	0.720	0.800	AML
	0.806	0.861	Weighted Average
Decision Stump	0.872	0.872	ALL
	0.760	0.760	AML
	0.833	0.833	Weighted Average

Table 13. F-Measure for Lung Cancer Dataset

LUNG CANCER - F-MEASURE			
Classifier	**Information Gain**	**Correlation Coefficient**	**Class**
Naive Bayes	1.000	1.000	ADCA
	1.000	1.000	Mesothelioma
	1.000	1.000	Weighted Average
Bagging	0.990	0.990	ADCA
	0.951	0.951	Mesothelioma
	0.983	0.983	Weighted Average
Random Forest	0.997	0.993	ADCA
	0.984	0.967	Mesothelioma
	0.994	0.989	Weighted Average
J48	0.961	0.973	ADCA
	0.793	0.871	Mesothelioma
	0.932	0.956	Weighted Average
Decision Stump	0.970	0.970	ADCA
	0.842	0.842	Mesothelioma
	0.949	0.949	Weighted Average

Table 14. F-Measure for Ovarian Cancer Dataset

OVARIAN CANCER - F-MEASURE			
Classifier	**Information Gain**	**Correlation Coefficient**	**Class**
Naive Bayes	0.947	1.000	Cancer
	0.909	1.000	Normal
	0.933	1.000	Weighted Average
Bagging	0.982	0.982	Cancer
	0.967	0.967	Normal
	0.976	0.976	Weighted Average
Random Forest	0.961	0.988	Cancer
	0.923	0.978	Normal
	0.948	0.984	Weighted Average
J48	0.984	0.975	Cancer
	0.973	0.956	Normal
	0.980	0.968	Weighted Average
Decision Stump	0.978	0.978	Cancer
	0.961	0.961	Normal
	0.972	0.972	Weighted Average

Table 15. F-Measure for Prostate Cancer Dataset

PROSTATE CANCER - F-MEASURE			
Classifier	**Information Gain**	**Correlation Coefficient**	**Class**
Naive Bayes	0.472	0.542	Tumor
	0.663	0.703	Normal
	0.555	0.612	Weighted Average
Bagging	0.916	0.935	Tumor
	0.889	0.915	Normal
	0.904	0.926	Weighted Average
Random Forest	0.859	0.948	Tumor
	0.789	0.932	Normal
	0.829	0.941	Weighted Average
J48	0.848	0.893	Tumor
	0.810	0.869	Normal
	0.831	0.883	Weighted Average
Decision Stump	0.882	0.882	Tumor
	0.804	0.804	Normal
	0.848	0.848	Weighted Average

datasets namely ALL/AML, Lung Cancer, Ovarian Cancer and Prostate Cancer is depicted in the Figure 9, Figure 10, Figure 11 and Figure 12 below

It is clearly evident from the above tables that the classifier accuracy of the correlation based filter approach produces the highest level of classifier accuracy. The main area of research is to identify the number of features that would be required for effective cancer classification. For the entire feature selection methods, the average accuracy of the correlation based filter was better than for the information gain based filter approach. Also the number of selected feature was also comparatively lesser for the correlation based filter than information gain filter approach.

5. CONCLUSION

In this paper, we have adopted the correlation based filter with best first search and compared it with information gain filter for microarray gene expression data. Later five different classifiers were used to evaluate the classification performance (percentage of accuracy and other related parameters). The correlation based filter with best first search which has higher potential in aiding further research in the area

Figure 9. ROC Plot Correlation Based Filter for ALL/AML dataset

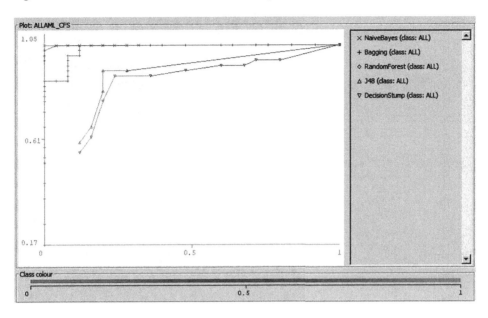

Figure 10. ROC Plot Correlation Based Filter for Lung Cancer dataset

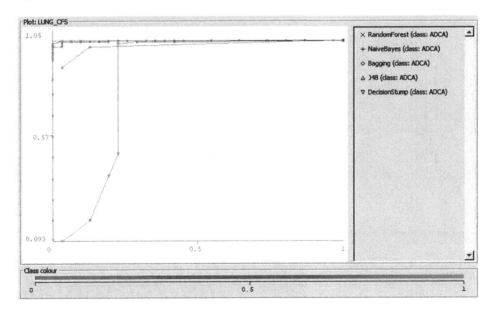

Figure 11. ROC Plot Correlation Based Filter for Ovarian Cancer dataset

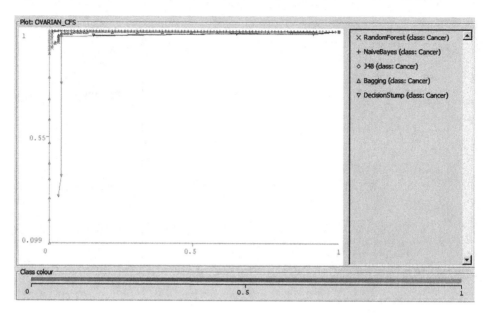

Figure 12. ROC Plot Correlation Based Filter for Prostate Cancer dataset

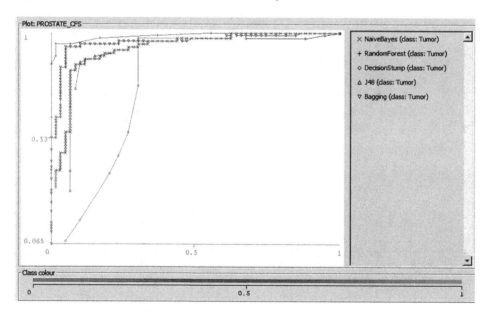

of feature selection simplified the process of gene selection which is evident from the experimental results. This method significantly reduced the number of genes needed for classification and has also contributed to the improvement in classifier accuracy. The correlation based filter has greater scope of application to problems in other domains in future.

REFERENCES

Acharjya, D. P., Roy, D., & Rahaman, M. A. (2012). Prediction of Missing Associations using Rough Computing and Bayesian Classification. *International Journal of Intelligent Systems and Applications*, 4(11), 1–13. doi:10.5815/ijisa.2012.11.01

Arunkumar, C., & Ramakrishnan, S. (2014). *Binary Classification of cancer microarray gene expression data using Extreme Learning Machines*. Paper presented at the 2014 IEEE International Conference on Computational Intelligence and Computing Research(ICCIC).

Arunkumar, C., & Ramakrishnan, S. (2015). *Hybrid Feature Selection using correlation coefficient and particle swarm optimization on microarray gene expression data: Innovations in Bioinspired computing and applications*. Paper presented at the 6th International Conference in Bioinspired computing and Applications, Advances in Intelligent Systems and Computing.

Bhagya Shree, S. R., & Sheshadri, H. S. (2014). *An initial investigation in the diagnosis of Alzheimer's disease using various classification techniques*. Paper presented at the 2014 IEEE International Conference on Computational Intelligence and Computing Research (ICCIC). doi:10.1109/ICCIC.2014.7238300

Chuang, Wu, & Yang. (2008). *Hybrid feature selection method using gene expression data*. Paper presented at the IEEE Conference on Soft Computing in Industrial Applications.

Doraisamy, Sulaiman, Udzir, & Norowi. (2008). Artificial Immune Recognition System with Nonlinear Resource Allocation Method and Application to Traditional Malay Music Genre Classification. Lecture Notes in Computer Science: Vol. 5132. Artificial Immune Systems (pp. 132-141). Berlin: Springer.

Govindarajan, M., & Chandrasekaran, R. M. (2011). Intrusion detection using neural based hybrid classification methods. *Computer Networks*, 55(8), 1662–1671. doi:10.1016/j.comnet.2010.12.008

Hall. (1999). *Correlation-based Feature Selection for Machine Learning.* University of Waikato.

Huang, J.-H., He, R.-H., Yi, L.-Z., Xie, H.-L., Cao, D., & Liang, Y.-Z. (2013). Exploring the relationship between 5'AMP-activated protein kinase and markers related to type 2 diabetes mellitus. *Talanta, 110,* 1–7. doi:10.1016/j.talanta.2013.03.039 PMID:23618167

Ji, G., Yang, Z., & You, W. (2011). PLS-Based Gene Selection and Identification of Tumor-Specific Genes. *IEEE Transactions on Systems, Man and Cybernetics. Part C, Applications and Reviews, 41*(6), 830–841. doi:10.1109/TSMCC.2010.2078503

Joaquim, F. (2011). A Weighted Principal Component Analysis and Its Application to Gene Expression Data. *IEEE/ACM Transactions on Computational Biology and Bioinformatics, 8*(1), 246–252. doi:10.1109/TCBB.2009.61 PMID:21071812

K, S., Subba Reddy, V., & B.Rananavare, L. (2011, February28). PCA Analysis of Few Parameters Role in Software Development. *International Journal of Computers and Applications, 14*(6), 15–20. doi:10.5120/1889-2506

Kumar, A. P., & Valsala, P. (2013). Feature Selection for high Dimensional DNA Microarray data using hybrid approaches. *Bioinformation, 9*(16), 824–828. doi:10.6026/97320630009824 PMID:24143053

Kumar, G., & Kumar, K. (2012). The Use of Artificial-Intelligence-Based Ensembles for Intrusion Detection: A Review. *Applied Computational Intelligence and Soft Computing, 2012,* 1–20. doi:10.1155/2012/850160

Kumaravel, A., & Aarthi, A. (2013). Malware Classification based on Clustering and classification. *International Journal of Advanced Research in Computer Science and Software Engineering, 3*(5), 121–123.

Lazar, C., Taminau, J., Meganck, S., Steenhoff, D., Coletta, A., Molter, C., & Nowe, A. et al. (2012). A Survey on Filter Techniques for Feature Selection in Gene Expression Microarray Analysis. *IEEE/ACM Transactions on Computational Biology and Bioinformatics, 9*(4), 1106–1119. doi:10.1109/TCBB.2012.33 PMID:22350210

Leon, F., Lisa, C., & Curteanu, S. (2010). Prediction of the Liquid-Crystalline Property Using Different Classification Methods. *International Journal of Molecular Crystals and Liquid Crystals, 518*(1), 129–148. doi:10.1080/15421400903574391

Leung, Y. (2010). A Multiple-Filter-Multiple-Wrapper Approach to Gene Selection and Microarray Data Classification. *IEEE/ACM Transactions on Computational Biology and Bioinformatics, 7*(1), 108–117. doi:10.1109/TCBB.2008.46 PMID:20150673

Li, M. (2003). Improving Reliability of Gene Selection From Microarray Functional Genomics Data. *IEEE Transactions on Information Technology in Biomedicine*, *7*(3), 191–196. doi:10.1109/TITB.2003.816558 PMID:14518732

Liu, S. (2012). Combined Rule Extraction and Feature Elimination in Supervised Classification. *IEEE Transactions on Nanobioscience*, *11*(3), 228–236. doi:10.1109/TNB.2012.2213264 PMID:22987128

Maji, P. (2012). Mutual Information-Based Supervised Attribute Clustering for Microarray Sample Classification. *IEEE Transactions on Knowledge and Data Engineering*, *24*(1), 127–140. doi:10.1109/TKDE.2010.210

Manne, & Fatima. (2011). A Novel Approach for Text Categorization of Unorganized data based with Information Extraction. *International Journal on Computer Science and Engineering*, *3*(7), 2846–2854.

Martin-Valdivia, M. T., Diaz-Galiano, M. C., Montejo-Raez, A., & Urena-Lopez, L. A. (2008). Using information gain to improve multi-modal information retrieval systems. *Information Processing & Management*, *44*(3), 1146–1158. doi:10.1016/j.ipm.2007.09.014

Martinez-Glez, V., Franco-Hernandez, C., & Rey, J. A. (2008). Microarray gene expression profiling in meningiomas and schwannomas. *Current Medicinal Chemistry*, *15*(8), 826–833. doi:10.2174/092986708783955527 PMID:18393851

Massinaei, M., Sedaghati, M. R., Rezvani, R., & Mohammadzadeh, A. A. (2014). Using Data Mining to Assess and Model the Metallurgical Efficiency of a Copper Concentrator. *International Journal of Chemical Engineering Communications*, *201*(10), 1314–1326. doi:10.1080/00986445.2013.808997

Mukras, R., Wiratunga, N., Lothian, R., Chakraborti, S., & Harper, D. (2007). Information gain feature selection for ordinal text classification using probability re-distribution. *Proceedings of IJCAI Textlink Workshop*, 1-10.

Pattekari, & Parveen. (2012). Prediction system for heart disease using Naïve Bayes. *International Journal of Advanced Computer and Mathematical Sciences*, *3*(3), 290–294.

Perez-Diez, Morgun, & Shulzhenko. (2007). Microarrays for Cancer Diagnosis and Classification. *Advances in Experimental Medicine and Biology*, 74–85.

Sanyog Choudhary, N., Yadav, H., & Jain, A. (2015). Enhanced Techniques for Filtering of Wall Messages over Online Social Networks (OSN) User Profiles. *International Journal of Wireless and Microwave Technologies*, *5*(4), 47–61. doi:10.5815/ijwmt.2015.04.05

Song, Q. (2013). A Fast Clustering-Based Feature Subset Selection Algorithm for High-Dimensional Data. *IEEE Transactions on Knowledge and Data Engineering*, *25*(1), 1–14. doi:10.1109/TKDE.2011.181

Yang, Chuang, Ke, & Yang. (2008). A Hybrid Feature Selection Method for Microarray Classification. *International Journal of Computer Science, 35*(3), 285-290.

Yang, Chuang, Li, & Yang. (2008). Information gain with chaotic genetic algorithm for gene selection and classification problem. *IEEE International Conference on Systems, Man and Cybernetics*, 1128-1123.

Yang, Chuang, & Yang. (2010). IG-GA: A Hybrid Filter/Wrapper Method for Feature Selection of Microarray Data. *Journal of Medical and Biological Engineering*, *30*(1), 23–28.

Yang, C.-S., Chuang, L.-Y., Ho, C.-H., & Yang, C.-H. (2008). Microarray Data Feature Selection Using Hybrid GA-IBPSO. *Trends in Intelligent Systems and Computer Engineering, Lecture Notes in Electrical Engineering*, *6*, 243–253. doi:10.1007/978-0-387-74935-8_18

Chapter 3
Bio–Inspired Algorithms for Text Summarization:
A Review

Rasmita Rautray
Siksha 'O' Anusandhan University, India

Rakesh Chandra Balabantaray
IIIT Bhubaneswar, India

ABSTRACT

In last few decades, Bio-inspired algorithms (BIAs) have gained a significant popularity to handle hard real world and complex optimization problem. The scope and growth of Bio Inspired algorithms explore new application areas and computing opportunities. This paper presents a review with the objective is to bring a better understanding and to motivate the research on BIAs based text summarization. Different techniques have been used for text summarization are genetic algorithm (GA), particle swarm optimization (PSO), differential evolution (DE), harmonic search (HS).

1 INTRODUCTION

Text summarization (TS) is the process of automatically creating a compressed version of a given text that provides useful information to users (Aliguliyev, 2009). It provides a solution to information overhead problem (Hahn & Mani, 2000; Mani & Maybury, 1999). A summary is the main objective of summarization method (Algu-

DOI: 10.4018/978-1-5225-2375-8.ch003

Copyright ©2017, IGI Global. Copying or distributing in print or electronic forms without written permission of IGI Global is prohibited.

liev & Aliguliyev, 2005), which highlights three important aspects that characterize the research on automatic summarization: (i) summaries may be produced from a single document or multiple documents; (ii) summaries should preserve important information; and (iii) summaries should be short. Summary generation evaluates each section (paragraph, sentence, word) of the document to decide whether to keep it or not and, then reformulate it to select output. Conceptually, summarization involves a tri-stage process (Gholamrezazadeh, Salehi & Gholamzadeh, 2009; Hovy & Lin, 1998; Lin & Hovy, 1997): topic identification or text representation, interpretation or compaction or summary representation and summary generation. First step transforms text document to source representation by identifying the main theme, second step interprets the meaning; distinguish relevant and irrelevant information, and then compact it to form summary representation. The last stage merges the previously identified information to generate summary. To achieve this goal, TS addresses both the problem of selecting a subset of the most important portions of sentences from the original documents (known as extractive summary) and the problem of generating coherent summaries by composing novel sentences and unseen in the original sources (known as abstractive summary) (Fattah & Ren, 2009). Depending on size of input document to be summarized, a summary can be single document summary or multi document summary. The producing summary for a single document is called single document summary and summary for multiple documents is called multi document summary (Mani & Maybury, 1999; Fattah & Ren, 2009; Alguliev, Aliguliyev & Isazade, 2012). The summary is generated based on different aspects such as content coverage, redundancy, length, readability, cohesion, diversity and relevancy, therefore summarization is considered as multi objective optimization problem. Such aspect which represents summary objectives is discussed below.

- **Content Coverage:** It is most important and major objective of summarization. Content Coverage of a summary should contain all salient sentences that cover all important subtopics and contents as much as possible from the original document (Alguliev, Aliguliyev & Isazade, 2012; Alguliev, Aliguliyev & Hajirahimova, 2012; Alguliev, Aliguliyev, & Isazade, 2013; Mendoza et al. 2014; Wei, Li & Liu, 2010).
- **Redundancy or Diversity:** The summary should expect non-redundant sentences. i.e. sentences with same meaning should be minimized (Alguliev, Aliguliyev & Hajirahimova, 2012; Alguliev et al., 2011; Alguliev, Aliguliyev & Mehdiyev, 2011).
- **Length:** A summary should be bounded in length (Alguliev, Aliguliyev & Hajirahimova, 2012; Alguliev, Aliguliyev, & Isazade, 2013; Alguliev et al., 2011; Alguliev, Aliguliyev & Mehdiyev, 2011).

- **Readability:** It is easiness of generated text or summary that can be understood by reader (Nandhini & Balasundaram, 2014).
- **Cohesion:** It determines the degree of relatedness of the sentences that make up a summary (Mendoza et al, 2014;Alguliev, Aliguliyev & Mehdiyev, 2011).
- **Relevancy:** A summary should contain information that is relevant to the source as well as for the user (Alguliev, Aliguliyev & Isazade, 2012; Alguliev et al., 2011).

In last few decades, for different input document size so many statistical techniques have been used to generate summary. But, due to impoverished performance of such techniques different global optimization techniques or bio inspired algorithms (BIA) have been used for summarization problem (Rautray & Balabantaray, 2015). Bio-inspired algorithms are based on design principles encountered in nature. The algorithms can provide an enhanced basis for problem-solving and decision-making (Reddy & Kumar, 2012). However these algorithms are devoted to tackle complex problems, design formulation for these algorithms involves choosing a proper representation of problem, evaluating the quality of solution using a fitness function and defining operators so as to produce a new set of solutions (Binitha & Sathya, 2012).

These algorithms are broadly classified as evolutionary computation (EC) and swarm intelligence (SI) algorithms. EC algorithms were inspired by 'survival of the fittest' or 'natural selection' principles3; whereas SI based algorithms distributed problems-solvers which were inspired by the cooperative group intelligence of swarm or collective behavior of insect colonies and other animal societies (Reddy & Kumar, 2012; Acharjya & Kauser, 2015). SI based algorithms are belongs to bio-inspired algorithms or theoretically SI is subset of bio-inspired algorithms. Mostly bio-inspired algorithms are not directly use swarm behavior. Therefore it is better to call bio-inspired, but not SI based algorithm. Many EC and SI based algorithms have been implemented and shown significant potential in solving text summarization problem such as genetic algorithm (GA), particle swarm optimization (PSO) and differential evolution (DE). Genetic algorithm is bio-inspired based algorithm, but not SI based. Differential evolution does not have direct link to any biological behavior. However, it has some similarity to GA and has keyword 'evolution'. Therefore tentatively it comes under bio-inspired algorithms category (Fister Jr Iztok et al., 2013). Whereas PSO is completely swarm based algorithm. Rest of the chapter is organized as follows. In section 2, BIAs are categorized into various sections. Section 3 explores genetic algorithm based text summarization whereas section 4 explores text summarization with respect to differential evolution. Section 5 explores text summarization pertaining to particle swarm optimization. In section 6, various aspects of text summarization due to harmonic search is explored. Chapter concluded in section 7.

2 BIO-INSPIRED ALGORITHMS FOR TEXT SUMMARIZATION

Bio-inspired algorithms acquire its sole inspiration from biological field with ability to illustrate and resolve complex problems. In information retrieval area, huge amount of literatures exist using bio inspired approaches. Especially most successful and prevalent algorithms such as Swarm based Algorithms and Evolutionary Algorithms, are inspired by collective behavior in animals and the natural evolution respectively (Binitha & Sathya, 2012). To improve the performance of text summarization problem as an optimization problem, so many BIAs have been used in literature. Therefore, this section provides a brief overview of BIAs and comprehensive review which has been used for text summarization problem.

3 GENETIC ALGORITHM

In the 1960s and 1970s, genetic algorithm (GA) is most popular as an optimization tool developed by Holland (Holland, 1975) that mimics the process of natural evolution and later on it became more popularized by Goldberg (Goldberg, 1989). The principle of GA is based on "select the best, discard the rest". Therefore, in early 1980s GA was being applied to a broad range of subjects. In genetic algorithm, each chromosome represents set of genes and a solution to the given problem. Individual variables are used as chromosomes. The selection of individual variables as best is based on evaluation of fitness function (Waleed, 2014). The basic steps involved in GA are discussed below.

Procedure Genetic Algorithm
Population Initialization
While (! Termination Condition) do
  Evaluation
  Reproduction
  Crossover
  Mutation
Result

3.1 GA based Text Summarization

For improvising the performance of text selection in document summarization using statistical tools, in 1990s a number of global optimization techniques were considered as effective solutions in literature (Rautray & Balabantaray, 2015). The first research used GA by (Gordon, 1988) to retrieve relevant document based on query and relevant judgments. López-Pujalte, Guerrero-Bote, & de Moya-Anegón, 2003 evaluates the efficiency of a GA with fitness functions for relevance feedback in information retrieval problem for maintaining the document order. Later on GA based programming technique is used for fuzzy retrieval system to extract information based on query by applying off-line adaptive process (García, de Moya Anegón, & Zarco, 2000). Genetic Algorithm used by Alguliev & Aliguliyev, 2005 for text summarization based on sentence score. Each sentence score is obtained through the comparison of each sentence with all other sentences as well as with the document title by cosine measure. The informative features weights are calculated by using GA to influence the words relevancy. Word relevancy defines relevancy and rank of the sentences having highest score with respect to a threshold, are selected as summary sentences. A single document generic summary has been extracted based on different sentence features using GA by comparing with some other techniques in (Fattah & Ren, 2009) and were evaluated using ROUGE score. Kogilavani & Balasubramanie, 2010 presents a feature based multi document generic summarization using GA & clustering to enhance the summary quality by maximizing length, coverage and informativeness while minimizing the redundancy. Whereas, by (He et al., 2006; Zhao & Tang, 2010), genetic algorithm based document summarization has been proposed to generate optimal summary by combining article sentences and query sentence to achieve satisfied length, high coverage, high informativeness and low redundancy in summary.

In the work, serial number 1-5 in Table 1 involves for single document summarization but, rest work involves for multi document summarization. As the solution based on GA needs more parameter tuning, to overcome the limitation of GA, DE used for summarization as it does not depend on fine tuning of parameters.

3.2 GA Advantages and Limitations

Advantages

- Every optimization problem can be solved using GA, if it is described with the chromosome encoding.
- It solves problems with multiple solutions.
- No mathematical analysis is required.
- GA can be efficiently used if search space is large complex or poorly unknown.

Limitations

- The basic disadvantage is unguided mutation due to slow convergence.
- Operating on dynamic dataset is difficult.
- It is not directly suitable for solving constraint optimization problem.

Table 1 Brief Description of GA based Summarization

Sl. no.	Authors, Years	NIAs	Fitness function	Summary Feature	Concept/ Theme	Source size	Language	Summary Type	Measure
1	M. Gordon, 1988	GA	-	Content coverage	-	Single	Monolingual	query	-
2	López-PujalteC., Guerrero-Bote, V. P., & de Moya-Anegón, F., 2003	GA	$F_1 - \dfrac{\sum r_d \cdot f_d}{\sum r_d}$ $F_2 - \alpha \dfrac{\sum r_d f_d}{\sum f_d} + \beta \dfrac{\sum r_d f_d}{\sum r_d}$	Relevancy	-	Single	Monolingual	query	Recall
3	García, O. C., de Moya Anegón, F., & Zarco, C., 2000	GA	$F = \dfrac{1}{D}\sum_{i=1}^{D}\left(r(d_i)\sum_{j=1}^{D}\dfrac{1}{j}\right)$	-	-	Single	Monolingual	query	Precision & Recall
4	Alguliev, R. M., & Aliguliyev, R. M., 2005	GA	$fitness(\alpha^i) = \dfrac{\sum_{j=1}^{N_{train}} F_1^{summary}(d_i)}{N_{train}}$	Relevancy	Clustering	Single	Monolingual	generic	F-score
5	Fattah, M. A., & Ren, F., 2009	GA	-	Content coverage, Relevancy	Feature	Single	Monolingual	generic	Rouge

continued on following page

Table 1. Continued

Sl. no.	Authors, Years	NIAs	Fitness function	Summary Feature	Concept/ Theme	Source size	Language	Summary Type	Measure
6	He, Y. X., Liu, D. X., Ji, D. H., Yang, H., & Teng, C., 2006	GA	$E(S) = \omega_{len} * LEN(S) + \omega_{con} * COV(S) + \omega_{info} * INFO(S) + \omega_{stm} * ANTI_{REDUN}(S)$	length, Content coverage, informativeness, anti-redundancy	-	Multi	Monolingual	query	Rouge
7	Kogilavani, A., & Balasubramanie, P., 2010	GA	$E(S) = LEN(S) + COV(S) + INFO(S) + ANTI_{REDUN}(S)$	length, Content coverage, informativeness, anti-redundancy	Clustering	Multi	Monolingual	generic	Precision, Recall & F-score
8	Zhao, X., & Tang, J., 2010	GA	$f = \dfrac{\lambda * QFF + \beta * IF + \gamma * NRF}{\lambda + \beta + \gamma}$	Query feature & anti-redundancy	Clustering	Multi	Monolingual	query	Rouge

4. DIFFERENTIAL EVOLUTION

Differential evolution (DE) is a population based paradigm of Evolutionary Algorithm unlike GA, was proposed in1997 by Storn and Price (Storn & Price, 1997). In both the algorithm populations are used to search for an optimal solution as well as use similar operators (Binitha & Sathya, 2012). But the difference is that GA is mostly relying on crossover parameter where as DE algorithm is relying on mutation parameter. In DE, different parameters are used as an operation in different aspect to reach at optimal solution such as mutation operation as search mechanism, reproduction as prospective region searching in search space and crossover as generation of possible combinations for better solution space (Karaboga & Akay, 2009). The expressions to evaluate such parameters are presented in following equation.

1. **Mutation:** It is the most important operation in DE. It produces mutant vector M_i with respect to each individual populations P_i, also called target vectors (Mallipeddi, 2011). Randomly selecting solutions r_1, r_2 and r_3 corresponding to target individuals generates M_i.

$$M_i = P_{r_1} + F(P_{r_3} - P_{r_2})$$

   where F is weighting factor within the range [0, 1] and, P_{r1}, P_{r2} and P_{r3} are solution vectors, which must satisfy $r_1 \neq r_2 \neq r_3 \neq i$.

2. **Crossover:** After completion of mutation operation, target vector P_i and its corresponding mutant vectors M_i are together generates trial vector t_i by performing crossover operation.

$$t_i^j = \begin{cases} M_i^j & t_i^j \ If \ rand_j \leq \\ P_i^j & otherwise \end{cases} \qquad (2)$$

   where $rand_j$ is randomly selected number and *CR* is crossover constant are specified within the range [0, 1] and j is the jth element of an array.

3. **Reproduction:** It is selection of better individuals from the current population.

$$P_{i,G+1} = \begin{cases} t_{i,G} & If \ f(t_{jG}) \leq f(P_{jG}) \\ P_{i,G} & otherwise \end{cases}$$

   The above steps are repeated until a termination condition is satisfied, is described below.

***Procedure** Differential Evolution*
Population Initialization
Evaluation
While** (! Termination Condition) **do
    Mutation
    Crossover
    Evaluation
    Reproduction
Result

4.1 DE based Summarization

The problem of summarization involves in different aspects of summary which need to optimize by minimizing or maximizing it. The aspects considered by (Rautray & Balabantaray, 2015; Rautray, Balabantaray & Bhardwaj, 2015) be the content coverage and redundancy that needs to maximize and minimize respectively to optimize the summary for single document. Where as (Alguliev & Aliguliyev, 2009) presents a sentence based extractive summarizer for a single document specifically focusing on clustering of sentences using inter sentence similarity measure. Whereas in (Abuobieda et al., 2013), a single document summarizer focuses on sentence feature as key ingredient instead of clustering to extract summary. A summarizer for single document based on clustering has been presented and made comparison of discrete DE and conventional DE for summarization and showed comparison result by the authors of (Karwa & Chatterjee, 2014). Nandhini & Balasundaram, 2014 have used DE algorithm to enhance sentence feature based summary by maximizing content coverage, readability and cohesion to improve text readability and informativeness of summary. As the problem of summarization is considered as discrete optimization problem in (Alguliev, Aliguliyev & Mehdiyev, 2011), to solve such problem the author has used adaptive DE to maximize informativeness of summary while reducing the redundancy of summary. In contrast the authors (Alguliev, R. M., Aliguliyev, & Isazade, 2012; Alguliev, Aliguliyev & Hajirahimova, 2012) consider same summarization problem as p-median problem and Quadratic Boolean programming problem, for that used a new variation of DE which is based on self adaptive mutation and crossover parameters and binary DE respectively. Where as in (Alguliev, Aliguliyev & Isazade, 2013) they only use adaptive crossover parameter to optimize the result. The models discussed in (Alguliev, R. M., Aliguliyev, & Isazade, 2012; Alguliev, Aliguliyev & Hajirahimova, 2012;Alguliev, Aliguliyev & Isazade, 2013) not only express sentence-to-sentence relationship, but also express summary-to-document and summary-to-subtopics relationships.

In the work, serial number 1-6 of Table 2 uses DE for single document summarization but, rest works uses DE for multi document summarization.

4.2 DE Advantages and Limitations

Advantages

- It requires less number of parameter tuning.
- It is a reliable, robust, accurate and fast optimization technique due to the nature of parallel processing.
- Capable of providing multiple solutions in a single run.

Limitations

- Finding best values for the problem dependent control parameter is a time consuming task.

5. PARTICLE SWARM OPTIMIZATION

The particle swarm optimization (PSO) is a population based heuristic search technique proposed by Eberhart and Kennedy in 1995(Eberhart & Kennedy, 1995). It is inspired by the social behavior of the bird flocking or fish schooling. In PSO, each individual in population (swarm) is denoted as 'particle'. Each particle of PSO algorithm is associated with position and velocity (Reddy & Kumar, 2012). The position of particle refers to possible solutions in the search space that need to be optimized. The function evaluation by the position of the particles provides fitness of the function. After each iteration the fitness of each particles defines two best values such as *Pbest* (personal best) and *Gbest* (global best). *Pbest* contains highest fitness value obtained by a specific particle, whereas *Gbest* contains highest fitness value in the entire population. The best value is considered as local best for a particle when particle takes part of the population as its topological neighbors. Then the particle move to good search space area for spreading of information to the population. After that the position of particles is changed by updating the velocity at each step *i*. The new position is expressed in terms of its previous value and updated value of velocity, but velocity can be expressed by taking some other parameters discussed in following equation.

Velocity:
$$v(i+1) = \omega \cdot v(i) + c_1 \cdot rand_1(pbest(i) - p(i)) + c_2 \cdot rand_2(gbest(i) - p(i))$$

Table 2 Brief Description of DE based Summarization

Sl. no.	Authors, Years	NIAs	Fitness function	Summary Feature	Concept/ Theme	Source size	Language	Summary Type	Measure
1	Rautray, R.., & Balabantaray, R. C., 2015	DE	$f = \dfrac{\beta * ISF + \delta * MF}{\beta + \delta}$	Content coverage, Redundancy	-	Single	Monolingual	Generic	Recall, Precision, F-score
2	Rautray, R.., Balabantaray, R. C., & Bhardwaj, A., 2015	DE	$f = \dfrac{\beta * ISF + \delta MF}{\beta + \delta}$	Content coverage, Redundancy	Feature	Single	Monolingual	Generic	Recall, Precision, F-score
3	Aliguliev, R., & Aliguliyev, R., 2009	DE	$F_1 = \sum_{p=1}^{k} \left(C_p \left(\sum_{S_i, S_l \in C_p} sim_{NGD}(S_i, S_l) \right)\right)$ $F_2 = \sum_{p=1}^{k-1} \frac{1}{|C_p|} \sum_{q=p+1}^{k} \frac{1}{|C_q|} \left(\sum_{S_i \in C_p} \sum_{S_l \in C_q} (S_i, S_l) \right)$	Content coverage	Cluster	Single	Monolingual	Generic	Rouge
4	Abuobieda, A., Salim, N., Binwahlan, M. S., & Osman, A. H.,2013	DE	$f_1 = \sum_{l=1}^{k} \left(C_l \left(\sum_{S_i, S_j \in C_l} sim_x(S_i, S_j) \right)\right)$ $f_2 = \sum_{l=1}^{k-1} \frac{1}{|C_l|} \sum_{m=l+1}^{k} \frac{1}{|C_m|} \left(\sum_{S_i \in C_l} \sum_{S_j \in C_m} sim_x(S_i, S_j) \right)$	Content coverage	Feature	Single	Monolingual	Generic	Rouge

continued on following page

Table 1. Continued

Sl. no.	Authors, Years	NIAs	Fitness function	Summary Feature	Concept/ Theme	Source size	Language	Summary Type	Measure
5	Karwa, S., & Chatterjee, N.,2014	DE	$f_1 = \sum_{p=1}^{k} \sum_{d_i, d_j \in C_p} sim(d_i, d_j) / (C_p($ $f_2 = \sum_{p=1}^{k-1} \sum_{q=k+1}^{k} \sum_{s_i \in C_p, s_j \in C_p} sim(d_i, d_j) / (C_p((C_q($	Content coverage	Cluster	Single	Monolingual	Generic	Recall, Precision, F-score
6	Nandhini, K., & Balasundaram, S. R., 2014	DE	$F_1 = \sum_{i=1}^{n} \dfrac{1}{\sum W_i * F_i}$ $F_2 = \sum_{i=1}^{n} \dfrac{1}{\sum Sim(S_i, S_j)}$	Content coverage, Cohesion, Readability	Feature	Single	Monolingual	Generic	Anova Analysis,FOG & SMOG score
7	Alguliev, R. M., Aliguliyev, R. M., & Mehdiyev, C. A.,2011	DE	$f(X) = \dfrac{\sum_{i=1}^{n-1} \sum_{j=i+1}^{n} [sim(S_i, O) + sim(S_j, O)]x_{ij}}{\sum_{i=1}^{n-1} \sum_{j=i+1}^{n} sim(S_i, S_j)x_{ij}}$	Content coverage, Redundancy	-	Multi	Monolingual	Generic	Rouge

continued on following page

Table 1. Continued

Sl. no.	Authors, Years	NIAs	Fitness function	Summary Feature	Concept/ Theme	Source size	Language	Summary Type	Measure
8	Alguliev, R. M., Aliguliyev, R. M., & Isazade, N. R., 2012	DE	$f(x) = f_{con}(x) + f_{red}(x) + f_{len}(x)$ $f_{con}(x) = sim(S,O) \cdot \sum_{i=1}^{n-1} sim(S, s_i) x_{ji}$ $f_{red}(x) = \sum_{i=1}^{n-1} \sum_{j=i+1}^{n} (1 - sim(s_i, s_j)) x_{ii}, x_{ji}$ $f_{len}(x) = \sum_{i=1}^{n-1} \sum_{j=i+1}^{n} sim(s_i, s_j) x_{ij}$	Content coverage, Redundancy, Length	-	Multi	Monolingual	Generic	Rouge
9	Alguliev, R. M., Aliguliyev, R. M., & Hajirahimova, M. S., 2012	DE	$f(X) = \omega \cdot f_{con}(X) + (1 - \omega) \cdot f_{red}(X)$ $f_{con}(X) = \sum_{i=1}^{n-1} sim(s_i, O) x_i$ $f_{red}(X) = \sum_{i=1}^{n-1} \sum_{j=i+1}^{n} (1 - sim(s_i, s_j)) x_i, x_j$	Content coverage, Redundancy	-	Multi	Monolingual	Generic	Rouge
10	Alguliev, R. M., Aliguliyev, R. M., & Isazade, N. R., 2013	DE	$f(X) = \dfrac{sim(O, O^s) \cdot \sum_{i=1}^{n} sim(O, s_i) x_i}{\sum_{i=1}^{n-1} \sum_{j=i+1}^{n} sim(S_i, S_j) x_i x_j}$	Content coverage, Redundancy	-	Multi	Monolingual	Generic	Rouge

83

Position: $p(i+1) = p(i) + v(i+1)$

Where ω is inertia weight and it controls magnitude of old velocity value. $c_1 \wedge c_2$ are cognitive and social parameters. $rand_1 \wedge rand_2$ are random numbers within the range [0, 1]. The steps involved in PSO algorithm is presented below.

Procedure Particle Swarm Optimization
Position and velocity Initialization
Do
      Particles fitness evaluation
      Compute Pbest (particles)& Gbest
      Calculate particles velocity
      Update particle positions
While *(! Termination Condition)*
Result

5.1 PSO based Summarization

The most of the features of PSO algorithm shares similarity with GA features. Unlike genetic algorithm, initially populations are generated randomly and optimum result is found by performing iterative search operation. The purpose of text summarization by considering the utilization of particle swarm optimization algorithm can be referred in literature. Rautray et al., 2015 presents a generic summarizer for single document by considering content coverage and redundancy feature of summary, taking weighted average of both the feature as an objective function. Whereas the aforementioned objective function is also used by (Rautray, Balabantaray & Bhardwaj, 2015) to generate summary taking features of text as an input arguments. Binwahlan et al., 2009 has proposed an extractive feature based summarizer where expression of ROUGE is used as fitness functions for extraction of summary sentences. The summary based on particle swarm optimization also presented in (Asgari, Masoumi, & Sheijani, 2014) by considering summary features such as content coverage, readability and length. A multi document summarization system has been presented in (Alguliev, Aliguliyev & Mehdiyev, 2011) based on the concept of clustering of sentences by calculating inter sentence similarity between sentences and sentence to document set to achieve content coverage & diversity of summary. In contrast, similarity metric also used in (Alguliev et al., 2011) to achieve content coverage, diversity and length of summary for multiple document sets.

In the work, serial number 1-4 in Table 3 uses PSO for single document summarization but, rest works use PSO for multi document summarization.

Table 3 Brief Description of PSO based Summarization

Sl. no.	Authors, Years	NIAs	Fitness function	Summary Feature	Concept/ Theme	Source size	Language	Summary Type	Measure
1	Rautray, R., & Balabantaray, R. C., 2015	PSO	$f = \dfrac{\beta * ISF + \delta * MF}{\beta + \delta}$	Content coverage, Redundancy	-	Single	Monolingual	Generic	Recall, Precision, F-score
2	Rautray, R., Balabantaray, R. C., & Bhardwaj, A., 2015	PSO	$f = \dfrac{\beta * ISF + \delta * MF}{\beta + \delta}$	Content coverage, Redundancy	Feature	Single	Monolingual	Generic	Recall, Precision, F-score
3	Binwahlan, M. S., Salim, N., & Suanmali, L., 2009	PSO	$f = \dfrac{\sum\limits_{S \in \{Referencesummary\}} \sum\limits_{gram_n \in S} count_{match}(gram_n)}{\sum\limits_{S \in \{Referencesummary\}} \sum\limits_{gram_n \in S} count(gram_n)}$	Content coverage	Feature	Single	Monolingual	generic	Rouge
4	Asgari, H., Masoumi, B., & Sheijani, O. S., 2014	PSO	-	Content coverage, Readability, length	-	Single	Monolingual	generic	Rouge
5	Alguliev, R. M., Aliguliyev, R. M., & Mehdiyev, C. A., 2011	PSO	$f = \dfrac{2}{3} \cdot \dfrac{f_{cover} + f_{diver}}{2} + \dfrac{1}{3}\sqrt{f_{cover} \cdot f_{diver}}$ $f_{cover}(X) = sim(O, O^a) + \sum sim(O, S_i)x_i$ $f_{diver} = \sum\sum (1 - sim(S_i, S_j))x_i x_j$	Content coverage, Diversity	cluster	Multi	Monolingual	Generic	Rouge
6	Alguliev, R. M., Aliguliyev, R. M., Hajirahimova, M. S., & Mehdiyev, C. A., 2011	PSO	$f = \sum\limits_{i=1}^{n-1}\sum\limits_{j=i+1}^{n} \left[sim(\vec{D}, \vec{S_i}) + sim(\vec{D}, \vec{S_j}) - sim(\vec{S_i}, \vec{S_j}) \right] x_{ij}$	Relevancy, Redundancy, length	-	Multi	Monolingual	Generic	Rouge

85

5.2 PSO Advantages

Advantages

- It requires less number of parameter tuning.
- There is no crossover and mutation calculation in PSO.
- It is more efficient in maintaining the diversity of the swarm.

6. HARMONIC SEARCH

The harmonic search (HS) is a stochastic meta-heuristic algorithm proposed by Zong Woo Geem et al. in 2001(Geem, Kim & Loganathan, 2001). The HS algorithm draws a motivation from music improvisation process (Chakraborty et al., 2009; Wang, Gao & Zenger, 2015) to obtain optimal output or perfect harmony by adjusting the input or pitches, unlike searching for the perfect state of harmony by improvising instrument pitches. To improvise the pitch a musician has to follow the any one of the rule given below:

1. Playing any one pitch from his (or her) memory,
2. Playing an adjacent pitch of one pitch from his (or her) memory, and
3. Playing totally random pitch from the possible range of pitches.

Similarly, in engineering optimization problem when each decision variable chooses one value in the HS algorithm, it follows any one of three rules (Chakraborty et al., 2009):

1. Choosing any one value from the HS memory (defined as memory considerations),
2. Choosing an adjacent value of one value from the HS memory (defined as pitch adjustments) and
3. Choosing totally random value from the possible range of values (defined as randomization).

Based on the above concept, the HS algorithm involves the following steps:

Procedure *Harmonic Search*
Harmony memory (population) and parameters Initialization
While *(! Termination Condition)* ***do***
    New Harmony improvisation

Harmony memory update
Result

6.1 HS based Summarization

The HS algorithm has gained a significant result in the field of optimization such as water distribution, signal processing, scheduling etc.. But in the year 2008, for the first time HS is used in text summarization problem by E. Shareghi considering three factors such as readability, cohesion and topic relation for web summary extraction (Shareghi & Hassanabadi, 2008). Brief description in this area of research is presented in Table 4.

6.2 HS Advantages

Advantages

- HS implementation is easier.
- Diversification is essentially controlled by the pitch adjustment and randomization.
- The intensification is dependent on memory acceptance rate. For high acceptance rate, good solutions from history or memory are more likely to be selected.

7 CONCLUSION

There are various bio-inspired algorithms, which have been used in text summarization problem either addressing single document or multi document sets. Among all bio-inspired algorithms, DE and PSO algorithms have gained more attention and also have been applied with some degree of success in text summarization problem.

Table 4 Brief Description of HS based Summarization

Sl. no.	Authors, Years	NIAs	Fitness function	Summary Feature	Concept/ Theme	Source size	Language	Summary Type	Measure
1	Shareghi, E., & Hassanabadi, L. S., 2008	HS	-	Content coverage, readability, cohesion	-	Single	Monolingual	-	Precision, Recall

But Harmonic Search algorithm has not been applied more in case of summarization problem. It is expected that in near future other similar bio-inspired approaches would also be tried for this text summarization problem.

REFERENCES

Abuobieda, A., Salim, N., Binwahlan, M. S., & Osman, A. H. (2013, August). Differential evolution cluster-based text summarization methods. In *Computing, Electrical and Electronics Engineering (ICCEEE), 2013 International Conference on* (pp. 244-248). IEEE. doi:10.1109/ICCEEE.2013.6633941

Acharjya, D. P., & Kauser, A. P. (2015). Swarm Intelligence in Solving Bio-Inspired Computing Problems: Reviews, Perspectives, and Challenges. In Handbook of Research on Swarm Intelligence in Engineering (pp. 74-98). IGI Global.

Alguliev, R., & Aliguliyev, R. (2009). Evolutionary algorithm for extractive text summarization. *Intelligent Information Management, 1*(02), 128–138. doi:10.4236/iim.2009.12019

Alguliev, R. M., & Aliguliyev, R. M. (2005, September). Effective summarization method of text documents. In *Web Intelligence, 2005. Proceedings. The 2005 IEEE/WIC/ACM International Conference on* (pp. 264-271). IEEE. doi:10.1109/WI.2005.57

Alguliev, R. M., Aliguliyev, R. M., & Hajirahimova, M. S. (2012). GenDocSum+ MCLR: Generic document summarization based on maximum coverage and less redundancy. *Expert Systems with Applications, 39*(16), 12460–12473. doi:10.1016/j.eswa.2012.04.067

Alguliev, R. M., Aliguliyev, R. M., Hajirahimova, M. S., & Mehdiyev, C. A. (2011). MCMR: Maximum coverage and minimum redundant text summarization model. *Expert Systems with Applications, 38*(12), 14514–14522. doi:10.1016/j.eswa.2011.05.033

Alguliev, R. M., Aliguliyev, R. M., & Isazade, N. R. (2012). DESAMC+ DocSum: Differential evolution with self-adaptive mutation and crossover parameters for multi-document summarization. *Knowledge-Based Systems, 36*, 21–38. doi:10.1016/j.knosys.2012.05.017

Alguliev, R. M., Aliguliyev, R. M., & Isazade, N. R. (2013). Multiple documents summarization based on evolutionary optimization algorithm. *Expert Systems with Applications, 40*(5), 1675–1689. doi:10.1016/j.eswa.2012.09.014

Alguliev, R. M., Aliguliyev, R. M., & Mehdiyev, C. A. (2011). An optimization model and DPSO-EDA for document summarization. *International Journal of Information Technology and Computer Science*, *3*(5), 59–68. doi:10.5815/ijitcs.2011.05.08

Alguliev, R. M., Aliguliyev, R. M., & Mehdiyev, C. A. (2011). Sentence selection for generic document summarization using an adaptive differential evolution algorithm. *Swarm and Evolutionary Computation*, *1*(4), 213–222. doi:10.1016/j.swevo.2011.06.006

Aliguliyev, R. M. (2009). A new sentence similarity measure and sentence based extractive technique for automatic text summarization. *Expert Systems with Applications*, *36*(4), 7764–7772. doi:10.1016/j.eswa.2008.11.022

Asgari, H., Masoumi, B., & Sheijani, O. S. (2014, February). Automatic text summarization based on multi-agent particle swarm optimization. In *Intelligent Systems (ICIS), 2014 Iranian Conference on* (pp. 1-5). IEEE. doi:10.1109/IranianCIS.2014.6802592

Bazghandi, M., Tabrizi, G. T., Jahan, M. V., & Mashahd, I. (2012). Extractive Summarization Of Farsi Documents Based On PSO Clustering. *International Journal of Computer Science Issues*, *9*(4), 329–332.

Binitha, S., & Sathya, S. S. (2012). A survey of bio inspired optimization algorithms. *International Journal of Soft Computing and Engineering*, *2*(2), 137–151.

Binwahlan, M. S., Salim, N., & Suanmali, L. (2009, April). Swarm based text summarization. In *Computer Science and Information Technology-Spring Conference, 2009. IACSITSC'09. International Association of* (pp. 145-150). IEEE. doi:10.1109/IACSIT-SC.2009.61

Chakraborty, P., Roy, G. G., Das, S., Jain, D., & Abraham, A. (2009). An Improved Harmony Search Algorithm with Differential Mutation Operator. *Fundamenta Informaticae*, *95*(4), 401–426.

Eberhart, R. C., & Kennedy, J. (1995, October). A new optimizer using particle swarm theory. In *Proceedings of the sixth international symposium on micro machine and human science* (Vol. 1, pp. 39-43). doi:10.1109/MHS.1995.494215

Fattah, M. A., & Ren, F. (2009). GA, MR, FFNN, PNN and GMM based models for automatic text summarization. *Computer Speech & Language*, *23*(1), 126–144. doi:10.1016/j.csl.2008.04.002

Fister, I., Jr., Yang, X. S., Fister, I., Brest, J., & Fister, D. (2013). *A brief review of nature inspired algorithms for optimization.* arXiv preprint, arXiv:1307.4186

García, O. C., de Moya Anegón, F., & Zarco, C. (2000). A GA-P algorithm to automatically formulate extended Boolean queries for a fuzzy information retrieval system. *Mathware & Soft Computing*, *7*(2), 309–322.

Geem, Z. W., Kim, J. H., & Loganathan, G. V. (2001). A new heuristic optimization algorithm: Harmony search. *Simulation*, *76*(2), 60–68. doi:10.1177/003754970107600201

Gholamrezazadeh, S., Salehi, M. A., & Gholamzadeh, B. (2009). A Comprehensive Survey on Text Summarization Systems. *Proceedings of CSA*, 1–6. doi:10.1109/CSA.2009.5404226

Golberg, D. E. (1989). *Genetic algorithms in search, optimization, and machine learning*. Reading, MA: Addison Wesley.

Gordon, M. D. (1988). Probabilistic and genetic algorithms for document retrieval. *Communications of the ACM*, *31*(10), 1208–1218. doi:10.1145/63039.63044

Hahn, U., & Mani, I. (2000). The challenges of automatic summarization. *IEEE Computer*, *33*(11), 29–36. doi:10.1109/2.881692

Hassan, R., Cohanim, B., De Weck, O., & Venter, G. (2005, April). A comparison of particle swarm optimization and the genetic algorithm. In *Proceedings of the 1st AIAA multidisciplinary design optimization specialist conference* (pp. 1-13). doi:10.2514/6.2005-1897

He, Y. X., Liu, D. X., Ji, D. H., Yang, H., & Teng, C. (2006, August). Msbga: A multi-document summarization system based on genetic algorithm. In *Machine Learning and Cybernetics, 2006 International Conference on* (pp. 2659-2664). IEEE. doi:10.1109/ICMLC.2006.258921

Holland, J. H. (1975). *Adaptation in natural and artificial systems: an introductory analysis with applications to biology, control, and artificial intelligence*. U Michigan Press.

Hovy, E., & Lin, C. Y. (1998, October). Automated text summarization and the SUMMARIST system. In *Proceedings of a workshop on held at Baltimore* (pp. 197-214). Association for Computational Linguistics. Automated Text Summarization And The Summarist System, TIPSTER III Final Report (SUMMAC).

Karaboga, D., & Akay, B. (2009). A comparative study of artificial bee colony algorithm. *Applied Mathematics and Computation*, *214*(1), 108–132. doi:10.1016/j.amc.2009.03.090

Karwa, S., & Chatterjee, N. (2014, December). Discrete Differential Evolution for Text Summarization. In *Information Technology (ICIT), 2014 International Conference on* (pp. 129-133). IEEE. doi:10.1109/ICIT.2014.28

Kogilavani, A., & Balasubramanie, P. (2010, December). Clustering based optimal summary generation using genetic algorithm. In *Communication and Computational Intelligence (INCOCCI), 2010 International Conference on* (pp. 324-329). IEEE.

Lin, C. Y., & Hovy, E. (1997). Identify Topic by Position. In *Proc. 5th Conference on Applied Natural Language Processing* (pp.283-290). doi:10.3115/974557.974599

López-Pujalte, C., Guerrero-Bote, V. P., & de Moya-Anegón, F. (2003). Order-based fitness functions for genetic algorithms applied to relevance feedback. *Journal of the American Society for Information Science and Technology*, *54*(2), 152–160. doi:10.1002/asi.10179

Mallipeddi, R., Suganthan, P. N., Pan, Q. K., & Tasgetiren, M. F. (2011). Differential evolution algorithm with ensemble of parameters and mutation strategies. *Applied Soft Computing*, *11*(2), 1679–1696. doi:10.1016/j.asoc.2010.04.024

Mani, I., & Maybury, M. T. (Eds.). (1999). *Advances in automatic text summarization* (Vol. 293). Cambridge, MA: MIT press.

Mendoza, M., Bonilla, S., Noguera, C., Cobos, C., & León, E. (2014). Extractive single-document summarization based on genetic operators and guided local search. *Expert Systems with Applications*, *41*(9), 4158–4169. doi:10.1016/j.eswa.2013.12.042

Nandhini, K., & Balasundaram, S. R. (2014). Extracting easy to understand summary using differential evolution algorithm. *Swarm and Evolutionary Computation*, *16*, 19–27. doi:10.1016/j.swevo.2013.12.004

Rautray, R., & Balabantaray, R. C. (2015). Comparative Study of DE and PSO over Document Summarization. In *Intelligent Computing, Communication and Devices* (pp. 371–377). Springer India. doi:10.1007/978-81-322-2012-1_38

Rautray, R., Balabantaray, R. C., & Bhardwaj, A. (2015). Document Summarization Using Sentence Features. *International Journal of Information Retrieval Research*, *5*(1), 36–47. doi:10.4018/IJIRR.2015010103

Reddy, J. M., & Kumar, N. D. (2012). Computational algorithms inspired by biological processes and evolution. *Current Science (Bangalore)*, *103*(4), 370–380.

Shareghi, E., & Hassanabadi, L. S. (2008). Text summarization with harmony search algorithm-based sentence extraction. In *Proceedings of the 5th international conference on soft computing as transdisciplinary science and technology* (pp. 226–231). Cergy-Pontoise, France: ACM. doi:10.1145/1456223.1456272

Storn, R., & Price, K. (1997). Differential evolution–a simple and efficient heuristic for global optimization over continuous spaces. *Journal of Global Optimization, 11*(4), 341–359. doi:10.1023/A:1008202821328

Waleed, J., Jun, H. D., Abbas, T., Hameed, S., & Hatem, H. (2014). A Survey of Digital Image Watermarking Optimization based on Nature Inspired Algorithms NIAs. *International Journal of Security and Its Applications, 8*(6), 315–334. doi:10.14257/ijsia.2014.8.6.28

Wang, X., Gao, X. Z., & Zenger, K. (2015). The Overview of Harmony Search. In *An Introduction to Harmony Search Optimization Method* (pp. 5–11). Springer International Publishing.

Wei, F., Li, W., & Liu, S. (2010). IRANK: A rank-learn-combine framework for unsupervised ensemble ranking. *Journal of the American Society for Information Science and Technology, 61*(6), 1232–1243.

Zhao, X., & Tang, J. (2010, March). Query-focused Summarization Based on Genetic Algorithm. In *2010 International Conference on Measuring Technology and Mechatronics Automation* (pp. 968-971). IEEE. doi:10.1109/ICMTMA.2010.429

Chapter 4

Issues and Challenges in Web Crawling for Information Extraction

Subrata Paul
Vignan Institute of Technology and Management, India

Anirban Mitra
Vignan Institute of Technology and Management, India

Swagata Dey
MIPS, MITS, Rayagada, India

ABSTRACT

Computational biology and bio inspired techniques are part of a larger revolution that is increasing the processing, storage and retrieving of data in major way. This larger revolution is being driven by the generation and use of information in all forms and in enormous quantities and requires the development of intelligent systems for gathering, storing and accessing information. This chapter describes the concepts, design and implementation of a distributed web crawler that runs on a network of workstations and has been used for web information extraction. The crawler needs to scale (at least) several hundred pages per second, is resilient against system crashes and other events, and is capable to adapted various crawling applications. Further this chapter, focusses on various ways in which appropriate biological and bio inspired tools can be used to implement, automatically locate, understand, and extract online data independent of the source and also to make it available for Semantic web agents like a web crawler.

DOI: 10.4018/978-1-5225-2375-8.ch004

Copyright ©2017, IGI Global. Copying or distributing in print or electronic forms without written permission of IGI Global is prohibited.

1. INTRODUCTION

Web search engines are today used by everyone with access to computers, and those people have very different interests. But search engines always return the same result, regardless of who did the search. Search results could be improved if more information about the user was considered. Web crawlers are computer programs that scan the web, 'reading' everything they find. Web crawlers are also known as spiders, bots and automatic indexers. These crawlers scan web pages to see what words they contain, and where those words are used. The crawler turns its findings into a giant index. The index is basically a big list of words and the web pages that feature them. So when you ask a search engine for pages about hippos, the search engine checks its index and gives you a list of pages that mention hippos. Web crawlers scan the web regularly so they always have an up-to-date index of the web. Archie is the first search engine, created in 1990. Downloaded directory listings of all files on anonymous FTP sites, and created searchable database (Gupta, 2011). In a generalized web crawler, two different users get different results for the same query, sometime when the transverse links-paths are from different direction. Web search engines have broadly three basic phases. These are crawling, indexing, and searching. The information available about the users' interest is considered in some of those three phases, depending on its nature.

Information retrieval (IR) is finding material of unstructured nature such as text, images, videos, and music. These materials are extracted from large collections usually stored on computers. For decades information retrieval is used by professional searchers, but now-a-days hundreds of millions of people use information retrieval daily. The field of IR also covers document clustering and document classification. Given a set of documents, clustering is the task of coming up with a good grouping of the documents based on their contents. Given a set of topics, and a set of documents, classification is the task of assigning each document to its most suitable topics, if any. IR systems can also be classified by the scale on which they operate. Three main scales are IR on the web, IR on the documents of an enterprise, and IR on a personal computer.

When doing IR on the web, the IR system will have to retrieve information from billions of documents. Furthermore, the IR system will have to be aware of some webs, where its owners will manipulate it, so that their web can appear on the top results for some specific searches. Moreover, the indexing will have to filter, and index only the most important information, as it is impossible to store everything. During the latest years, the Web 2.0 has emerged. With this development, web users not only retrieve information from the web but also add value to the web. If the search engines are capable to retrieve implicit information (such as the number of visits), or explicit information (such as rankings) given by the users, they will get more accurate results.

When the IR is executed on a personal computer, IR will be based on the documents on same computer, and on its e-mails. In such case, the IR is a lot more personalized than the one done on the web. This allows the user to classify the documents according to his topics of interest. This classification will fit better interests than the one done by a web search engine. IR on an enterprise documents is in the middle of the other two cases. In this case, the IR system is placed on a separate computer and the system will cover the internal documents of the enterprise. Therefore, information retrieval is now an extremely wide field (Kleinberg, 1998; Liu, Yu & Meng, 2002; Markov & Larose, 2007).

2. SEARCHES BY CONTENT

To do a search by content, the user needs to enter the query. The search engine will return the documents that satisfy the query. This feature can be achieved by reading the content on all of the documents, and search for the words specified by the user. The problem on this technique is that it requires a lot of computational effort at query time which makes it infeasible. The solution to such problem is to index the content of the files. If an inverted index is build prior to the searches, it will speed-up the searches. An inverted index is composed by a dictionary of terms, which will contain all the terms in the lexicon. Then, for each entry in the dictionary, one will have a list of documents; this list contains references to the documents where the term appears. Each item in this list is called a posting, and so the list is called postings list. This index will make it very easy and fast to know whether a word appears or not into a document. Moreover, it will also be easy to retrieve the document frequency of a term from the index. The document frequency of the terms is very useful to retrieve information from a collection of documents. Some additional information can be stored in the inverted index, for example, a user can also store the term frequency for each posting. The following steps are used to build the inverted index (Manning, Raghavan, and Schtze, 2009).

1. Collect the documents to be indexed.
2. Tokenize each text, turning each document into a list of tokens.
3. Do a linguistic pre-processing: normalize each token to produce the list of indexing terms and drop useless tokens.
4. Create the dictionary containing the indexing terms.
5. Read each document to add its postings into the postings lists.

Once the inverted index is obtained we will store the dictionary in main memory, meanwhile posting lists will be stored in the hard disk, as they are too large to be on main memory. The various model to this extent are discussed below.

2.1 Boolean Retrieval Model

Boolean queries only can express the appearance or nil appearance of some terms in a document. This model of queries is very limited, and cannot rank the results: a document satisfies the query or it does not, but there is no middle course. Extended Boolean model is similar to the Boolean Retrieval Model, but with some additional operators as term proximity operators. The extended Boolean model was most used during the early 90's (Kleinberg, 1998).

2.2 Ranked Retrieval Model

Ranked Retrieval Model is more complex than the Boolean retrieval model, and allows the user to execute queries in free text (without Boolean or proximity operators). This feature makes ranked retrieval model more user-friendly than Boolean retrieval model and extended Boolean model. Furthermore, the results of the search are ranked by score, so that the most representative documents of the search will appear on the top of the results. Additionally, structure of a ranked retrieval model query is the same as the structure of a document. This makes it possible to have a similarity function that works for both document-query comparisons and document-document comparisons. This function cannot exist for the Boolean retrieval model, as a Boolean query structure and a document structure are different. Nowadays, ranked retrieval model is mostly used. Ranked retrieval model queries do not need to have any Boolean operators, which makes them more user friendly than Boolean queries. Furthermore, a plain-text ranked retrieval model query will usually return a good result. However, Ranked Retrieval Model queries may not be enough in some cases. Therefore search engines also allow the execution of Boolean queries when using an advanced search option, as using Boolean operators in the queries can help to get a more selective result. This makes Boolean queries especially useful when the user knows what the user is looking for (Kleinberg, 1998).

3. CRAWLING APPLICATION AND WEB CRAWLERS

A search engine needs to have an index containing information about a set of web pages. Before indexing the documents, it is necessary to have the documents. The component that will provide the documents and their content is the crawler or spider.

The crawler will surf the Internet, or a part of it, searching for the most interesting web pages. The interesting pages will be stored locally, so that they can be indexed later. Crawlers can be classified as focused or unfocused. Unfocused crawlers store information about a page, regardless of its topic and its site whereas unfocused crawling is used by large scale web search engines. By contrast, focused crawlers store information only of some of the web pages, thus focusing their crawling on some topics, or some sites, or some type of documents, or to interesting pages according to information retrieved from the user (Ahuja & Bal, 2014), (Malhotra, 2013).

3.1 Crawler Architecture

A web crawler is one of the main components of the web search engines. The growth of web crawler is increasing in the same way as the web is growing. A list of URLs is available with the web crawler and each URL is called a seed. Crawler visits each pages and then it also add other URLs available from those visited pages in the queue. The list of URLs is called crawl frontier. This queue is scheduled by a scheduler. Some suitable algorithms are also used by web crawler to find the relevant links for the search engine (Ahuja & Bal, 2014). Databases are very big machines like DB2, used to store large amount of data (Malhotra, 2013). The architecture of a web crawler has been given in Figure 1.

Figure 1. Architecture of web crawler

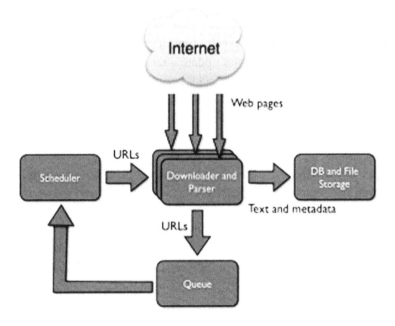

3.2 Crawler Design Issues

Depending on how the crawler updates its collection, the crawler can be classified as one of the following.

1. **Batch-Mode Crawler:** A batch-mode crawler runs periodically (say, once a month), updating all pages in the collection in each crawl.
2. **Steady Crawler:** A steady crawler runs continuously without any pause. Further, as the crawler updates pages in the collection, it may visit the pages either at the same frequency or at different frequencies.
3. **Uniform Frequency:** The crawler revisits Web pages at the same frequency, regardless of how often they change.
4. **Variable Frequency:** A crawler may increase the freshness of its collection by 10%–23% if it adjusts page revisit frequencies based on how often pages change.

3.3 Types of Web Crawler

Different types of web crawlers are available depending upon how the web pages are crawled and how successive web pages are retrieved for accessing next pages. Some of which are following ones:

1. **Breadth First Crawler:** Searching starts with some pages and then continues exploring related pages using Breadth first searching mode. But may not be strictly BFS, it can also search for important pages first (Ahuja & Bal, 2014).
2. **Incremental Web Crawlers:** In this type of crawling, instead of searching start from scratch each time, crawler update a set of existing pages related a topic. Using some methods crawler checks periodically if previously downloaded pages needs any updates or not and keep high freshness in low peak (Ahuja & Bal, 2014). Figure 2 shows the architecture of incremental web crawler.
3. **Form Focused Crawler:** This type of crawler use some stopping criteria to stop searching and focus on sparse distribution in the web (Ahuja & Bal, 2014). Form Crawler (Sharma, 2008) avoids crawling through unproductive paths by limiting the search to a particular topic. Figure 3 shows the architecture of form focused crawler.
4. **Focused Crawler:** It has three components such as a classifier, a distiller and a crawler classifier makes relevance judgments on pages crawled to decide on link expansion, distiller determines a measure of centrality of crawled pages

Figure 2. Architecture of incremental model

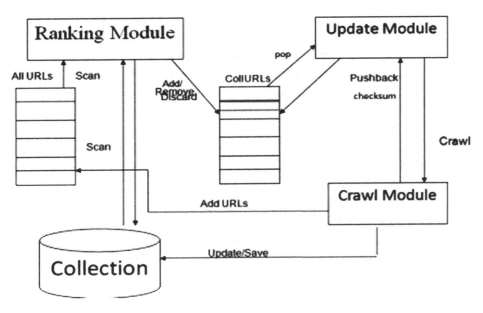

Figure 3. Architecture of Form Focused Crawler

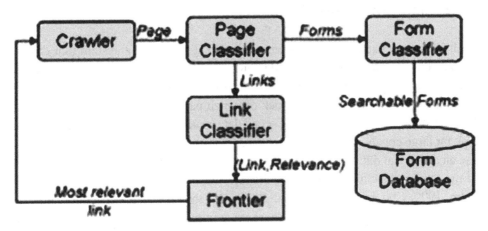

to determine visit priorities, and crawler dynamically reconfigurable priority controls which is governed by the classifier and distiller (Ahuja & Bal, 2014).

5. **Hidden Web Crawlers:** Some high quality data are only retrieved from database by an appropriate query or by submitting a form in web, known as hidden web or deep web (Ahuja & Bal, 2014). Crawlers that automatically fill

in forms to reach the content behind them are called hidden web or deep web crawlers. Content of this type of crawler may be unstructured or structured. Query interface can also be either structured or unstructured (Olston & Najork, 2010). Deep web crawling has three steps.

    a.   Locate deep web content sources, means first find which website lead a client to deep web content.

    b.   Select relevant sources.

    c.   **Extract Underlying Content**: Extract original content lying behind the form interfaces of the selected content sources (Olston & Najork, 2010).

6.   **Parallel Crawlers:** Many search engines often run multiple processes in parallel to perform the searching, so that download rate is maximized. This type of crawler is known as a parallel crawler (Ahuja & Bal, 2014).

7.   **Distributed Web Crawler:** Because of huge and ever growing situation of web, Parallel crawler or a single crawling process even with multithreading will be insufficient. So process need to be distributed to multiple processes to make the process scalable. Pages are downloaded by multiple processes and sent to a central indexer to extract those links (Ahuja & Bal, 2014). A pictorial representation of this type of crawler is given in Figure 4.

3.4 Basic Crawler Structure

With known scenarios, this work intends to design a flexible system that can be adapted to different applications and strategies with a reasonable amount of work. There are significant differences between the scenarios. For example, a broad breadth first crawler has to keep track of which pages have been crawled already. It is commonly done using a "URL seen" data structure that may have to reside on disk for large crawls. A link analysis based focused crawler, on the other hand, may use an additional data structure to represent the graph structure of the crawled part of the web, and a classifier to judge the relevance of a page (Chakrabarti, Berg & Dom, 1999; Cho & Garcia-Molina, 2000). But the size of the structures may be much smaller. On the other hand, there are a number of common tasks that need to be done in all or most scenarios, such as enforcement of robot exclusion, crawl speed control, or DNS resolution. For simplicity, the crawler design is restricted to two main components, referred to as crawling application and crawling system. The crawling application decides what page to request next given the current state and the previously crawled pages, and issues a stream of requests (URLs) to the crawling system. The crawling system (eventually) downloads the requested pages and supplies them to the crawling application for analysis and storage. The crawling system is in charge of tasks such as robot exclusion, speed control, and DNS resolu-

Figure 4. Architecture of distributed crawler

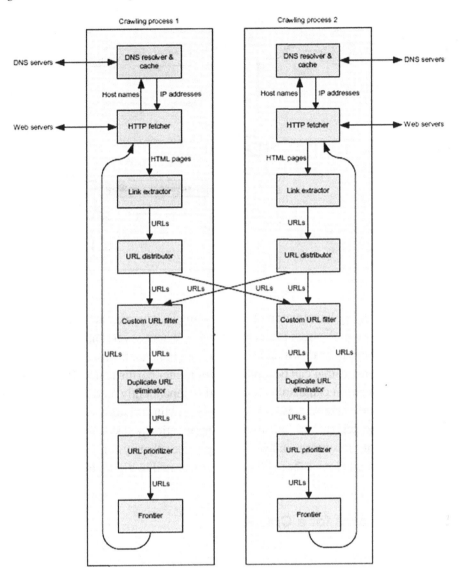

tion that are common to most scenarios, while the application implements crawling strategies such as "breadth-first" or "focused". Thus, to implement a focused crawler instead of a breadth-first crawler, one would use the same crawling system but a significantly different application component, written using a library of functions for common tasks such as parsing, maintenance of the "URL seen" structure, and communication with crawling system and storage. The working of the web crawler has been demonstrated in Figure 5.

Figure 5. Flowchart showing the working of the web crawler

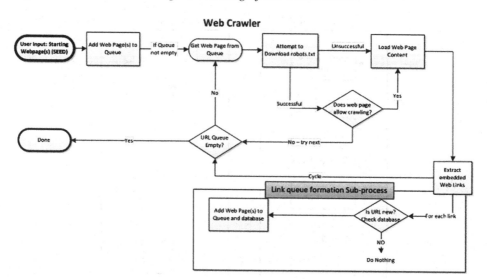

At first glance, implementation of the crawling system may appear trivial. This is however not true in the high performance case, where several hundred or even a thousand pages have to be downloaded per second. In fact, crawling system consists of several components that can be replicated for higher performance. Both crawling system and application can also be replicated independently, and several different applications could issue requests to the same crawling system, showing another motivation for the design. This partition into application and system components is a design choice of the system, and not used by some other systems. The implementation of the web crawler has been clearly demonstrated in Figure 6 (Cho & Garcia-Molina, 2000).

3.5 Requirements for a Crawler

The following section reviews the requirements for a good crawler, and approaches for achieving them. Figure 7 demonstrates the two basic components of the crawler. Details on the solutions are given in the subsequent sections (Chakrabarti, Berg & Dom, 1999).

1. **Flexibility:** The system should be developed in such a way that it would be able to use in a variety of scenarios, with as few modifications as possible.
2. **Low Cost and High Performance:** The system should scale to at least several hundred pages per second and hundreds of millions of pages per run, and should run on low cost hardware. Note that efficient use of disk access is crucial to

Figure 6. Flowchart demonstrating the implementation of the web crawler

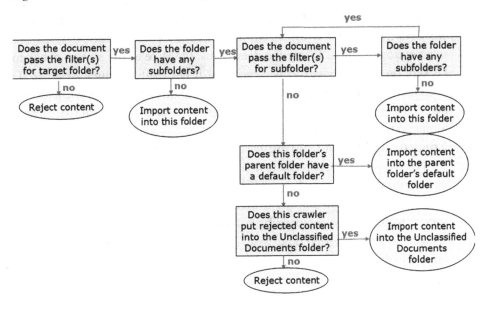

Figure 7. Basic two components of the crawler

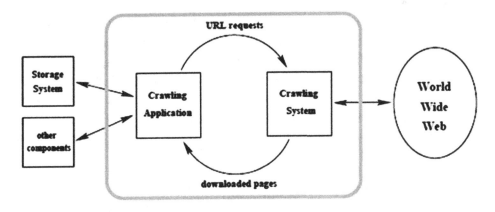

maintain a high speed after the main data structures, such as the "URL seen" structure and crawl frontier, become too large for main memory. This will only happen after downloading several million pages.

3. **Robustness:** There are several aspects under this category. First, since the system will interact with millions of servers, it has to tolerate bad HTML, strange server behaviour and configurations, and many other odd issues. The goal here is to err on the side of caution, and if necessary ignore pages and

even entire servers with odd behaviour, since in many applications one can only download a subset of the pages anyway. Secondly, since a crawl may take weeks or months, the system needs to be able to tolerate crashes and network interruptions without losing the data. Thus, the state of the system needs to be kept on disk. It needs to be noted that it not really requires strict ACID (Atomicity, Consistency, Isolation, and Durability) properties. Instead, we decided to periodically synchronize the main structures to disk, and to re-crawl a limited number of pages after a crash.

4. **Etiquette and Speed Control:** It is extremely important to follow the standard conventions for robot exclusion to supply a contact URL for the crawler, and to supervise the crawl. In addition, one needs to control access speed in several different ways. Further avoiding in putting too much load on a single server; which can be achieved by contacting each site only once in every 30 seconds unless specified otherwise. It is also desirable to throttle the speed on a domain level, in order not to overload small domains, and for other reasons to be explained later. One needs to control the total download rate of our crawler. In particular, it is observed that crawl at low speed during the peek usage hours of the day, and at a much higher speed during the late night and early morning, limited mainly by the load tolerated by router.

5. **Manageability and Re-Configurability:** An appropriate interface is needed to monitor the crawl, including the speed of the crawler, statistics about hosts and pages, and the sizes of the main data sets. An administrator should have privileges to adjust the speed, add and remove components, shut down the system, force a checkpoint, or add hosts and domains to a "blacklist" of places that the crawler should avoid. After a crash or shutdown, the software of the system may be modified to fix problems, and one may want to continue the crawl using a different machine configuration. The software at the end of mentioned, first huge crawl was significantly different from that at the start, due to the need for numerous fixes and extensions that became only apparent after tens of millions of pages had been downloaded.

4. PARALLEL CRAWLER- A NEW CRAWLING APPROACH

A parallel crawler consists of multiple crawling processes, called C-proc's. Each c-pros works like single crawler, searching starts from a set of URL and then retrieve all other URLs linked with that page and keep them into a queue. Depending on how the C-proc's split the download task, there are different types of parallel crawler. A general architecture of a parallel crawler is depicted in Figure 8.

1. **Intra-Site Parallel Crawler:** When all C-proc's run on the same local network and communicate through a high speed interconnect such as local area network (LAN), it is called an intra-site parallel crawler.
2. **Distributed Crawler:** When C-proc's run at geographically distant locations connected by the Internet or wide area network, we call it a distributed crawler.

In case of parallel crawler, same pages can be downloaded multiple times. To avoid this overlap, C-proses need to coordinate using some logical methods as discussed below.

1. **Independent:** C-proc's may download pages independently without any coordination. Every C-proc's starts searching from different set of URL seed and continue searching. In this case, overhead of coordination is minimum and very scalable.
2. **Dynamic Assignment:** A central coordinator logically divides the Web into small partitions using a certain partitioning function and dynamically assigns each partition to a C-proc for download. Each C-proc reports the link to the central coordinator. The central coordinator later uses this link as a seed URL for the appropriate partition.
3. **Static Assignment:** Partitioning and division of web is predefined before starting the crawling, and there is no existence of any coordinator. Each C-pros is responsible for their allocated page during a crawl (Cho & Garcia-Molina, 2002).

Figure 8. General architecture of a parallel crawler

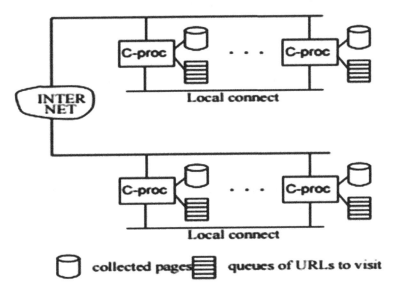

4.1 Crawling Modes for Static Assignment

In this process, C-Proc already know about their crawling segments, but there may exist some pages which have connecting links to other segment, they are known as inter-partition link. Depending on handling process of these links, there can be some modes of static assignment. These are defined below (Cho & Garcia-Molina, 2002).

1. **Firewall Mode:** In firewall mode, each C-proc downloads only the pages within its partition and does not follow any inter-partition link. All inter-partition links are ignored and thrown away.
2. **Cross-Over Mode:** Primarily, each C-proc downloads pages within its partition, and if necessary, it also follows inter-partition links. In this case, pages may overlap, but web coverage is better than firewall mode.
3. **Exchange Mode:** Here C-pros do not follow inter-partition links. They periodically and incrementally exchange inter-partition URLs.

4.2 URL Exchange Minimization

The URL exchange also follows some process. To maintain the performance of crawler, no of URL exchange must be reduced. There are some techniques, like batch communication, and replication.

Batch communication partitions do not exchange immediately after finding an inter-communicational link. It waits until it gathers some URLs and exchange them as a batch. It only keeps track of links of current batch. After exchanging a batch of URL, it again starts gathering a new batch of URLs to be transferred.

In replication, a small number of Web pages have an extremely large number of links pointing to them, while a majority of pages have only a small number of incoming links. It is known that the number of incoming links to pages on the Web follows a Zipfian distribution (Barabasi & Albert, 1999; Border et. al, 2000; Zipf, 1949).

So, it significantly reduce URL exchanges, if it is replicated the most "popular" URLs at each C-proc and stop transferring them between C proc's. That is, before starting crawling pages, identify the most popular URLs based on the image of the Web collected in a previous crawl. Then replicate these URLs at each C-proc, so that the C-proc's do not exchange them during a crawl. Since a small number of Web pages have a large number of incoming links, this scheme may significantly reduce URL exchanges between C-proc's even if we replicate a small number of URLs (Cho & Garcia-Molina, 2002).

4.3 Partitioning Function

It is mainly assumed that the Web pages are partitioned by Web sites. Clearly there exists multitude of ways to partition the Web. These are URL hash based, site hash based and hierarchical based.

In URL-hash based partitioning, based on the hash value of the URL of a page, a C-proc is assigned to the page. In this scheme, pages in the same site can be assigned to different C-proc's. Therefore, the locality of link structure is not reflected in the partition, and there will be many inter-partition links (Cho & Garcia-Molina, 2002).

In site-hash based portioning, instead of computing the hash value on an entire URL, the hash value only on the site name of a URL is computed. In this scheme the pages in the same site will be allocated to the same partition. Therefore, only some of the inter-site links will be available in inter-partition links, and thus reduces the number of inter-partition links quite significantly compared to the URL-hash based scheme (Cho & Garcia-Molina, 2002).

In hierarchical partitioning, instead of using a hash-value, a partition of the Web is done hierarchically based on the URLs of pages. For example, the Web can be divided into three partitions and allocate them to three C-proc's (Cho & Garcia-Molina, 2002).

4.4 Comparative Evaluation of Models

Different crawling models are evaluated by their performance. These are listed below.

1. **Overlap:** While working simultaneously, multiple C-pros can download same URL multiple times. The overlap of downloaded pages can be defined as $\frac{N-I}{I}$, where N is the total no of pages downloaded by the crawler and I is the total no of unique pages downloaded. This overlapping problem can clearly be avoided if 'Firewall model' or 'Exchange Model' is used. As they download URL only from their own partition, so chance of overlap is zero (Cho & Garcia-Molina, 2002).

2. **Coverage:** In Firewall model, one can see that C-pros run independently and they do not follow inter-partition link. In that case they may not coverage all the web. In this case we can define the coverage of downloaded pages as $I\,/\,U$, where I is the total no of unique pages downloaded and U is the total no of pages a crawler has downloaded (Cho & Garcia-Molina, 2002).

3. **Quality:** To represent most possible information to the user, crawler always want to download most important pages as it can not download the whole web. Therefore, it has enough space to keep 1 million pages. In this case, crawler

always tries to download most important 1 million pages (Cho, Garcia-Molina & Page, 1998).

A crawler considers a page to be important, when a lot of other pages point to that page. This is known as backlink count. For a single crawler, it keeps track of backlink count of pages and then hit those 1 million pages which have maximum backlink counts and maintain the quality of crawler.

Hypothetically, consider an oracle crawler. Say, oracle crawler downloads most important N pages and P_N represents the set of N pages, A_N to represent the set of N pages that an actual crawler would download, which would not be necessarily the same as P_N. Then the ratio $\dfrac{|A_N \cap P_N|}{|P_N|}$ provides the quality of downloaded pages by the actual crawler. To maintain the Quality of parallel crawler C-proc's need to periodically exchange information on page importance.

4. **Communication Overhead:** In order to coordinate, C-proc's need to exchange their work. C-proc's swap their inter-partition URLs periodically based on the exchange mode. To quantify how much communication is required for this exchange, the communication overhead is defined as the average number of inter-partition URLs exchanged per downloaded page. For example, if a parallel crawler has downloaded 1,500 pages in total and if its C-proc's have exchanged 3,000 inter-partition URLs, its communication overhead is 3, 000/1, 500 = 2. The firewall and the cross-over based crawler do not have any communication overhead, because they do not exchange any inter-partition URLs (Cho & Garcia-Molina, 2002).

4.5 Crossover Mode and Overlap

Crossover mode based crawler follows inter-partitioning link. It provides good coverage and quality. However, this mode incurs overlap in download, because a page can be downloaded by multiple C-proc's. In most cases the overlap stays at zero until the coverage becomes relatively large. By applying the partitioning scheme to C-proc's, each C-proc stay in its own partition in the beginning and suppress the overlap as long as possible (Cho & Garcia-Molina, 2002).

An exchange mode crawler constantly exchanges inter-partition URLs between C-proc's to avoid overlapping and coverage problem (Cho & Garcia-Molina, 2002).

5. CRAWLING ALGORITHMS

There are many crawling algorithms available till date. The basic steps which are involved in the working of the crawler are removing a URL from the URL list, determining the IP address of its host name, downloading of the related documents, and extracting any links available in the documents (Ahuja & Bal, 2014). A crawler must have a good crawling strategy, as noted in the previous sections, but it also needs a highly optimized architecture.

5.1 Pseudo-Code for a Generalized Web Crawler

The following is a pseudo code summary of the algorithm that can be used to implement a web crawler. The algorithm, asks user to specify the starting URL on web and file type that crawler should crawl.Algorithm:

Add the URL to the empty list of URLs to search
While not empty (the list of URL to search)

```
{
        Take the first URL in the form to the list of URLs
        Mark this URL as already searched URL
        If the URL protocol is not HTTP then
                break;
                go back to while
        If robots.txt file exist on the site then
                If file includes.Disallow statement then
                        Break;
                        Go back to while
        Open the URL
        If the opened URL is not HTML file then
                Break;
                Go back to while
        Iterate the HTML file
        While the html text contails another link
        {
                If robots.txt file exists on the URL/site then
                        If file includes.Disallow statement
then
                                Break;
                                Go back to while
                        If the opened URL is HTML file then
```

```
                                If the URL isn't marked as
searched then
                                     Mark this URL as al-
ready searched URL
                        Else if type of file is user requested
                            Add to list of files found.

        }
}
```

6. APPLICATIONS FOR VARIOUS CRAWLERS

There are a number of different scenarios in which crawlers are used for data acquisition. This section describes few examples and how they differ in the crawling strategies used.

6.1 Breadth First Crawler

In order to build a major search engine or a large repository such as the internet archive (Raghavan & Garcia-Molina, 2001), high-performance crawlers start out at a small set of pages and then explore other pages by following links in a "breadth first-like" fashion. In reality, the web pages are often not traversed in a strict breadth-first fashion, but using a variety of policies such as for pruning crawls inside a web site, or for crawling more important pages first.

6.2 Re-Crawling Pages for Updates

After pages are initially acquired, they may have to be periodically re-crawled and checked for updates. In the simplest case, this could be done by starting another broad breadth-first crawl, or by simply requesting all URLs in the collection again. However, a variety of heuristics can be employed to crawl more important pages, sites, or domains more frequently. Good re-crawling strategies are crucial for maintaining an up-to-date search index with limited crawling bandwidth (Cho & Garcia-Molina, 2000; Diligenti, Coetzee, Lawrence, Giles & Gori, 2000).

6.3 Focused Crawling

More specialized search engines may use crawling policies that attempt to focus only on certain types of pages such as pages on a particular topic or in a particular language, images, mp3 files, or computer science research papers. In addition to heuristics, more general approaches have been proposed based on link structure analysis (Chakrabarti, Berg & Dom, 1999; Cho & Garcia-Molina, 2000) and machine learning techniques (Henzinger, Heydon, Mitzenmacher & Najork, 1999; Medigue, Viari, Henaut & Danchin, 1992). The goal of a focused crawler is to find many pages of interest without using a lot of bandwidth. Thus, most of the previous work does not use a high-performance crawler, although doing so could support large specialized collections that are significantly more up-to-date than a broad search engine.

6.4 Random Walking and Sampling

Several techniques have been studied that use random walks on the web graph to sample pages or estimate the size and quality of search engines (Chakrabarti, Berg & Dom, 1999; Henzinger, Heydon, Mitzenmacher & Najork, 2000; Kahle, 1997).

6.5 Crawling the Hidden Web

A lot of the data accessible via the web actually resides in databases and can only be retrieved by posting appropriate queries and filling out forms on web pages. Recently, a lot of interest has focused on automatic access to this data, also called the Hidden Web or Deep Web, or Federated Facts and Figures. (Rennie & McCallum, 1999) has looked at techniques for crawling hidden web. A crawler such as described here could be extended and used as an efficient front-end for such a system. However that there are many other challenges associated with access to the hidden web, and the efficiency of the front end is probably not the most important issue.

7. DATA RETRIEVAL AND ITS ACQUISITION IN BIOLOGICAL ENVIRONMENTS

In general, a molecular biology database provides with at least one of the following data retrieval approach. These are query interface, indirect data retrieval with database browsers, and database downloading. The query interfaces found in molecular biology databases can be classified in "free-form/ adhoc" query interfaces and "fixed-form" query interfaces. Free-form/ad-hoc query interfaces provide the possibility to express a query in a query language depending on the underlying data model of the database. Although the query languages used are often powerful, free-form/ad-hoc query interfaces consists of certain drawback. Biologists are usually not familiar with the principles of these languages, and of database query languages in general.

But a user of such a language must have a detailed knowledge of the schema of the database (Davidson, Overton, Tannen & Wong, 1997).

Fixed-form query interfaces provide one or several views on the database. With such a query interface, queries can only be posed against a predetermined set of tables, classes, or other database components, and in queries only a predetermined set of attributes for each database component can be used. The view underlying a fixed-form query interface to a molecular biology database not necessarily reflects the internal structure of the database, i.e., the storage structure. (Anuradha J. and B.K. Tripathy, 2011) Fixed-form query interfaces do not have the above mentioned drawbacks of free-form/ad-hoc query interfaces at the price of strongly restricting data retrieval. Figure 9 demonstrates the fixed-form query interface of EMGLib as an example.

In some molecular biology databases, hierarchical classifications of the data can then be browsed for data retrieval. This approach to data retrieval has been called "indirect data retrieval". Interestingly, browsers are also available for flat file databases. Most molecular biology databases, support flat file download via the file transfer protocol (FTP), including databases that are not implemented as flat files but with a database management system. Flat files are the de facto data interchange standard in molecular and computational biology. A sample browser for Colibri for exptraction of biological data has been shown in Figure 10.

Figure 9. Fixed-form query interface of EMGLib

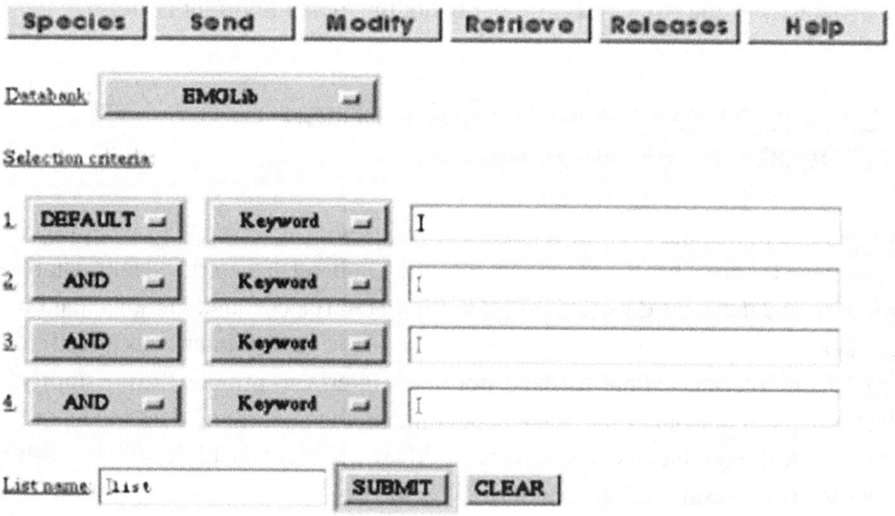

Figure 10. Browswer for Colibri

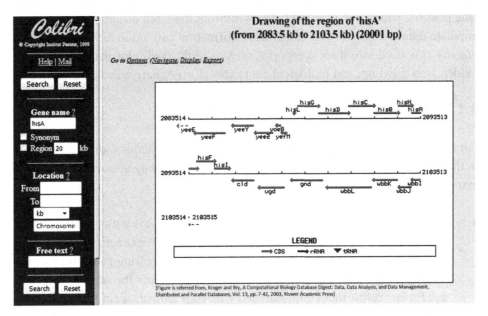

Molecular biology databases collect their data using some of the following approaches:

1. **From Other Databases:** The collected data in general have to be reformatted.
2. **From the Research Community:** Many molecular biology databases acquire their data from submissions by researchers. Fill-in forms often make sure that the data fit the database schema.
3. **From the Literature:** Usually, data acquisition from the scientific literature is done manually and is therefore work intensive. The update frequency is an interesting aspect of a molecular biology database, for it considerably varies between databases (Baumgartner, Flesca & Gottlob, 2001).

8. INFORMATION EXTRACTION

Currently, with the fast development of the internet, both the amount of useful data and the number of web sites are growing rapidly. The web is becoming an increasingly useful information tool for computer users. However, there are so many web pages that no human being can traverse all of them to obtain the information needed. Even in the narrow domain of molecular biological data, no human can traverse all the pages that may be of interest for finding needed information. A system that can allow users to query web pages like a database is becoming increasingly desirable. One possible strategy is to extract useful information from different web pages to populate databases for further handling. Information extraction techniques can be broadly classified into three categories such as traditional information extraction, hidden web crawling, and biological data extraction (Acharjya & Ahmed, 2015).

8.1 Traditional Information Extraction

For traditional information extraction, five major data extraction tools are presented in the discussion. Each tool represents a different major way of doing information extraction.

- **Lixto:** Lixto (Baumgartner, Flesca & Gottlob, 2001) is a tool for supervised wrapper generation and automated web information extraction. It generates wrappers semi-automatically and interactively by creating patterns in a hierarchical order. The user can define extraction patterns through the interface and further refine them until satisfied with the elements identified by the system. Then Lixto uses the wrapper to extract the relevant information from an HTML document and translate it into XML which can be easily queried and further processed. Lixto has a friendly interface and does not require users to know any specific language. However, it is not robust to changes in web pages and does not work well with unstructured data.

  The Lixto toolkit consists of the following modules: The Interactive Pattern Builder provides the visual UI that allows a user to specify the desired extraction patterns and the basic algorithm for creating a corresponding Elog wrapper as output. The Extractor is the Elog program interpreter that performs the actual extraction based on a given Elog program. The extractor, provided with an HTML document and a previously constructed program, generates as its output a pattern instance base, a data structure encoding the extracted instances as hierarchically ordered trees and strings. One program as input of the extractor can be used for continual extraction on changing pages, or to extract from several HTML pages of similar structure. With the controller of the XML Generator, the user chooses how to map extracted information to XML. Its transformer module performs the actual translation from the extracted pattern instance base to XML. Lixto offers two basic mechanisms of data extraction: tree and string extraction. For tree extraction, we identify elements with their corresponding tree paths and possibly some properties of the elements themselves (Baumgartner, Flesca & Gottlob, 2001).
- **Road Runner:** Road Runner (Crescenzi, Mecca & Merialdo, 2001) does fully automatic wrapper generation. It does not need any interaction with the

user during the wrapper generation process. It compares two HTML pages from one web site and analyses the similarities and dissimilarities between them in order to discover the pattern of how this web site presents data. The system discovers data fields by string mismatches. For more complex cases, the system may need more than two pages to capture more accurate structural variations. Although this approach is fully automatic, it does not generate robust wrappers and thus has to generate one wrapper for each web site. Another problem is that, it only works for web pages that are highly regular, usually only those that are generated automatically (Crescenzi, Mecca & Merialdo, 2001).

- **SRV**: SRV (Freitag, 1998) combine natural language processing (NLP) techniques with machine learning algorithms. It is a general-purpose top-down learner for information extraction. It learns extraction rules and extracts useful information from text documents based on a set of token-oriented features. There are two basic varieties of token- oriented features: simple and relational. A simple feature is a function mapping a token to some discrete value, such as length, character type, orthography, part of speech, or lexical meaning. A relational feature considers relationships between tokens, such as adjacency or linguistic syntax. In addition, it is not robust to changes; its training documents need to be labelled; and it does not work well as a "multiple slot" filler.

- **RAPIER:** RAPIER (Embley, Campbell, Jiang, Liddle, Lonsdale, Ng & Smith, 1999; Califf & Mooney, 1999; Crescenzi, Mecca & Merialdo, 2001) is a bottom-up relational learner of pattern-matching rules for information extraction. The pattern-matching rules are indexed by template name and slot name. Each rule consists of three parts: pre-filler pattern, slot filler pattern, and post-filler pattern. A slot filler pattern matches the information that needs to be extracted, and a pre-filler and post-filler match the context of the information of interest. An extraction pattern considers features such as word lengths, symbols, part-of-speech tags, and semantic classes. It induces the extraction pattern from a pre-tagged training set. It is a single-slot approach and can only work with free text. RAIPER make use of limited syntactic and semantic information, using freely available, robust knowledge sources such as a part-of-speech tagger and a lexicon with semantic classes, such as the hypernym links in WordNet (Miller et al., 1993).

- **BYU Ontos:** BYU Ontos (Embley, Campbell, Jiang, Liddle, Lonsdale, Ng & Smith, 1999) is an ontology-based data extraction system. Domain specific extraction ontology describes the data of interest by using objects, relationships, and data frames which contain data-value recognizers. The ontology guides the extraction process by providing conceptual expectations which can be matched using pre-specified heuristics. This approach is robust to changes in source pages and can extract and integrate information from different web sites in the same application domain. It works for unstructured, semi-structured, or structured source documents that require multiple slot filling. The drawback of this system is that it requires human experts to build extraction ontologies manually.

For HTML documents with multiple records that are generated manually, it is usually true that the creator of these documents follows certain patterns, though these patterns are not necessarily rigid or well-formed. To deal with inconsistency within a Web page and variation across individually consistent pages, multiple heuristics is used in identifying record separators. The experimental results of applying the different heuristics on randomly chosen sets of HTML documents show a high success rate in determining the correct record separators (Embley, Jiang & Ng, 1999). The results support the tag-tree approach is reliable and general.

8.2 Hidden Web Crawling

Traditional information extraction tools only work on the publicly index able web. However, large numbers of web pages are hidden behind search forms. These pages are dynamically generated through searchable online databases according to users' queries submitted through the search forms. HiWE (Hidden web Exposer) (Raghavan & Garcia-Molina, 2001) is a hidden web crawler that can crawl the hidden web according to a user's query. When it encounters a form page, the crawler first builds an internal representation of the form. It then tries to match the internal form representation with the concepts in a task-specific database. Once concepts are matched, HiWE can assign values to each internal form field according to the database. HiWE uses value assignments to fill out and submit the search form. It then can retrieve the information hidden behind the form.

8.3 Biological Data Extraction

Current biological information extraction approaches mainly extract data from plain text such as online abstracts and articles. Systems recognize biological terms such as protein and gene names (Krauthammer, Rzhetsky, Morozov & Friedman, 2000) and relationships between biological terms (Gaizauskas, Demetriou, Artymiuk & Willett, 2003). Recognizing biological terms from a plain text document is a non-trivial problem. It is, however, one of the first steps toward achieving the goal of biological information extraction. The approaches to named-entity extraction can be divided into two categories: rule-based and dictionary-based. Rule-based approaches generate heuristic rules based on text features such as morphologic characteristics, part-of-speech tagging, or keywords. Dictionary-based approaches consist of first constructing named entity dictionaries and then detecting dictionary terms in documents. Rule-based approaches are particularly useful in identifying new names. However, if a biological object has multiple synonyms, rule-based approaches are not able to unify them. This problem can be solved by the dictionary-based approaches. Here a system has been introduced for protein and gene name recognition which is mainly a dictionary-based, but also considers spelling variations in names to recognize biological terms (Krauthammer, Rzhetsky, Morozov & Friedman, 2000). The system works based on BLAST (Basic Local Alignment Search Tool) which provides a method for rapid DNA and protein sequence comparison and a database for gene and protein names. First an exhaustive list of gene and protein names is translated into an alphabet of DNA sequences by substituting each character in the name with a pre- determined unique nucleotide combination and then the encoded names are imported into BLAST. Once the system has a source article, the system encodes it using the same nucleotide combination. The system then matches the translated article against the nucleotide representation of gene and protein names. BLAST finds any exact match; it also considers similar sequences. Therefore, this tool can find both exact names and names that are closely similar to the names in the dictionary.

In addition to extracting biological element names, it is also important to extract relationships among these biological elements. PASTA (Protein Active Site Template Acquisition) (Gaizauskas, Demetriou, Artymiuk & Willett, 2003) is one of the tools to automatically extract amino acid residues in protein molecules from online articles and abstracts. A PASTA template stores information about an entity, a relation, and an event. The system fills out the slots in a template using the following four steps.

Step 1: In a text pre-processing step, the system analyses each section in a source document and discards those sections that are not related to the domain of interest. It also splits those sections that are related to the domain of interest into sentences and character sequence units.

Step 2: In a terminological processing step, the system identifies and classifies instances of the term classes by analysing the morphological features of each term and looking them up in biological databases. It also combines related adjacent terms into phrases.

Step 3: In a syntactic and semantic processing step, the system builds a "semantic" representation of the text on a sentence-by-sentence basis by using NLP syntactical and grammatical analysis.

Step 4: In a discourse processing and template extraction step, the system fills out the templates, links information from sentences, and merges the related information together.

9 CONCLUSION

This chapter reviews a generalize web search engines as a web crawler as an approach towards the searching problem considering the users topics of interest and the navigation context. In a generalized web crawler, two different users get different results for the same query, sometime when the transverse links-paths are from different direction. Web search engines have, broadly classified in three basic phases. They are crawling, indexing and searching. The information available about the users interest can is considered in some of those three phases, depending on its nature. Web Crawler is the vital source of information retrieval which traverses the Web and downloads web documents that suit the users need. Web crawler is used by the search engine and other users to regularly ensure that their database is up-to-date. The overview of different crawling technologies has been presented in this chapter. Crawlers are being used more and more often to collect Web data for search engine, caches, and data mining. The size of the Web is growing and it becomes increasingly important to use crawlers. This chapter has enumerated the major components of the crawler and their algorithmic details. Parallelization of crawling system is very vital from the point of view of downloading documents in a reasonable amount of time. Also it is designed to be scalable Web crawler.

There are obviously many improvements to the system that can be made. A major open issue for future work is a detailed study of database indexing and normalization that can be done so as to increase the work efficiency of the overall system. Inter-processes communication can also be added. Some mechanism for removing duplicate downloads shall also be included in cases where different URLs point to same page.

REFERENCES

Acharjya, D. P., & Kauser Ahmed, P. (2015). Swarm Intelligence in Solving Bio-Inspired Computing Problems – Reviews, Perspectives, and Challenges. In S. Bhattacharyya & P. Dutta (Eds.), *Swarm Intelligence in Engineering* (pp. 74–98). IGI Global Publishers.

Ahuja, M. S., & Dr, J. S. B. (2014). Varnica Web Crawler: Extracting the Web Data. *International Journal of Computer Trends and Technology, 13*(3).

Anuradha, J., & Tripathy, B. K. (2011). *Improved Intelligent Dynamic Swarm PSO Algorithm and Rough Set for feature Selection, Obcom 2011 conference.* VIT, Vellore.

Barabasi, A., & Albert, R. (1999). Emergence of scaling in random networks. *Science, 286*(509). PMID:10521342

Baumgartner, R., Flesca, S., & Gottlob, G. (2001), Visual Web information extraction with Lixto.*Proceedings of the 27th International Conference on Very Large Data Bases (VLDB'01)*, 119-128.

Broder, A. Z., Kumar, S. R., Maghoul, F., Raghavan, P., Rajagopalan, S., Stata, R., & Wiener, J. L. et al. (2000). Graph structure in the web.*Proc. Of WWW Conf.*

Califf, M. E., & Mooney, R. J. (1999). Relational learning of pattern-match rules for information extraction.*Proceedings of the Sixteenth National Conference on Artificial Intelligence (AAAI-99)*, 487-493.

Chakrabarti, S., van den Berg, M., & Dom, B. (1999). Distributed hypertext resource discovery through examples. *Proc. Of 25th Int.Conf. on Very Large Data Bases*, 375–386.

Chakrabarti, S., van den Berg, M., & Dom, B. (1999). Focused crawling: A new approach to topic-specific web resource discovery.. doi:10.1016/S1389-1286(99)00052-3

Cho, J., & Garcia-Molina, H. (2000). The evolution of the web and implications for an incremental crawler.*Proc. of 26th Int. Conf. on Very Large Data Bases*, 117–128.

Cho, J., & Garcia-Molina, H. (2000). Synchronizing a database to improve freshness. *Proc. of the ACM SIGMOD Int. Conf. on Management of Data*, 117–128.

Cho, J., Garcia-Molina, H., & Page, L. (1998). Efficient crawling through URL ordering.*Proc. of WWW Conf.*

Cho & Garcia-Molina. (2002). *Parallel Crawlers*. ACM.

Crescenzi, V., Mecca, G., & Merialdo, P. (2001). Roadrunner: Towards automatic data extraction from large web sites.*Proceedings of the 27th International Conference on Very Large Data Bases (VLDB'01)*, 109-118.

Davidson, S. B., Overton, C., Tannen, V., & Wong, L. (1997). Biokleisli: A Digital Library for Biomedical Researchers. *International Journal on Digital Libraries, 1*(1), 36–53.

Diligenti, M., Coetzee, F., Lawrence, S., Giles, C., & Gori, M. (2000). Focused crawling using context graphs.*Proc. of 26th Int. Conf. on Very Large Data Bases.*

Embley, D., Jiang, S., & Ng, Y.-K. (1999). Record-boundary discovery in Web documents. *Proceedings of the 1999 ACM SIGMOD International Conference on Management of Data*, 467-478. doi:10.1145/304182.304223

Embley, D. W., Campbell, D. M., Jiang, Y. S., Liddle, S. W., Lonsdale, D. W., Ng, Y.-K., & Smith, R. D. (1999). Conceptual-model-based data extraction from multiple-record Web pages. *Data & Knowledge Engineering*, *31*(3), 227–251. doi:10.1016/S0169-023X(99)00027-0

Freitag, D. (1998). Information extraction from HTML: Application of a general machine learning approach. In *Proceedings Fourteenth National Conference on Artificial Intelligence (AAAI-1998) / the Tenth Innovative Applications of Artificial Intelligence Conference,* 517-523.

Gaizauskas, R., Demetriou, G., Artymiuk, P. J., & Willett, P. (2003). Protein structures and information extraction from biological texts: The PASTA system. *Bioinformatics (Oxford, England)*, *19*(1), 135–143. doi:10.1093/bioinformatics/19.1.135 PMID:12499303

Gupta. (2011). *Search Engines and Web Crawler: Part I*. Dept. of Computer Science & Engg., I.I.T. Kharagpur.

Henzinger, M. R., Heydon, A., Mitzenmacher, M., & Najork, M. (1999), Measuring index quality using random walks on the web. *Proc. of the 8th Int. World Wide Web Conference (WWW8)*, 213–225. doi:10.1016/S1389-1286(99)00016-X

Henzinger, M. R., Heydon, A., Mitzenmacher, M., & Najork, M. (2000), On near-uniform URL sampling.*Proc. of the 9th Int. World Wide Web Conference.*

Kahle, B. (1997). Archiving the internet. *Scientific American.*

Kleinberg, J. (1998), Authoritative sources in a hyperlinked environment.*9th ACM-SIAM Symposium on Discrete Algorithms.*

Krauthammer, M., Rzhetsky, A., Morozov, P., & Friedman, C. (2000). Using BLAST for identifying gene and protein names in journal articles. *Gene*, *259*(1-2), 245–252. doi:10.1016/S0378-1119(00)00431-5 PMID:11163982

Liu, Yu, & Meng. (2002). Personalized web search by mapping user queries to categories. *CIKM'02.*

Malhotra. (2013). *Web Crawler And It's Concepts*. Academic Press.

Manning, C. D., Raghavan, P., & Schtze, H. (2009). *An Introduction to Information Retrieval*. Cambridge University Press.

Markov & Larose. (2007). *Data mining the web*. Wiley Interscience.

Medigue, C., Viari, A., Henaut, A., & Danchin, A. (1992). Colibri: A Functional Database for the Escherichia coli Genome. *Microbiology and Molecular Biology Reviews, 57*(3), 623–654.

Olston & Najork. (2010). Web Crawling, Foundations and Trend sRF. *Information Retrieval, 4*(3), 75–246. DOI: 10.1561/1500000017

Raghavan, S., & Garcia-Molina, H. (2001). Crawling the hidden web.*Proceedings of the 27th International Conference on Very Large Data Bases (VLDB'01)*, 129-138.

Rennie, J., & McCallum, A. (1999), Using reinforcement learning to spider the web efficiently.*Proc. of the Int. Conf. on Machine Learning (ICML)*.

Sharma, S. (2008). *Web-Crawling Approaches in Search Engines, Report*. Patiala: Thapar University.

Zipf, G. K. (1949). *Human Behaviour and the Principle of Least Effort: an Introduction to Human Ecology*. Addison-Wesley.

Section 2
Bio- and Nature-Inspired Computing and Information Retrieval

Chapter 5
Swarm–Based Clustering for Gene Expression Data

P. K. Nizar Banu
B. S. Abdur Rahman University, India

S. Andrews Samraj
Mahendra Engineering College, India

ABSTRACT

Clustering is one of the most important techniques, which group genes of similar expression pattern into a small number of meaningful homogeneous groups or clusters. Gene expression data has certain special characteristics and is a challenging research problem. There are many applications for clustering gene expression data. Clustering can be applied for genes called gene clustering. Hard clustering allows a gene to get placed in exactly one cluster and converges in local optima. Soft clustering approach allows gene to get placed in all the clusters with some membership values. As the hard clustering approach converges in local optimum, an evolutionary computation technique like swarm clustering is required to find the global optimum solution. This chapter studies swarm clustering techniques such as Particle Swarm Clustering K-Means, Cuckoo Search Clustering, Cuckoo Search Clustering with levy flight, harmony search, Fuzzy PSO and Ant Colony Optimization based Clustering for clustering gene expression data. Evaluation measures for clustering gene expression data are also discussed.

DOI: 10.4018/978-1-5225-2375-8.ch005

Copyright ©2017, IGI Global. Copying or distributing in print or electronic forms without written permission of IGI Global is prohibited.

1. INTRODUCTION

The revolution in the development of DNA microarray technology for examining gene expression has created a new era for further exploration of living systems, source of disease and drug development (He & Hui, 2009). Clustering is concerned with representing a new cancer or disease as a new class. It involves analyzing a given set of gene expression profiles with the goal of discovering subgroups that share common features. It involves grouping together specimens that are based on the similarity of their expression profiles with regard to the genes represented on the array (Tarca, Romero, & Draghici, 2006). Clustering of microarray gene expression data helps to understand the gene functions, gene regulation and cellular processes (Daxin, Chaun, & Aidong, 2004). Genes in the same cluster exhibit similar expression patterns and are likely to be co-regulated. Clustering gene expression data emphases on finding new biological classes or refining the existing ones (Gregory & Pablo, 2003). Gene groups enable researchers to predict the functional role or regulatory control of a novel gene, based on the similarity in expression patterns of tissue samples collected from various people including healthy persons and people affected by cancer helps in effective classification of unknown samples which in turn can lead in the early diagnosis of diseases (Marcilio, Ivan, Daniel, Teresa, & Alaxander, 2008). According to Jiang *et al.,* (2004), elucidating the patterns hidden in gene expression data offers a tremendous opportunity for enhanced understanding of functional genomics. In cancer studies, (Golub *et al.,* 1999; Alon *et al.,* 1999; Spellman *et al.,* 1998; Eisen, Spellman, Brown, & Botstein, 1998; Wen *et al.,* 1998) both gene expression, signatures for cell types and signatures for biological processes have been successfully identified by clustering (Alizadeh *et al.,* 2000). GenClust is a gene based clustering approach which is capable of identifying clusters and sub-clusters of arbitrary shapes of any gene expression dataset is proposed (Sauravjyoti & Dhruba, 2010). A novel harmony search K-Means hybrid algorithm for clustering gene expression dataset is proposed by Abdul, Sebastian, & Madhu (2013). Fuzzy C-Means (Bezdek, 1981) and Genetic Algorithms (Bandyopadhyay, Mukhopadhyay, & Maulik, 2007; Maulik, Mukhopadhyay, & Bandyopadhyay, 2009) have been used effectively in clustering gene expression data. Lu, Lu, Fotouhi, Deng, & Brown, (2004) has applied Fast Genetic K-means Algorithm (FGKA) for clustering genes.

Swarm based clustering algorithms for gene expression datasets adopts the similarity of gene expression patterns and gives good clusters to predict benign and malignant tumors. Though Particle Swarm Optimization is extensively used for many practical applications, it fails in finding the initial seeds. Harmony search PSO introduced by (Nizar & Andrews, 2015a) solves the issue of finding initial seed. The most important issue in using microarray technology is the huge amount of data produced. Finding meaningful information pattern and dependencies among genes to provide a basis for hypothesis test, includes the initial step of organizing gene expression data into group of genes that has similar expression patterns. The expression levels of different genes can be viewed as attributes of the samples, or the samples as the attributes of different genes (Sushmita, 2006).

Meta-heuristic optimization algorithms are also used effectively in clustering problem as it converges to global minima. Cuckoo search is implemented and analyzed by (Yang & Deb, 2009) and compared with PSO and GA by using standard benchmark functions. Levy flight property with cuckoo search is used in their study and is found that cuckoo search with levy flight property works well than GA and PSO. Few research studies have been presented in this chapter for clustering gene expression data.

2. CLUSTERING METHODS

Discovery of a new class is achieved with the help of a clustering technique such as hierarchical clustering and K-Means clustering. Grouping is not driven by any phenotype external to the expression profiles such as tissue type, stage, grade or response to treatment (Tarca, Romero, & Draghici, 2006; Tjaden & Cohen, 2006). Hard clustering places gene in exactly one cluster; in contrast, soft clustering approaches places genes in all the clusters with its associated membership values. Swarm clustering approach finds the best possible solution for every gene to get placed in the cluster. These three clustering types are discussed in the following sections.

2.1 Hard Clustering

K-Means (MCQueen, 1967), is a typical partition based hard clustering algorithm used for clustering gene expression data. It divides data into predefined number of clusters in order to optimize a predefined criterion. The major advantages of K-Means clustering are its simplicity and its speed, which allows running on large datasets. The disadvantage is that it gets trapped in local optimum.

2.2 Soft Clustering

In the hard clustering each gene has to be assigned exclusively to one cluster. This approach works well when the physical boundaries are well defined. Boundaries between clusters for real world applications might be vague. So, fuzzy clustering; one of the soft clustering technique extends the traditional clustering concept by allowing each gene to be assigned to every cluster with an associated membership value. Hence, for unclear cluster boundaries, fuzzy clustering may produce more reasonable results.

Clustering algorithms which permit genes to belong to more than one cluster are highly more applicable for gene expression, since the impact of noisy data on clusters obtained is minimized. Noisy genes are unlikely to belong to any one cluster but are equally likely to be members of several clusters. The basic principal of clustering gene expression is, genes with similar change in expression for a set of samples are involved in a similar biological function. Biologists are not only interested in the clusters of genes, but also in the relationships among the clusters and their sub-clusters and association of genes within a cluster. Though the soft clustering techniques provide promising results, growth of the tumor and the spread of cancer cells towards other organs of the body cannot be diagnosed at an early stage. To alleviate this problem, swarm clustering approaches, a computational intelligence method to cluster microarray gene expression dataset is studied in this chapter.

3. SWARM BASED CLUSTERING

Swarm based clustering is inspired from the behavior of swarms such as ants and fish. Swarms have different ways of moving around the search space. Swarm clustering techniques require some special characteristics to adopt the intelligence of swarms. The intelligence of inspiring from nature is complemented to the clustering techniques in terms of fitness functions and is widely known as swarm based clustering.

Particle Swarm Optimization

Swarm based clustering algorithms for gene expression datasets gives good clusters to predict benign and malignant tumors. Particle Swarm Optimization (PSO) algorithm is based on the principles of collective behavior of swarms. They are highly efficient, adaptive and robust search method in producing near optimal solutions and have a large amount of implicit parallelism. Particle Swarm Optimization (PSO) and Genetic Algorithm (GA) are the two most popular population-based globalized search algorithms used for clustering gene expression data. The major disadvantage of these two algorithms is, they get trapped in local optimum in an entire solution space if the parameters are not tuned properly. Genetic Algorithms (GAs), as an evolutionary approach, work well for small datasets, but have prohibitive time constraints for anything larger, so are less desirable for gene expression analysis. Although GAs find the global optimum, they are sensitive to user defined input parameters and must be fine-tuned for each specific problem (Kerr, Ruskin, Crane, & Doolan, 2008).

PSO K-Means

Particle Swarm Optimization is a heuristic global optimization method originally designed and introduced by Kennedy and Eberhart in 1995. It is inspired from the behavior of swarms such as bird and fish flock movement. With evolutionary computation methods, a swarm is similar to population and a particle is similar to an individual. Basic notion behind PSO is that each particle represents a potential solution which updates according to its own experience and that of neighbors. PSO algorithm searches in parallel with a group of individuals. Individuals or particles in a swarm move towards the optimum through their present velocity, previous experience and the experience of its neighbors (Shi & Eberhart, 1998). PSO searches the problem domain by adjusting the path of moving points in a multidimensional space. The motion of the individual particles for the optimal solution is governed through the interaction of the position and velocity of each individual, their own previous best performance and the best performance of their neighbors (Sandeep, Sanjay, & Rajesh, 2010). Exploration and exploitation are the two basic strategies used by meta-heuristic optimization algorithms while searching for the global optimum (Rashedi, Nezamabadi, & Saryazdi, 2009). The exploration process succeeds in enabling the algorithm to reach the best local solutions within the search space, while the exploitation process expresses the ability to reach the global optimum solution which is likely to exist around the local solutions obtained. Widely adopted clustering techniques for gene expression datasets converge either in local or global optimum solutions and produce different types of clusters depending upon the random choice of the initial centroids. None of the existing clustering methods find to be the best for gene expression datasets as initial centroids are chosen randomly and so it suffers from incorrect grouping of genes.

PSO algorithm includes some tuning parameters that greatly influence the performance of the algorithm. PSO starts with a population of particles whose positions represent the potential solutions for the problem domain and velocities are randomly initialized in the search space. The search for optimal position is achieved by updating the particle velocities and positions in every iteration. Once a particle is placed in a cluster, possibility of the particle belonging to that particular cluster and its position should be determined using a fitness function. The velocity of each particle is updated using two best positions, personal best position and global best position. The personal best position (pbest) is the best position, the particle has visited and global best (gbest) is the best position the swarm has visited since the first time step (Hesam & Ajith, 2011). A particle's velocity and position are updated as follows.

$$V\big(t+1\big) = w * V\big(t\big) + c_1 * r_1\big(pbest\big(t\big) - X\big(t\big)\big) + c_2 * r_2\big(gbest\big(t\big) - X\big(t\big)\big)$$

$$(1)$$

$$X(t+1) = X(t) + V(t+1) \tag{2}$$

where, X and V are position and velocity of a particle respectively. w is the inertia weight, c1 and c2 are positive constants, called acceleration coefficients which controls the influence of pbest and gbest on the search process, r1 and r2 are random values in range [0, 1].

Swarm clustering inspired from swarms, strives to update every genes personal best position to produce better clusters. This process is carried out as follows: Every gene expression pattern (gene vector) from the dataset is taken and compared with the existing cluster centroids. Gene vector is placed in the cluster to which it is more similar. As the proposed algorithm is inspired from the swarm, personal best position of a particle (gene vector) and global best position of a particle is recorded to check the fitness of the cluster. Acceleration coefficients c1 and c2 should be set, which controls personal best position (pbest) and global best position (gbest) in search process. Random variables r1 and r2 should be between 0 and 1.

Algorithm: PSO K-Means

Input: K – Number of Clusters; D – Dataset containing n genes and m samples;
       tmax - Maximum number of iterations
Output: Set of K clusters
Procedure:

```
Initialize parameters including population size
```
$P, C_1, C_2, r_1, r_2, w \, and \, tmax$
```
Create swarms with P particles
```
$\left(X, P_i, g \, and \, v \right)$
```
        For it = 1: tmax
                Calculate cluster centroids using the follow-
ing equation
```

$$z_i(K+1) = \frac{1}{N_i} \sum_{x \in C_i(K)} x; i = 1, 2, \dots K \tag{3}$$

```
                Calculate fitness of each particle using Xie-
Beni Index
                Update pbest for each particle
                Update gbest for the swarm
                Update velocity for each particle using equa-
tion (1)
```

```
                Update position for each particle using equa-
tion (2)
        End
```

Cuckoo Search based Clustering

This sub-section focuses on applying meta-heuristic clustering approaches such as cuckoo search based clustering on gene expression data. Gene expression exploits the information from a gene to synthesize a functional gene product. Tumor is an abnormal growth of tissues that grow more rapidly than normal cells and it continues to grow if not treated. Tumors can be either benign or malignant. Benign tumors are harmless; removal of such tumors may not cause danger to other organs, whereas removal of malignant tumors may cause danger. Clustering methodology for gene expression dataset finds the similarity of gene expression patterns and assists in producing clusters to predict benign and malignant tumors. Cuckoo search optimization technique is introduced by Yang and Deb (Yang, & Deb, 2010) in 2009. It is one of the latest nature inspired meta-heuristic algorithms. Recent studies show cuckoo search is far more efficient than PSO and Genetic Algorithms.

Breeding Behavior of Cuckoo

Breeding behavior of cuckoo is matched with the genes that causes tumor to grow and affect other organs. Some species of cuckoos like Ani and Guira have aggressive reproduction strategy that involves female laying her fertilized eggs in the nest of another species (Yang & Deb, 2009; Yang & Deb, 2010). As stated in (Yang & Deb, 2010), the possibility of occurrence of such act leads to

The host birds' eggs being destroyed by the cuckoo itself or the cuckoo chick upon hatching

The host birds may realize the presence of a foreign egg in its nest and may throw away these eggs or abandon the nest altogether and build a new nest elsewhere

Cuckoo search optimization algorithm considers various design parameters and constraints, three main idealized rules (Yang & Deb, 2009; Yang & Deb, 2010) on which it is based are as follows.

Each cuckoo lays one egg at a time, and dumps its egg in randomly chosen nest

Best nests with high quality of eggs will carry over to next generations

Number of available host nests is fixed, and the egg laid by a cuckoo is discovered by the host bird with a probability $p_a \in [0, 1]$. In this case, the host bird can either throw the egg away or abandon the nest, and build a completely new nest

The above said breeding behavior can be applied for gene expression pattern for clustering. It is discussed in detail and applied for brain tumor gene expression dataset (Nizar & Andrews, 2015a).

Algorithm: Cuckoo Search based Clustering

Input: K – Number of Clusters; D – Dataset containing n genes with m samples;
    tmax - Maximum number of iterations
Output: Set of K clusters
Procedure:

```
Begin
Consider K hostnests (clusters) containing 1 egg solution each
For each solution of host i
Initialize C_i to contain K randomly selected cluster centroids
```

$C_i = (z_1 \ldots z_K)$ `where` z_i `represents the Kth cluster centroid vector of ith host`

```
End
For it = 1: tmax
For each solution of host i
                For each data point x_j
                    Calculate distance d(x, z_i) from all
cluster C_i using
```

$$d\left(x_j, z_i\right) = \sqrt{\sum_{j=1}^{n_K} x_j - z_i}$$

(4)

```
                    where, n_K is the number of data points
in the cluster,
assign x_j to z_i where
```

$$d\left(x_j, z_i\right) = min_{\forall k=1 \ldots K}\left\{d\left(x_j, z_i\right)\right\}$$

(5)

```
End
        Calculate fitness function f(C_i) for each host nest i
```

```
End
Select a fraction  p_a  of worse nests
For each  y ∈ p_a
                    Build new ones using New_Cuckoo func-
tion
End
Keep the best solutions
Find the current best solution
End
```

Consider the clustering solution represented by best solution

New_Cuckoo function $q \in \{0.1\}$ q_1 = random number $\in \{0,1\}$

If $\left(q_1 < q\right)$

For each cluster centroid $z_{new,k}$

For each dimension

$$n_d \; x_{new}\left(z_{new,k,n_d}\right) = x_{best} + pow\left(-1, n_d\right) * rand\left(1\right) \tag{6}$$

where, x_{best} is the best solution of current iteration

```
End
End
Else
Select another set of clusters randomly from the search space
End
```

3.3 Levy Flight Cuckoo Search

Cuckoo search clustering using levy flight is similar to cuckoo search based clustering except, the former has levy flight property, which ensures that the whole search
space is covered. Each nest represents a solution and a cuckoo egg represents a
new solution. Initial population of host nest is generated randomly. The algorithm
runs for maximum number of iterations. For every iteration, a cuckoo is selected at
random using levy flight (Yang and Deb, 2009).

$$x_j\left(t+1\right) = x_j\left(t\right) + \propto * L \tag{7}$$

where α is the step-size, it determines how far a random walker can go for a fixed
number of iterations. L is a value from the levy distribution, i=1,2,…K, K is the

number of nests (clusters) considered for clustering genes. Cuckoo search based clustering using levy flight is applied for brain tumor gene expression dataset (Nizar & Andrews, 2015a).

Algorithm: Cuckoo Search based Clustering using Levy Flight
Input: K – Number of Clusters; D – Dataset containing n objects; tmax - Maximum number of iterations
Output: Set of K clusters
Procedure:

```
Initialize n nests
Repeat till stopping criteria is met
Randomly select a cuckoo using levy flight by equation (7)
Calculate its fitness (F_c)
Randomly select a nest
Calculate its fitness (F_n)
If (F_c < F_n) then replace the nest with the cuckoo
A fraction p_a of nest are replaced by new nests
Calculate fitness and keep best nests
Store the best nest as optimal fitness value
Cluster center will be the best nest position
```

3.4 Harmony Search PSO

Harmony search is a novel process, conceptualized from music performance process to improve synchronization and to find perfect state of harmony (Babak, Liaquat & Seyyed, 2010). Harmony search makes use of a harmony memory which is initialized with randomly generated feasible solutions to provide a global solution space. This process is applied to find initial centroids for clustering genes (Nizar & Andrews, 2014).

Harmony Search PSO algorithm finds the initial centroids to cluster the genes precisely in order to find the genes that lead to the growth of tumor or spread of cancer. Fixing proper centroids produce good clusters even if the order of genes in the dataset is changed (Nizar & Andrews, 2014). This method includes two phases. In the first phase gene expression data is normalized and initial centroids are determined using harmony search optimization technique. The centroids thus determined are used in the second phase to form final clusters by assigning the data points to the nearest centroids.

Swarm-Based Clustering for Gene Expression Data

Algorithm: Harmony Search PSO (HSPSO)
Input: Gene Expression data matrix – D (n genes, m samples);
Number of desired clusters – K
Output: K clusters of gene
Procedure:

```
For each column of the data matrix i = 2 to n + 1
Sort the first column of the data matrix based on column i
Divide the sorted columns into K equal parts
For each part j = 1 to K, determine the middle data item
Initialize Harmony Memory with K middle data item called cen-
troid
End For
End For
Calculate fitness of each data item with centroid using
```

$$fitc\left(C\right) = \frac{1}{K}\left\{\sum_{k=1}^{K}\frac{\sum_{j=1}^{n_k}D\left(C_i, x_{ij}\right)}{n_k}\right\} \tag{8}$$

```
For MI = 1 to mi // Maximum number of iterations
Compute the distance of each data point x_i (1 ≤ i ≤ n) to all the
centroids
```

$$C_j\left(1 \leq j \leq K\right) \text{ as } D\left(x_i, C_j\right)$$

```
For each data point x_i find the closest centroid C_j and assign
x_i to cluster C_j
Calculate fitness of each particle as follows
```

$$fit\left(k\right) = \frac{1}{\pi/s} \tag{9}$$

where, $\pi = \dfrac{\sum_{i=1}^{K}\sum_{j=1}^{n}x - C_i^2}{n}$; $s = \left(d_{min}\right)^2$ \hfill (10) where $d_{min} = min_{ij} C_i - C_j$; $C_i = \dfrac{1}{n_k} \displaystyle\sum_{i=1}^{n_k} x_i$ $\qquad$ (11)

Move all the particles towards the gbest position as follows

$$V_i(t+1) = w * V_i(t) + c_1 * r_1 \left(pbest_i(t) - C_i(t) \right) + c_2 * r_2 \left(gbest(t) - C_i(t) \right)$$

(12)

$$C_i(t+1) = C_i(t) + V_i(t+1)$$

(13)

For each particle if $fit(k) < fit(pbest)$ // Fitness of k

$pbest = fit(k)$

Update pbest for each particle
End For
For each cluster $(1 \leq j \leq k)$ recalculate the centroids
Until there are no more genes in the data matrix
End For
End For
End For

3.5 Fuzzy PSO

Pang, Wang, Zhou, & Dong (2004) proposed a modified particle swarm optimization for TSP called Fuzzy Particle Swarm Optimization (FPSO). In their proposed method the position and velocity of particles are redefined to represent the fuzzy relation between variables. In this section, fuzzy clustering method is described for gene expression data. In FPSO algorithm, X the position of particle, shows the fuzzy relation from set of data objects, O = {o1, o2... on}, to set of cluster centers, Z = {z1, z2... zc}. Hence, the dataset X can be expressed as follows:

$$\begin{bmatrix} \mu_{11} & \cdots & \mu_{1c} \\ \vdots & \ddots & \vdots \\ \mu_{n1} & \cdots & \mu_{nc} \end{bmatrix}$$

in which µij is the membership function of the ith object with the jth cluster. Therefore the position matrix of each particle becomes the same as fuzzy matrix µ in FCM algorithm. As other evolutionary algorithms, fuzzy PSO algorithm also requires a function for evaluating the generalized solutions called fitness function. For the experiments, Xie-Beni index discussed in evaluation measures section can also be used as fitness function. After evaluating the fitness of genes to the clusters, membership of every gene to the cluster is computed. Maximum number of iterations is used as the stopping criteria for FPSO and FCM algorithm.

$$\mu_{ij} = \frac{1}{\sum_{k=1}^{K} \left(\dfrac{d_{ij}}{d_{ik}} \right)^{\frac{2}{m-1}}} \qquad (14)$$

where k = 1,2...K is the number of clusters, m is the fuzzification parameter. The Fuzzy PSO algorithm for fuzzy clustering problem is presented below.

Algorithm: Fuzzy PSO Clustering
Input: K – Number of Clusters; D – Dataset containing n genes and m samples;
    tmax - Maximum number of iterations
Output: Set of K clusters
Procedure:

```
1. Initialize the parameters of FPSO including population size
P, c1, c2, w, and m.
2. Create a swarm with P particles (X, pbest, gbest and V are
n × c matrices)
3. Initialize X, V, pbest for each particle and gbest for the
swarm
4. FPSO algorithm:
    4.1 Calculate the cluster centers
    4.2 Calculate the fitness value of each particle using
Xie-Beni Index
    4.3 Calculate pbest for each particle
    4.4 Calculate gbest for the swarm
    4.5 Update the velocity matrix of each particle
    4.6 Update the position matrix of each particle
    4.7 If FPSO terminating condition is not met, go to Step 4.
5. FCM algorithm
```

```
    5.1 Calculate the cluster centers for each particle
    5.2 Compute Euclidian distance dij, i = 1,2,..., n; j =
1,2,..., c;
For each particle
    5.3 Update the membership function μij, i = 1,2,..., n; j =
1,2,..., c;
For each particle
    5.4 Calculate pbest for each particle.
    5.5 Calculate gbest for the swarm.
    5.6 If FCM terminating condition is not met, go to Step 5.
6. If FCM-FPSO terminating condition is not met, go to Step 4.
```

3.6 Ant Colony Optimization Based Clustering

Ant Colony Optimization is nature inspired swarm intelligence based algorithm which is derived from a model inspired by the collective foraging behavior of ants. Investigation of ant-based algorithms for clustering gene expression data is presented (Yulan & Siu, 2009). Early approaches in applying ACO to clustering (Lumer & Faieta, 1994) are to first partition the search area into low-dimensional regular 2D grid. A population of ant-like agents then moves around this 2D grid and carries or drops object based on certain probabilities so as to categorize the objects. This results in too many clusters. Therefore, usually K-means is normally combined with ACO to minimize categorization errors (Wu, Zheng, Lu, & Shi, 2002). Hybrid ant-based clustering model (Wafa'a, Amr, & AbdEl-Fattah, 2013) is developed and applied on real and artificial datasets.

4. EVALUATION MEASURES FOR SWARM CLUSTERING

The result of a clustering algorithm can be very different from each other on the same dataset as the other input parameters of an algorithm can extremely modify the behavior and execution of the algorithm. The process of evaluating the results of a clustering algorithm is called cluster validity assessment. A good clustering method will produce high quality clusters with high intra cluster similarity and low inter cluster similarity. Two measurement criteria, to evaluate and select an optimal clustering scheme namely compactness and separation is proposed (Berry & Linoff, 1996). Compactness is defined as the number of each cluster that should be as close to each other as possible. A common measure of compactness is the variance. Separation is defined as the clusters themselves should be widely separated. There are three common approaches to measure the distance between two different clusters: distance between the closest members of clusters, distance between the most distant members and distance between the centers of the clusters. Most widely used cluster validity indices for clustering gene expression dataset are discussed below. These validity indices are also used as fitness functions in swarm clustering. Fitness functions for swarm clustering are evaluated in (Nizar & Andrews, 2015b).

4.1 Davies-Bouldin Index

Davies-Bouldin (DB) index is based on the similarity measure of clusters $\left(R_{ij}\right)$ whose bases are the dispersion measure of a cluster $\left(S_i\right)$ and the cluster dissimilarity measure $\left(d_{ij}\right)$. DB index measures the average of similarity between each cluster and its most similar one. As the clusters have to be compact and separated, the lower DB index means better cluster configuration. It is a function of the ratio of the sum of within-cluster distance to between cluster separations. The DB index according Pal and Bezdek (1995); Davies and Bouldin (1979) is defined as

$$DB = \frac{1}{K}\sum_{i=1}^{K}R_i \tag{15}$$

where, $R_i = \underset{\substack{j=1,\ldots,K, \\ i\neq j}}{max}\left(R_{ij}\right), i = 1,\ldots K$. The similarity measure of clusters $\left(R_{ij}\right)$ is computed using equation 16.

$$R_{ij} = \frac{S_i + S_j}{d_{ij}} \tag{16}$$

where $d_{ij} = d\left(v_i, v_j\right)$ is the cluster dissimilarity measure and S_i is computed as follows

$$S_i = \frac{1}{C_i}\sum_{x \in c_i}d\left(x, v_i\right) \tag{17}$$

The Fuzzy DB index (Xuejian & Kian, 2004) uses fuzzy within-cluster distance, which is formulated as

$$S_i = \frac{\sum_{j=1}^{m} \mu_{ij}^{m'} d\left(S, C_i\right)}{\sum_{j=1}^{n} \mu_{ij}^{m'}} \tag{18}$$

where $1 \le i \le K$ *and* m' is a fuzzification parameter.

4.2 Xie-Beni Validity Index

Xie-Beni (XB) index (Xie & Beni, 1991) is defined as a well-known validity index. It is used to measure overall average compactness against separation of the fuzzy partition. The minimum value of this index indicates the better performance of the predicted clusters, which reflects that the clusters have greater separation from each other and are more compact.

Thus Xie-Beni validity index is the combination of two functions. The first one calculates the compactness of data in the same cluster and the second one computes the separation of data in different clusters. Let XB represent the overall validity index, π be the compactness and s be the separation of the K-clusters of the data set. The Xie-Beni validity can now be expressed as:

$$XB = \frac{\pi}{s} \tag{19}$$

where $\pi = \dfrac{\sum_{i=1}^{K} \sum_{j=1}^{n} \mu_{ij}^{2} s - z_{i}^{2}}{n}$ and $s = \left(d_{min}\right)^2$. d_{min} is the minimum distance between cluster centers, given $d_{min} = min_{ij} z_i - z_j$, where n is the number of genes, K is the number of clusters, and Z_i is the cluster center, μ_{ij} be the membership value of gene. Smaller values of π indicate that the clusters are more compact and larger values of s indicate the clusters are well separated.

4.3 Dunn's Index

If a dataset contains well-separated clusters, the distances among the clusters are usually large and the diameters of the clusters are expected to be small. Therefore larger value of Dunn's Index (DI) means better cluster configuration. The Dunn's Index (Dunn, 1973) is defined as

$$DI = min_{i=1...K} \left\{ min_{j=i+1...K} \left(\frac{d\left(C_i, C_j\right)}{max_{k=1...K}\left(diam\left(C_k\right)\right)} \right) \right\} \tag{20}$$

where $d\left(C_i,C_j\right)=min_{x\in C_i,y\in C_j}\left\{d\left(x,y\right)\right\}and\ diam\left(C_i\right)=max_{x,y\in C_i}\left\{d\left(x,y\right)\right\}$ and d is a distance function and C_j is the set whose elements are the data points assigned to the ith cluster. The main drawback with direct implementation of Dunn's index is computational complexity, since calculation becomes computationally very expensive as K and m increase.

4.4 Mean Absolute Error

Mean Absolute Error (MAE) (Decastro, DeFranca, Ferreira, & Von, 2007) evaluates the average magnitude of the errors without considering their direction. It is defined as the average distance between the data and their cluster center as shown in equation 21.

$$MAE=\frac{1}{N}\sum_{i=1}^{N}\left(\left|X_i-C_i\right|\right) \tag{21}$$

where N is the number of objects, X_i is the value of object i, and C_i is corresponding cluster center.

4.5 Root Mean Squared Error

Root Mean Squared Error (RMSE) (Decastro, DeFranca, Ferreira, & Von, 2007) is a frequently used measure to find the distance between the object and the cluster center. This value is computed by taking the average of the squared differences between each data value and its corresponding cluster center. The root mean squared error is simply the square root of the mean-squared-error as given in equation 22.

$$RMSE=\sqrt{\frac{1}{N}\sum_{i=1}^{N}\left(X_i-C_i\right)^2} \tag{22}$$

The MAE and RMSE can be used together to diagnose the variation in the errors in a clustering techniques. The greater difference between MAE and RMSE means the greater variance in the individual errors in the sample. If MAE and RMSE are same, then all the errors are of the same magnitude (Goran & Zarko, (2011).

4.6 Sum of Intra Cluster Distances

Sum of Intra Cluster Distances (SICD) is the most known evaluating criteria for clustering data. Less value of SICD means higher quality clustering is performed (Neshat, Yazdi, Yazdani, & Sargolzaei, 2012).

$$SICD = \sum_{i=1}^{K} \sum_{x_j \in C_i} Z_i - x_j \qquad (23)$$

In equation 18, Euclidean distance between each gene vector in a cluster and the centroid of that cluster is calculated and summed up. Here, in K clusters $C_i \left(1 \leq i \leq K\right)$, each of N gene vector x_j are clustered on the basis of distance from each other of these cluster centers $z_i \left(1 \leq i \leq K\right)$.

5. EXPERIMENTAL ANALYSIS

This section presents and discusses the results and performances of PSO-K-Means, Harmony Search PSO, Cuckoo Search based Clustering and Cuckoo Search based Clustering using levy flight algorithms. These clustering algorithms are applied for brain tumor gene expression. Merits and demerits of the clustering algorithms discussed in this chapter are tabulated in Table 1.

- **Data Source:** Brain tumor gene expression dataset is available in http://www. Broadinstitute.Org/cgibin/cancer/datasets.cgi. Dataset comprises 7129 genes with 40 samples.
- **Performance Analysis of Clustering Algorithms:** The performance of K-Means algorithm, executed for 40 iterations is shown in Figure 1. According to K-Means clustering, error produced for 5 clusters is less. Fuzzy C-Means clustering finds the similarity between genes and places genes in more than one cluster. Initial centroids are chosen randomly, initial membership of gene vector to k desired cluster is taken as zero Figure 2 demonstrates the results of Fuzzy C-Means clustering, error is less for 2 clusters.

Compactness and separation of genes in the same cluster and in different clusters are analyzed using Mean Absolute Error (MAE), Root Mean Squared Error (RMSE) (Decastro, DeFranca, Ferreira, & Von, 2007) and Dunn's Index (Dunn, 1973). Figure 3 presents the MAE produced for brain tumor gene expression dataset using

Table 1. Merits and Demerits of Various Clustering Algorithms

Clustering Approach	Clustering Algorithm	Input	Merits	Demerits
Hard Clustering	K-Means	Gene expression matrix K – Number of clusters	Simple and easy to implement	Converges in local optimum Sensitive to input parameter and order of input
Soft Clustering	Fuzzy C-Means (FCM)	Gene expression matrix K – Number of clusters Fuzzy Index	Produces overlapping cluster partitions Genes can belong to a cluster partially and to multiple clusters at the same time with different membership degrees	Converges in local optimum Sensitive to input parameter and order of input
Swarm based Clustering	PSO	Gene expression matrix K – Number of clusters Maximum number of iterations	Converges in global optimum	Sensitive to input parameter and order of input Choice of fitness function is significant It may produce empty cluster
	Fuzzy PSO	Gene expression matrix K – Number of clusters Maximum number of iterations	Converges in global optimum Produces overlapping cluster partitions	Sensitive to input parameter and order of input Choice of fitness function is significant
	Harmony Search PSO	Gene expression matrix K – Number of clusters Maximum number of iterations	Converges in global Optimum Finds initial seeds No change in performance even if the order of input is changed	Choice of fitness function is significant
Meta-heuristic Clustering Approach	Cuckoo Search based Clustering	Gene expression matrix K – Number of clusters Maximum number of iterations	Converges in global Optimum Helps to identify other organs that may get affected in short duration	Choice of fitness function is significant
	Levy Flight Cuckoo Search based Clustering	Gene expression matrix K – Number of clusters, Maximum number of iterations	Converges in global Optimum Helps to identify other organs that may get affected in short duration It has levy flight property, which ensures whole search space is covered	Choice of fitness function is significant

Figure 1. Performance Analysis of K-Means Clustering

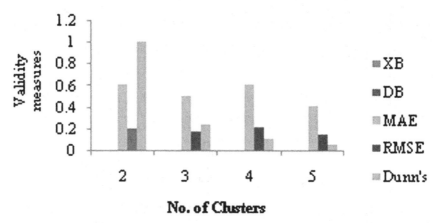

Figure 2. Performance Analysis of Fuzzy C-Means Clustering

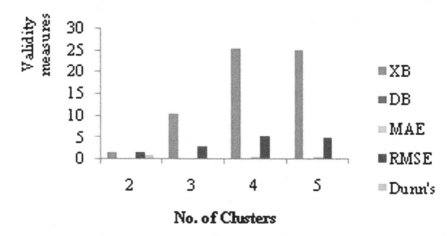

PSO K-Means and Cuckoo Search based clustering methods. In Figure 4, values of RMSE for brain tumor gene expression data set are presented. From the results, it is observed that cuckoo search based clustering and cuckoo search based clustering using levy flight performs better than PSO-K-Means. Best clustering is the one, which produces less error. With respect to MAE and RMSE, cuckoo search based clustering and levy flight cuckoo search clustering generates very less error.

In the experiments, SICD and Dunn's index finds how well genes in the clusters are compactly packed. SICD should be less and Dunn's index should be high for the HSPSO approach (Nizar & Andrews, 2014). It is observed from the experimental results that XB index and SICD of HSPSO method gives minimum values, and

Figure 3. Mean Absolute Error of Clusters

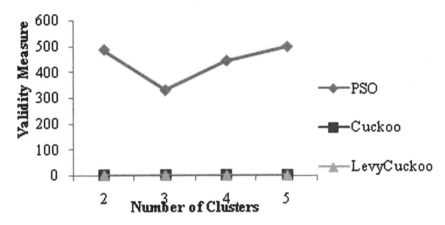

Figure 4. Root Mean Squared Error of Clustering Algorithms

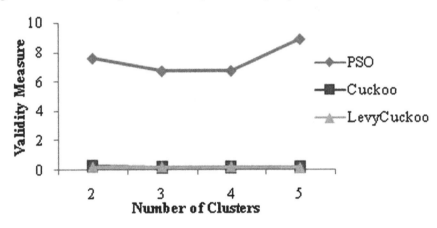

Figure 5. Performance of Dunn's Index

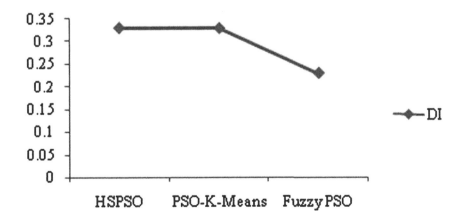

Figure 6. Performance of SICD

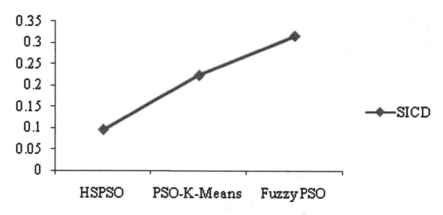

maximum value is found for Dunn's index for brain tumor dataset. Values of Dunn's index and SICD for brain tumor gene expression data set are shown in Figures 5 and 6 respectively.

6. CONCLUSION

Many researchers have criticized the limitations of hard and soft clustering methods which develop clusters that are not much useful in diagnosis. But the widespread use of swarm clustering approaches develops methods to realistically and accurately assess the clusters and the organs that get affected by the tumors or cancer. Though clustering helps in finding the genes that are either highly expressed or suppressed, global solution suggests in locating the significant gene and its function. This is significant and evolution of advanced algorithms is extremely curious. Thus this chapter, on swarm based clustering for gene expression data discussed PSO K-Means, cuckoo search with and without levy flight, harmony search, fuzzy PSO, ACO for clustering gene expression dataset. The work discussed in this chapter for brain tumor gene expression dataset determines the initial centroid which has high significance in characterizing the gene function. The breeding pattern of cuckoo adopted in cuckoo search based clustering prompts the physicians to diagnose other organs that get affected in short span of time. This kind of research work helps in immediate identification of tumors even before the laboratory work. The future work can be carried out using other swarm intelligent techniques like bat based optimization algorithm and Ant-Lion Optimization algorithm.

REFERENCES

Abdul Nazeer, , & Sebastian, , & Kumar. (2013). A Novel harmony search-K means hybrid algorithm for clustering gene expression data. *Bioinformatics (Oxford, England)*, *9*(2), 84–88. PMID:23390351

Alizadeh, A. A., Eisen, M. B., Davis, R. E., Ma, C., Lossos, I. S., Rosenwald, A., & Staudt, L. M. et al. (2000). Distinct types of diffuse large B-cell lymphoma identified by gene expression profiling. *Nature*, *403*(6769), 503–511. doi:10.1038/35000501 PMID:10676951

Alon, U., Barkai, N., Notterman, D. A., Gish, K., Ybarra, S., Mack, D., & Levine, A. J. (1999). Broad patterns of gene expression revealed by clustering analysis of tumor and normal colon tissues probed by oligonucleotide arrays. *Proceedings of the National Academy of Sciences of the United States of America*, *96*(12), 6745–6750. doi:10.1073/pnas.96.12.6745 PMID:10359783

Amiri, B., Hossain, L., & Mosavi, S. E. (2010) Application of Harmony Search Algorithm on Clustering.*Proceedings of World Congress on Engineering and Computer Science*, 1, 20-22.

Bandyopadhyay, S., Mukhopadhyay, A., & Maulik, U. (2007). An improved algorithm for clustering gene expression data. *Bioinformatics (Oxford, England)*, *23*(21), 2859–2865. doi:10.1093/bioinformatics/btm418 PMID:17720981

Berry, M. J. A., & Linoff, G. (1996). *Data Mining Techniques for Marketing, Sales and Customer Support*. John Wiley & Sons, Inc.

Bezdek, J. C. (1981). *Pattern Recognition with Fuzzy Objective Function Algorithms*. New York: Plenum Press. doi:10.1007/978-1-4757-0450-1

Bryan, J. (2004). Problems in gene clustering based on gene expression data. *Journal of Multivariate Analysis*, *90*(1), 44–66. doi:10.1016/j.jmva.2004.02.011

Davies, D. L., & Bouldin, D. W. (1979). A cluster separation measure. *IEEE Transactions on Pattern Analysis and Machine Intelligence*, *1*(4), 224–227. doi:10.1109/TPAMI.1979.4766909 PMID:21868852

De Castro, P. A. D., de França, O. F., Ferreira, H. M., & Von Zuben, F. J. (2007). Applying Biclustering to Perform Collaborative Filtering.*Proceedings of the Seventh International Conference on Intelligent Systems Design and Applications*. 421-426.

de Souto, M. C. P., Costa, I. G., de Araujo, D. S. A., Ludermir, T. B., & Schliep, A. (2008). Clustering Cancer Gene Expression Data: A Comparative Study. *BMC Bioinformatics*, *9*(1), 497. doi:10.1186/1471-2105-9-497 PMID:19038021

Dunn, J. C. (1973). A Fuzzy Relative of the ISODATA Process and its Use in Detecting Compact Well-Separated Clusters. *Journal Cybernetics*, *3*(3), 32–57. doi:10.1080/01969727308546046

Eisen, M. B., Spellman, P. T., Brown, P. O., & Botstein, D. (1998). Cluster Analysis and Display of Genome-Wide Expression Patterns. *Proceedings of the National Academy of Sciences of the United States of America*, *95*(25), 14863–14868. doi:10.1073/pnas.95.25.14863 PMID:9843981

Golub, T. R., Slonim, D. K., Tamayo, P., Huard, C., Gaasenbeek, M., Mesirov, J. P., & Lander, E. S. et al. (1999). Molecular classification of cancer: Class discovery and class prediction by gene expression monitoring. *Science*, *286*(5439), 531–537. doi:10.1126/science.286.5439.531 PMID:10521349

He, Y., & Hui, S. C. (2009). Exploring ant-based algorithms for gene expression data analysis. *Artificial Intelligence in Medicine*, *47*(2), 105–119. doi:10.1016/j.artmed.2009.03.004 PMID:19376690

Izakian, H., & Abraham, A. (2011). Fuzzy C-means and fuzzy Swarm for fuzzy clustering problem. *Expert Systems with Applications*, *38*(3), 1835–1838. doi:10.1016/j.eswa.2010.07.112

Jiang, D., Tang, C., & Zhang, A. (2004). Cluster Analysis for Gene Expression Data: A Survey. *IEEE Transactions on Data and Knowledge Engineering*, *16*(11), 1370–1386. doi:10.1109/TKDE.2004.68

Kerr, G., Ruskin, H. J., Crane, M., & Doolan, P. (2008). Techniques for Clustering Gene Expression data. *Computers in Biology and Medicine*, *36*(3), 283–293. doi:10.1016/j.compbiomed.2007.11.001 PMID:18061589

Lu, Y., Lu, S., Fotouhi, F., Deng, Y., & Brown, S. (2004). Fast genetic K-means algorithm and its application in gene expression data analysis. *Proceedings of the ACM Symposium on Applied Computing (SAC)*.

Lumer, E., & Faieta, B. (1994) Diversity and adaptation in populations of clustering ants. *Proceedings of the 3rd International Conference on Simulation of Adaptive Behaviour: From Animals to Animats*, *3*, 501–508.

Maulik, U., Mukhopadhyay, A., & Bandyopadhyay, S. (2009). Combining pareto-optimal clusters using supervised learning for identifying coexpressed genes. *BMC Bioinformatics*, *10*(27). PMID:19154590

McQueen, J. (1967) Some methods for classification and analysis of multivariate observations.*Proceedings of the Fifth Berkeley Symp. Math. Statistics and Probability,* 1, 281–297.

Mitra, S., Banka, H., & Pedrycz, W. (2006). Rough Fuzzy Colloborative Clustering. *IEEE Transactions on Systems, Man, and Cybernetics, 36*(4), 795–805. doi:10.1109/TSMCB.2005.863371 PMID:16903365

Neshat, M., Yazdi, S. F., Yazdani, D., & Sargolzaei, M. (2012). A New Cooperative Algorithm Based on PSO and K-Means for Data Clustering. *J. of Computer Science, 8*(2), 188–194. doi:10.3844/jcssp.2012.188.194

Nizar Banu, P. K., & Andrews, S. (2014). Harmony Search PSO Clustering for Tumor and Cancer Gene Expression Dataset. *International Journal of Swarm Intelligence Research, 5*(3), 1–22. doi:10.4018/ijsir.2014070101

Nizar Banu, P. K., & Andrews, S. (2015a). Gene Clustering Using Metaheuristic Optimization Algorithms. *International Journal of Applied Metaheuristic Computing, 6*(4), 14–38. doi:10.4018/IJAMC.2015100102

Nizar Banu, P. K., & Andrews, S. (2015b). Evaluation of Fitness Functions for Swarm Clustering Applied to Gene Expression Data. Smart. *Innovation Systems and Technologies., 33*, 571–581. doi:10.1007/978-81-322-2202-6_52

Pal, N. R., & Bezdek, J. C. (1995). On cluster validity for the fuzzy c-means model. *IEEE Transactions on Fuzzy Systems, 3*(3), 370–379. doi:10.1109/91.413225

Pang, W., Wang, K., Zhou, C., & Dong, L. (2004) Fuzzy Discrete Particle Swarm Optimization for Solving Traveling Salesman Problem. *Proceedings of the Fourth International Conference on Computer and Information Technology*, 796–800. doi:10.1109/CIT.2004.1357292

Petrovic, G., & Cojbasic, Z. (2011) Comparison of Clustering Methods for Failure Data Analysis: A Real Life Application.*Proceedings of International Scientific Conference on Industrial Systems,*14-16.

Rana, S., Jasola, S., & Kumar, R. (2010). A hybrid sequential approach for data clustering using K-Means and particle swarm optimization algorithm.*International Journal of Engineering Science and Technology, 2*(6), 67–176.

Rashedi, E., Nezamabadi-pour, H., & Saryazdi, S. (2009). GSA: A Gravitational Search Algorithm. *Information Sciences, 179*(13), 2232–2248. doi:10.1016/j.ins.2009.03.004

Sarmah, , & Bhattacharyya. (2010). An Effective Technique for Clustering Incremental Gene Expression data. *International Journal of Computer Science Issues*, *7*(3), 31–41.

Shapiro, G. P., & Tamayo, P. (2003). Microarray Data Mining: Facing the Challenges. *SIGKDD Explorations*, *5*(2), 1–5. doi:10.1145/980972.980974

Shi, Y., & Eberhart, R. C. (1998) A modified particle swarm optimizer.*Proceedings of the IEEE International Conference on Evolutionary Computation*, 69–73.

Spellman, P. T., Sherlock, G., Zhang, M. Q., Iyer, V. R., Anders, K., Eisen, M. B., & Futcher, B. et al. (1998). Comprehensive Identification of cell cycle-regulated genes of the Yeast Saccharomyces Cerevisiae by Microarray Hybridization. *Molecular Biology of the Cell*, *9*(12), 3273–3297. doi:10.1091/mbc.9.12.3273 PMID:9843569

Tarca, L., Romero, R., & Draghici, S. (2006). Analysis of microarray experiments of gene expression profiling. *American Journal of Obstetrics and Gynecology*, *195*(2), 373–388. doi:10.1016/j.ajog.2006.07.001 PMID:16890548

Tjaden, & Cohen, J. (2006). A Survey of computational methods used in microarray data interpretation. *Applied Mycology and Biotechnology, Bioinformatics*, *6*, 7-18.

Wafaa, O., Badr, A., & Hegazy, A. E.-F. (2013). Hybrid Ant-Based Clustering Algorithm with Cluster Analysis Techniques. *Journal of Computer Science*, *9*(6), 780–793. doi:10.3844/jcssp.2013.780.793

Wen, X., & Fuhrman, S. (1998). Large-scale temporal gene expression mapping of central nervous system development. Proc. Natl. Acad. Sci. USA, Neurobiology, 95(1), 334-339.

Wu, B., Zheng, Y., Liu, S., & Shi, Z. (2002). CSIM: a document clustering algorithm based on swarm intelligence. *Proceedings of the 2002 congress on Evolutionary Computation*, 477–482.

Xie, X. L., & Beni, G. (1991). A Validity Measure for fuzzy Clustering. *IEEE Transactions on Pattern Analysis and Machine Intelligence*, *13*(8), 841–847. doi:10.1109/34.85677

Xiong, X., & Tan. (2004). Similarity-Driven Cluster Merging Method for Unsupervised Fuzzy Clustering.*Proceedings of the 20th Conference in Uncertainty in Artificial Intelligence*, 611-627.

Yang, X.-S., & Deb, S. (2009) Cuckoo search via Levy flights. *Proceedings of World Congress on Nature & Biologically Inspired Computing*, 210-214. doi:10.1109/NABIC.2009.5393690

Yang, X.-S., & Deb, S. (2010). Engineering optimization by cuckoo search. *International Journal of Mathematical Modelling and Numerical Optimization*, 1(4), 330–343. doi:10.1504/IJMMNO.2010.035430

Chapter 6
Significance of Biologically Inspired Optimization Techniques in Real–Time Applications

Sushruta Mishra
C. V. Raman College of Engineering, India

Brojo Kishore Mishra
C. V. Raman College of Engineering, India

Hrudaya Kumar Tripathy
KIIT University, India

ABSTRACT

The techniques inspired from the nature based evolution and aggregated nature of social colonies have been promising and shown excellence in handling complicated optimization problems thereby gaining huge popularity recently. These methodologies can be used as an effective problem solving tool thereby acting as an optimizing agent. Such techniques are called Bio inspired computing. Our study surveys the recent advances in biologically inspired swarm optimization methods and Evolutionary methods, which may be applied in various fields. Four real time scenarios are demonstrated in the form of case studies to show the significance of bio inspired algorithms. The techniques that are illustrated here include Differential Evolution, Genetic Search, Particle Swarm optimization and artificial bee Colony optimization. The results inferred by implanting these techniques are highly encouraging.

DOI: 10.4018/978-1-5225-2375-8.ch006

Copyright ©2017, IGI Global. Copying or distributing in print or electronic forms without written permission of IGI Global is prohibited.

1. INTRODUCTION

Today computers are so well developed that it can perform all sorts of complex computations and act as a huge repository to store massive quantity of data. Still its memory usage depends on the available resources used to develop a system. Many memory enhancement methodologies are initiated to maximize the computing capacity of a computer that can solve complex problems. In spite of great advancements made, still nature forms a formidable force that decides the outcome of several approaches. Bio-inspired approach is one of the nature binding techniques that can be capitalized in handling complex domains that are complicated to deal with in normal circumstances. This approach of computation is a defining aspect of nature that is derived from the semantics, behaviour and methods of a natural system. In present era complex and real time problems are being solved very easily through the evolving techniques of computation. These computation techniques may be sophisticated, but still they are not flexible enough and lack a well-defined mathematical structure. To counter these techniques new natural approaches are starting to emerge to increase the simplicity in problem solving.

Bio-inspired methods of computing work in a decentralized manner which generate specific rules and apply such rules to find a suitable solution to a problem. Such techniques are generally very adaptable to environment and work in distributed platforms. In addition to its potential applications, such as DNA computation, nanofabrication, storage devices, sensing, and health care, bio-computation also has implications for basic scientific research. It can provide biologists, for example, with an IT-oriented paradigm for looking at how cells compute or process information, or help computer scientists construct algorithms based on natural systems, such as evolutionary and genetic algorithms. It has the potential to be a very powerful tool. The environmental demands of such organisms are different and this helps them to deal with complex issues that are different than engineering approach (Ullas, 2008). These methods started to show its presence since early days when the first digital computer was discovered by Von Newman and it was based on the human brain. But recent development of algorithms directly mimicking natural organisms' behaviour and has proved more adaptive and precise than conventional methods. It deals with field of research that allow the development of new computational methods (in software or hardware) to solve problems that leads to the formation of natural patterns and behaviours and may result in designing systems that implements natural media to compute. The nature is in itself has parallel, asynchronous, decentralised and collective behaviour. The nature-inspired techniques are an excellent match for computing environments that exhibit these characteristics. It is vital that disciplined scientific and engineering investigations are undertaken to successfully transfer

Table 1. Comparisons between bio-inspired computing and conventional computing

Criteria	Bio-inspired computing	Conventional computing
Performance	Exhibits good performance even if work is ill-defined.	Performance level gets saturated after a threshold value.
Flexibility in decision making	It determines the alternate optimal solution for a problem.	Depends on programmer's understanding of the It is dependent on User interpretation of a task.
Overhead involved	Significant computation overhead incurred in allotting a fitness function.	Computation overhead incurred is relatively less.
Intelligence	It involves a bottom-up approach which generates simple basic rules.	It involves top down approach and rules generation is problem dependant.
Improvement	Enhancing a Bio-inspired algorithm is cumbersome.	It can be improved if a more suitable solution exists.
Adaptability to practical situations	Not applicable for solutions to practical problems.	Developed for a more realistic scenario that always yield result.
Scalability	It is highly scalable.	Scalable, but only to a certain extent.

these algorithms, techniques and infrastructures into emerging computing environments (Gupta, Bhardwaj & Bhatia, 2011). A brief comparison between conventional technique and bio-inspired technique is presented in Table 1.

1.1. Agent based Solving Using Bio-Inspired Computing

Biologically motivated computation is highly dependent on component behaviour. They employ a bottom-up mechanism in a decentralized manner while dealing with problem solving. They are perceived as computationally intelligent since they are highly adaptive and the method to solve a problem is not known at prior. It reaches the solution by cohesive and iterative behaviour of its components thereby developing an emergent behaviour. This emergent nature propels to find a suitable solution to a problem. Basically three concepts are followed to acquire this bottom-up emergent nature (Brownlee, 2005). These are:

Emergent Effects: Potential features are developed when a certain problem is encountered by the bio-inspired computational system. This is very well recognized in systems as a result of interaction of individual components which results in complicated associations among individual behavioural patterns causing emergent effects.

Local Interactions: These interactions are very much local and simple in the sense they are easily implemented and are used by various components in the interchange of local data thereby enhancing synchronization.

Intermediate Dynamics: These are the system processes which analyze various aspects of discrete units and other localized rules causing emergent behavioural patterns. These aspects are tough to design but still these methods can offer an optimal solution which is applicable to target engineering problems (Abbott, 2005).

1.2. Agent Based Optimization Using Bio-Inspired Computing

Problem solving optimization is an important issue in all aspects. It is useful in determining the best possible solution to a problem. Optimization problems are numerous, hence methods for solving these problems is a hot area of interest. These techniques are either deterministic or stochastic in nature. Deterministic methods require much higher computational efforts and effectiveness decreases when the input size of a problem increases. This is a motivating factor in implementing nature inspired stochastic optimization algorithms which proves to be computationally efficient alternatives to such deterministic methods. These biologically inspired techniques receive its sole inspiration from nature. It uses computer to simulate the natural model on analyzing various processes of life to enhance the usage of computers. It incur the capability to analyze and resolve complicated associations from intrinsically very simple start up conditions and rules with very less information regarding the search space. Thus it can be said that nature is the best example for optimization. Also it appears that persistent problems in the field of computer science draw its similarity with problems nature has encountered and resolved long back. So these two fields can strongly be mapped together. Bio inspired computing has emerged in this modern new era in computing, covering a wide range of areas that includes computer networks, security, robotics, bio-medical engineering, control systems, parallel processing, data mining, power systems, production engineering and many more. Several decisions are made in random for classification. Basically three aspects are involved in the design of a bio-inspired technique. These include selecting a suitable problem denotation, proper choice of fitness function to get a good solution and representing operators to develop a new series of solutions. There exist a number of techniques in this area to solve a very diverse set of problems and it has been inferred that several of these techniques are helpful in solving critical problems in a wide range of areas.

This chapter is prepared as follows. Initiating with introductory discussion in section 1, section 2 explains taxonomy of bio optimization approach. Section 3 mainly focuses on concepts of swarm intelligence followed by discussion on applications of swarm intelligence in Section 4. Section 5 focuses on some of the practical illustrations of bio inspired techniques and evolutionary computation in optimization problems. Section 6, concludes the about chapter.

2. TAXONOMY OF BIO OPTIMIZATION APPROACH

There exists a massive literature work on bio inspired techniques for handling various types of problems and, until now, numerous studies have been reported that have successfully implemented such techniques in solving complicated problems in variety of areas of computer science. Evolutionary based algorithms and Swarm based Algorithms are the two most widely accepted categories of bio-inspired computing. While evolutionary algorithms are based on adopting Darwinian principle, the main idea of swarm intelligence lies in the aggregated nature of individuals that interact with each other and their surroundings in a local manner. Due to increasing complexity of real-world space it motivates the researchers to search for efficient methods. The basic taxonomy of bio-inspired approach is illustrated in Figure 1.

2.1 Evolutionary Computing Concepts and Computation

Usually a solution is termed as computationally efficient if it can be developed with a closed form equation or some mathematical judgments. The main advantage of such solutions is the rate at which the computation is performed while the accuracy of computation is ignored. But the problem arises when certain unreasonable assumptions are made in the course of getting to the solution. In fact problems whose

Figure 1. Taxonomy of bio optimization approach

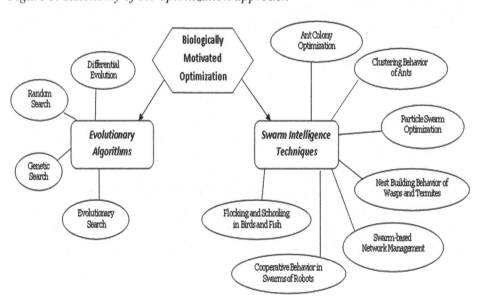

solutions can be achieved by sampling techniques in iterative manner do not require any other method of computation. But still complexity is seen when the calculation technique is difficult. In such scenarios evolutionary techniques are handful tools which can be quite effective in handling imprecision and to avoid lengthy computation. If there is any uncertainty and confusion in selecting an accurate method of computation then evolutionary technique is the preferred approach. It is suitable to problems where there is no mechanical solution is available so that several unreasonable assumptions are taken into account. Some of common problems that can be handled in better way using evolutionary computing include the following.

1. Assignment of individuals into groups, wherever simple ranking and truncation will not work. This usually involves interactions, whereby whether an individual should be in a group depends on what other individuals will be in that group.
2. Problems where thresholds are involved, for example when the value of a solution depends on whether certain thresholds have been passed, or the fate of an individual depends on passing one or more thresholds.
3. Combinatorial tedious problems, where many combinations of components can exist.

2.2 Basic Architecture of Evolutionary Computation

The basic architecture consists of problem notification, objective function and optimization module. Problem notification includes writing algorithm to produce the input variables or states from a vector of simple numbers. Such a vector is converted into a pattern of mating and selection (Kinghorn & Shepherd, 1999). This algorithm should ideally produce only legal solutions to the problem. Objective function able to return a single value known as Fitness that represents the value of a single solution. The single solution is represented by variable input values and states. Optimization module is the heart of an evolutionary algorithm. It is where operations such as recombination and mutation are carried out, to make genotypes of progeny out of the genotypes of parents. However, the optimization engine is quite simple. It generates vectors of numbers ("Genotypes") and seeks the vector that gives the highest fitness. A general architecture design is depicted in Figure 2.

An optimal solution implies absolute knowledge of the problem, but frequently knowledge of the problem's domain is incomplete and sparse, the solution space is unknown, and data sources are noisy. In other types of problems optimality may vary over time or there are multiple optimal solutions. And, sometimes problems are heavily constrained and simply finding a single set of parameters that comply with the bounds is unwieldy. Biological problems seem to fall under all these cat-

Figure 2. Architecture of Evolutionary computing

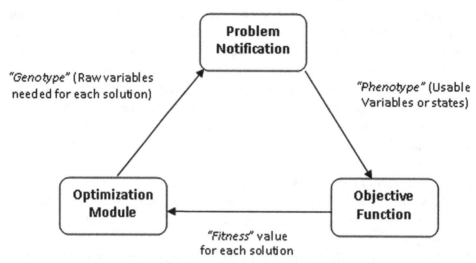

egories. For such complex problems a compromise must be sought. Instead of deterministic algorithms which yield optimal solutions but can only be used in specific and frequently unrealistic problems, stochastic algorithms that are not mathematically guaranteed to converge on a optimal solution can be adopted (Michalewicz & Fogel, 2000). Evolutionary computation falls under this last category. These techniques are loosely inspired on evolutionary processes such as selection, mutation and crossover. All algorithms have in common the use of populations of candidate solutions which reproduce, compete, and are subjected to selective pressures and random variation (Atmar, 1994).

Evolutionary computing has been sub divided into various categories. The chapter briefly focus on the main branches of evolutionary computing. Keeping the topics within the boundary of this chapter, the sole intent is to give a taste for the different variants.

1. **Random Search:** This search is a stochastic based global optimization method that is derivative-free in its search. The probability distribution of sample solutions in the search space is uniform. The solution samples are different in every generation with no two samples alike. It only requires two things for its evaluation that include construction module and a solution module that are integrated with each other during its evaluation.

2. **Evolutionary Search:** This is a global optimization method where a progeny is developed on reproduction of a species of population. Based on the suitability of environment, the parent with their progeny competes and the fittest

individual is passed to the next generation and undergoes reproduction again. The process continues thereby increasing the fitness individuals adaptive to surroundings. Optimizing the candidate solutions suitability with respect to the objective function in a domain is the main aim of evolutionary search.

3. **Differential Evolution:** This technique is an instance of an evolutionary algorithm. It may be used for optimization of nonlinear and non-differentiable functions. Several rounds of recombination, evaluation, and selection are applied to a set of candidate solution population. In recombination new candidate solutions are produced that is based on the weighted difference between two members chosen at random which is added to a third population member. This perturbs population members relative to the spread of the broader population. In conjunction with selection, the perturbation effect self-organizes the sampling of the problem space.

4. **Genetic Search:** In genetic search, every species of a population contribute their genotype which is proportional to the phenotype suitability in the form of offspring. It produces the subsequent generations by mating where genomes of two species are recombined whereby mutation occurs creating the diversity in population. Maintaining an optimal trade off between candidate solutions of a population and the fitness function from the problem domain is the prime motive of a genetic search algorithm. Surrogates are repeatedly applied for recombination and mutation functions on the candidate solution set where the fitness function is applied to a decoded representation to the subsequent generation of candidate solutions.

3. SWARM INTELLIGENCE

Swarm intelligence is the field of study dealing with natural and artificial phenomena of individuals that act in a coordinated manner with self-organizing capability. Basically it deals with collective behaviour resulting from individual's local coordination with their surroundings. The five vital rules of swarm intelligence are depicted in Table 2. Various examples illustrating this behaviour include ants colonies and that of termites, schools of fish, flocks of birds etc. It also includes human simulation models like models depicting multi-robot and some software agents capable of handling optimization and data analysis problems. Basically there are two criteria based on research activities in swarm intelligence. They are comparison between natural to artificial and science to engineering.

Classification of natural to artificial is according to the analysis of nature of systems. Natural swarm intelligence refers to biologically based systems while artificial swarm intelligence means system models based on human artifacts. The

Table 2. Five rules of swarm intelligence and respective properties

Rules	Properties
Rule of proximity	Ability to carry out simple space and time computations.
Rule of quality	Ability to respond to quality criterions in the environment.
Rule of diverse response	No commitment in its activity along excessively narrow channels.
Rule of stability	No change in its mode of behavior every time the environment changes.
Rule of adaptability	Ability to change its behavior according to its computational price

scientific study means that the system model should behave in a coordinated manner as a result of local individual-individual and individual-environment interactions but engineering stream refers in designing a swarm intelligence model capable of solving more practical problems of real life relevance. A general swarm intelligence system is comprised of the following features.

1. It constitutes several species or individuals.
2. These species are homogeneous or identical in nature.
3. Individual interaction is dependent on simple behavioural guidelines based on local information exchange among individuals.
4. The system overall behaviour is the impact of individual behaviour with each other and their surroundings.

Scalability means that the functionality of a system remains unchanged while the input size may increase without redefining the manner its parts interact. In swarm intelligence system, interactions involve only neighbouring individuals and the number of interactions tends not to grow with the overall number of individuals in the swarm. In artificial systems, scalability is interesting because a scalable system can increase its performance by simply increasing its size, without the need for any reprogramming.

Parallel action is possible in swarm intelligence systems because individuals composing the swarm can perform different actions in different places at the same time. In artificial systems, parallel action is desirable because it can help to make the system more flexible, that is, capable to self-organize in teams that take care simultaneously of different aspects of a complex task. Fault tolerance is an inherent property of swarm intelligence systems due to the decentralized, self-organized nature of their control structures. Because the system is composed of many interchangeable individuals and none of them is in charge of controlling the overall system behaviour, a failing individual can be easily dismissed and substituted by another one that is fully functioning.

3.1 Behaviour of Swarm Intelligence

The behaviour of swarm intelligence basically deals with clustering behaviour of ants, nest building behaviour of wasps, flocking and schooling in birds and fish etc. These behaviours are briefly discussed below.

1. **Clustering Behaviour of Ants**: Cemeteries are constructed by ants by aggregating dead stuffs into a single coherent area. The disposition of larvae is organized into clusters with a small young larvae being located at its centre while the older ones reside in territory. This phenomenon has motivated in the building of many models and simulated them accordingly (Bonabeau et al., 1999). The main idea is that the probability of an unloaded ant to carry a larva or corpse is inversely related to the local density of identical matter. This model has been verified with the actual ant behaviour.

2. **Nest building Behaviour of Wasps and Termites**: The nest building method of wasps are quite complex. The nest building of termites involves massive dimensions when compared to a single species. Research was being conducted on these coordination mechanisms of such termites and wasps and has developed models based on probability and statistics that analyzes behaviour of insects. Various models are being applied in software programs which are used in simulating structures to recognize the morphology of the real nests (Bonabeau et al., 1999).

3. **Flocking and Schooling in Birds and Fish**: This is a characteristics noticed in massive groups of birds and fish which is very much coordinated. It occurs in an environment where there is no leader of troop and every species directs its location coordinate completely based on locally available data like distance, anticipated speed and its neighbours movement direction. Such methods are highly used in the field of computer graphics to generate a realistic model of vision in movies and computer games.

3.2 Applications of Swarm Intelligence

The concept for swarm based technique in management of network was proposed first time in 1996 (Schoonderwoerd et. al, 1996). Working with this concept, the team of researchers (Schoonderwoerd et. al, 1996) developed an algorithm called ant-based control (ABC) used in efficient routing and balancing of loads in circuit-switched networks. It may be applicable to networks with heavy and dynamic traffic like Internet. Ad-hoc networks (Di Caro, Ducatelle & Gambardella, 2005) successfully implemented a variation of ant net which is yet a very effective artificial/engineering swarm intelligence system. Another application is swarm robotics.

Swarm robotics is an innovation that may be applied to solve problems based on behaviours of swarms in natural systems. It can add a new scientific or a technical angle to a problem. A bright example is the clustered analysis in a swarm of robots. A simplified illustration is a collective effort of multiple robots to carry a heavy object which is a distinctive feature of ant colonies.

4 BIO-INSPIRED TECHNIQUES IN OPTIMIZATION PROBLEMS

Bio-inspired computation approach is implemented in various real time applications to serve humanity. This nature based computation techniques have helped in solving complex problems and provides optimum solution. Parallel, dynamic, decentralized, asynchronous and self organizing behaviour of nature inspired algorithms are best suited for soft computing applications. This chapter discus some vital case studies where such approaches have been successfully used.

4.1 Ant Colony Optimization

Ant colony optimization (Dorigo, Maniezzo & Colorni, 1991; Dorigo & Stützle, 2004) is a population based meta-heuristic approach and can be used to find approximate solutions to difficult optimization problems. It is inspired by the above described foraging behaviour of ant colonies. In ant colony optimization (ACO), a set of software agents called "artificial ants" search for good solutions to a given optimization problem transformed into the problem of finding the minimum cost path on a weighted graph. The artificial ants incrementally build solutions by moving on the graph. The solution construction process is stochastic and is biased by a pheromone model, that is, a set of parameters associated with graph components (either nodes or edges) the values of which are modified at runtime by the ants. ACO has been applied successfully in many classical combinatorial optimization problems, as well as to discrete optimization problems that have stochastic and dynamic components.

4.2 Particle Swarm Optimization

This is a widely used stochastic optimization technique to solve optimization problems of continuous domains (Kennedy & Eberhart, 1995; Kennedy, Eberhart & Shi, 2001). It draws its inspiration from social behaviours in flocks of birds and schools of fish. In this technique series of agents are in search of a good optimal solution for a continuous optimization problem. Here every particle has its own start up velocity and coordinate position. An objective function is associated with a particle's position to denote a solution to a problem. At every round a particle moves with a velocity which constitutes summation of three parts which include the previous velocity, the velocity component with which the previously best solution was determined by that particle and the velocity component in search space where neighbour particles found the best solution so far.

This algorithm starts with a set of random solutions which updates the subsequent generations in search of optimal solutions. In each round a particle updates two best values. One is the pbest value which denotes its best solution till the very instant. While the other is the global best value achieved so far by any other particle in the entire population which is called as gbest. When a particle becomes part of its topological neighbor the best value is local in nature called 'lbest'. Once these two values are computed the velocity and position of every particle is updated as below.

$$v[\,] = v[\,] + c_1\, rand(\,)(pbest[\,] - present[\,]) + c_2\, rand(\,)(gbest[\,] - present[\,])$$
(1)

$$present[\,] = present[\,] + v[\,]$$
(2)

$v[\,]$ denotes the velocity of particle, $present[\,]$ is the current particle (solution). $pbest[\,]$ and $gbest[\,]$ are already defined above, $rand(\,)$ is a random number between (0,1). c_1 and c_2 represent learning factors such that $c_1 = c_2 = 2$ holds true for many cases.

4.3 Artificial Bee Colony

Artificial bee colony (ABC) draws its inspiration from foraging and dance behaviours of real honey bee colonies. This optimization technique was proposed by Karaboga to solve continuous optimization problems. It is attributed with the simulating behaviour of honey bee colonies. The bees may be categorized into three distinct types which are employed bees, onlooker bees and scout bee. Employed bees are required during the start of the algorithm to enhance self-food source to get the feasible solution for an optimization problem. They help in foraging food sources and locate position information about them to the hive. Onlooker bees analyze data shared by employed bees to reach the possible solutions. If an employed bee fails to optimize its self-solution within a certain time frame it is changed into a scout bee. As soon as a new solution is generated for a scout bee, it is changed back to employed bee. In order to update the food source positions, the employed bees use equation given as follows:

Let $V_i = X_i$, then

$$V_{i,j} = X_{i,j} + \Psi(X_{i,j} - X_{k,j}) \tag{3}$$

where, $i \neq k$ and $i, k \in \{1, 2, \cdots, N\}$, $V_{i,j}$ is the candidate food source position for i^{th} food source position on the jth dimension for the solution space. $X_{i,j}$ is the jth dimension of the ith food source position. $X_{k,j}$ is the jth dimension of the kth food source position, Ψ is the scaling factor randomly produced in the range of $[-1, 1]$ and N is number of employed bees. After all the employed bees update self-solutions, fitness values of the solutions of employed bees are calculated as

$$f_i t_i = \begin{cases} 1 / (1 + f_i) & \text{if } f_i \geq 0 \\ 1 + abs(f_i) & \text{if } f_i < 0 \end{cases} \tag{4}$$

where, f_i is the fitness value of the solution of ith employed bee, $f_i t_i$ is the objective function value specific for the problem. The onlooker bees select an employed bee in order to improve its solution by using (4). The selection probabilities of the employed bees by the onlooker bees are calculated (Karaboga, Ozturk, Karaboga, & Gorkemli, 2012) using equation (5).

$$P_i = (0.9 f_i t_i) / f_i t_{best} + 0.1 \tag{5}$$

where, P_i is being selected probability of the solution of ith employed bee, $f_i t_i$ is the fitness value of the solution of the ith employed bee and $f_i t_{best}$ is the maximum fitness value of the solutions of the employed bees. In the initialization phase of the algorithm, a food source position is produced for each employed bee using equation (6).

$$X_{i,j} = X_j^{\min} + r(X_j^{\max} - X_j^{\min}); \, i = 1, 2, \cdots, N \text{ and } j = 1, 2, \cdots, D \tag{6}$$

where, $X_j^{\min}$ is the lower bound of the jth dimension, $X_j^{\max}$ is the upper bound of the jth dimension, and D is the dimensionality of the optimization problem. Also it is mentioned that if a scout bee occur, a new food source position is produced for this scout bee by using equation (6). The ABC algorithm is iterative algorithm and consists of four phases, named as initialization phase, employed bee phase, onlooker bee phase and scout bee phase, sequentially realized.

Pseudocode of ABC Algorithm

Initialization Phase

1. Determine the number of employed bees or food source number (N)
2. Determine the limit value for the population
3. Generate food source positions for each employed bee using equation (6)
4. Calculate the objective function values of the solutions of the employed bees
5. Calculate the fitness values of the solutions of the employed bees using (4)
6. Reset the trial counters of the food sources
7. Repeat {

Employed Bee Phase

8. For each employed bee
9. Update the solution of the employed bees using (3)
10. Calculate the objective function value of candidate solution
11. Calculate the fitness value of the candidate solution
12. If the fitness value of the candidate solution is better than the fitness value of the solution of employed bee, memorize the candidate solution and reset its trial counter. Otherwise increase its trial counter by 1.

Onlooker Bee Phase

13. Calculate the selection probabilities using (5)
14. For each onlooker bee
15. Select an employed bee
16. Update the solution of employed bee using (3)
17. Calculate the objective function values of the solution of the onlooker bee
18. If the fitness value of the solution of the onlooker bee is better than the fitness value of the solution of employed bee, memorize the solution of the onlooker bee and reset its trial counter. Otherwise increase its trial counter by 1.

Scout Bee Phase

19. Fix the maximum content of the trial counters
20. If the counter with maximum content is higher than the limit, generate a new solution for this bee, calculate the objective function value of this solution, calculate the fitness value of this solution and reset trial counters of this bee.
21. } Until (A termination condition is met)

4.4 Differential Evolution Algorithm

Differential algorithm is a part of evolutionary computation coined by Price and Storn (1997). It is defined as a parallel stochastic evolution based optimization technique that deals with problems that are non differentiable, nonlinear and multimodal objective in nature. These algorithms are quite fast and are robust. Neural networks with real and constrained integer weights are trained with differential algorithm. The main features of this algorithm lie in its simplicity, speed of operation and its robustness. Mutation is used here as a search method while it uses selection to move the search in the suitable direction in the feasible area. Basic difference between it and genetic search is quite simple. Genetic search uses crossover operator to find better solutions while differential evolution implements mutation function to evaluate the search process. In this process, a real number is used to denote a variable. The main motive is to produce trial parameter vectors. A parameter vector is generated by adding the weighted difference vector between two species of a population to a third species. A newly produced vector replaces the older one only if the predetermined species member is more than the lower objective function value. Each generation yield a best parameter value to track the optimization process in every generation. This algorithm is adaptive in the sense it produces great convergence features if random deviations are generated by extracting distance and direction information (Price et al., 2005). The two distinct arrays are maintained. Each array has a population size NP and consists of real-valued vectors. Current vector population is contained in the primary array while vectors that are chosen for the next round are stored in the secondary array. For every round NP competes to compute the next generation population. A vector differential in the form of $(X_a - X_b)$ is denoted for every vector pair (X_a, X_b). Another vector selected at random X_c is perturbed with the weighted differential expressed as in equation (7).

$$X_{c'} = X_c + F(X_a - X_b) \tag{7}$$

A user defined constant factor called scaling factor F lies in the range of 0.5 to 1.0. Every round generates a trial vector X_t by crossover operation between a primary array vector X_i and another vector X_c. So, the trial vector is the child of two parents, a noisy random vector and the target vector against which it must compete. An optimum range of 0.5 to 1.0 is chosen where a uniform crossover (CR) occurs using a crossover constant. This denotes the possibility that the parameter values are inherited from the noisy random vector by the child vector. Every trial vector parameter comes from $X_{c'}$ when $CR = 1$. But when $CR = 0$, all but one trial vector parameter comes from the target vector. The final trial vector always arrive from the noisy random vector when $CR = 0$ so that X_t varies from X_i by minimum one value. After comparing the objective function corresponding to the trial vector to the target vector, the vector with minimum valued objective function goes to the next generation. This process goes on till the end condition of a predefined number of generations is satisfied such that the objective function between two successive generations is kept at minimum. The entire working of differential algorithm is illustrated in Figure 3.

Example 1: A simple numerical example is presented to illustrate the differential evolution algorithm. Considering the objective function $f(x)$ as

$$Minimize \ f(x) = x_1 + x_2 + x_3 \qquad (8)$$

The initial population is selected at random among the bounds of decision variables between 0 and 1 for the decision variables. Table 3 denotes the population and its corresponding objective function. The target vector is set as the first member of the population "Individual 1". "Individual 2", "Individual 4" and "Individual 6" are picked up randomly to produce the noisy random vector. "Individual 1" is already set as the target vector hence it is not selected. Thus the noisy random vector is produced by adding "Individual 6" to the weighted difference of "Individual

Figure 3. Working of differential algorithm

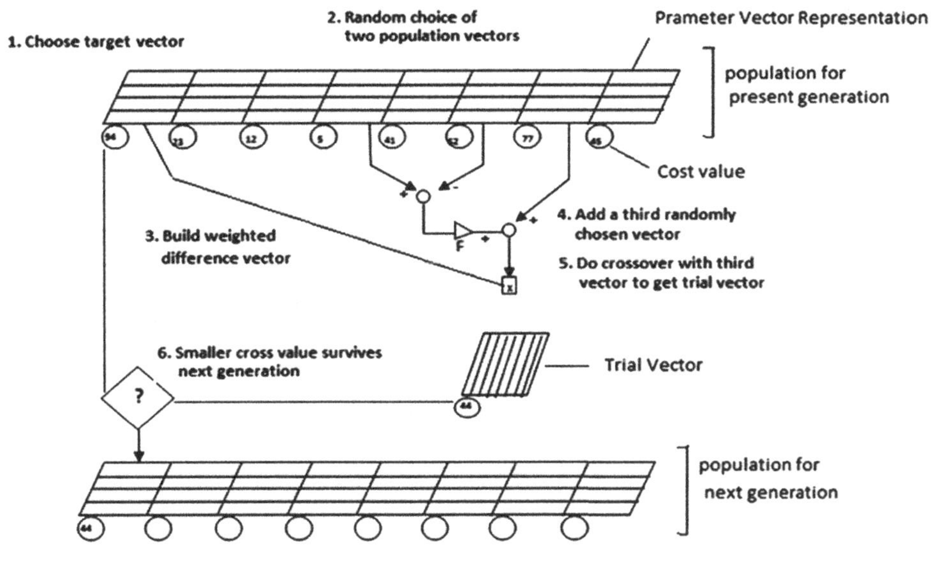

2" and "Individual 4". The weighted factor 0.8 is selected while Table 4 represents the weighted difference vector. The noisy random vector is illustrated in Table 5.

The noisy random vector does a crossover with the target vector to generate the trial vector as shown in Table 6. This is carried out by (1) generating random numbers equal to the dimension of the problem (2) for each of the dimensions: if random number > CR; copy the value from the target vector, else copy the value from the noisy random vector into the trial vector. In this example, the crossover constant CR is chosen as 0.50.

The objective function of the trial vector is compared with that of the target vector and the vector with the lowest value of the two becomes "Individual 1" for the next generation. To evolve "Individual 2" for the next generation, the second member of the population is set as target vector and the above process is repeated. This process is repeated NP times till the new population set array is filled which completes one generation. Once the termination criterion is met, the algorithm ends. The new population for subsequent generation is shown in Table 7.

Table 3. An illustrated example showing population with their objective functions

			Population Size NP = 6 (user defined), D = 3			
	Individual 1	Individual 2	Individual 3	Individual 4	Individual 5	Individual 6
x_1	0.68	0.92	0.22	0.12	0.40	0.94
x_2	0.89	0.92	0.14	0.09	0.81	0.63
x_3	0.04	0.33	0.40	0.05	0.83	0.13
$f(x)$	1.61	2.17	0.76	0.26	2.04	1.70

Table 4. Computation of the weighted difference vector for the illustrative example

	Individual 2	Individual 4	Difference Vector	X F (F = 0.80)	Weighted Difference Vector
x_1	0.92	0.12	= 0.80		= 0.64
x_2	0.92	0.09	= 0.83		= 0.66
x_3	0.33	0.05	= 0.28		= 0.22

Table 5. Calculation of the noisy random vector for the illustrative example

	Weighted Difference Vector	+	Individual 6	Noisy random Vector
x_1	0.64		= 0.94	= 1.58
x_2	0.66		= 0.63	= 1.29
x_3	0.22		= 0.13	= 0.35

Table 6. Generation of the trial vector for the illustrative example

	Target Vector	Crossover (CR = 0.50)	Noisy random Vector	Trial Vector
x_1	0.68		1.58	= 1.58
x_2	0.89		1.29	= 0.89
x_3	0.04		0.35	= 0.04
$f(x)$	1.61		3.22	2.51

Table 7. New population for next generation for the illustrative example

	Individual 1	Individual 2	Individual 3	Individual 4	Individual 5	Individual 6
x_1	0.68	0.9	0.21	0.11	0.4	0.91
x_2	0.89	0.91	0.12	0.07	0.8	0.62
x_3	0.04	0.31	0.37	0.04	0.83	0.09
$f(x)$	1.61	2.15	0.74	0.24	2.02	1.68

4.5 Genetic Algorithm in Testing Phase Optimization of Software Development

Genetic algorithm offer solutions to optimization problems through simulated evolution. Natural selection based processes like selection, crossover, and mutation are subjected iteratively to a series of binary strings denoting potential solutions. Subsequently more optimized and good solutions are combined from various individuals to compute potentially better solution to a problem. The basic building block of a genetic algorithm has five constituents such as chromosomes denoting a gene, starting pool of chromosomes, a fitness function, a selection function, and a crossover operator and a mutation operator.

Usually a chromosome is a binary string. The starting chromosomes are randomly generated. To evaluate the suitability of a particular chromosome meeting the desired objective fitness function is present. Decision of chromosome participation in the evolution phase is done by selection and mutation function. To retain the diversity in population crossover operator is applied to interchange parts of two chromosomes thereby generating a new one.

Pseudocode of Genetic Algorithm

1. Select initial population
2. Determine fitness function of each individual
3. Compute average fitness function
4. Repeat
5. Choose individuals that are top ranked to reproduce
6. Randomly mate pairs
7. Crossover operator is applied
8. Mutation operator is applied
9. Find fitness of every individual
10. Calculate average fitness of population
11. Till the process is terminated (At least one individual has the expected level of fitness or several generations have gone)

There has been less growth in software engineering area as far as dynamic testing is concerned. Still now test data design is done manually. Software testing process is a huge task which consumes a lot of resources (Mathur & Aditya, 2008). The basic aim of testing phase is to design a minimal test case set so that many faults are disclosed. Previously much research is being conducted in the field to produce test data in an automated manner. (Mansour & Salame, 2004; Srivastava et al, 2008; Wegener, Baresel, & Sthamer, 2002; Berndt, & Watkins, 2004; Korel, 1990; Sthamer & Eyres, 1996). The new techniques has to be developed that can support software testing automation in a cost effective way. Evolutionary approach is a potential solution where genetic algorithms based test data tool are developed (Wegener, Baresel & Sthamer, 2002; Berndt & Watkins, 2004; Korel, 1990; Jones, Sthamer & Eyres, 1996; Goldberg, 1989). Several methods of generating test data have been proposed (Berndt, Fisher, Johnson, Pinglikar & Watkins, 2003; Lin & Yeh, 2000; Baresel, Sthamer, & Schmidt, 2002; Rajappa Biradar & Panda, 2008) which may be classified into structural and functional testing. Here a simple approach based on generic algorithm is discussed to determine the path with more errors in a software development.

4.6 Methodology for Software Testing

In the entire cited process of test data generation along with the fitness function is discussed in detail using genetic algorithm. It uses a weighted control flow graph (CFG). A path testing search involves searching of suitable test cases that covers every possible path in the software to be developed. But a program may have infinite paths in an iterative program. Then the paths present in a program may grow exponentially with the branches in it making it technically unfeasible. Due to these constraints the path testing issue may be a NP complete problem for which total path coverage becomes practically inefficient. Hence a considerable subset of paths is selected and a test data is chosen at random to cover it. The proposed technique involves a control flow graph (CFG) which denotes the flow of control. An independent path is said to be a path in the program that introduces at least one new condition. In context of a flow graph an independent path must move along at least edge that has not been traversed before the path is defined. The algorithm is initiated by assigning weights to CFG. Paths which are more prone to errors are assigned more weights. While an initial credit of 100 is taken if large number of edges is present else a credit of 10 is considered if the CFG is not so dense.

At first weights are allotted to CFG. Paths that are more prone to error are assigned more weights. A start up credit of 100 is assumed if the CFG considered is dense while a start up credit of 10 is considered if the CFG is sparse with less number of edges. The summation of the weights of incoming edges is divided at every node which is further distributed to all outgoing edges in the certain manner that has been discussed in the next paragraph.

Let us assume the number of outgoing edges be n. Based on 80-20 rule the loops and branches are given a weightage of 80% while 20% is devoted to edges in linear path. For a given node let n_1 be the edge count in linear path while n_2 represent the edge count in the paths where most of branching and looping occurs. 20% of incoming weights are retained with n_1 edges which are divided equally among them while the rest 80% is allotted to n_2 edges. The incoming weight is allotted to the outgoing edge if there is a single outgoing edge present from a particular node. Figure 4 shows the CFG of the code where node-1 represents the predicate node since line-1 denotes if statement. Node-6 has two outgoing edges in the CFG since

Figure 4. A sample code and its corresponding control flow graph

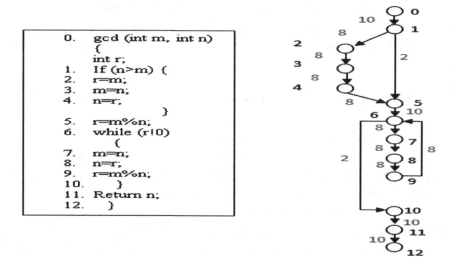

line6 is awhile statement. A loop is seen connecting an edge from node-9 to node-6. As the code is quite small so the credit taken here is 10. As the CFG is accessed in top down approach 80-20 rule is followed by dividing the incoming credit at every node.

In the figure shown the start up credit of 10 is distributed to many edges as per their significance. The weight value is shown close to the edges in the figure. The symbols, represented are:

X : Denotes our test data set

$F(x)$: Corresponding fitness value determined for each test data, by having a cumulative sum of the weights of the path followed by it in the CFG.

P_i : Probability for the corresponding data

C_i : Cumulative probability

Ran : Random number generated for the test data

Ns : Test data number that has cumulative probability just greater than the corresponding random number.

Thus, the expression is given as:

$$P_i = F(X_i) / \Sigma(F(X_i)) \tag{9}$$

Mating Pool suggest the number of times a test data appears in Ns column. Binary code is used to denote the data of Ns values. Exchange of the second half binary representation of data is facilitated by pair-wise crossover with a condition of $Ran < 0.8$. Crossover occurs if its respective random number is less than 80% probability. Bit-wise random number is produced for each entry in the new dataset. If the random number value is below 0.3 then that bit is flipped and a new data entry is the result. Till optimal values for the fitness function $F(x)$ is obtained similar process is undertaken with further crossover followed by mutation.

Given the initial population: (n, m) having values (12, 8), (2, 3), (6, 2), (15, 4).

Table 8, 9, 10, 11, 12, 13 and Table 14 represent iterations followed with the results obtained. The third column denotes the fitness function values of input species. Probability is found by using equation (3). The cumulative probability is shown in the fifth column.simulation of genetic algorithm occurs by the help of random numbers.

This work proved experimentally that genetic algorithm proves to be more efficient method than just generating random test data. The genetic search technique is much more efficient than earlier exhaustive search and other locality based search methods. In this case study an innovative way of software testing is been examined by taking the critical paths and thereby useful in cost and effort determination dur-

Table 8. First Iteration

Serial Number	X	$F(x)$	P_i	C_i	Ran	Ns	Mating pool
1	(12,8)	76	0.228	0.228	0.934	4	0
2	(2,3)	106	0.317	0.545	0.474	2	2
3	(6,2)	44	0.132	0.677	0.374	2	1
4	(15,4)	108	0.323	1.000	0.618	3	1

Table 9. First iteration continued

Serial Number	Ns	Mating pool	Crossover	Mutation
1	4	(15,4) 1111010	(15,4) 11001010	(15,5) 11001010
2	2	(2,3) 00100110	(2,3) 11001010	(3,3) 11001010
3	2	(2,3) 00100110	(2,2) 11001010	(2,2) 11001010
4	3	(6,2) 01100010	(6,3) 11001010	(10,3) 11001010

Table 10. Second iteration

Serial Number	X	$F(x)$	P_i	C_i	Ran	Ns	Mating pool
1	(15,5)	44	0.212	0.212	0.217	2	0
2	(3,3)	44	0.212	0.424	0.999	4	1
3	(2,2)	44	0.212	0.636	0.979	4	1
4	(10,3)	76	0.364	1.000	0.533	3	2

Table 11. Second iteration continued

Serial Number	Ns	Mating pool	Crossover	Mutation
1	2	(3,3) 00110011	(3,2) 00110010	(5,10) 01011010
2	4	(10,3) 10100011	(10,3) 10100011	(9,10) 10001010
3	4	(10,3) 10100011	(10,3) 10100011	(11,6) 10110110
4	3	(2,2) 00100010	(2,3) 00100011	(2,2) 00100010

Table 12. Third iteration

Serial Number	X	$F(x)$	P_i	C_i	Ran	Ns	Mating pool
1	(5,10)	74	0.223	0.223	0.934	4	0
2	(9,10)	106	0.319	0.542	0.474	2	2
3	(11,6)	108	0.325	0.867	0.374	2	1
4	(2,2)	44	0.123	1.000	0.618	3	1

ing testing stage. This study is useful to develop several test cases during software development. It can be useful in comparing much larger test data set with the chosen paths and hence can be implemented in more complex examples.

Table 13. Third iteration continued

Serial Number	Ns	Mating pool	Crossover	Mutation
1	4	(2,2) 00100010	(2,2) 00100010	(4,3) 01000011
2	2	(9,10) 10011010	(9,10) 10011010	(7,12) 01111100
3	2	(9,10) 10010010	(9,10) 10011010	(13,10) 11011010
4	3	(11,6) 10110110	(11,6) 10110110	(2,6) 00100110

Table 14. Final outcome

Serial Number	X	$F(x)$	P_i	C_i	Ran	Ns	Mating pool
1	(4,3)	76	0.178	0.178	0.098	1	1
2	(7,12)	170	0.399	0.577	0.275	2	3
3	(13,10)	106	0.249	0.826	0.325	2	0
4	(2,6)	74	0.174	1.000	0.487	2	0

4.7 Attribute Optimization in Healthcare Using PSO

Particle Swarm optimization is a technique used in non-linear and multidimensional optimization problem capable of achieving the desired solution with less parameterization. PSO algorithm as discussed earlier may be implemented as an attribute reduction technique to select the optimal set of features required to classify in healthcare datasets. As a simple case study a fitness function in the form of a filter like correlation-based feature selection (CFS) can be taken with PSO and combined with a search technique to evaluate the feature subset worthiness. The basic principle of CFS is that more correlated features are present in good subset of features but not related with each other (Hall & Lloyd A, 1997). This work constitutes the implementation of PSO with CFS as the fitness function and a comparison is drawn with (Karegowda, Jayaram & Manjunath, 2011) where genetic algorithm is used as a search technique with CFS as the fitness function.

Three different datasets were collected from University medical centre, Institute of oncology which includes that of breast cancer, heart statlog and dermatology. The breast cancer set consists of 286 instances, 201 instances of one class while

85 instances of the other class. It has a total of 9 features with a combination of linear and nominal types. The heart statlog dataset has total of 270 instances which are represented by 13 input features with the output class predicting the presence or absence of heart disease. The multi class dermatology dataset consists of 366 instances, 34 inputs and the output class to be predicted has 6 class labels. The diseases in this group are seboreic dermatitis, psoriasis, pityriasisrosea, lichen planus, pityriasisrubra pilaris, and chronic dermatitis. This database contains 34 attributes, one of them is nominal and the rest are linear valued (Hall & Lloyd, 1997).

4.8 Observations and Analysis of CFS

CFS is used as a subset evaluating technique with PSO algorithm to determine the potential disease risk of various categories. The size of population and the number of iterations are kept at 20. The individual weight is kept at 0.34 and inertia weight is 0.33. The result analysis is represented in Table 16 to Table 18 for different datasets. It depicts the number of features selected for a particular technique used with its accuracy level and error rate. The entire set has been conducted with WEKA a widely popular machine learning tool. Various classifiers under consideration involve Naive Bayes, Decision tree C3.4, RBF, K-NN and Bayesian classifier. These classifiers were being demonstrated with the clinical datasets using the important set of attributes as calculated with CFS filter. K-NN was experimented with different values of K-neighbors that have been used in various set up.

Table 16 shows the enhancement in classification process where there is improvement in accuracy as well as the root-mean-square error (RMSE) of the five classifiers on the breast cancer dataset as result of attribute selection. The number of features selected by our proposed wrapper model for three classifiers - Naive Bayes and RBF classifier- is less while keeping higher classification accuracy. Classification accuracy of Bayesian classifier is the same for the two proposed models.

Table 17 denote the result analysis of the heart stat log dataset on these classifiers as discussed above. Here the classification accuracy of KNN classifier does not vary much with inputs and with attributes chosen by proposed filter PSO - CFS, representing that removal of 6 noisy attributes has not got the classification accuracy worse. But the classification accuracy obtained with GA-CFS for KNN classifier has exceeded our proposed wrapper model by a value of 2%.

Table 18 shows the classification accuracy and the RMSE for the Dermatology dataset. The results show that using feature subset selection enhances the classification accuracy and the RMSE of all the five classifier for Dermatology dataset. Only the RBF classifier performance has not enhanced accuracy with our proposed models against the enhancement with GA-CFS.

Table 16. Classification analysis with PSO search in breast cancer dataset

Classifier	Approach	No of features	Accuracy	RMSE
Naïve Bayes	PSO and NBay.	4	75.52	0.44
	PSO and CFS	5	74.13	0.45
Bayesian	PSO and NBay.	3	73.08	0.43
	PSO and CFS	5	73.43	0.45
RBF	PSO and NBay.	4	76.22	0.43
	PSO and CFS	5	72.03	0.44
Decision Tree	PSO and NBay.	5	74.13	0.44
	PSO and CFS	5	72.03	0.44
KNN	PSO and NBay.	5	76.22	0.43
	PSO and CFS	5	74.83	0.45

Table 17. Classification analysis with PSO search in heart statlog dataset

Classifier	Approach	No of features	Accuracy	RMSE
Naïve Bayes	PSO and NBay.	7	85.56	0.35
	PSO and CFS	7	85.19	0.36
Bayesian	PSO and NBay.	5	84.82	0.35
	PSO and CFS	7	84.44	0.36
RBF	PSO and NBay.	9	85.19	0.35
	PSO and CFS	7	83.70	0.35
Decision Tree	PSO and NBay.	4	83.33	0.37
	PSO and CFS	7	80.74	0.39
KNN	PSO and NBay.	7	83.70	0.37
	PSO and CFS	7	82.59	0.37

The result indicates that classification with PSO algorithm enhances the accuracy rate for the clinical datasets taken. The classification accuracy for dermatology dataset has been enhanced with Naïve Bayes, decision tree, RBF and K-NN. Here also few exceptions were determined as the case with GA-CFS has better accuracy than our methods in a scenario where KNN classifier was used on Heart Statlog dataset, and the second with RBF.

Table 18. Classification analysis with PSO Search in Dermatology dataset

Classifier	Approach	No of features	Accuracy	RMSE
Naïve Bayes	PSO and NBay.	22	99.18	0.47
	PSO and CFS	20	99.45	0.05
Bayesian	PSO and NBay.	23	99.45	0.04
	PSO and CFS	20	99.45	0.04
RBF	PSO and NBay.	15	89.62	0.20
	PSO and CFS	20	86.07	0.22
Decision Tree	PSO and NBay.	14	97.27	0.09
	PSO and CFS	20	97.54	0.08
KNN	PSO and NBay.	22	98.63	0.09
	PSO and CFS	20	97.27	0.11

4.9 Application of ABC for Coronary Artery Disease Diagnosis

Artificial bee colony algorithm can be integrated with K- nearest neighbour algorithm for diagnosing coronary artery disease. Classification technique K-Nearest neighbour is a very common classification algorithm. It has a very less computation cost because of absence of training phase. Various distance computation methods like Euclid, Hamming and Manhattan are used to determine the distance between samples and the evaluated sample. A simple Euclidian distance based calculation is shown in equation (10). The majority voting of the K nearest samples determines the class of the evaluated sample (Duda, Hart, & Stork, 2001; Shakhnarovish, Darrell & Indyk, 2005).

$$d = \sqrt{\Sigma_{i=1}^{n}(p_i - q_i)^2} \tag{10}$$

where p is the evaluated sample and q represent a random sample in the training data while n is the size of features.

The proposed technique constitutes about 80% of training dataset used to get two centroid vectors related to healthy and unhealthy data samples. Then the remaining 20% sample undergoes classification with K-NN algorithm with the help of two centroids. Reliability of the proposed model is ensured by repeating the same process around 50 times. The result analysis is depicted in the Table 19. In a similar analysis K-NN algorithm was used with PSO technique in a previous work (Babaoglu, Fındık, Ülker & Aygül, 2012). The comparison of both methods is presented in Table 20. It is seen that the classification accuracy obtained with ABC-KNN approach proved

Table 19. Results obtained for ABC-KNN technique

Iteration	Population	Sensitivity	Specificity	PPV (%)	NPV (%)	Accuracy (%)
500	40	95.79	91.42	96.60	89.00	94.48
1000	10	96.83	91.68	96.65	91.75	95.28
1500	100	95.60	90.98	96.50	88.50	94.27

Table 20. comparative analysis of ABC-KNN with PSO-KNN model

Technique	Sensitivity	Specificity	PPV(%)	NPV(%)	ACC(%)
ABC-KNN	96.83	91.68	96.65	91.75	95.28
PSO-KNN	97.39	79.94	92.87	93.13	92.49

to be more optimal than PSO-KNN model. Apart from accuracy, other metric like sensitivity, positive predictive value (PPV), negative predictive value (NPV) etc also illustrated better outcome with ABC-KNN model.

5. CONCLUSION

This chapter represents various techniques that has been developed and implemented to solve complicated optimization problems. As observed that algorithms motivated from the natural behaviour attract special attention due to its high performance in term of efficiency and time complexity. Bio Inspired computation techniques proved to be a powerful tool in providing collaborative solution to uncommon and real life and real time problems. Nature based techniques of computing provides many alternatives for solving the real world problems more efficiently and quickly with accuracy. This chapter deals with a precise analysis of two broad optimization categories of Bio inspired techniques involving Evolutionary methods and Swarm Intelligence methods. These methods find a wide range of applications in various sectors. In the subsequent sections of this chapter, the authors had discussed and demonstrated the implementation issues of some widely used biologically motivated techniques in various domains and a brief illustration on impacts of these techniques on betterment of human society.

REFERENCES

Abbott, R. (2005). Challenges for Bio-inspired Computing. In *Proceedings of The BioGEC workshop* (pp. 12-22). New York. ACM.

André, B., Harmen, S., & Michael, S. (2002). Fitness function design to improve evolutionary structural testing. *Proceedings of the genetic and evolutionary computation conference*, 1329-1336.

Gowda Asha, K., Jayaram, M.A., & Manjunath, A.S. (2011). Feature Subset Selection using Cascaded GA & CFS: A Filter Approach in Supervised Learning. *International Journal of Computer Applications, 23*(2).

Atmar, W. (1994). Notes on the Simulation of Evolution. *IEEE Transactions on Neural Networks, 5*(1), 130–147. doi:10.1109/72.265967 PMID:18267786

Babaoglu, İ., Fındık, O., Ülker, E., & Aygül, N. (2012). A novel hybrid classification method with particle swarm optimization and k-nearest neighbor algorithm for diagnosis of coronary artery disease using exercise stress test data. *International Journal of Innovative Computing, Information and Control,8*(5), 3467-3475.

Berndt, D. J., Fisher, J., Johnson, L., Pinglikar, J., & Watkins, A. (2003). Breeding Software Test Cases with Genetic Algorithms. *Proceedings of the Thirty-Sixth Hawaii International Conference on System Sciences,*1-10. doi:10.1109/HICSS.2003.1174917

Berndt, D. J., & Watkins, A. (2004). Investigating the Performance of Genetic Algorithm-Based Software Test Case Generation. *Proceedings of the Eighth IEEE International Symposium on High Assurance Systems Engineering*, 261-262. doi:10.1109/HASE.2004.1281750

Bonabeau, E., Dorigo, M., & Theraulaz, G. (1999). *Swarm Intelligence: From Natural to Artificial System*. New York: Oxford University Press.

Brownlee, J. (2005). *On Biologically Inspired Computation a.k.a. The Field* (PhD Thesis). Swinburne University of Technology.

Di Caro, G., Ducatelle, F., & Gambardella, L. M. (2005). An adaptive nature-inspired algorithm for routing in mobile ad hoc networks. *European Transactions on Telecommunications, 16*(5), 443–455. doi:10.1002/ett.1062

Dorigo, M., Maniezzo, V., & Colorni, A. (1991). *Positive feedback as a search strategy*. Milan, Italy: Technical Report, InDipartimento di Elettronica, Politecnico di Milano.

Dorigo, M., & Stützle, T. (2000). *Ant Colony Optimization*. Cambridge, MA: MIT Press.

Duda, R. O., Hart, P. E., & Stork, D. G. (2001). *Pattern classification*. New York: John Wiley and Sons.

Goldberg, D. E. (1989). Genetic Algorithms. In *Search, Optimization & Machine Learning*. Addison Wesley.

Hall, M. A., & Smith, L. A. (1997). Feature subset selection: a correlation based filter approach. *University of Waikato Research-Computing and Mathematical Sciences Papers,* (pp. 855-858). Berlin: Springer.

Jones, B. F., Sthamer, H., & Eyres, D. E. (1996). Automatic structural testing using genetic algorithms. *Software Engineering Journal, 11*(September), 299–306. doi:10.1049/sej.1996.0040

Karaboga, D., Ozturk, C., Karaboga, N., & Gorkemli, B. (2012). Artificial bee colony programming for symbolic regression. *Information Sciences, 209*, 1–15. doi:10.1016/j.ins.2012.05.002

Kennedy, J., & Eberhart, R. C. (1995). Particle swarm optimization. In *Proceedings of IEEE International Conference on Neural Networks* (pp. 1942-1948). IEEE. doi:10.1109/ICNN.1995.488968

Kennedy, J., Eberhart, R. C., & Shi, Y. (2001). *Swarm Intelligence (book)*. San Francisco, CA: Morgan Kaufmann.

Kinghorn, B. P., & Shepherd, R. K. (1999).Mate selection for the tactical implementation of breeding programs.*AAABG Conference Proceedings*, 13, 130-133.

Korel, B. (1990). Automated software test data generation. *IEEE Transactions on Software Engineering, 16*(8), 870–879. doi:10.1109/32.57624

Lin, J. C., & Yeh, P. L. (2000). Using Genetic Algorithms for Test Case Generation in Path Testing.*Proceedings of the 9th Asian Test Symposium (ATS'00)*.

Mathur, P., & Aditya, P. (2008). *Foundation of Software Testing* (1st ed.). Pearson Education.

Michalewicz, T., & Fogel, D. B. (2000). *How to solve it: modern heuristics*. Heidelberg, Germany: Springer-Verlag. doi:10.1007/978-3-662-04131-4

Nashat, M., & Miran, S. (2004). Data Generation for Path Testing. *Software Quality Journal, 12*(2), 121–136. doi:10.1023/B:SQJO.0000024059.72478.4e

Price, K. V. S., & Rainer, M. (1997). Differential evolution - A simple evolution strategy for fast optimization. Dr. Dobb's Journal, 22, 18-24.

Price, V. K., Storn, M. R., & Lampinen, A. J. (2005). Differential evolution: A practical approach to global optimization. Springer-Verlag.

Schoonderwoerd, R., Holland, O., Bruten, J., & Rothkrantz, L. (1996). Ant-based load balancing in telecommunications networks. *Adaptive Behavior, 5*(2), 169–207. doi:10.1177/105971239700500203

Shakhnarovish, G., Darrell, T., & Indyk, P. (2005). *Nearest-Neighbor Methods in Learning and Vision*. MIT Press.

Shilpi, Shweta, & Parul. (2011). A Reminiscent Study of Nature Inspired Computation. *International Journal of Advances in Engineering & Technology*, 117-125.

Srivastava. (2008). *Generation of test data using Meta heuristic approach. In IEEE TENCON* (pp. 1–6). IEEE.

Ullas, M. (2008). *Bio Inspired Computing*. Cochin, India: Seminar Report School of Engineering Cochin University of Science & Technology.

Velur, R., Arun, B., & Satanik, P. (2008). Efficient Software Test Case Generation Using Genetic Algorithm Based Graph Theory. *First International Conference on Emerging Trends in Engineering and Technology, ICETET '08,* (pp. 298-303). IEEE.

Wegener, J., Baresel, A., & Sthamer, H. (2002). Suitability of Evolutionary Algorithms for Evolutionary Testing. *Proceedings of the 26th Annual International Computer Software and Applications Conference*. doi:10.1109/CMPSAC.2002.1044566

Chapter 7
Classification of Faults in Power Transmission Systems Using Modern Techniques:
An Overview

Avagaddi Prasad
VIT University, India

J. Belwin Edward
VIT University, India

K. Ravi
VIT University, India

ABSTRACT

Power system constitute a major part of the electrical system relating in the present world. Every single portion of this system assumes a major part in the accessibility of the electrical power one uses at their homes, enterprises, workplaces, industrial facilities and so on. Any deficiency in power system causes a ton of inconvenience for the maintenance of the system. So transmission system needs a proper protection scheme to ensure continuous power supply to the consumers. The countless extent of power systems and applications requires the improvement in suitable techniques for the fault classification in power transmission systems, to increase the efficiency of the systems and to avoid major damages. For this purpose, the technical literature proposes a large number of methods. This chapter analyzes the technical literature,

DOI: 10.4018/978-1-5225-2375-8.ch007

Copyright ©2017, IGI Global. Copying or distributing in print or electronic forms without written permission of IGI Global is prohibited.

summarizing the most important methods that can be applied to fault classification and advanced technologies developed by various researchers in power transmission systems.

1. INTRODUCTION

Power system is developing in size and complex nature in all divisions such as generation, transmission, distribution and load systems. Generation and usage of electrical energy in nowadays is to a greater extent need than an extravagance. In the seasons of innovative headway anything that qualities must be take well care of. The working of a significant number of the businesses and organizations beginning from ranchers to governments is currently depending to a great extent on a ton of electrical vitality. Continuous supply of power is vital for the functioning of the society which now calls for research and development in this field to guarantee this. Power system can be extensively separated into 4 primary divisions. This is a general order or segment regardless of where we are. These incorporate generation, transmission, distribution and utilization. With regards to generation a ton of endeavors have been taken to enhance the models of power generation. A ton of examination and cash goes into this segment in each nation. This is so on the grounds that if a nation can spare and proficiently create energy, it would give a major help to its economy. The generation of power is accompanied by a couple of misfortunes like eddy current, copper, iron losses and so forth. These are normally taken well care of during generation and don't act like the greatest risk. Consequently the amount of focus and research on these elements satisfies the normal needs.

Discussing the distribution, the energy must be proficiently transmitted to places both residential and modern in the most ideal way that is available. The amount of misfortunes in these regions are additionally less and don't act like a noteworthy risk. And still, after all that there are lots of facilities and devices to guarantee the way that not a lot of energy is lost all the while. The significant components in these areas are transformers both step up and step down. Utilization is the territory which chooses the entire situation of the power system in light of the fact that the estimation of the measure of energy to be produced is landed at just by comprehending what the prerequisite at this end of the power system. Presently the heart of the power system is the transmission. This is the place the significant faults are acquired. The generation happens at specific areas just though the usage happens all over. Along these lines, there is a need to exchange this energy to these places. Transmission now can be in both of the two ways. It can either be through overhead transmission lines or through underground lines. Presently underground lines have but rather been utilized as they are in principle, for the most part as a result of reasons like its expense of establishment or the way that if there should arise an occurrence of a single fault the entire scope of link will must be taken out, which would cost a great deal. In spite of the fact that underground links have a considerable measure of advantages, they are not utilized as much. Presently the most utilized method for transmission is the overhead lines and there are a considerable measure of ways in which energy is lost, with regards to overhead lines. The causes can be outer or inside. In the outer causes incorporate lighting, vegetation impacts, debacles and so forth. These cause real interruption in the power system and that too all the time. Inside faults incorporate the consonant issues and then some. The classification of deficiencies is significantly open conductor and short circuit faults. Open conductor faults can be single open or two open faults.

Here transmission lines shield against uncovered deficiency is the most basic errand in the assurance of power system. Faults in overhead lines are an unusual condition, brought on by climate conditions, human mistakes, smoke of flames, hardware letdowns, for example, pivoting machines and transformers, and so on. These issues cause intrusion to electric streams, hardware harms and even cause passing of people, winged creatures and creatures. These issues are hazard to the congruity of power supply. Transmission line faults are either be single phase to ground or phase to phase or double phase to ground or a three phase fault. Fault is the deviation of currents and voltages from ostensible values or states. Under typical working conditions, power system hardware or lines convey ordinary currents and voltages which bring about a more secure operation of the power system. However, when deficiency happens, it causes unnecessarily high currents to stream which causes the harm to hardware. Fault investigation is important to choose or plan appropriate switchgear hardware. Thus, power system requires a good protective scheme to identify and isolate faults quickly so that the harm and interruption brought on to system is reduced. The need of a protective system is to detect the faults in overhead lines.

Recent technological advancement in soft computing techniques creates an interest to engineers to do research in this area. Earlier various researchers have proposed different schemes for fault classification. The problem is raised, whenever a new user starts his research in this area, authors may get confusion to select the method to classify the nature of the fault. Because, so many researchers have already developed different methods such as fuzzy logic (Das & Reddy, 2005; Ferrero, Kumar, Jamil & Thomas, 1999; Mahanty & Gupta,2007; Prasad, Edward, Roy, Divyansh & Kumar, 2015; Razi, Hagh & Ahrabian, 2007; Samantaray, 2013;Sangiovanni& Zappitelli, 1994; Youssef, 2004a), rough computing with formal concept analysis (Acharjya & Ezhilarasi, 2011), wavelet technique (Guillen, Paternina, Zamora, Ramirez, & Idarraga, 2015;Megahed, Moussa, & Bayoumy, 2006; Pérez, Orduna & Guidi, 2011; Prasad & Edward, 2016), rough computing with Bayesian classification (Acharjya,

Roy & Rahaman, 2012), artificial neural networks (Dalstein & Kulicke, 1995; He, Lin, Deng, Li, & Qian, 2014; Seyedtabaii, 2012), neural network and rough set hybridization (Anitha & Acharjya,2015), neuro-fuzzy (Dash, Pradhan & Panda, 2000; Vasilic& Kezunovic, 2005; Wang & Keerthipala, 1998), rough set on two universal sets (Acharjya, 2014), rough set on fuzzy approximation spaces with soft set techniques (Das & Acharjya, 2014), wavelet-neural networks (Silva, Souza, & Brito, 2006), dominance based rough set (Ahmed & Acharjya, 2015),wavelet-fuzzy (Reddy& Mohanta, 2007;Youssef, 2004b), rough set on fuzzy approximation space and ordering of objects for mining knowledge (Tripathy & Acharjya, 2010),wavelet-neuro-fuzzy (Jung, Kim, Lee, & Klöckl, 2007), rough set on two universal sets (Tripathy & Acharjya, 2013)and other methods (Girgis & Johns, 1989;Moravej, Pazoki, & Khederzadeh, 2015;Pan, Morris, & Adhikari, 2015;Ruiz,Zhang, & Coombs,2015). All these methodsare very popular and have their own advantages and disadvantages.As of late some different strategies actualized for classifying faults in transmission lines. These new methods are not familiar to all.This chapter will give the clear idea about all the recent methods in fault classification.

This chapter is prepared as follows. Following introduction in section 1, section 2 explains classical techniques used in fault classification. Section 3 mainly focuses on modern tools for fault classification. Section 4, presents the comparison of modern fault classification techniques in transmission lines followed by Section5, concluding the explanations.

2. CLASSICAL TECHNIQUES IN FAULT CLASSIFICATION

There are a couple of strategies that can be utilized in the Simulink for this purpose. The significant methods are wavelet technique, artificial neural networks (ANN) and fuzzy logic. There are a considerable measure routes in which these real strategies can be coupled together to apply reenactments and procedures in an approach to give more proficiency. Certain strategies function admirably in detection while the others are most ideal approach to classify or locate the faults. Consequently, these techniques when connected together can work for various angles all the while and enhance the time reaction.

Wavelets are a numerical tool for signal processing. The essential thought in wavelet transform (WT) is to choose a reasonable wavelet function "mother wavelet" and afterward execute examination utilizing moved and expanded forms of this wavelet. Wavelet can be picked with exceptionally desirable frequency and time attributes when contrasted with fourier procedures. The fourier expansion has just frequency determination and no time determination. This implies it decides every one of the frequencies present in the signal yet it doesn't tell at what time they introduce. To defeat this issue WT is proposed. WT (Guillenet al., 2015; Megahedet al., 2006; Pérezet al., 2011; Prasad & Edward, 2016)gives time and frequency data all the while. WT can split signals into various frequency bands with the assistance of multi resolution analysis (MRA). It has been in operation in a variety of places and gives an additional favorable position of low time reaction which enhances systemefficiency and issue resolve. It has the capacity of performing neighborhood examination to the best level without hampering a considerable measure of the time recurrence information. It can be utilized as a part of distinguishing faults and to evaluate the phasors of the current and voltage signals, which are vital for security of transmission lines.

Neural networks are a standout amongst the most primitive and most ideal routes for fault examination and determining. These methods are under the audit of analysts for a long time. The elements of this strategy give a dynamic change ability to the system in light of the adjustments in it. The progressions that occur in the system are more often than not at fast and this proves to be useful in such a circumstance. Design acknowledgment and order are additionally solid in ANN strategies (Dalstein& Kulicke, 1995; Heet al., 2014; Seyedtabaii, 2012) as they have the ability to learn complex info yield mapping. These give a major help in the under span and overextend issues of separation transfers. They can develop the main zone of transfers and upgrade the security. To make this method more receptive to time shifting voltage and current waveforms, the learning system is sustained with shrouded units of their own past yield to enhance it and give better results. These ANN systems are exceptionally dependable in light of the fact that the operations inside these methods are clear. The precision and time reaction of ANN methodology is superior to anything the various significant strategies and when utilized with different systems it gives much better results. Keeping in mind the end goal to recognize fault zone manufactured neural system methods are known not the complexities of the assurance of transmission lines. ANN show qualities, for example, pattern association or mapping abilities, adaptation to internal failure, robustness, generalization and rapid data preparing. Neural systems can be learnt by cases. They can in this manner be prepared with known case of an issue to "gain" information about it. Once fittingly prepared, the system can be put to powerful use in explaining "untrained" or "obscure" cases of the issue.

Another of the significant strategies is the fuzzy logic approach (Das& Reddy, 2005; Ferreroet al., 1999; Mahanty & Gupta, 2007; Prasadet al., 2015; Raziet al., 2007; Samantaray, 2013; Sangiovanni& Zappitelli, 1994; Youssef, 2004a) The utilization of fuzzy logic has gotten a great deal of consideration lately as a result of its adequacy in diminishing the requirement for complex numerical models in critical thinking. Fuzzy rationale utilizes linguistic terms, which manage the easy-going relationship amongst information and yield variables. Consequently, fuzzy rationale strategy makes it less demanding to control and to tackle numerous issues, especially where the scientific model is not unequivocally known, or is hard to illuminate. Fluffy rationale gives not just a capable representation for estimation of vulnerabilities additionally a vital representation for indistinct ideas communicated in natural language. It is a scientific hypothesis, which incorporates the sign of ambiguity while depicting an importance or idea. Fuzziness is essentially one method for portraying instability. Such ideas are helpful in issue fault classification.

Fuzzy control is generally utilized with ANN methods, and gives a powerful system of security and fault location. These fuzzy control strategies are significantly utilized to solve the uncertainty in the continuously varying system parameters. The changes in the system make these system parameters shift to basic qualities for little times. The key advantage of utilizing this procedure is that the classification of the faults to be genuinely basic by the restrictive flowchart of the control system. Fuzzy logic procedure is a good tool for unverifiable information circumstances while ANN is a decent device for gaining from illustrations. This is a standout amongst the most inquired about types of hybrid systems and has brought about a marvelous amount of publications and examination comes about. Neural systems that perceive designs and adjust to adapt to evolving situations, fuzzy systems that join human information and perform approaches, together with certain subsidiary – free advancement methods, brings about another strategy called neuro – fuzzy.

3. MODERN TOOLS IN FAULT CLASSIFICATION

All the above popular methods have their own advantages and disadvantages. Apart from the above mentioned techniques, there are some other strategies which are useful for fault classification. This chapter deals with the explanation of all the modern techniques. Now a days, these modern techniques are being implemented for fault analysis in power transmission systems. The modern techniques divided into several types. These are support vector machine, genetic algorithm, DWT-ELM approach, theory and FPGA-based implementation, GSM technique, PMU-based protection scheme, decision tree based method, multi-information measurements, fast estimation of phasor components, PCA based framework, pilot scheme, functional analysis and computational intelligence, and Euclidean distance based function.

3.1 Support Vector Machine

A novel strategy for learning isolating capacities in characterization (design acknowledgment) assignments or for performing practical estimation in relapse issues is support vector machine (SVM). It is a computational learning system in light of the measurable learning hypothesis. In this the information vectors are nonlinearly mapped into a high dimensional element space. It has been effectively applied to many classification problems. Malathi and Marimuthu (2008) has presented a method for the classification of faults using multi-class support vector machine in power transmission systems. This strategy utilizes information from the wavelet deterioration of post issue streams as contribution to SVM for fault characterization.. The strength of this methodology is SVM prepared to end up streamlined classifier and with less measure of preparing tests. The Figure 1 gives the clear idea on fault classification using SVM. Wang and Zhao (2009) proposed a different approach for location of faults based on SVM in power transmission systems. This technique also used fuzzy set theory for solving uncertainty linear division relations. The error rates of SVM models low compared to multilayer perceptions (MLP) for the steady-state information. Youssef (2009) has developed a novel technique to real-time fault analysis using Support-Vector- Machines in transmission lines. Classification of faults in this approach depends on phase angles between the line currents and offline nonlinearly separable limitations between these angles generated by the SVM through training. Singh, Panigrahi, and Maheshwari (2011) has proposed a novel approach that is combination of SVM and wavelet techniques. This is used to detect and classify the types of the faults. Tripathi, Sharma, Pillai, and Gupta (2011) has implemented a technique for accurate fault classification scheme in thyristor controlled series compensator (TCSC) compensated transmission line with the help of SVM. In this approach one SVM is trained for classification of faults and its input is independent of firing angle. Thus it does not need wavelet transform, communication setup and calculation of zero-sequence-current component etc.

The advantages of SVM are successful in high dimensional spaces furthermore viable in situations where number of measurements is more prominent than the quantity of tests. SVM utilizes a subset of preparing focuses in the choice capacity (called support vectors), so it is additionally memory effective. SVM classifier is an intense classifier that functions admirably on an extensive variety of classification problems, even issues in high measurements and that are not straightly distinct. But it has certain limitations such as, on the off chance that the quantity of elements is much more prominent than the quantity of tests, the strategy is prone to give poor exhibitions. SVMs don't straightforwardly give likelihood evaluates, these are ascertained utilizing a costly five-fold cross- validation, along these lines runs moderate.

3.2 Genetic Algorithm

Genetic algorithm (GA) work with a coding of variables. The significant distinction between Genetic algorithm and conventional improvement strategies is that GA utilizes a populace of focuses at one time as opposed to the single point meth-

Figure 1. Block diagram of fault classification

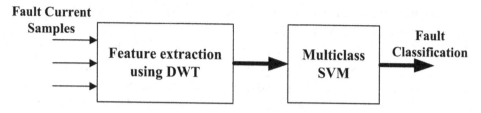

odology by conventional techniques. This implies GA forms various plans in the meantime. Song, Johns, Xuan, and Liu (1997) proposed a novel technique using genetic algorithm based neural networks (GANN) for fault classification. This paper was also made comparison between a genetic algorithm based neural network and a BP (Back Propagation) network based scheme. Upendar, Gupta, and Singh (2008) proposed a novel method for classifying different types of transmission line faults by merging wavelet transform (WT) and genetic algorithm. The proposed method contains a preprocessing unit depends on both discrete wavelet transform (DWT) and GA, in which DWT has been used to extract characteristic features from the input current signal collected at source end. The data is given as an input to GA for fault classification. The major benefits of GA is concepts are straightforward and characteristically parallel. It requires less time for some extraordinary applications and probabilities of getting optimal solution are more. But this method is restricted in mutation rate ought to be low, the choice of technique ought to be suitable and writing of fitness function must be exact.

3.3 DWT-ELM Approach

Extreme learning machine (ELM) is a straightforward and viable learning calculation of single-hidden layer feed-forward neural network (SLFNN), where the era of information weights and inclination of concealed hubs are done arbitrarily without tuning. At the same time the yield weight is discovered systematically and depends on likelihood thickness capacity which is a uniform appropriation capacity in the reach from - 1 to +1. The heart of ELM over other ordinary strategies is that tuning of concealed layer is not obliged, easy to utilize, speculation execution is vastly improved at a speedier learning speed with minimum human interference, doesn't have issues like neighborhood minima and overfitting as in slope based learning calculation, and reasonable for any nonlinear initiation capacity and part work. Distinctive sorts of initiation capacity which are utilized as a part of ELM incorporate sine, sigmoidal, spiral premise and triangular premise capacity. Other than this, the other value of ELM is that it can deal with a non-straight piecewise constant capacity which incorporates the limit capacity and makes it much prevalent than other learning calculation utilized by other specialist's as a part of the previous decade. A hybrid DWT-ELM based method (Ray, Panigrahi, & Senroy, 2012) for classification of faults in an arrangement remunerated transmission line is exhibited. Current specimens of three stages for one cycle after the beginning of shortcoming are taken from the transferring end of the transmission line. From there on the gathered examples are decayed and components are removed from it by DWT took after by standardization of the aggregate list of capabilities and ideal element choice from it by forward element choice strategy. To decide the power of the proposed strategy, reproduction condition for creating test information set is made not the same as the train one. From that point chose elements are nourished as contribution to the ELM for deficiency characterization.

This strategy utilizes daubechies (db2) as mother wavelet to disintegrate the sign and forward element determination technique to pick best component from the aggregate list of capabilities, which upgrades its precision. An examination of the proposed issue classifier is made with DWT-ANN fault classifier and it is watched that the proposed classifier gives high exactness and little learning time contrasted with the other one. To stress the significance of the proposed highlight determination strategy in the present plan, a correlation is finished with other element choice technique and it is found that proposed highlight choice strategy gives better characterization precision. In this way, it can be reasoned that consolidated DWT-ELM approach characterizes the issue quick and precisely and can be prescribed to arrange the deficiency in an arrangement remunerated transmission line. The key advantages of DWT-ELM method are, it needs less preparing time contrasted with other methods. The forecast execution of ELM is typically somewhat superior to other techniques in numerous applications. The issue of this method is in spite of the fact that author can prepare them truly quick, author pay for it by having moderate assessment. For most applications, assessment velocity is more vital than training speed.

3.4 FPGA-Based Implementation

Valsan and Swarup (2009) has presented a better hardware-efficient logic using a field-programmable gate array (FPGA) for fault analysis in transmission lines. FPGA gives a reasonable altered choice to testing the execution of new systems. Since FPGAs are reusable, on the off chance that outline issues are recognized at the testing stage, the chip can be reconstructed after changes are made in the configuration. Recent developments in FPGA technology at both hardware and software levels, as well as the rapidly reducing cost, increases the usage of FPGA in the field of power systems. The application of an FPGA is a recently emerging method in the field of power systems for fault classification. The real advantages of this method is, it can be redesigned and overhauled. It can be used for execution pick up for programming applications, hugely parallel information handling. The accessibility of this approach is more. But this method falls short on execution, restricted in size, not useful for high volume applications. In the event that utilized for prototyping, still may have huge changes when relocate to higher execution outline and bundle arrangement.

3.5 GSM Technique

Sujatha and Kumar(2011) has developed a global system for mobile communication (GSM) method, it can be effectively apply to the previous established special protection systems to increase its reliability during network interruptions. In this approach a powerful GSM is considered to send data from a network to other network, any variation in parameters of transmission is detected to protect the whole transmission and distribution. Increment sought after of power for whole applications in any nation, need to create reliably with cutting edge assurance outline. Numerous unique security schemes are accessible taking into account volume of power dispersed and frequently the heap changes without forecast required a progressed and extraordinary correspondence based schemes to control the electrical parameters of the generation. The majority of the current systems are solid on different applications however not ideal for electrical applications. Electrical environment will have bunches of aggravation in nature, due to regular fiascos like tempests, violent winds or substantial downpours transmission and circulation lines may prompt harm.

The electrical wire may cut and fall on ground, this prompts exceptionally unsafe for people and may get to be lethal. Along these lines, an unbending, solid and hearty interchanges like GSM innovation rather than numerous correspondence strategies utilized before. This upgrades pace of correspondence with separation independency. This innovation spares human life from this electrical threat by giving the shortcoming discovery and consequently stops the power to the harmed line furthermore passes on the message to the power board to clear the issue. An Embedded based equipment configuration is created and should obtain information from electrical detecting system. A capable GSM systems administration is intended to send information from a system to other system. Any adjustment in parameters of transmission is detected to ensure the whole transmission and appropriation. This GSM technique exhibits greater advantages like a message will be sent to the administrator when the deficiency happen, easy to install and less maintenance required. The proposed system gives the answer for a portion of the principle issues confronted by the current Indian grid system, for example, manual billing system, power robbery, wastage of vitality, and overhead line fault. This technique will diminish the vitality wastage and recovery a ton of vitality for future use. But this approach falls short on extensive variety of frequencies is required for large systems. On the off chance that actualized on an extensive scale it might require lot of investment and manual information.

3.6 PMU-Based Protection Scheme

A phasor measurement unit (PMU) based protection system was proposed by Jiang, Chen, Fan, Liu, and Chang (2002) and Jiang, Chen, and Liu (2003). It presented a versatile protection scheme using synchronized phasor measurements for transmission systems. This PMU method very useful of fault analysis. This scheme used synchronized phasor quantities to enterprise a multi-function protection relay to reach the entire line protection. Rahideh, Gitizadeh, and Mohammadi (2013) has presented a model for location of faults for two-terminal multi segment compound transmission lines, which was the combination of underground power cables and overhead lines. The procedure is reached out from a two-terminal fault location technique with synchronized phasor measurements as sources of info. This proposed technique has the capacity to find a deficiency regardless of where the defect is on overhead line or underground power link. The received system has a strong hypothetical establishment and is immediate and basic as far as computational many-sided quality. Both broad reenactment results and field test results are exhibited to show the adequacy of the proposed plan. This proposed strategy has as of now been actualized in the Taiwan power system since the year 2008. To date, the proposed strategy yields amazing execution in practice. Even though PMU-based protection technique gives Post disturbance investigations of power system, system protection, Wide region estimation and control, power system real-time monitoring and automation. It has certain restrictions, for example, PMU positions, communication delays, low frequency oscillation checking.

3.7 Decision Tree Based Method

The decision tree (DT) mechanism is straightforward and we can take after a tree structure effectively to clarify how a choice is made. It is maybe the most exceptionally created method for parceling test information into a gathering of choice tenets. DT for classification issues are frequently called classification trees. The authors of Jamehbozorg, and Shahrtash (2010) and Shahrtash, and Jamehbozorg (2008) has developed a DT technique. It is actualized for fault classification in power transmission system. It decides the exact fault inception time using traveling waves.. For this technique, information of one side of the ensured line is required and basic leadership has been performed in only 2msec, which is the best time among prior methodologies. Samantaray (2009) has developed another technique for defective area location and classification for thyristor controlled series compensator and unified power flow controller line utilizing decision tree. The decision tree based procedure uses one cycle data from fault inception of three phase currents along with zero-sequence voltage and current to constructs the optimal decision tree for fault analysis in transmission lines. This decision tree based method shows more noteworthy points of interest like ready to create reasonable guidelines. They give clear sign of which fields are most essential for prediction or classification. They can deal with both numerical and absolute characteristics. While weaknesses are some decision tree can just manage with binary-valued target classes. The way toward growing a decision tree is computationally costly.

3.8 Multi-Information Measurements

Fu, He, and Bo (2009) has presented a novel procedure using multi-information measurements of fault transients. Because of the unpredictability of transient parts, careful numeric examination is strange. Along these lines, taking data hypothesis into record, this work extricates transient elements through data estimations, so as to diminish the impact of system instability and increment the unwavering quality of fault examination. Data estimations principally incorporate information entropy estimations and unpredictability measurements. Data entropy estimations, which incorporate data entropy, contingent entropy, common entropy and relative entropy, quantificationally portray the entire normal instability and peculiarity of signs by measurement investigation. Unpredictability estimations, which incorporate inexact entropy, math many-sided quality and change many-sided quality, quantificationally portray the characteristic circulation and unpredictability of signs. This work utilizes the data entropy to correct entire recurrence range highlight from high-recurrence transient and utilizations the inexact entropy to separate the time-succession inside multifaceted nature from low-recurrence and non-occasional drifters. Along these lines, fault classification calculation taking into account multi-data estimations can be figured it out. This method can works under different transient components. This strategy can classify nature of faults with distinctive transient segments and simulations turned out to be helpful particularly for the condition under which the fault voltage beginning point is zero and the high-recurrence transient part is low. Along these lines, this calculation would be accessible in giving a decent way to deal with inexhaustible fault data for transient security. The major limitation of this method is it only detects fault type. It doesn't shows in which phase fault occurred.

3.9 Fast Estimation of Phasor Components

Saha et al. (2010a, 2010b) has proposed a novel method for transmission system to identify the faulty phases. The suggested algorithm is based on readings of phase currents and fast estimation of phasor components in relatively short data window. The key selection technique utilizes the relations among magnitudes of current for different possible fault loops. This method can differentiate grounded and ungrounded faults with the help of the neutral and phase currents. To learn the viability of the strategy, it was tried with ATP-EMTP reproduced information. Acquired results appear exact and stable conduct of the proposed calculation which can precisely distinguish all transmission uncompensated furthermore, arrangement repaid line deficiencies. The other favorable position of this system is that it can be utilized where numerous transmission lines are available. The key benefits of this technique is independent of the system configuration, and the system operating conditions during faults. This method is computationally efficient. On the off chance that actualized on an extensive scale it might require lot of investment and manual information.

3.10 PCA Based Framework

A critical trait of an electrical power system is the coherence of administration with an abnormal state of unwavering quality. This inspired numerous specialists to examine power system with an end goal to enhance dependability by centering on deficiency recognition. A novel fault classification method (Alsafasfeh, Abdel-Qader, &Harb, 2010) has been proposed. This work is based on phase currents during the first (¼) th of a cycle in an combined technique that gives better results using symmetrical components method and principal component analysis (PCA). The advantage of this algorithm is used at any end of a transmission line, so data communication devices are not necessary. The Figure 2 shows the clear procedure how fault signatures generated using the symmetrical patterns. The real advantages of PCA are, it can diminishes the amount of excess data by decorrelating the information vectors. The input vectors, with high measurement and connected, can be spoken to in a lower measurement space and decorrelated. PCA is a capable device to pack information. Turns multivariate dataset into another setup which is less demanding to decipher. Purposes disentangle information take a look at connections between variables take a look at examples of units. But this method depends only on the mean vector and the covariance matrix of the information.

Figure 2. Generating fault signatures using the symmetrical patterns

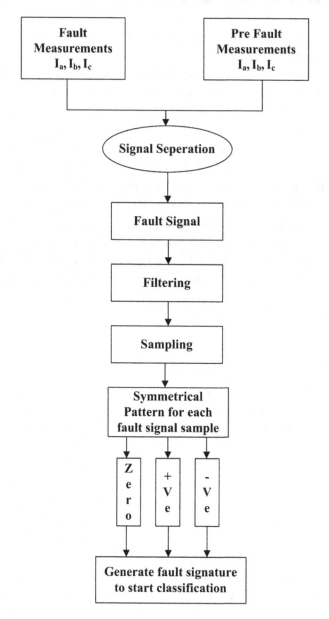

3.11 Pilot Scheme

Mahamedi (2011) has presented a novel fault classification technique utilizing reactive power under normal and fault conditions. A pilot method needs to relate the sign of reactive power measured by one relay to other relay. The key benefit of this technique is that it does not need any setting. The relay is not needed to set a threshold for any parameter. Thus, this technique can also called as setting free. This technique is independent on inception time and location of fault. Hence, all type of faults are characterized and the defective locations are identified. There are a few points of interest to the proposed technique over other existing strategies. The most vital one is that it doesn't have to set any parameter and it works just with the indication of reactive power. This is a restrictive highlight the proposed strategy presents. The prerequisite to actualize the strategy is to utilize a pilot plan. Since pilot plans are basic in today utilization of power system assurance, this is not of concern. There are a few points of interest to the pilot scheme over other existing strategies. The most imperative one is that it doesn't have to set any parameter and it works just with the indication of reactive power. This is a restrictive component the proposed technique presents. Another preferred standpoint of the strategy is that it doesn't rely on upon fault inception time and fault location. The restriction of this approach is, if implementing in real time due to high investment cost and it requires more time.

3.12 Functional Analysis and Computational Intelligence

De Souza Gomes, Costa, De Faria, and Caminhas (2013) proposed a method to discovery and characterization system are created from the examination of the model parameters and are assessed utilizing an arrangement of reenacted deficiencies and a genuine database. The introduced scientific model incorporates stochastic segments which represent current and voltage stochastic deviations under typical working conditions. The evaluations of the coefficients of the post fault are accomplished, immediately, by method for a straight condition arrangement. Another significant favorable position of the proposed strategy comprises in its capacity to produce deficiency grouping space with low many-sided quality. Subsequently, high order rates can be accomplished with low many-sided quality models. So it gives novel stochastic representation of the transmission lines, which empowers quicker location of faults. The Figure 3 explains monitoring procedure of phases. This scheme shows greater advantages like give an approach to analyzing waveforms limited in both

Figure 3. Flowchart for monitoring the phases of a transmission line

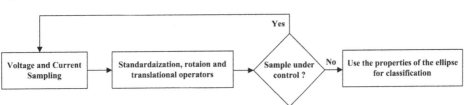

frequency and time length, permit signals to be put away more effectively than by fourier transform, have the capacity to better rough certifiable signals, appropriate for approximating information with sharp discontinuities. While it shortcomings are because of the excess, and the amount of accessible wavelets (not the same is best for various purposes), they could show up somewhat less productive for the examination of unadulterated stationary and sounds signals, for which fourier is more qualified.

3.13 Euclidean Distance Based Function

A Euclidean Distance based methodology is proposed (Prasad & Prasad, 2014) for the discovery of faults in overhead lines. The relative execution of the calculation is considered with signs containing noise, spike, recurrence deviation, load change, and blames at various circumstances of the power system. The strategy is observed to be a superior instrument to be utilized with relays and the same technique is stretched out to distinguish defective stage choice. It can be striven for different applications such as fault classification, area and in power quality unsettling influence discovery. The major benefits of this method is representation of capacities that have discontinuities and sharp pinnacles. Precisely deconstructing and reproducing limited, non-intermittent and/or non-stationary signals. Permit signals to be put away more proficiently. The primary downsides are for fine examination, it turns out to be computationally concentrated, and its discretization is less productive. It take some vitality to put resources into wavelets to end up ready to pick the best possible ones for a particular reason, and to actualize it correctly.

4. COMPARISONS

The following Table 1 gives the clear idea about the review on fault classification approaches in transmission lines based on techniques, simulation tools, advantages and limitations/drawbacks.

5. CONCLUSION

This work has included many recent fault classification techniques along with their key features. All these techniques have their own features and researches are still going on to obtain lesser operating time of relay at high speed. So there is a necessity for developing new algorithms using advanced optimization techniques and flexible

Table 1. Comparison of fault classification approaches

Name of the approach	Techniques used	Simulation tools used	Advantages	Limitations
Support Vector Machine	SVM Classifier, Wavelet	MATLAB SVM Toolbox, EMTP	Produce very accurate classifiers, robust to noise.	Computationally expensive.
Genetic Algorithm	GA, NN	EMTP, MATLAB	Easy to understand, less time required.	Mutation rate should be low.
DWT-ELM Approach	DWT, ELM	MATLAB/ SIMULINK	Prediction performance is more	Local minima issue, easy overfitting.
Theory and FPGA-Based Implementation	Field-programmable gate array (FPGA)	Real Time Windows Target Toolbox of MATLAB	Performance gain for software applications, fast and efficient.	Limited size options.
GSM Technique	Global System For Mobile Communication (GSM)	Embedded based hardware design	Easy to install and less maintenance required	Implementing time is more.
PMU-based protection scheme	Phasor measurement unit	EMTP/ATP	Real-time monitoring.	Communication delays.
Decision Tree Based Method	Discrete Fourier Transform	EMTDC/PSCAD	Can deal with both numerical and absolute characteristics	Computationally expensive.
Multi-information Measurements	Multi-information measurements	MATLAB	Depends on data entropy estimations.	Implementation time is more.
Fast estimation of phasor components	Zero-component current phasors	ATP-EMTP	Independent of the system configuration	Require lot of investment and manual information.
PCA Based Framework	Principal component analysis	PSCAD	Diminishes the amount of excess data.	Depends on the mean vector and the covariance matrix of the data
Pilot Scheme	Pilot Scheme	MATLAB	Independent on inception time and location of fault.	High cost and requires more time to installation.
Functional Analysis and Computational Intelligence	Wavelet Transform	MATLAB	Analyzing waveforms limited in both frequency and time duration.	Somewhat less productive.
Euclidean Distance Based Function	DWT	MATLAB/ SIMULINK	Be able to better approximate real-world signals.	Computationally intensive.

alternating current transmission systems (FACTS) devices that have higher computational effectiveness and suitability for real time applications. This review will be useful for power system planners and designers of transmission system protection.

REFERENCES

Acharjya, D. P. (2014). Rough set on two universal sets and knowledge representation. In B. Issac & N. Israr (Eds.), *Case Studies in Intelligent Computing* (pp. 79–108). CRC Press. doi:10.1201/b17333-6

Acharjya, D. P., & Ezhilarasi, L. (2011). A knowledge mining model for ranking institutions using rough computing with ordering rules and formal concept analysis. *International Journal of Computer Science Issues*, *8*(2), 417–425.

Acharjya, D. P., Roy, D., & Rahaman, M. A. (2012). Prediction of missing associations using rough computing and Bayesian classification. *International Journal of Intelligent Systems and Applications*, *4*(11), 1–13. doi:10.5815/ijisa.2012.11.01

Ahmed, N. S. S., & Acharjya, D. P. (2015). Detection of denial of service attack in wireless network using dominance based rough set. *International Journal of Advanced Computer Science and Applications*, *6*(12), 267–278.

Alsafasfeh, Q., Abdel-Qader, I., & Harb, A. (2010). Symmetrical pattern and PCA based framework for fault detection and classification in power systems. In *Proceedings of International Conference on Electro / Information Technology (EIT)* (pp. 1-5). doi:10.1109/EIT.2010.5612179

Anitha, A., & Acharjya, D. P. (2015). Neural network and rough set hybrid scheme for prediction of missing associations. *International Journal of Bioinformatics Research and Applications*, *11*(6), 503–524. doi:10.1504/IJBRA.2015.073237 PMID:26642360

Dalstein, T., & Kulicke, B. (1995). Neural network approach to fault classification for high speed protective relaying. *IEEE Transactions on Power Delivery*, *10*(2), 1002–1011. doi:10.1109/61.400828

Das, B., & Reddy, J. V. (2005). Fuzzy-logic-based fault classification scheme for digital distance protection. *IEEE Transactions on Power Delivery*, *20*(2), 609–616. doi:10.1109/TPWRD.2004.834294

Das, T. K., & Acharjya, D. P. (2014). A decision making model using soft set and rough set on fuzzy approximation spaces. *International Journal of Intelligent Systems Technologies and Applications*, *13*(3), 170–186. doi:10.1504/IJISTA.2014.065172

Dash, P. K., Pradhan, A. K., & Panda, G. (2000). A novel fuzzy neural network based distance relaying scheme. *IEEE Transactions on Power Delivery*, *15*(3), 902–907. doi:10.1109/61.871350

De Souza Gomes, A., Costa, M. A., de Faria, T. G. A., & Caminhas, W. M. (2013). Detection and classification of faults in power transmission lines using functional analysis and computational intelligence. *IEEE Transactions on Power Delivery*, *28*(3), 1402–1413. doi:10.1109/TPWRD.2013.2251752

Ferrero, A., Sangiovanni, S., & Zappitelli, E. (1994, April). A fuzzy-set approach to fault-type identification in digital relaying. In *Proceedings of Transmission and Distribution Conference, IEEE Power Engineering Society* (pp. 269-275). IEEE. doi:10.1109/TDC.1994.328391

Fu, L., He, Z., & Bo, Z. (2009, March). Novel approach to fault classification in EHV transmission line based on multi-information measurements of fault transients. In *Proceedings ofAsia-Pacific Power and Energy Engineering Conference* (pp. 1-4). doi:10.1109/APPEEC.2009.4918524

Girgis, A. A., & Johns, M. B. (1989). A hybrid expert system for faulted section identification, fault type classification and selection of fault location algorithms. *IEEE Transactions on Power Delivery*, *4*(2), 978–985. doi:10.1109/61.25578

Guillen, D., Paternina, M. R. A., Zamora, A., Ramirez, J. M., & Idarraga, G. (2015). Detection and classification of faults in transmission lines using the maximum wavelet singular value and Euclidean norm. *IET Generation. Transmission & Distribution*, *9*(15), 2294–2302. doi:10.1049/iet-gtd.2014.1064

He, Z., Lin, S., Deng, Y., Li, X., & Qian, Q. (2014). A rough membership neural network approach for fault classification in transmission lines. *International Journal ofElectrical Power & Energy Systems*, *61*, 429–439. doi:10.1016/j.ijepes.2014.03.027

Jamehbozorg, A., & Shahrtash, S. M. (2010). A decision tree-based method for fault classification in double-circuit transmission lines. *IEEE Transactions on Power Delivery*, *25*(4), 2184–2189. doi:10.1109/TPWRD.2010.2050911

Jiang, J. A., Chen, C. S., Fan, P. L., Liu, C. W., & Chang, R. S. (2002). A composite index to adaptively perform fault detection, classification, and direction discrimination for transmission lines. In *Proceedings of Power Engineering Society Winter Meeting, IEEE* (Vol. 2, pp. 912-917). IEEE.

Jiang, J. A., Chen, C. S., & Liu, C. W. (2003). A new protection scheme for fault detection, direction discrimination, classification, and location in transmission lines. *IEEE Transactions on Power Delivery*, *18*(1), 34–42. doi:10.1109/TPWRD.2002.803726

Jung, C. K., Kim, K. H., Lee, J. B., & Klöckl, B. (2007). Wavelet and neuro-fuzzy based fault location for combined transmission systems. *International Journal of Electrical Power & Energy Systems*, *29*(6), 445–454. doi:10.1016/j.ijepes.2006.11.003

Kumar, P., Jamil, M., & Thomas, M. S. (1999, December). Fuzzy approach to fault classification for transmission line protection. In *Proceedings of the IEEE Region 10 Conference* (Vol. 2, pp. 1046-1050). IEEE. doi:10.1109/TENCON.1999.818602

Mahamedi, B. (2011, November). A novel setting-free method for fault classification and faulty phase selection by using a pilot scheme. In *Proceedings of 2nd International Conference on Electric Power and Energy Conversion Systems (EPECS)* (pp. 1-6). IEEE. doi:10.1109/EPECS.2011.6126835

Mahanty, R. N., & Gupta, P. D. (2007). A fuzzy logic based fault classification approach using current samples only. *Electric Power Systems Research*, *77*(5), 501–507. doi:10.1016/j.epsr.2006.04.009

Malathi, V., & Marimuthu, N. S. (2008, November). Multi-class support vector machine approach for fault classification in power transmission line. In *Proceedings of IEEE International Conference on Sustainable Energy Technologies* (pp. 67-71). IEEE. doi:10.1109/ICSET.2008.4746974

Megahed, A. I., Moussa, A. M., & Bayoumy, A. E. (2006). Usage of wavelet transform in the protection of series-compensated transmission lines. *IEEE Transactions on Power Delivery*, *21*(3), 1213–1221. doi:10.1109/TPWRD.2006.876981

Moravej, Z., Pazoki, M., & Khederzadeh, M. (2015). New pattern-recognition method for fault analysis in transmission line with UPFC. *IEEE Transactions on Power Delivery*, *30*(3), 1231–1242. doi:10.1109/TPWRD.2014.2365674

Pan, S., Morris, T., & Adhikari, U. (2015). Classification of disturbances and cyber-attacks in power systems using heterogeneous time-synchronized data. *IEEE Transactions on Industrial Informatics*, *11*(3), 650–662. doi:10.1109/TII.2015.2420951

Pérez, F. E., Orduna, E., & Guidi, G. (2011). Adaptive wavelets applied to fault classification on transmission lines. *IET generation, transmission & distribution*, *5*(7), 694-702.

Prasad, A., & Edward, J. B. (2016). Application of wavelet technique for fault classification in transmission systems. *Procedia Computer Science*, *92*, 78–83. doi:10.1016/j.procs.2016.07.326

Prasad, A., Edward, J. B., Roy, C. S., Divyansh, G., & Kumar, A. (2015). Classification of faults in power transmission lines using fuzzy-logic technique. *Indian Journal of Science and Technology, 8*(30), 1–6. doi:10.17485/ijst/2015/v8i1/77065

Prasad, C. D., & Prasad, D. J. V. (2014, January). Fault detection and phase selection using Euclidean distance based function for transmission line protection. In *Proceedings of International Conference on Advances in Electrical Engineering* (pp. 1-4). IEEE. doi:10.1109/ICAEE.2014.6838516

Rahideh, A., Gitizadeh, M., & Mohammadi, S. (2013). A fault location technique for transmission lines using phasor measurements. *International Journal of Engineering and Advanced Technology, 3*(1), 241–248.

Ray, P., Panigrahi, B. K., & Senroy, N. (2012, December). Extreme learning machine based fault classification in a series compensated transmission line. In *Proceedings of IEEE International Conference on Power Electronics, Drives and Energy Systems* (pp. 1-6). IEEE. doi:10.1109/PEDES.2012.6484297

Razi, K., Hagh, M. T., & Ahrabian, G. (2007, December). High accurate fault classification of power transmission lines using fuzzy logic. In *Proceedings of International Power Engineering Conference* (pp. 42-46). IEEE.

Reddy, M. J., & Mohanta, D. K. (2007). A wavelet-fuzzy combined approach for classification and location of transmission line faults. *International Journal of Electrical Power & Energy Systems, 29*(9), 669–678. doi:10.1016/j.ijepes.2007.05.001

Ruiz, H. S., Zhang, X., & Coombs, T. A. (2015). Resistive-type superconducting fault current limiters: Concepts, materials, and numerical modeling. *IEEE Transactions on Applied Superconductivity, 25*(3), 1–5. doi:10.1109/TASC.2014.2387115

Saha, M. M., Rosolowski, E., Izykowski, J., Pierz, P., Balcerek, P., & Fulczyk, M. (2010a, March). An efficient method for faulty phase selection in transmission lines. In *Proceedings of 10th IET International Conference on Developments in Power System Protection. Managing the Change,* (pp. 1-5). IET. doi:10.1049/cp.2010.0320

Saha, M. M., Rosolowski, E., Izykowski, J., Pierz, P., Balcerek, P., & Fulczyk, M. (2010b). A novel fault classification technique for high speed protective relaying of transmission lines. In *Proceedings of the Modern Electric Power Systems (MEPS), International Symposium* (pp. 1-6). IEEE.

Samantaray, S. R. (2009). Decision tree-based fault zone identification and fault classification in flexible AC transmissions-based transmission line. *IET generation, transmission & distribution, 3*(5), 425-436.

Samantaray, S. R. (2013). A systematic fuzzy rule based approach for fault classification in transmission lines. *Applied Soft Computing, 13*(2), 928–938. doi:10.1016/j.asoc.2012.09.010

Seyedtabaii, S. (2012). Improvement in the performance of neural network-based power transmission line fault classifiers. *IET generation, transmission & distribution, 6*(8), 731-737.

Shahrtash, S. M., & Jamehbozorg, A. (2008, April). A decision tree based method for fault classification in transmission lines. In *Proceedings of IEEE/PES Transmission and Distribution Conference and Exposition* (pp. 1-5). IEEE. doi:10.1109/TDC.2008.4517258

Silva, K. M., Souza, B. A., & Brito, N. S. D. (2006). Fault detection and classification in transmission lines based on wavelet transform and ANN. *IEEE Transactions on Power Delivery, 21*(4), 2058–2063. doi:10.1109/TPWRD.2006.876659

Singh, M., Panigrahi, B. K., & Maheshwari, R. P. (2011, March). Transmission line fault detection and classification. In *Proceedings of International Conference on Emerging Trends in Electrical and Computer Technology*(pp. 15-22). IEEE. doi:10.1109/ICETECT.2011.5760084

Song, Y. H., Johns, A. T., Xuan, Q. Y., & Liu, J. Y. (1997, March). Genetic algorithm based neural networks applied to fault classification for EHV transmission lines with a UPFC. In *Proceedings of Sixth International Conference on Developments in Power System Protection* (pp. 278-281). IET. doi:10.1049/cp:19970081

Sujatha, M., & Kumar, M. V. (2011). On-line monitoring and analysis of faults in transmission and distribution lines using GSM. *Journal of Theoretical and Applied Information Technology, 33*(2), 258–265.

Tripathi, P., Sharma, A., Pillai, G. N., & Gupta, I. (2011). Accurate fault classification and section identification scheme in TCSC compensated transmission line using SVM. *World Academy of Science. Engineering and Technology, 60*, 1599–1605.

Tripathy, B. K., & Acharjya, D. P. (2010). Knowledge mining using ordering rules and rough sets on fuzzy approximation spaces. *International Journal of Advances in Science and Technology, 1*(3), 41–50.

Tripathy, B. K., & Acharjya, D. P. (2013). Approximation of classification and measures of uncertainty in rough set on two universal sets. *International Journal of Advanced Science and Technology, 40*, 77–90.

Upendar, J., Gupta, C. P., & Singh, G. K. (2008, December). Discrete wavelet transform and genetic algorithm based fault classification of transmission systems. *Proceedings ofNational Power Systems Conference*, 323-328.

Valsan, S. P., & Swarup, K. S. (2009). High-speed fault classification in power lines: Theory and FPGA-based implementation. *IEEE Transactions on Industrial Electronics*, *56*(5), 1793–1800. doi:10.1109/TIE.2008.2011055

Vasilic, S., & Kezunovic, M. (2005). Fuzzy ART neural network algorithm for classifying the power system faults. *IEEE Transactions on Power Delivery*, *20*(2), 1306–1314. doi:10.1109/TPWRD.2004.834676

Wang, H., & Keerthipala, W. W. L. (1998). Fuzzy-neuro approach to fault classification for transmission line protection. *IEEE Transactions on Power Delivery*, *13*(4), 1093–1104. doi:10.1109/61.714467

Wang, Z., & Zhao, P. (2009, August). Fault location recognition in transmission lines based on support vector machines. In *Proceedings of 2nd IEEE International Conference on Computer Science and Information Technology* (pp. 401-404). IEEE.

Youssef, O. A. (2004a). A novel fuzzy-logic-based phase selection technique for power system relaying. *Electric Power Systems Research*, *68*(3), 175–184. doi:10.1016/j.epsr.2003.06.006

Youssef, O. A. (2004b). Combined fuzzy-logic wavelet-based fault classification technique for power system relaying. *IEEE Transactions on Power Delivery*, *19*(2), 582–589. doi:10.1109/TPWRD.2004.826386

Youssef, O. A. (2009, March). An optimised fault classification technique based on Support-Vector-Machines. In *Proceedings of Power Systems Conference and Exposition, IEEE/PES* (pp. 1-8). doi:10.1109/PSCE.2009.4839949

Chapter 8
Generating Efficient Techniques for Information Extraction and Processing Using Cellular Automata

Subrata Paul
Vignan Institute of Technology and Management, India

Anirban Mitra
Vignan Institute of Technology and Management, India

ABSTRACT

The evolution of Cellular automaton has proved to be very efficient in carrying out arbitrary information processing. A significant application lies in the theory and practice of finding a technique for unifying the information processing. But, in this case the structures used in conventional computer languages are largely inappropriate. The definite organization of computer memory into named areas, stacks, and so on, is not suitable for cellular automata in which processing elements are not distinguished from memory elements. Rather it can be assumed that the data could be represented by an object like a graph, on which transformations can be performed in parallel. This chapter initiate with basic literature on cellular automata, related definitions and notations and focuses on its applications in information processing.

DOI: 10.4018/978-1-5225-2375-8.ch008

Copyright ©2017, IGI Global. Copying or distributing in print or electronic forms without written permission of IGI Global is prohibited.

1. INTRODUCTION

Automata theory is an exciting, theoretical branch of computer science. It established its roots during the 20th Century, as mathematicians began developing - both theoretically and literally - machines which imitated certain features of man, completing calculations more quickly and reliably. The word automaton itself, closely related to the word "automation", denotes automatic processes carrying out the production of specific processes. Simply stated, it deals with the logic of computation with respect to simple machines, referred to as automata. Through automata, computer scientists are able to understand how machines compute functions and solve problems and more importantly, what it means for a function to be defined as computable or for a question to be described as decidable (Yan, 1998).

The major objective of automata theory is to develop methods by which computer scientists can describe and analyse the dynamic behaviour of discrete systems, in which signals are sampled periodically. The behaviour of these discrete systems is determined by the way that the system is constructed from storage and combinational elements (Chakraborty, Saxena & Katti, 2011). Characteristics of such machines include inputs, outputs and states. Inputs are assumed to be sequences of symbols selected from a finite set I of input signals. Namely, set I is the set $\{x_1, x_2, x_3, \cdots, x_k\}$ where k is the number of inputs. Outputs are sequences of symbols selected from a finite set Z. Namely; set Z is the set $\{y_1, y_2, y_3, \cdots, y_m\}$ where m the number of outputs is. States are denoted as Q, whose definition depends on the type of automaton.

There are four major families of automaton. These are finite state machine, pushdown automata, linear bounded automata, and Turing machine. The families of automata can be interpreted in a hierarchal form, where the finite state machine is the simplest automata and the Turing machine is the most complex. A Turing machine is a finite state machine yet the inverse is not true (Amadek & Trnkova, 1990). The following Figure 1 depicts the families of automaton.

2. FINITE AUTOMATA

A finite automaton is the mathematical model of some machine whose state may change in time, the set of possible states being finite. Its behaviour is the succession of its states throughout time. Its characteristically features are the set of states, Q, and the rules for their changes. The number of states being finite, there is no question of a continuous course, so the time-scale will be N. Changes are ruled by the function δ mapping state of automaton at time t, denoted (a, t), on state at time $(t + 1)$

Figure 1. Families of Automata

Automata theory

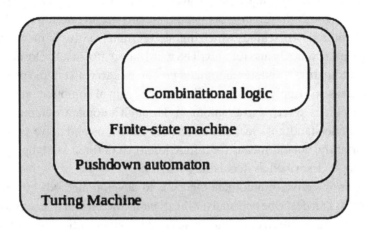

$$(a, t+1) = \delta(a, t)$$

The behaviour of the automaton is studied from an initial state a, it is the sequence:

$$a, \delta(a, 1), \delta(a, 2), \delta(a, 3), \cdots, \delta(a, n)$$

As just described, isolated and independent from any outer surrounding, automaton presents very little interest; indeed, if k is the number of states in Q, two out of the $(k+1)$ states from time 0 to time k must be the same (Lane, 1971).

$$\exists \, i, j \text{ such that } (a, i) = (a, j) \text{ for } 0 \leq i < j \leq k$$

Providing an input and an output to automaton, where input alphabets are the set of possible inputs (denoted by X). The state of the automaton a at certain time will depend not only on its previous state but also on its present input at the preceding time which can be expressed as,

$$<(a, t+1)> = \delta(<a, t>, x(t))$$

where $x(t)$ denotes input at time t. The set of possible outputs will be called the output alphabet, noted Y, the output at a certain time depending only on the state:

Figure 2. DFA of even number of 0's

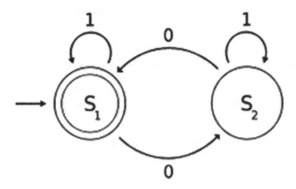

$y(t) = \sigma(< a, t >)$, σ being the output function

Figure 2 is a visualization of an automaton that recognizes strings containing an even number of 0s. The automaton starts in the state s_1 and transitions to the non-accepting state s_2 upon reading the symbol 0. Reading another 0 causes the automaton to transition back to the accepting the state s_1. In both states the symbol 1 is ignored by making a transition to the current state. It means that the input alphabet is 1 and 0 whereas output is either accepted or rejected. This is known as the classical theory of finite automata (Vivien, 2003).

3 CELLULAR AUTOMATA AND ITS EVOLUTION

The origins of cellular automata can be traced back to mathematician John von Neumann's (Neumann, 1958; Neumann, 1966)attempt to create a self replicating machine. He then proceeds to outline the following argument to show that this is entirely feasible in principle. One starts with a machine, A that has the ability to construct any other machine once it is furnished with a set of instructions denoted by I. Machine A is envisaged to float in the reservoir of liquid with all the necessary component parts that it requires for any particular construction. Now attach to machine A with another component called B, which can make a copy of any instruction that is supplied to it. A final component, labelled C, Von Neumann called the "control mechanism" which has the functions of initiating A to construct a machine as described by the instructions I, and then cause B to make a copy of the instructions I and supply the copy of the instructions to the machine newly formed by A. Then the entire apparatus can be denoted by $M = A + B + C$.

A simpler 8-state self-replicating cellular automaton was created by (Codd, 1968) with some computer assistance. Then in 1984, Christopher Langton demonstrated self-reproduction in an 86 cell looped pathway using 8 states with a 5-cell neighborhood, which simply reproduced itself. Langton's loop has a construction arm attached to it and consists of an outer sheath of cells that remain in a fixed state and an inner sequence of 'DNA' cells in various states that circulate around the loop which has been viewed in Figure 3 where different colors represent the different cell states. At the junction of the loop and arm, the 'DNA' cells are replicated: one copy goes back around the loop and the other copy travels down the construction arm where it is translated at the tip of the arm spawning new growth.

Once a side of the offspring loop is fully generated, the growth pattern makes a left turn and propagates another side and so on until the offspring loop is complete. Then the connection between parent and offspring is severed and both parent and offspring propagate separate construction arms to begin the process anew which has been viewed in Figure 4 where parent and offspring loops each propagating new constructions.

Construction continues in this fashion with each new loop generating at least one new offspring. When a loop tries to extend an arm into a region already occupied, it will retract the arm and the 'DNA' of that loop is erased and the loop becomes inert. The Langton loops will continue this replication process indefinitely expanding outward with time and filling the plane. Although each loop

Figure 3. The Langton looped pathway in its initial configuration

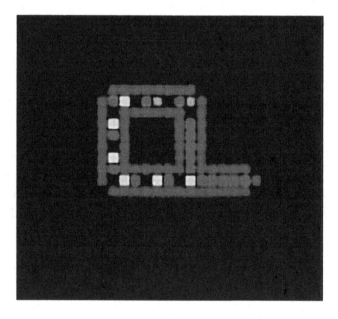

Figure 4. The parent and offspring loops each propagating new construction

contains the same 'DNA' sequence, the number of times it can replicate itself will depend on the space available in its immediate environment. A somewhat simpler self-replicating loop that dispenses with the outer sheath but also having 8 states was constructed. Another approach was taken by Morita and Imai (Morita & Imai, 1996) who devised cellular configurations that were able to reproduce by self-inspection rather than from any stored self-description. Recently, Hod Lipson (Lipson, 2005) and colleagues at Cornell University have created a self-replicating robot consisting of a tower of cubes that can swivel around and pick up other cubes and stack them to create another tower identical to itself. According to Lipson, this opens up the possibility of using robotic systems in future space travel that can repair themselves (Wolfram, 1983).

A cellular automaton consists of a regular grid of cells, each in one of a finite number of states, such as on and off (in contrast to a coupled map lattice). The grid can be in any finite number of dimensions. For each cell, a set of cells called its neighborhood is defined relative to the specified cell. An initial state (time t = 0) is selected by assigning a state for each cell. A new generation is created (advancing t by 1), according to some fixed rule (generally, a mathematical function) that determines the new state of each cell in terms of the current state of the cell and the states of the cells in its neighborhood. Typically, the rule for updating the state of cells is the same for each cell and does not change over time, and is applied to the whole grid simultaneously.

One way to simulate a two-dimensional cellular automaton is with an infinite sheet of graph paper along with a set of rules for the cells to follow. Each square is called a "cell" and each cell has two possible states, black and white. The neighborhood of a cell is the nearby, usually adjacent, cells. The two most common types of neighborhoods are the von Neumann neighborhood and the Moore neighborhood. The former, named after the founding cellular automaton theorist, consists of the four orthogonally adjacent cells. The latter includes the von Neumann neighborhood as well as the four remaining cells surrounding the cell whose state is to be calculated. For such a cell and its Moore neighbourhood as seen in Figure 5, there are $512 (= 29)$ possible patterns. For each of the 512 possible patterns, the rule table would state whether the center cell will be black or white on the next time interval. Conway's Game of Life is a popular version of this model. Another common neighborhood type is the extended von Neumann neighborhood, as seen in Figure 6, which includes the two closest cells in each orthogonal direction, for a total of eight. (Amadek & Trnkova, 1990)

The general equation for such a system of rules is kks, where k is the number of possible states for a cell, and s is the number of neighboring cells (including the cell to be calculated itself) used to determine the cell's next state.(Wolfram, 1983).

It is usually assumed that every cell in the universe starts in the same state, except for a finite number of cells in other states; the assignment of state values is called a configuration. (Schiff, 2008) More generally, it is sometimes assumed that the universe starts out covered with a periodic pattern, and only a finite number of cells violate that pattern. The latter assumption is common in one-dimensional cellular automata.

Figure 5. The red cells are the Moore neighborhood for the blue cell

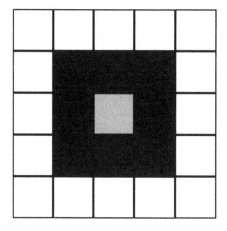

Figure 6. The red cells are the von Neumann neighborhood for the blue cell, the extended neighborhood includes the pink cells as well

Cellular automata are often simulated on a finite grid rather than an infinite one. In two dimensions, the universe would be a rectangle instead of an infinite plane. The obvious problem with finite grids is how to handle the cells on the edges. One possible method is to allow the values in those cells to remain constant. Another method is to define neighborhoods differently for these cells. One could say that they have fewer neighbors, but then one would also have to define new rules for the cells located on the edges. These cells are usually handled with a toroidal arrangement: when one goes off the top, one comes in at the corresponding position on the bottom, and when one goes off the left, one comes in on the right. This can be visualized as taping the left and right edges of the rectangle to form a tube, then taping the top and bottom edges of the tube to form a torus (doughnut shape). (Schiff, 2008), (Wolfram 1983).

The term cellular automaton is plural. A cellular automaton is a model of a system of "cell" objects with the following characteristics.

- The cells live on a grid.
- Each cell has a state. The number of state possibilities is typically finite. The simplest example has the two possibilities of 1 and 0.
- Each cell has a neighborhood. This can be defined in any number of ways, but it is typically a list of adjacent cells.

4. CLASSIFICATION OF CELLULAR AUTOMATA

A major problem stemming from Wolfram's work (Wolfram, 1963) is classifying cellular automata rules according to their behaviour. His classification is based on entropy measures and identifies the following four classes.

1. Evolution leads to a homogeneous state.
2. Evolution leads to a set of separated simple stable or periodic structures.
3. Evolution leads to a chaotic pattern.
4. Evolution leads to complex localized structures which are sometimes long-lived. It is believed that this class is capable of universal computation.

Later work concentrated on formalizing the intuitive classifications by Wolfram (Wolfram, 1983 & 1984) and Culik II and Yu (Culik II and Yu, 1988) who proposed the following classification.
Let r be the local rule for a cellular automata, then

1. Rule r is in class one iff every finite configuration, i.e. configurations in which only a finite number of cells are in no quiescent states, evolves to a stable configuration in finitely many steps.
2. Rule r is in class two iff every finite configuration evolves to a periodic configuration in finite number of steps.
3. Rule r is in class three iff it is decidable whether a configuration occurs in the orbit of another.
4. Class four comprises all local rules (Wolfram, 1984), (Culik & Yu,1988).

A classification of periodic boundary condition based on cellular automata (whose configurations can be thought of as spatially periodic configurations of an infinite cellular automata) have also been proposed (Sutner 1990). Using a nonstandard simulation of a truing machine a cellular automata, it is shown that the problem of deciding membership in the hierarchy is undecidable (Sutner, 1989 and 1990).
In a recent study, Braga et al. (Braga et al. 1995) provided a classification of cellular automata based on pattern growth. Hence forth, the author represents Cellular automata as CA in some places in this chapter for simplicity. The pattern growth properties are shown to be dependent on the truth table of the local rule of the corresponding CA. This provides an algorithm for classifying CA rules, and hence defines an effective hierarchy of CA rules, in sharp contrast to the undecidability results discussed. (Culik & Yu,1988), (Braga, Cattaneo, Flocchini, & Vogliotti, 1995).
A preliminary study of 2-d CA (Packard & Wolfram, 1985) shows that it is possible to classify 2-d CA along the same lines as 1-d CA. This suggests that the

global behaviour of 2-d CA is similar to 1-d CA. However, 1-d and 2-d CA show marked differences with respect to other properties. Golze has shown that for 1-d CA every recursive configuration (a configuration where each cell value can be calculated effectively) has a recursive predecessor; but in the 2-d case, even a finite configuration may fail to have a recursive predecessor. (Packard, 1985; Golze, 1976).

5. MAJOR REQUIREMENTS TO BE FULFILLED BY CELLULAR AUTOMATA

In the past decade a lot of cellular automata environments have been implemented on current computing machines (Toffoli & Margolus, 1987). There are two main alternatives that allow achieving needed performance in the implementation of cellular automata. The first one consists in the design of special hardware devoted to the execution of cellular automata. The second alternative is based on the use of the commercially-available parallel computers for developing parallel cellular automata applications and environments.

Cellular automata modelling software and hardware systems belong to the class of problem solving environments. The community has formulated the following common recommendations for a general problem solving environment:

1. It should reduce the difficulty of the simulation.
2. It should reduce costs and time of complex solutions development.
3. It should allow performing experiments reliably.
4. It should have a long lifetime without getting obsolete.
5. It should support the plug-and-play paradigm.
6. It should exploit the paradigm of the multilevel abstractions and complex properties of science (Houstis, Gallopoulos, Bramley & Rice, 1997).
7. User should be able to use the environment without any specialized knowledge of the underlying computer hardware or software.
8. It should be addressed to the wide scope of problems.
9. It should be able to coordinate large computational power (Gallopoulos, Houstis & Rice, 1994).
10. It should be complete, containing and providing all facilities, which might be required for solving a problem in a target domain (Abrams, Allison, Kafura, Ribbens, Rosson, Shaffer & Watson, 1998).
11. Extensibility of the environment will provide an ability to enlarge the target problem domain and to enrich the set of supported functions. This can be achieved with the help of a component-based design. A component approach also complies with the modern trend in distributed problem-solving facili-

ties design, which is based on web- and grid services (Houstis, Gallopoulos, Bramley & Rice, 1997) or Common Object Request Broker Architecture (CORBA) objects (Walker, Li, Rana, Shields & Huang, 2000)

Basing on common considerations, the software or hardware modelling facility, which allows performing experiments using cellular automata, should have the following set of features:

1. It should hide the complexity of a computational architecture, operating system, networking mechanism and other technical aspects, which are far from a research domain.
2. It should allow to setup and tune a cellular automaton for the computational experiment, granting the researcher as much freedom as it is possible.
3. It should provide tools to run and control a computational experiment.
4. It should support visualization of the grid's state and other experimental data.
5. It should provide a set of tools to analyse grid's state or any computational experiment's characteristics, which is possible to obtain.
6. It should provide reproducibility and allow sharing experiments description between researchers (Walker, Li, Rana, Shields & Huang, 2000), (Toffoli & Margolus, 1987).

6. AN APPLICATION OF CELLULAR AOTOMATA IN INFORMTION FLOW

It is assumed for the case of an educational institution where 4 levels of entities are described as Director in the first, HOD's in the second, and faculties in the third and students in the last level. Let's assume the case where a particular instruction such as the deadline of project submission of the final year Master students and some general instructions regarding the project are to be conveyed to the students from the highest level. In a certain situation, director does not have a direct link with the students. Hence, the instruction is to be conveyed step by step from one level to another so that it finally reaches the students. This hierarchical order of transfer of message is demonstrated in Figure 7.

The director has a direct link with the HOD's of all the departments of the institution and so he can easily convey the set of instructions to the HOD's of all departments. This forms the first level of relationship where the information is passed from one level to another. In the next level, the HOD has a direct link with faculties of his concerned department under him. So now he can easily convey the information that he has received from the Director to his subordinate faculties. Dur-

Figure 7. Transfer of Information through different levels in case of Regular Faculty

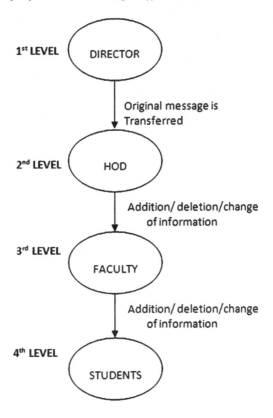

ing the process of passing the information any new additions or deletions to the original set of instructions can be made. The faculty has a direct link with the students and so he conveys the instruction to the students in order to guide them for submitting the project at an appropriate date. This forms the final level of the relationship and there lies the possibility that the instructions can be added, deleted or modified before it finally reaches the students. Thus the authors visualize that even though the director has no direct link with the students, the set of instructions generated by him is conveyed to the students through an orderly manner in a stepwise process (Mitra, Paul, Panda & Padhi, 2016).

In a specific instance, where a student feels difficulty in completing all criteria required for the project. The particular student has completed two modules out of five modules within the given deadline and had submitted the report to project guide, who is a faculty of the Department. Faculty has certain restriction, where, he cannot forward the same report to Department head or other higher authorities. So he completes the task of the remaining modules himself within the deadline and then explains the same to the student who finally submits the project within the deadline.

This scenario has been demonstrated in Figure 8. Thus, with finite output alphabet, the theory of General Sequential Machines can be obtained (Mitra et. al, 2016)

The first automaton may also communicate with a second automaton, or several others, which, the authors have assumed to be all identical and identical to the first one. It then becomes the generic element of a colony, hence the name cell given to each such automaton. In this colony, the state of each cell depends on the state of some of the others, usually the nearest neighbours. One can immediately imagine many varieties of such colonies, called cellular automata that one may fancy to study (Vivien, 2003). Figure 9 presents the successive states of a piled up above state at time 0, so the time scale is upwards.

7. APPLICATION OF CELLULAR AUTOMARA IN TRAFFIC MODELLING

Traffic congestion on major routes is an enduring problem and it is getting worse year on year due to the unrestricted trends in traffic growth. The volume of the traffic is too close to the maximum capacity of the roads. One approach to reducing congestion would be to construct new or widen existing roads to provide additional

Figure 8. State diagram representing relationship

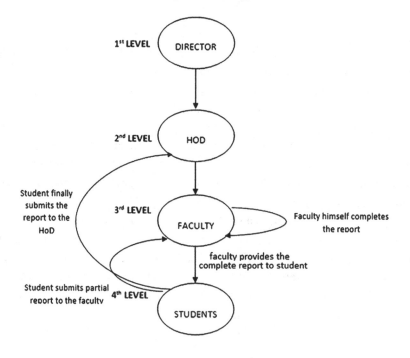

Figure 9. Diagram of a single automaton with input and output

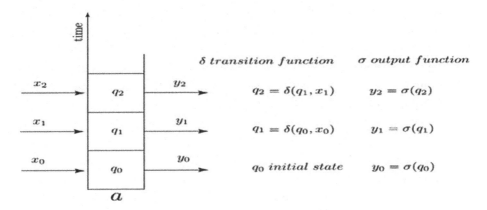

lanes and hence increase the capacity of the road infrastructure. However, this approach can be very costly and delays may worsen while road works are in progress. Sometimes it is difficult to improve the existing road system due to environmental or social objectives. Another approach may be to control the traffic in such a way that congestion would be solved with the use of traffic lights or making adjustments to road marking.

The use of a traffic model is needed to predict the behaviour of vehicles and the interactions between them on the roads.

7.1 Approaches

Approaches to traffic modelling can be divided into three groups: traffic flow theory, car-following theory, and the particle hopping traffic model (Nagel, 1996)

- **Traffic Flow Theory:** Fluid-dynamics and the kinetic theory of vehicular traffic belong to the group of traffic ow theories [Sone, 2002]. These theories describe traffic as a continuous traffic flow with varying density and an average velocity. They are a type of macroscopic theory as traffic is treated on a large scale and the movements of vehicles are not modelled individually.
- **Car-Following Theory:** The optimal velocity model and intelligent driver model were based on the car-following theory. These models are defined by ordinary differential equations and are able to simulate each vehicle individually (Nagel, 1996). Therefore, these models are a type of microscopic model that describes the one by one following process of vehicles on the same lane. Traffic is represented using the spacing and speed differential between each pair of adjacent cars.

- **Particle-Hopping Model:** Particle hopping models are known to be numerically robust with complex geometries and the interconnections of realistic road networks. The Nagel-Schreckenberg model (Henceforth, the NaSch model) (Nagel & Schreckenberg, 1992) and Rule 184 belong to the group of particle-hopping models. The one-dimensional rule 184 is fundamental to traffic simulation by cellular automata. The NaSch model can be seen as an elaboration of this rule with additional features such as a discrete velocity for each vehicle, acceleration, deceleration and a random tendency to slow down the vehicle (Gershenson and Rosenblueth, 2009). Depending on the global density and probability, the slowdown function in the NaSch model attempts to model the human tendency to overreact when braking. These models use integer state variables within each cell to describe the dynamic properties of the system. Cellular automata based traffic models generate velocity distribution as a function of position on the road network. These models are also a type of the microscopic model like the car-following theories. Traffic modelling is a vast complex subject and the choice of the model to be used can be difficult. Each cell of the automaton can reflect individual object characteristics and small changes in the rules or the cells state can produce dramatic consequences (Benjamin et al., 1996).

8 SELF-REPRODUCTION NATURE OF CELLULAR AUTOMATA AND ITS BIOLOGICAL CORRESPONDENCE

Originally, von Neumann had in mind a self-reproducing machine built of actual, physical parts such as girders, motors, sensors, and computer elements. The parts would be floating on the surface of a pond and the self-reproducing machine would have organs to recognize, grasp, and assemble the parts required to build a copy of its own. Von Neumann soon realized that the actual manipulation of physical parts in this kinematic model increased the difficulty of the task without benefiting its conceptual side. Following a suggestion of Stan Ulam, von Neumann thus switched to a cellular model, where the environment of the self-reproducing machine is a two-dimensional CA.

The mathematical study of cellular systems was born. The first problem that von Neumann faced in defining his self-reproducing automaton was the choice of the state set and transition function of the CA, that is, of the elementary "objects" of his synthetic universe and their rules of behavior.

The transition function is defined so as to let the automaton operate on its own matter under the control of its built-in logic i.e it permits the definition of a self-modifying computer. The next problem was to define the self-reproduction strategy.

Von Neumann discarded from the outset the idea of reproduction by self-inspection for fear of logical paradoxes and of potential undesired interactions between the activity of the automaton and that of the self-inspection organ. He relied instead on the use of a quiescent description of the automaton in the form of a tape (Floreano and Mattiussi, 2008).

8.1 Correspondences with Biology

When von Neumann was formulating his formal model of robust self-reproduction the molecular details of the process of reproduction in living cells were not known. Now that molecular biology has revealed many aspects of the working of cells we can compare von Neumann's formal model with its biological counterpart.

It can be note that the correspondence between what is observed in biology and von Neumann's model is not complete. In von Neumann's model the whole reproduction process is guided step by step by the instructions issued by the control unit and by those read in the tape. On the contrary, in biological cells the control of the self-reproduction activity is only in part controlled by dedicated molecular machinery and by the genome. In biology an essential role is played by processes of self-organization, which ensure that in the physicochemical environment of the cell several steps of the structuring of the newly created molecules will self-assemble in the right way. This does not happen in von Neumann's model because the "laws" of the synthetic universe represented by the state set and transition function of von Neumann's CA are defined at a higher level than the laws of physics holding at the microscopic scale and which produce the self-organization observed in biological cells.

A useful property of the formal model proposed by von Neumann is that it lets us better understand the role and the information represented in the various parts of biological cells and dispel some myths related to the genome and to its role. A virus should not be considered a self-reproducing organism but merely a free-floating tape with some minimalistic machinery that allows it to invade cells and force them to use their tape copier to replicate the virus genetic information (Floreano and Mattiussi, 2008).

9 APPLICATION OF CELLULAR AUTOMATA IN ENGINEERING AND COMPLEX INDUSTRIAL SYSTEM

Cellular automata have simple structures and appropriate to concurrent operation, they have been used to engineer and industry fields, such as traffic, image processing, machine learning and control.

10.1 Applications of Cellular Automata in Traffic System Study

The most important application of CA in traffic system study is the study of CA traffic models, in which the 184 CA model established by Wolfram is the most classical one (Wolfram, 1986). In order to simulate more real and more complex cases, the others are obtained by improving Wolfram's model. The classical improved models are N-S model (Kai & Michael, 1992) and F-I model (Fukui & Ishibashi, 1996). N-S model is a simplified model, and every step of it is necessary for simulating various behaviours of real traffic flow. N-S model presents fundamental principles for more complex cases or urban traffic flow.

These models reveal the nonlinear changing law of vehicle speed, and reproduce the process of complex traffic phenomena in real traffic flow. These models have played important roles in urban traffic development and offered fundamental principles to the establishment of cellular automata based pedestrian flow model rules (Zhang, 2001), (Hugo & M-Brain, 1996).

In empirical observations of highway traffic, it is possible to notice two different regimes (Hall, Allen & Gunter, 1986). For low densities (number of vehicles per length unit), the flux (number of vehicles per time unit) shows an approximately linear behavior. For higher densities, however, the flux exhibits strong fluctuations resulting in a complex behavior that is still not clearly understood (Chowdhury, Santen & Schadschneider, 2000). First, such fluctuations prevent the use of a functional model. Second, hysteresis has been noticed, where the flux is greater when the density increases than when the density decreases. Third, metastable states (i.e., states in a precarious equilibrium) have been observed. Authors normally distinguish between at least two different congested (jammed) regimes: the synchronized and the stop-and-go phases (Chowdhury, Santen & Schadschneider, 2000).

As a result of this complexity, myriad highway traffic models have appeared which says Macroscopic models view traffic as a one dimensional compressible fluid (Chowdhury, Santen & Schadschneider, 2000). The microscopic approaches, by contrast, model each individual vehicle. Within the microscopic treatments kinetic theories model traffic as a gas in which each particle represents a vehicle (Huang, 1987). The class of follow-the-leader models represents each vehicle with a motion equation in a system of interacting classical particles (Chowdhury, Santen & Schadschneider, 2000). Coupled-map lattice models treat time as a discrete variable and the dynamical equations for each vehicle become a discrete dynamical map (Kaneko, 1993). Finally, CA models play a prominent role. One of the main reasons is that these models are computationally cheap.

Possibly the first traffic model that could be viewed based on cellular automata was that of Cremer and Ludwig (Cremer & Ludwig, 1986). By using binary one-dimensional arrays, this model represents the presence/absence of a vehicle with each of the two states of a cell, so that each vehicle occupies exactly one cell.

The traffic model of Nagel and Schreckenberg (Nagel & Schreckenberg, 1992) (NaSch) can be seen as an elaboration of rule 184 with the following extensions: (1) a variable (discrete) velocity is associated with each vehicle, (2) acceleration (tending to attain the maximum velocity), (3) deceleration (due to the presence of other vehicles), and (4) a random tendency to slow down (an attempt to model a human tendency to overreact when decelerating).

8.2 Applications of CA in Image Processing

Preston et al. (Preston, Du, Levialdi, Norgen, & Toriwaki, 1979) proposed cellular logics for some applications in medical image processing. Wongthanavasu and Sadananda (Wongthanavasu & Sadananda, 2000) presented a CA for pixel-level edge detection on binary, which presented a new edge detector based on a cellular automata model and showed that a cellular automata-based model often provides an optimum edge map on binary images, and on average is better than the compared edge operators for gray-scaled images.

A digital image is a bi-dimensional array of n x n pixels. Each pixel can be characterized by a triplet (i, j, k) where (i, j) represents its position in the array and k the associated color. The image may then be considered as a particular configuration state of a cellular automaton that has as cellular space the n x n array defined by the image. Each site in the array corresponds to a pixel.

A dynamical rule derived from properties of cellular automata can solve the problem. This rule must be such that in a given noisy image as initial configuration it produces a trajectory whose final configuration corresponds to a noise reduced version of the image. It is desirable that the dynamics be applied to any kind of images without distinction (monographic, gray level or color) (Lim, 1990). Such models are based on a bi-dimensional symmetric non-deterministic CA of the form A= (S, N, δ) with S={ #, 0,1,......,k-1}. A pixel color is represented by a state in { 0,1,......,k-1} (k=2 for a monochromatic image; k=16 for an image with 16 colors and/or gray levels), # is the quiescent state associate to the cells outside the grid, N the von Neumann neighbourhood, while the local transition function δ is based on the comparison criteria of the central cell state with those cells from its neighbourhood. Thus δ: $S^5 \rightarrow S$ and is defined by

$$\delta(s_i)_{i=1}^5 = \begin{cases} j(\neq \#); & \text{if } s_3 \neq \# \text{ and } |\{i \mid s_i = j\}| = \max_{l=0}^{k-1}\{s_i = l\} \\ \#; & \text{if } s_3 = \# \end{cases}$$

A cell (not being in the quiescent state) changes its state to the state of the majority of cells in the neighbourhood. The cells disposed outside the lattice of n x n pixels are assumed to be in the quiescent state. We can compare the results obtained in this model and analyse the better image enhancement using cellular automata (von Neumann, 1966).

10 MACHINE LEARNING WITH CELLULAR AUTOMATA

CA has been used widely in machine learning and control fields. CA has been used as highly parallel multipliers, sorters and prime number sieves (Wolfram, 1986). Pseudorandom number generators (Tsalides, 1990) and for pattern classification (Tzionas, Tsalides and Thanailakis, 1992) are some of the known applications in machine learning and control. Further, CA has been used to study parallel evolutionary algorithms. A programming of CA algorithms on parallel computers (Spezzano & Talis, 1999). Moshe Sipper and Marco Tomassini studied non-uniform cellular automata focusing on the evolution of such systems to perform computational tasks, via a parallel evolutionary algorithm, known as cellular programming (Sipper & Tomassini, 1999).

10.1 Multiple Classifier Systems (MCS)

In recent years there has been a growing interest in the area of combining classifiers into MCS (also known as ensembles or committees). An important characteristic of MCS is that using the classification capabilities of multiple classifiers (experts), where each classifier may make different and perhaps complementary errors, tends to yield an improved performance over single experts. Therefore many researchers have focused on developing various approaches for combining classifiers by selection and/or fusion. However, the diversity of combined classifiers is emphatically a key factor for the success of the combination approach. Some MSC approaches actively try to perturb some aspects of the training set, such as training samples, attributes or classes, in order to force classifier diversity. One of the most popular perturbation approaches are Bootstrap Aggregation – Bagging and Boosting. Bagging, first introduced by Breiman (Breiman, 1996) in 1996, works by manipulating the training samples and forming replicate training sets. The final classification is based on a majority vote.

Boosting was introduced by Freund and Schapire in 1996 (Freund & Schapire, 1996). Boosting combines classifiers with weighted voting and is more complex since the distribution of training samples in the training set is adaptively changed according to the performance of sequentially constructed classifiers.

10.2 Cellular Automata as a MSC Model

In general MCS approaches can be divided into two groups: (1) MCS approaches that combine different independent classifiers (such as: Bayesian Voting, Majority Voting, etc.) and (2) MCS approaches which construct a set of classifiers on the basis of one base classifier with perturbation of training set (such as: Bagging, Boosting, Windowing, etc.) (Dietterich, 2000). The most essential deficiency in first group is their restriction of a predefined way of combining classifiers induced on the basis of different predefined methods of machine-learning. On the contrary, the MCS approaches that are based on improving one base classifier of second group use only one method for constructing all classifiers in MCS. Therefore the problem of choosing the appropriate method for solving a specific task can be decided accordingly. The idea was to combine different classifiers induced on the basis of various methods of machine-learning into MCS in a non-predefined way. After several iterations of applying adequate transaction rules only the set of the most appropriate classifiers will be get preserved. Thus, the problem of choosing the right machine learning method or a combination of them would be solved automatically (Dietterich, 2000).

11 CLASSIFICATIONAL CELLULAR AUTOMATA (CCA)

CCA is usually known as a classifier. Generally, learning a classifier is based on samples from a learning set. Every learning sample is completely described by a set of attributes (sample properties) and class (decision).

CCA is initially defined as a 2D lattice of cells. Each cell can contain a classifier and according to its classification of an input sample the cell can be in one of the k states, where k is the number of possible classes and the state "cannot classify". The last state has an especially important role when such a classifier is used, which is not defined on a whole learning set, i.e. when using the if-then rule. Therefore, from the classification point of view in the learning process the outcome of each cell can be:

1. Either, the same as the learning sample's class,
2. Or, different from the learning sample's class or
3. Cannot be classified.

However, a cell with an unknown classification for the current learning sample should be treated differently as a misclassification.

In addition to the cell's classification ability, the neighbourhood plays a very important role in the self-organization ability of a CCA. Transaction rules depend on the specific neighbourhood state to calculate a new cell's state and must be defined in such a way that enforces self-organization of CCA, which consequently leads to generalization process (Breiman, 1996).

The diversity of classifiers in CCA cells is ensured by using different machine-learning methods for classifier induction. However, there is only a limited number of machine learning methods, which can be a problem for a large CCA. Most methods have some tuning parameters that affect classification and therefore, by changing those parameters, many different classifiers can be obtained. Another possibility for obtaining several different classifiers is by changing the expected probability distributions of the input samples, which may also result in different classifiers, even by using the same machine learning method with the same parameters (Freund and Schapire, 1996; Dietterich, 2000).

12 CONCLUSION

Throughout this chapter authors have visualized that cellular automata excel at modelling physical systems because the properties of the physical world and cellular lattices are very similar. These tools may provide powerful solutions for researchers and engineers that need to implement real-life applications. This approach allows scientists to concentrate on "how to model a problem" rather than on architectural details.

There has been perhaps an under-explored approach to using automata which could be applied to other areas. Envisage a traffic simulation in which congestion forced roads to widen or the lack of sufficiently direct route to their destination caused the cars to bore new roads through the country-side. There are several advantages of simple traffic models. Such models are, on the one hand, easy to implement and reproduce, and on the other hand, computationally cheap. Also, by abstracting most details from real traffic, one can observe properties more clearly. A two-dimensional cellular automaton with a very simple transition rule may be used as a very efficient border detector in digital images. The border detection method based on a cellular automaton has a general applicability to monochromatic, gray level and colour images. A cellular automata approach for solving the robot path planning problem that yields very efficient experimental performance on real life path planning situations is proposed. The cellular automata algorithms were tested with different workspace configurations and cellular space sizes over real time images from a digital camera. Important research directions in the future are to analyse the resulting self-organized structure, the impact of transaction rules on classification accuracy, the introduction of other social aspects for cell survival and enlarging the classifier diversity by implementing even more machine-learning methods.

REFERENCES

Abrams, M., Allison, D., Kafura, D., Ribbens, C., Rosson, M. B., Shaffer, C., & Watson, L. (1998). PSE research at Verginia Tech: An Overview. Technical Report: TR-98-21. Virginia Polytechnic Institute & State University.

Amadek & Trnkova. (1990). *Automata and Algebras in Categories*. Dordrecht: Kluwer Academic Publishers.

Benjamin, S. C., Johnson, N. F., & Hui, P. M. (1996). Cellular automata models of traffic ow along a highway containing a junction. *Journal of Physics. A, Mathematical and General*, *29*(12), 3119–3127. doi:10.1088/0305-4470/29/12/018

Braga, G., Cattaneo, G., Flocchini, P., & Vogliotti, C. Q. (1995). Pattern growth in elementary cellular automata. *Theoretical Computer Science*, *145*(1-2), 1–26.

Breiman, L. (1996). Bagging Predictors. *Journal of Machine Learning*, *24*(2), 123–140. doi:10.1007/BF00058655

Chakraborty, P., Saxena, P. C., & Katti, C. P. (2011). Fifty Years of Automata Simultion: A Review. *ACM Inroads*, *2*(4), 59–70. doi:10.1145/2038876.2038893

Chowdhury, D., Santen, L., & Schadschneider, A. (2000). Statistical Physics of Vehicular Traffic and Some Related Systems. *Physics Reports*, *329*(4–6), 199–329. doi:10.1016/S0370-1573(99)00117-9

Cremer, M., & Ludwig, J. (1986). A Fast Simulation Model for Traffic Flow on the Basis of Boolean Operations. *Mathematics and Computers in Simulation*, *28*(4), 297–303. doi:10.1016/0378-4754(86)90051-0

Culik, K. II, & Yu, S. (1988). Undecidability of Cellular Automata classification schemes. *Complex Systems*, *2*(2), 177–190.

Dietterich, T. G. (2000). Ensemble Methods in Machine Learning. In *First International Workshop on Multiple Classifier Systems*. Springer Verlag. doi:10.1007/3-540-45014-9_1

Floreano & Mattiussi. (2008). *Bio-Inspired Artificial Intelligence- Theories, Methods, and Technologies*. The MIT Press.

Freund, Y., & Schapire, R. E. (1996). Experiments with a new boosting algorithm. In *Proceedings Thirteenth International Conference on Machine Learning*. Morgan Kaufman.

Fukui, M., & Ishibashi, Y. (1996). Traffic Flow in 1D Cellular Automaton Model Including Cars Moving with High Speed. *Journal of the Physical Society of Japan, 65*(6), 1868–1870. doi:10.1143/JPSJ.65.1868

Gallopoulos, E., Houstis, E., & Rice, J. R. (1994). Computer as thinker/doer: Problem-solving environments for computational science. *IEEE Computational Science & Engineering, 1*(2), 11–23. doi:10.1109/99.326669

Garis & Brain. (1996), ATR's Bbillion Neuron Artificial Brain Project: A Three Year Progress Report. *Proceedings of the International Conference on Evolutionary Computation*, 886-891.

Gershenson & Rosenblueth. (2009). Modeling self-organizing traffic lights with elementary cellular automata. *Complex Systems, 19*(4), 305-322.

Golze, U. (1976). Differences between 1- and 2-dimensional cell spaces. In Automata, Languages. Development. North-Holland Publishing Co.

H'el`ene. (2003). *An Introduction to Cellular Automata.* IRIF.

Hall, F. L., Allen, B. L., & Gunter, M. A. (1986). Empirical Analysis of Freeway Flow-Density Relationships. *Transportation Research Part A, General, 20*(3), 197–210. doi:10.1016/0191-2607(86)90094-4

Houstis, E., Gallopoulos, E., Bramley, J., & Rice, J. R. (1997). Problem-solving environments for computational science. *IEEE Computational Science & Engineering, 4*(3), 18–21. doi:10.1109/MCSE.1997.615427

Huang, K. (1987). Statistical Mechanics (2nd ed.). New York: Wiley.

Kai, N., & Michael, S. (1992). A Cellular Automaton Model for Freeway Traffic. *Journal de Physique. I, 2*(12), 2221–2229. doi:10.1051/jp1:1992277

Kaneko, K. (Ed.). (1993). *Theory and Applications of Coupled Map Lattices.* Wiley.

Marc Lane, S. (1971). *Categories for the working Mathematician* (2nd ed.). Springer Publication. doi:10.1007/978-1-4612-9839-7

Mitra, A., Paul, S., Panda, S., & Padhi, P. (2016). A Study on the representation of the various models for Dynamic Social Networks. *Procedia Computer Science, 79*, 624–631. doi:10.1016/j.procs.2016.03.079

Morita, K., & Imai, K. (1996). Self-reproduction in a reversible cellular space. *Theoretical Computer Science, 168*(2), 337–366. doi:10.1016/S0304-3975(96)00083-7

Nagel, K. (1996). Particle hopping models and traffic ow theory. *Physical Review E: Statistical Physics, Plasmas, Fluids, and Related Interdisciplinary Topics*, *53*(5), 4655–4672. doi:10.1103/PhysRevE.53.4655 PMID:9964794

Nagel, K., & Schreckenberg, M. (1992). A cellular automaton model for freeway traffic. *Journal de Physique. I*, *2*(12), 2221–2229. doi:10.1051/jp1:1992277

Packard, N., & Wolfram, S. (1985). Two-dimensional cellular automata. *Journal of Statistical Physics*, *30*(5-6), 901–942. doi:10.1007/BF01010423

Preston, K.J., Du, M.J.B., Levialdi, S., Norgen, P., & Toriwaki, J. (1979). Basics of Cellular Logic with Some Applications in Medical Image Processing. *Proc. IEEE*, (67), 826-857.

Schiff, J. L. (2008). *Cellular Automata*. Wiley.

Sipper, M., & Tomassini, M. (1999). Computation in Artificially Evolved Non-Uniform Cellular Automata. *Theoretical Computer Science*, *217*(1), 81–98. doi:10.1016/S0304-3975(98)00151-0

Sone, Y. (2002). *Kinetic theory and fluid dynamics. Birkhauser*. Springer. doi:10.1007/978-1-4612-0061-1

Spezzano, G., & Talis, D. (1999). Programming Cellular Automata Algorithms on Parallel Computers. *Future Generation Computer Systems*, *16*(2-3), 203–216. doi:10.1016/S0167-739X(99)00047-3

Stephen, W. (1983). Statistical Mechanics of Cellular Automata. *Reviews of Modern Physics*, *55*(3), 601–644. doi:10.1103/RevModPhys.55.601

Sutner, K. (1989). A note on the Culik-Yu classes. *Complex Systems*, *3*(1), 107–115.

Sutner, K. (1990). Classifying circular cellular automata. *Physica D. Nonlinear Phenomena*, *45*(1-3), 1–3, 386–395. doi:10.1016/0167-2789(90)90196-V

Toffoli, T., & Margolus, N. (1987). *Cellular Automata machines: A new environment for modelling*. The MIT Press.

Tsalides, P. (1990). Cellular Automata based Built-in Self Test Structures for VLSI Systems. *Electronics Letters*, *26*(17), 1350–1352. doi:10.1049/el:19900869

Tzionas, P., Tsalides, P., & Thanailakis, A. (1992). Design and VLSI Implementation of a Pattern Classifier Using Pseudo-2D Cellular Automata. *IEEE Proceedings Part G*, *139*(6), 661-668.

von Neumann. (1958). The General and Logical theory of Automata. In L.A. Jeffress (Ed.), *Cerebral Mechanisms in Behaviour – The Hixon Symposium*. John Wiley & Sons.

von Neumann, J. (1966). *Theory of Self-Reproducing Automata*. University of Illinois Press.

Walker, D. W., Li, M., Rana, O. F., Shields, M. S., & Huang, Y. (2000). The software architecture of a distributed problem solving environment. *Concurrency (Chichester, England)*, *12*(15), 1445–1480. doi:10.1002/1096-9128(20001225)12:15<1455::AID-CPE538>3.0.CO;2-#

Wolfram, S. (1984). Universality and complexity in cellular automata. *Physica D. Nonlinear Phenomena*, *10*(1-2), 1–35. doi:10.1016/0167-2789(84)90245-8

Wolfram, S. (1986). *Theory and Applications of Cellular Automata*. Singapore: World Scientific.

Wongthanavasu, S., & Sadananda, R. (2000). *Pixel-level Edge Detection Using a Cellular Automata-Based Model. In Advances in Intelligent Systems: Theory and Applications* (Vol. 59, pp. 343–351). IOS Press.

Yan, S. Y. (1998). An Introduction to Formal Languages and Machine Computation. Singapore: World Scientific Publishing Co. Pte.

Zhang, S. Y. (2001). A Brief Introduction to Complex Systems and Complexity Science. *Journal of Qingdao University*, *16*(4), 25–28.

Section 3
Human-Centric and Behavior-Based Computing

Chapter 9
A Novel Hybrid Genetic Algorithm for Unconstrained and Constrained Function Optimization

Rajashree Mishra
KIIT University, India

Kedar Nath Das
NIT Silchar, India

ABSTRACT

During the past decade, academic and industrial communities are highly interested in evolutionary techniques for solving optimization problems. Genetic Algorithm (GA) has proved its robustness in solving all most all types of optimization problems. To improve the performance of GA, several modifications have already been done within GA. Recently GA has been hybridized with many other nature-inspired algorithms. As such Bacterial Foraging Optimization (BFO) is popular bio inspired algorithm based on the foraging behavior of E. coli bacteria. Many researchers took active interest in hybridizing GA with BFO. Motivated by such popular hybridization of GA, an attempt has been made in this chapter to hybridize GA with BFO in a novel fashion. The Chemo-taxis step of BFO plays a major role in BFO. So an attempt has been made to hybridize Chemo-tactic step with GA cycle and the algorithm is named as Chemo-inspired Genetic Algorithm (CGA). It has been applied on benchmark functions and real life application problem to prove its efficacy.

DOI: 10.4018/978-1-5225-2375-8.ch009

Copyright ©2017, IGI Global. Copying or distributing in print or electronic forms without written permission of IGI Global is prohibited.

1. INTRODUCTION

Optimization problems arise in almost in every field i.e. Mathematics, Science, Business Administration, Management, and Medicine. These occur in almost every engineering discipline such as Civil Engineering, Mechanical Engineering, Electrical Engineering, Telecommunication Engineering, Chemical and Bio-Chemical Engineering, Design and Manufacturing Systems. Most of the practical problems viz. analysis of electrical circuits, design of chemical production plant, the structural design of buildings or bridges, aircraft scheduling can be modeled through the nonlinear relationships. The problems also involve linear or nonlinear constraints. So, in real life situation we come across many nonlinear optimization problems. Thus, a requirement arises for developing efficient and effective optimization techniques for solving such problems. Many Evolutionary algorithms have been designed in recent past to tackle such problems (Das, 2013; Goldbarg, Goldbarg, Menzes, & Luna,2016; Hu et al, 2015; Qu, Liang, Wang, Chen& Suganthan,2016; Russo,2016;Singh &Das,2016;Wang, Yu & Cheung,2014). In recent past many interesting book came describing the application of Evolutionary technique (Tripathy & Acharjya, 2014a; Tripathy & Acharjya, 2014b). In general; a nonlinear optimization problem may have one or more local optimal solution. In case of linear programming problem, every local optimal solution is also its global optimal solution. Particularly, in case of non linear programming problem, locating the global optimal solution is a difficult task. It is not possible to find the global maxima (or minima) without searching in the neighborhood of every feasible point. As a result, there do not exist such computational algorithm, which can guarantee the solution of an optimization problem in a finite number of steps.

According to (Wolpert & Macready, 1997), all algorithms designed for finding the extremum of the cost function performs equally well when averaged over all the cost functions. According to the authors, if algorithm A outperforms algorithm B in some optimization problems, there exist as many other problems where algorithm B outperforms algorithm A. Hence, from the problem solving perspective, no single state of the art algorithm can handle all sorts of optimization problems. That's why; Now-a-days researchers are more focused on hybridized techniques.

GA and BFO have been hybridized with many nature inspired algorithms for the improvement of the searching capability of the algorithm. To list a few, GA has been successfully hybridized with Baldwin effect (Yuan, Qian, & Du, 2010), with Ant colony optimization (Ciornei & Kyriakides, 2012), with Particle swarm optimization (Kao & Zahara, 2008; Fan, Liang, & Zahara, 2006), with Simulated annealing (Hwang & He, 2006), with Quasi-simplex technique (Zhang & Lu, 2006), with niche technique and Nelder–Mead's simplex method (Wei & Zhao, 2005) and with Quadratic approximation (Deep & Das, 2008).

Similarly, based on the concept of foraging behavior of living organism, and deriving concepts from natural genetics, researchers have started imitating food search strategies of living organism. Those algorithms are coming under the umbrella of Swarm intelligence techniques. BFO is the popular algorithm which is newer in rank to the swarm intelligence techniques proposed by (Passino, 2002). BFO has also been effectively hybridized with PSO (Pattanaik, Bakward, Devi, Panigrahi, & Das, 2010; Shen, Zhu, Zhou, Guo, & Chang, 2009), with gradient PSO (Fa & Ling, 2012), with parameter free PSO (Bakward et al., 2009).

Amongst, the hybridization of GA and BFO, the hybridization of GA with BFO (GA-BF) is proven to be much robust in recent past (Kim, Abraham, Cho, 2007). The author hybridized the entire steps of GA with entire steps of BFO. It is found that while hybridizing GA with BFO, the behavior/mechanism of some of the operators seems to be repeated and it may lead to hamper the solution quality as well as increases the computational time. Hence, instead of taking the whole BFO to hybridize with GA (called GA-BF); in this Chapter a novel method has been developed where only the chemo-taxis step is picked from BFO mechanism and hybridized with GA. It is named as Chemo-Inspired Genetic Algorithm (CGA). The brief overviews of GA and BFO have been discussed in Section 2 and Section 3 followed by the literature review in Introduction Section. Then, discussion is given about the proposed design of Chemo-inspired Genetic Algorithm in Section 4. The hybridized algorithm CGA is next applied for function optimization for unconstrained problems in Section 5 and compared with GA and GA-BF. Again, it is applied to constrained optimization real life problem described in Section 6. Next the conclusions have been drawn in Section 7.

2. GENETIC ALGORITHM (GA)

Among, the Evolutionary Algorithms GA is most popular due to John Holland. GA is based on the concept of "survival of the fittest". The basic principle of GA was first proposed by (Holland, 1975). A series of literature surveys are available (Michalewicz, 1994; Beasley, Bull, & Martin, 1993; Srinivas & Patnaik, 1994; Goldberg, 1989; Das, 2013). GA has been applied to task scheduling problem by (Fatma &Mona2010). GA has been used to Decision Support System problem by (Bukharov & Bogolyubov, 2015), Image/ Video Processing problem (Hashemi, Kiani, Noroozi, & Moghaddam,2010), Fractal Image Compression problem (Wu, Jeng & Hsieh, 2006), Digital Road map problem (Costa & Baldo,2015), finger print matching problem (Tan & Bhanu, 2006)) respectively. GA works on a population of individuals. The operators used in the GA are Selection, crossover, mutation and elitism respectively. The details of the operators have been discussed below.

2.1 Encoding of Chromosomes

In GA, initially the decision variables are encoded to another space. Encoding is a mapping from phenotype space to genotype space. There exist several types of encoding such as binary encoding, value encoding, permutation encoding, and tree encoding. In general binary encoding is a popular approach in Binary GA. Binary encoding is very popular. So, it has been discussed below.

Binary Encoding

The simplest and popular approach among the Encoding is Binary Encoding. The potential solutions are represented in sequence of 0's and 1's shown in Table 1. Binary encoding gives many possible chromosomes even with a small number of alleles. It has been used in the first research of GA.

2.2 Selection

Selection operator follows certain criteria of fitness function evaluation of the strings. It extracts the above average strings and forms multiple copies of best strings from an existing population. It quantifies the optimality of the solution and pick up the string in a probabilistic manner. The fitter individuals are selected and undergo the transformation in cross over phase and the string of population advances towards the next generation of the mating pool and expected to reach to the optimal solution. It is the first genetic operator found by (Holland, 1975). The population may converge to suboptimal solution due to strong selection and too slow selection lowered the process of evolution. Selection strategy is analogous to Darwinians principle of the survival of the fittest. Several methods exist for the selection procedure. These are roulette wheel selection, Boltzmann selection, rank selection, steady state selection, and tournament selection. Tournament Selection operator is discussed below.

Table 1. Binary Encoding

Chromosome 1	0	1	1	0	1	0	1	0	1
Chromosome 2	0	0	0	1	1	0	1	1	0

- **Tournament Selection:** Tournament Selection has the benefit that it can be implemented in non parallel and parallel architectures having simple coding procedures and easier implementation process. Basically, the tournament is held between S competitors and individual having highest fitness value is the winner of the tournament. It can be adjusted according to the selection pressure in Genetic Algorithm. The better will be the fitness value as better will be the selection pressure. As the fitness of the individuals is increased and algorithm is driven into better candidate solutions in the next generation as compared to the previous generation.

Out of several Tournament selection operators, in this Chapter, Binary tournament Selection has been used which has been explained in detail. In this case tournaments are played between two candidate solutions and the better solution is picked up and placed in the mating pool. This is depicted in Figure 1. Initially, 1st and 2nd solution are picked up and the string which is more fit is placed in 1st slot of the mating pool. Next, to fill the 2nd slot, the 2nd and 3rd solutions are chosen. The process continues till all the slots are filled up. In this way, each solution participates in two tournaments. The best solution will win both times and makes two copies of it in the new population. The worst solution will lose both the tournaments and will be eliminated from the population. Thus, the solution may have zero, one or two copies in the population

Figure 1. Pictorial representation of binary tournament selection

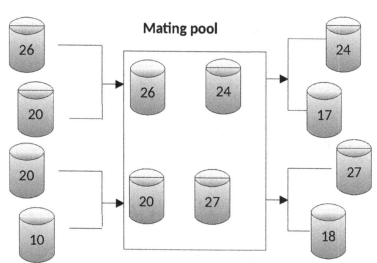

2.3 Cross Over

Generally cross over operator is the amalgamation of the two parent strings for producing two child strings. In this case, the exchange of discovered knowledge occurs in the form of genes between the two parent chromosomes. The main idea behind the operator is that it may create two better strings in comparison to the parent strings if it takes best characteristics of the parent strings. Various crossovers are one point crossover, two point crossover, uniform crossover, arithmetic crossover, and heuristic crossover. One point cross over is explained below.

- **One Point Crossover:** In this case, two parent strings are selected randomly and the one cross over site is selected randomly. The chromosomes after the crossover site are swapped between the parents strings and the two child strings are produced. It is shown in Figure 2.

2.4 Mutation

In genetic search, mutation has an important role. It maintains the diversity of the population by creating a small perturbation in the population. It prevents the stagnation of population at any local optima by dint of restoring lost or unexplored regions in the space. The main task of mutation is to drag the potential solutions from falling into a local optimum. Various types of mutation operators are bitwise mutation, non uniform, boundary, uniform, and Gaussian. Bit wise mutation is popular in Binary GA which is described below.

Figure 2. Pictorial representation of one point crossover

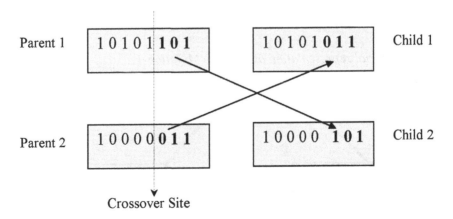

- **Bitwise Mutation:** It is applied in case of binary strings. In this process a bit is chosen randomly within the chromosome with a very small mutation probability. The randomly chosen bit is then mutated to create a new chromosome in the neighborhood of the current chromosome. The value of the chosen gene is inverted randomly from 0 to1 and vice versa. It is shown in Figure 3. The 2nd and 7th bits of the chromosome have participated in the mutation process and are mutated to create new chromosomes. The changed bits are bold faced and depicted in Figure 3.

2.5 Elitism

The process of elitism operator is to keep the better individuals in the population and eliminate the worst strings. There exist several types of elitism viz. complete elitism, partial elitism and alternate elitism. The mechanism is defined as follows.

1. Store the population of strings with their fitness function value before and after the GA cycle.
2. Mingle the two set of population of strings to make the population size double.
3. Arrange the strings in descending order of their fitness function value for a minimization problem.
4. Keep the first half of the population of strings to participate for the next GA cycle.

2.6 Pseudo Code of GA

```
Simple GA ()
{
Randomly initialize the population of strings.
```

Figure 3. Pictorial representation of Bit-wise Mutation

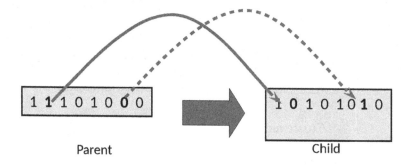

Parent   Child

```
Evaluate fitness of the strings.
Initialize the control parameters of GA.
While stopping criterion is not satisfied
    {
Apply Selection operator
Apply the Crossover operator with cross over probability
Apply Mutation Operator with Mutation probability
Evaluate the fitness of the individuals.
Perform Elitism by selecting the best half of the population
    }
}
```

3. BACTERIAL FORAGING OPTIMIZATION

It mimics the foraging behavior of E. coli bacterium found in human intestine. BFO is successfully applied on harmonic estimation (Ray & Subudhi, 2012), transmission loss reduction (Tripathy, Mishra, Lai, & Zhang, 2006), Stock Market prediction (Yudong & Lenin, 2009), Port folio Optimization (Niu, Fan, Xiao, & Xue, 2012), real Power loss and Voltage Stability problem (Tripathy & Mishra, 2007), Traffic Signal Timing Optimization (Liu and Xu, 2012), Congestion Management in Power system (Panigrahi &Pandi, 2009) respectively. It has also been applied to Multi objective optimization problem (Niu, Wang, Wang, & Tan, 2013).The E. Coli bacterium that are present in our intestine undergo the foraging behavior and it is used as the optimization process. The foraging strategies of the bacteria are subdivided into 4 sections i.e. Chemo-taxis, Swarming, Reproduction & Elimination-Dispersal.

- **Chemo-Taxis:** Swimming and Tumbling are the major processes in controlling the Chemo-taxis step. An E. Coli bacterium can move in two ways. It can run (swim for a period of time) or it can tumble and alternate between these two modes of operation in the entire life time. In particular, the chemo-taxis step is defined as follows.

$$\theta^i\left(j+1,k,l\right) = \theta^i\left(j,k,l\right) + c\left(i\right)\delta\left(i\right) \tag{1}$$

$\theta^i\left(j,k,l\right)$ represents the ith bacterium at j^{th} chemo tactic step in k^{th} reproductive step and l^{th} elimination dispersal step. $c\left(i\right)$ is the step size taken in the random direction specified by the tumble(run length unit). $\delta\left(i\right)$ represents the random vector whose elements are lying in [-1, 1]. The cost function at $\theta^i\left(j,k,l\right)$ is defined as $J\left(i,j,k,l\right)$.

- **Swarming:** In swarming, the bacterium signals other bacteria by releasing attractants and the bacteria swarm together with high bacterial density. The cell to cell repellant and attractant function for i^{th} bacterium is denoted as $j^i_{cc}\left(\theta,\theta^i\left(j,k,l\right)\right), i=1,2,3,...,S.$

$$J_{cc}\left(\theta,\theta^i\left(j,k,l\right)\right)=\sum_{i=1}^{s}J^i_{cc}\left(\theta,\theta^i\left(j,k,l\right)\right)$$

$$=\sum_{i=1}^{s}\left[-d_{aattract}\exp\left(-w_{attract}\sum_{m=1}^{p}\left(\theta_m-\theta^i_m\right)^2\right)\right]+\sum_{i=1}^{s}\left[h_{repellant}\exp\left(-w_{repellant}\sum_{m=1}^{p}\left(\theta_m-\theta^i_m\right)^2\right)\right]$$

(2)

where $h_{repellant}$ is called the height of the repellant effect, $w_{repellant}$ is called the width of the repellant and $w_{repellant}=10$. The depth of the attractant is denoted by $d_{attract}=0.1$, the width of the attractant is defined as $w_{attract}=0.2$. The cell also repels nearby cell because it is not practically possible to have two cells at the same location. The model of this equation is defined as $d_{attract}=w_{attract}$. The J_{cc} is the swarming effect due to the bacteria which is added to the actual cost function to be minimized to present a time varying cost function. If swarming effect is considered then total cost function is computed as follows.

$$J\left(i,j,k,l\right)=J\left(i,j,k,l\right)+J_{cc}\left(\theta,\theta^i\left(j,k,l\right)\right)$$

(3)

- **Reproduction:** Reproduction step is started after the completion of Chemotactic steps. The bacteria having poor foraging behavior dies and the healthier bacteria replicate themselves. The health of each bacterium is evaluated as sum of the nutrient got over the entire life time. The health of the ith bacterium is defined as follows.

$$J^i_{health}=\sum_{j=1}^{N_c+1}j\left(i,j,k,l\right)$$

(4)

- **Elimination-Dispersal:** After a pre specified number of reproduction steps, elimination Dispersal events take place. According to the fixed elimination-Dispersal probability P_{ed}, few bacteria are eliminated and dispersed to random positions in the optimization domain.

3.1. Bacterial Foraging Optimization Algorithm (BFOA)

```
Algorithm 1: BFO_ Algo ()
```
$//S$: Number of bacteria to be initialized within the search space

$//P$: Number of parameters to be optimized

$//N_s$: Swim length step

$//N_c$: Number of Chemo tactic steps of the Chemo tactic loop

$//N_{re}$: Number of reproduction steps

$//N_{ed}$: Numbers of Elimination Dispersal steps

$//P_{ed}$: Probability of Elimination-Dispersal

```
1.              Set  j = k = l = 0
2.                   l = l + 1 // Elimination-Dispersal loop
3.              k = k + 1 // Reproduction loop
4.          j = j + 1 // Chemotatic loop

          // Bacteria loop
5.          For each bacterium  i = 1, 2, .., S , take the Chemo taxis
operator as follows
```

    (a) Evaluate the swarming effect $J_{cc}\left(\theta, \theta^i\left(j, k, l\right)\right)$ at $\theta^i\left(j, k, l\right)$ as equation(2)

    (b) Evaluate the fitness function $J\left(i, j, k, l\right)$ at $\theta^i\left(j, k, l\right)$ as

$$J\left(i, j, k, l\right) = J\left(i, j, k, l\right) + J_{cc}\left(\theta, \theta^i\left(j, k, l\right)\right)$$

    (c) $J_{last} = J\left(i, j, k, l\right)$

    (d) **Tumble:** Randomly generate P dimensional vector $\delta\left(i\right)$ with each element in the range [-1,1]

    (e) **Move:** Update move of the bacteria as

$$\theta^i\left(j + 1, k, l\right) = \theta^i\left(j, k, l\right) + c\left(i\right)\delta\left(i\right)$$

    (f) Evaluate fitness function $J\left(i, j + 1, k, l\right)$ at $\theta^i\left(j + 1, k, l\right)$ $J\left(i, j + 1, k, l\right) = J\left(i, j + 1, k, l\right) + J_{cc}\left(\theta, \theta^i\left(j + 1, k, l\right)\right)$

(g) **Swim:** $m = 0$

$$\text{while}\left(m < N_s\right)$$

{

$m = m + 1$

If $(J(i, j+1, k, l) < J_{last})$

$$J_{last} = J(i, j+1, k, l)$$

Update move of the bacteria as 5(e)

Evaluate new fitness $\theta^i(j+1, k, l)$ of the bacteria at new position $\theta^i(j+1, k, l)$

Else $m = N_s$

}

// End of the swim loop

6. If $(i < S)$ Go to Step 5 to process the next bacterium $(i+1)$ if $i \neq S$

// End of Bacteria loop

7. If $(j < N_c)$ Go to Step 4

// End of Chemo taxis step

8. //Reproduction step:

(a) Evaluate the health of the ith bacterium defined as J_i^{health} as per equation (4).

(b) Sort the bacteria in ascending order of their health. Select the first half of the bacterial population and copy those strings in the lower half of the population. The least healthy bacteria die and the healthier bacteria replicate themselves.

(c) If $(k < N_{re})$ Go to Step 3

// End of Reproduction Step

9. //Elimination and Dispersal:

(a) For $(i = 1 \ to \ S)$

Eliminate and disperse the bacteria in the search domain with probability P_{ed}

(b) If $(l < N_{ed})$ Go to Step 2

Else Exit.

// End of Elimination and Dispersal Step.

4. DESIGN OF CHEMO-INSPIRED GENETIC ALGORITHM

The brief overview of both GA and BFO are presented above. Collectively, the objectives of both the mechanism are the same as to explore the search space and coming up with a near optimal solution. Each of them has some pitfalls in their inherent mechanism. Previously many researchers tried to improve the performances of BFO (Chen, Ksai, Chu, & Pan, 2007; Kim, Abraham, & Cho, 2007). (Kim, Abraham, & Cho, 2007) tried to hybridize the GA with BFO by taking the entire steps of GA with the entire steps followed in case of BFO. In CGA, the hybridization of GA and BFO has been done in a novel fashion. Motivation behind the Novel Hybridization the motivation behind the novel hybridization draws its inspiration from the following two similarities found out while closely looking through the mechanism of GA and BFO.

1. Based on the Darwinian's principle of survival of the fittest, Selection operator quantifies the optimality of the solution. It picks up the above average strings and forms multiple copies of the best strings from the existing population. The strings of the previous generation pass towards the next generation and reach the optimal solution. Basically, selection operator in GA does the work of the exploitation (intensification) of the search space. Similarly, Reproduction operator eliminates the worst half of the population and creates the replica of the best strings. So, it does the same work of exploitation in case of BFO.

2. Again in Complete Elitism in GA, the selection is based on elite operation. It passes the best strings of the previous generation onto the next generation. There by, it restores the best strings in the population and eliminates the worst strings. As a result, it avoids the unnecessary stagnation of the solutions and escapes the potential solutions from being trapped into the suboptimal solutions. Similarly, Elimination-Dispersal is the process where some strings are liquidated and some strings are generated in the search space to avoid the solutions from converging into the local optimum.

So the following analyses can be drawn before hybridizing the entire steps of GA with entire steps of BFO.

Selection in GA and Reproduction in BFO are doing the operation of exploitation. Also, Elitism in GA and Elimination–Dispersal in BFO are doing the exploration of the search space. It is realized and experimented that too much exploitation and also too much exploration of the search space decrease the performance improvement of the solution. The repetition of steps will take more number of function evaluations and increase the computational time also. Therefore, keeping in view the above, it is experienced that while hybridizing to BFO with GA, probably the reproduction and elimination-dispersal steps of BFO become inefficient or it just repeats few of the existing operators in GA. Therefore, the Chemo taxis step only seems to have a greater contribution in finding the global optimal solution in the hybridization process. Hence, the chemo taxis step of BFO has been picked up from BFO to hybridize with GA as an additional operator in GA and the hybridized algorithm has been designed. The hybrid algorithm thus formed is named as Chemo-inspired Genetic Algorithm (CGA). Thus an attempt has been made in this Chapter to apply the designed CGA algorithm for solving unconstrained benchmark problem and later it has been applied to constrained real life problem.

The detailed mechanism of CGA is as follows. Clearly, CGA has 5 major steps viz. Selection, Crossover, Mutation, Complete Elitism and Chemo taxis. The proposed CGA also implemented the Adaptive Step size & Squeezed search space as proposed by (Chen & Lin, 2009). The Adaptive step size proposed by (Chen & Lin, 2009) is further modified and implemented in the proposed CGA. These are discussed as follows.

- **Adaptive Step Size:** The adaptive step-size C_{step} as proposed by (Chen & Lin, 2009) is implemented in CGA is as follows.

$$C_{step} = C_{max}(i) - \frac{C_{max}(i) - C_{min}(i)}{N_c} j \tag{5}$$

where, $C_{max}(i)$, $C_{min}(i)$ are maximum and minimum step sizes. N_c is the number of chemo tactic step. The adaptive step size can exploit and explore the search space in a better way.

- **Squeezed Search Space:** In order to improve the search performance in subsequent step the search space has been reduced as proposed by (Chen &Lin, 2009) is described below. The range of the search space is as follows. Range $= (Min(j), Max(j))$.

$$\left. \begin{aligned} Min(j) &= X_{best} - \frac{R}{2^j} \\ Max(j) &= X_{best} + \frac{R}{2^j} \end{aligned} \right\} \tag{6}$$

where,. X_{best} .is the current best position in the search space R, where R is the sphere of activity of the bacteria swarm.

- **The Proposed Modified Chemo Tactic Step Size:** In order to avoid the premature convergence, care has been taken in modifying the Adaptive chemo tactic step size proposed by (Chen &Lin, (2009) and implemented in the proposed algorithm. If the solution remains unchanged for continuously 10 steps then a new and modified step size C_{step} is proposed as

$$C_{step} = i..k + C_{step},$$ (7)

where, i is the ith bacterium and k is a constant. This is acting as a mutation operator. If the solution is trapped in the local optima a sudden change in step size is required to get out of that. The pseudo code of CGA has been discussed below and also the flow diagram is given in Figure 4.

4.1 Chemo-Inspired Genetic Algorithm (CGA)

```
Algorithm 2: CGA_ Algo ()
// n : Dimension of the variable
// S : Number of bacteria used in the Chemo tactic loop
// N_c :Number of chemo tactic steps
// N_s : Swim steps
// P(t): Initial population
// C(t): Off spring generated after Crossover
// C'(t): Off spring generated after Mutation
// C_step : Step size of the bacterium
// X^i : Initial position of the i^th bacterium
// fit X^i(j): The fitness function value i^th bacterium in j^th
chemo tactic step
// X^i(j): Position of the  i^th bacterium at j^th chemo tactic
step
// F_best : The best fitness value of the bacteria swarm
// X_best : Position corresponding to F_best
```

$// Min(j), Max(j)$: Range of the search space reinitialized in the Chemo tactic loop

1.   Set $i = j = 0. \ S = 4$
2.   Generate the initial population $P(t)$
3.   Evaluate the objective function value
4.   Apply Selection operator
5.   Create offspring $C'(t)$ applying crossover
6.   Create offspring $C'(t)$ applying Mutation
7.   Apply Complete Elitism
8.   Evaluate the objective function value
9.   Update F_{best} and X_{best} :
10.   If (Gen> 10) Go to   Step 11
                 Else Go to Step 4

//Chemo taxis Step

11. $j = j + 1$// for Chemo tactic Loop
12. $i = i + 1$// for Bacteria loop
13.   //Tumble and Move:

               (a) Reinitialize the Search space within $Min(j) \ \& \ Max(j)$ as equation (6)

               (b) Create population and Evaluate objective function $fit \ X^i(j)$

               (c)   Update F_{best} and X_{best} :

             (d)   Randomly generate p dimensional vector

$$\delta(j), \delta(i) = \left[\delta_1^j, \delta_2^j, ..., \delta_n^j \right], \delta_m^j \in \left[-1, 1 \right]$$

               (e) Evaluate step size C_{step} as equation(5) or equation(7).

               (f)   Evaluate the new position in $j + 1^{th}$ chemo tactic step

$$X^i(j+1) = X^i(j+1) + C_{step} \left(\delta(i) \Big/ \sqrt{\delta(i) \delta^T(i)} \right) \tag{8}$$

(e) Update F_{best} and X_{best} :

14.   //Swim loop: Set m=0
          While ($m < N_s$) do

$m = m + 1$

$$\text{If}\left(fit\left(X^i \left(j+1 \right) \right) < F_{best} \right)$$

          {
              Update F_{best} and X_{best} :
          Evaluate the modification of new position in $j+1^{th}$
step

$$X^i \left(j+1 \right) = X^i \left(j+1 \right) + C_{step} \left({\delta(i)} \middle/ {\sqrt{\delta(i)\delta^T(i)}} \right) \tag{9}$$

Evaluate $fit\, X^i \left(j+1 \right)$

          }

                      Else
$X^i \left(j+1 \right) = X^i \left(j \right)$ and Set $m = N_s$

                      End While
15.   If$\left(i < S \right)$Go to step 12
16.   If ($j < N_c$) Go to Step 11
17.   If $\left(gen < gen\_max \right)$Go to Step 4
              Else Exit

5. UNCONSTRAINED OPTIMIZATION PROBLEMS

The performance of the proposed CGA is tested on 5 most typical benchmark problems which are complex in nature of finding the global optimal solution as shown below. Again, CGA has been further compared with GABF over some benchmark problems of various dimensions to test its efficacy. The list of benchmark functions have been listed in Table 3.

Figure 4. Flow diagram of CGA

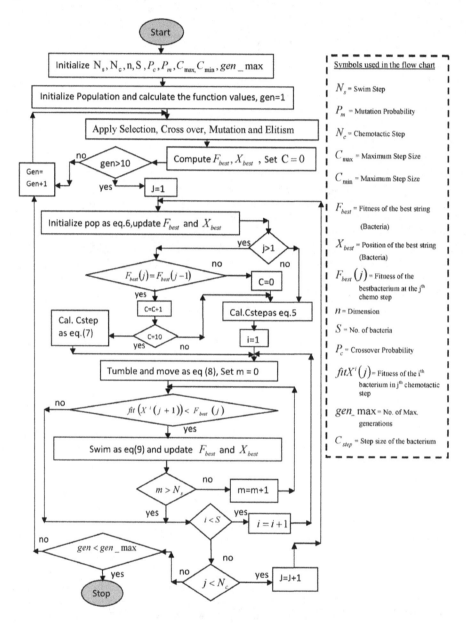

5.1. List of Five Most Typical Benchmark Problem

All the problems having fixed dimension 10. The result comparison of CGA has been done with GA over the following test problems and comparison has been shown graphically also.

(I) Ackley Problem (ACK)

$$Min_x \ f(x) = -20 \exp\left(-0.02\sqrt{n^{-1}\sum_{i=1}^{n} x_i^2}\right) - \exp\left(n^{-1}\sum_{i=1}^{n} \cos(2\pi x_i)\right) + 20 + e$$

$$(10)$$

The range of the search space is $(-37.5, \ 37.5)$ for each x_i where $i = 1, 2, ..., n$. The number of local minima is unknown. The global minimum is located at $x = (0, 0, 0, ..., 0)$ and the objective function value $f(x) = 0$. For n=10, the tests are carried out.

(II) Griewank Problem (GW)

$$Min_x \ f(x) = 1 + \frac{1}{4000}\sum_{i=1}^{n} x_i^2 - \prod_{i=1}^{n} \cos\left(\frac{x_i}{\sqrt{i}}\right)$$

$$(11)$$

where, $-600 \le x_i \le 600$ for $i \in (1, 2, 3, ..., n)$. The number of local minima is unknown for arbitrary n. But it has 500 local minima when $n = 2$. Tests were performed when $n = 10$. The function become flatter if the range of the search space is increased.

(III) RastiriginProblem (RG)

$$Min_x \ f(x) = 10n + \sum_{i=1}^{n}\left[x_i^2 - 10\cos(2\pi x_i)\right]$$

$$(12)$$

Where, $i \in (1, 2, 3, ..., n)$. The total number of minima is unknown. But the global minimum is located at $x = (0, 0, 0, ..., 0)$ with $f(x) = 0$.

(IV) Rosen Brock Problem

$$Min_x \ f(x) = \sum_{i=1}^{n-1}\left[100\left(x_{i+!} - x_i^2\right)^2 + \left(x_i - 1\right)^2\right]$$

$$(13)$$

The range of the search space $\left(-30, 30\right)$ for each x_i, $i = 1, 2, 3, ..., n$. This is known as Extended Rosenbrock function. It is function. But due to the presence of saddle point it is very difficult to locate the global minima. The function has a very narrow ridge. The objective function value $f\left(x\right) = 0$, where $x = \left(1, 1, 1, 1, ..., 1\right)$.

(V) Schwefel Problem (SWF)

$$Min_x \; f\left(x\right) = 418.9829n - \sum_{i=1}^{n} x_i \sin\left(\sqrt{|x_i|}\right) \tag{14}$$

The function is calculated in the hypercube lying in the range $\left(-500, \;\; 500\right)$, for each x_i. The function is very complex having many local minima. The objective function value is $f\left(x\right) = 0$, where $x = \left(420.9867, 420.9867, 420.9867, ..., 420.9867\right)$.

5.2. Experimental Set up and Parameter Setting

The proposed CGA program is designed in C++ and the experiment is carried out on a P-IV, 2.8 GHz machine with 512 MB RAM under WINXP platform. Here, in the first part, five benchmark functions have been solved and the result is being compared with simple GA (Deep and Das, 2007) that uses 4 types of combinations of operators of GA. (i) Tournament Selection and Single point crossover, (ii) Tournament Selection and Uniform Crossover, (iii) Roulette Wheel Selection and Single Point Crossover, and (iv) Roulette Wheel Selection and Uniform Crossover. For a fair comparison, the following parameters of GA and CGA are kept fixed as in (Deep & Das, 2007). They are as follows.(i)Population size=100,(ii) Maximum generation=500,(iii)Probability of Crossover and Probability of Mutation defined for 4 types of combinations of GA described in Table 1(Deep & Das, 2007). Apart from these fixed parameters, the parameters recommended for CGA which are found experimentally are also considered for implementation of the algorithm on 5 benchmark functions as follows. The minimum step size is ($C_{min} = 0.007$). The maximum step size is ($C_{max} = 0.1$). Number of Chemo tactic steps are 600. Next the CGA has been tested on few benchmark functions of various dimensions and compared with GABF with above parameter setting.

5.3. Result Discussion

Based on the parameter setting defined above, CGA is tested on 5 benchmarking functions and compared with GA. Everywhere in the study GA refers the best version of GA as reported in (Deep & Das, 2007). All the benchmark problems have been solved for 10 variables. 30 independent runs are carried out and the results for minimum function value are reported in Table 2. The convergence graphs of five functions have been shown from Figure 5, Figure 6, Figure 7, Figure 8, and Figure 9 respectively. It is observed that CGA outperforms for the entire considered benchmark problem (Table 2). It is worth here to realize the comparison of the convergence graphs from both GA and CGA. From the convergence graphs from Figure 5 to Figure 9, it is found that CGA converges sooner and hence faster than GA. Again, CGA has been further compared with GABF. The list of benchmark functions have been listed in Table 3. Taking the same parameter setting as recommended earlier, the average minimum function values of 30 independent runs both from GA-BF and CGA are reported in Table 4 and the convergence graphs have been plotted in Figure 10, Figure 11, Figure 12, & Figure 13 respectively. It also contains the comparison of CPU time for both the algorithms. It is observed that CGA outperforms GA-BF for the entire considered benchmark problem which is shown in Table 4. It is found from the tabular data as well as from the convergence graphs that CGA converges sooner and hence faster than GA-BF.

6. CONSTRAINED OPTIMIZATION PROBLEM

The designed algorithm is also made capable of handling constraints. It is named as Chemo-Inspired Genetic Algorithm for Constrained Optimization (CGAC). It has been applied to Non-convex Economic load dispatch problem i.e. to 15 generator system where all the operational constraints such as Generator capacity constraint, Power balance constraint, Ramp rate limit and Prohibited Operating Zones (POZ) constraints are taken into consideration and it has been compared with recent state of the art algorithm i.e. Iteration Particle Swarm Optimization (IPSO) and other algorithms also to test its efficacy.

Table 2. Comparison of Objective Function Values of GA and CGA

Fun. Sl.	Name of the Function	GA	CGA
1	ACK	0.28534 (C3)	**0.250668**
2	GWK	0.23567 (C3)	**0.029577**
3	RG	0.987788 (C3)	**1.07E-14**
4	RB	15.59604 (C4)	**0.0037**
5	SWF	1.131254 (C3)	**0.000127**

Figure 5. Convergence graph of Ackley's Problem (ACK)

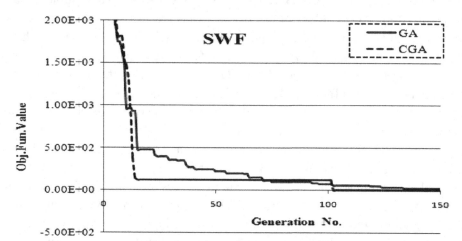

Figure 6. Convergence graph of Griewank Problem (GWK)

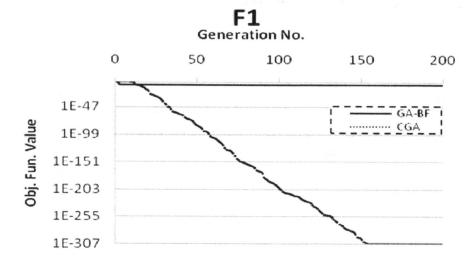

6.1. Problem Definitions of Economic Load Dispatch with Valve Point Loading, Ramp Rate Limit and POZ Constraints

The objective of the Economic Load Dispatch (ELD) problem is the determination of the optimal combination of power generations by minimizing the total generation cost satisfying all generational constraints at the same time. Here the Quadratic cost function is taken including the power loss. The overall problem can then be

Figure 7. Convergence graph of Rastrigin Problem (RG

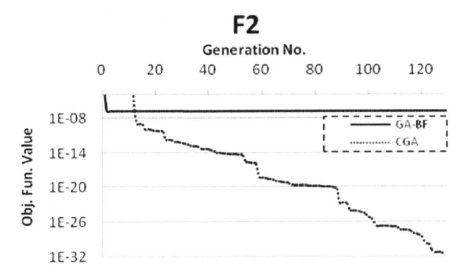

Figure 8. Convergence graph of Rosenbrock Problem (RB)

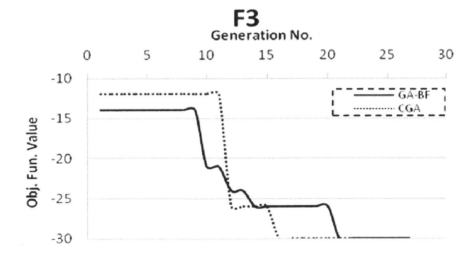

formulated as a constrained optimization problem as follows. The Economic Load Dispatch problem can be modeled mathematically as equation (15).

$$Min \ F = \sum_{i=1}^{n} F_i \left(P_i \right) \tag{15}$$

Figure 9. Convergence graph of Shewefel Problem (SWF)

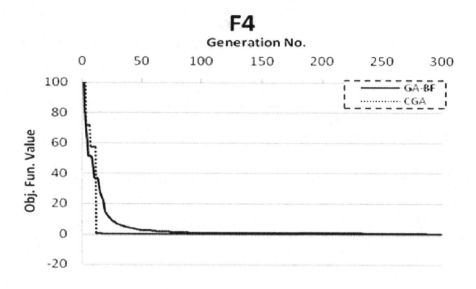

Table 3. List of test functions with the bounds of the decision variables

Test Functions		$x_i^{(L)}$	$x_i^{(U)}$
$F_1(x) = \sum_{i=1}^{3} x_i^2$		-5.12	5.11
$F_2(x) = 100\left(x_1^2 - x_2\right)^2 + \left(1 - x_1\right)^2$		-2.048	2.047
$.\, F_3(x) = \sum_{i=1}^{5}\left[x_i\right]$		-5.12	5.12
$F_4(x) = \sum_{i=1}^{30} i\,.\,x_i^4 + N(0,1)$		-1.28	1.27

Here f is the objective function describing the total generation cost. P_i, the power output of the unit. $f_i(P_i)$ is generation cost for the generator of unit i to produce power output P_i having quadratic cost function defined by equation (16). n is number of committed units.

Table 4. Comparative result (Minimum function Value) of GA-BF and CGA

Factors		Name of the Technique	$F1$	$F2$	$F3$	$F4$
Minimum objective Function value		GA-BF	2.54e-06	1.15e-07	-30	0.286627
		CGA	**4.94066e-324**	**1.2326e-032**	**-30**	**0.00699286**
CPU TIME (in Sec.)		GA-BF	11	9	13	78
		CGA	**1**	**2**	**1**	**17**

Figure 10. Convergence graph of F1

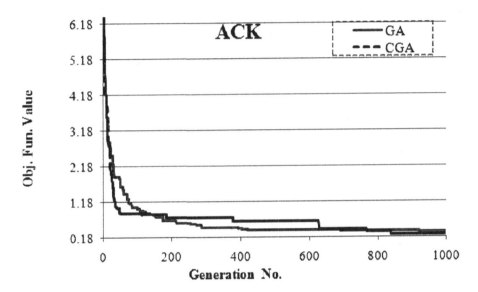

$$f_i = a_i P_i^2 + b_i P_i + c_i \qquad (16)$$

where, a_i, b_i & c_i are the coefficients of the generator.

The ELD problem is solved Subject to the following constraints four constraints:

(I) Generator Capacity Constraints: The power output of the unit should vary within its minimum & maximum limits which is defined as equation (17).

$$P_i^{\min} \leq P_i \leq P_i^{\max} \qquad (17)$$

Figure 11. Convergence graph of F2

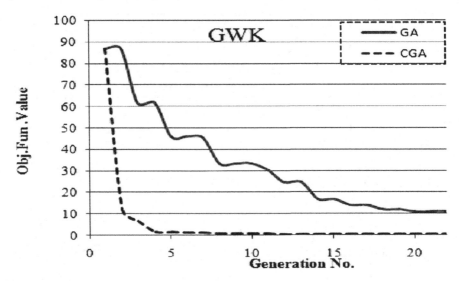

Figure 12. Convergence graph of F3

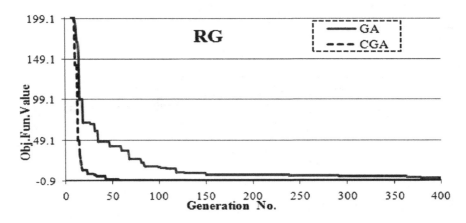

where, P_i^{min} and P_i^{max} are the minimum and maximum power output of the unit i

(II) Power Balance constraint: The power output P_i of the ith unit defined in equation (11) is subject to the power balance constraint as defined in equation (18).

Figure 13. Convergence graph of F4

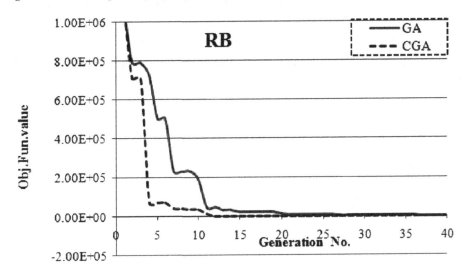

$$\sum_{i=1}^{n} P_i = P_{\mathrm{D}} + P_{\mathrm{L}} \tag{18}$$

Where P_{D} is system load demand and P_{L} is the entire transmission network losses of the system.

The power loss P_L is calculated by means of the B-coefficients matrix, which can be expressed as the quadratic function of unit power output defined as equation (19).

$$P_L = \sum_{i=1}^{n}\sum_{j=1}^{n} P_i B_{ij} P_j + \sum_{i=1}^{n} B_{0i} P_i + B_{00} \tag{19}$$

Where, B_{ij} is the ij^{th} component of loss co-efficient square matrix of size n.

(III) Ramp rate limits : If the power increases, then

$$P_i - P_i^0 \le UR_i \tag{20}$$

If the power decreases, then

$$P_i^0 - P_i \le DR_i \tag{21}$$

where P_i is the present power output of unit i and P_i^0 is the previous power output of unit i.

UR_i and DR_i are respectively the up-ramp and down-ramp limits of the ith generator (in units of MW/time-period). The inclusion of the ramp rate limit included in the generator constraints as follows.

$$Max\left(P_i^{\min}, P_i^0 - DR_i\right) \leq P_i \leq Min\left(P_i^{\max}, P_i^0 + UR_i\right) \tag{22}$$

(IV) Prohibited Operating Zones: The limitation of machine components and instability concerns of the operation zones impose certain restrictions on the generating units. So, the Prohibited operating zones can be mathematically formulated as follows.

$$\begin{cases} P_i^{\min} \leq P_i \leq P_{i,1}^{lb} \\ P_{i,j-1}^{ub} \leq P_i \leq P_{i,j}^{lb}, j = 2, 3, \ldots, nP_i \\ P_{i,j}^{ub} \leq P_i \leq P_i^{\max}, j = nP_i \end{cases} \tag{23}$$

where, $P_{i,j}^{lb}$ is the lower bound and $P_{i,j}^{ub}$ is the upper bound of prohibited operating zone j of the generator i respectively. The total number of POZ of generator i is nP_i.

6.2. Methodology Adopted in the Proposed CGAC Algorithm to Solve ELD Problem

In the proposed CGAC method to solve ELD problem with ramp rate limit and POZ constraints, the calculation for slack generator, Calculation of power output of dependent unit violating the capacity constraints and handling the POZ constraints are implemented in this algorithm and are discussed as follows.

(I) Calculation of Slack Generator (Bhattacharya & Chattopadhya, 2010)

Let P_n be the power output of the dependent generator.

$$P_n = P_D + P_L - \sum_{i=1}^{n-1} P_i \tag{24}$$

where the transmission loss is a function of all the generator outputs including the slack generator and it is given by

$$P_L = \sum_{i=1}^{n-1}\sum_{j=1}^{n-1} P_i B_{ij} P_j + 2P_n\left(\sum_{i=1}^{n-1} B_{ni} P_i\right) + B_{nn} P_n^2 + \sum_{i=1}^{n-1} B_{0i} P_i + B_{0n} P_n + B_{00}$$

(25)

Substituting the power loss term P_L into equation (24), the quadratic equation obtained is given in equation (26)

$$B_{nn} P_n^2 + 2\left(\sum_{i=1}^{n-1} B_{ni} P_i + B_{0n} - 1\right)P_n + \left(P_D + \sum_{i=1}^{n-1}\sum_{j=1}^{n-1} P_i B_{ij} P_j + \sum_{i=1}^{n-1} B_{0i} P_i - \sum_{i=1}^{n-1} P_i + B_{00}\right) = 0$$

(26)

It is a quadratic equation of the form $xP_n^2 + yP_n + z = 0$ 　　　　　　　　(27)

where $x = B_{nn}$

$$y = \left(2\sum_{i=1}^{n-1} B_{ni} P_i + B_{0n} - 1\right)$$

(28)

$$z = \left(P_D + \sum_{I=1}^{n-1}\sum_{j=1}^{n-1} P_i B_{ij} Pj + \sum_{i=1}^{n-1} B_{0i} P_i - \sum_{i=1}^{n-1} P_i + B_{00}\right)$$

(29)

$$P_n = \frac{-y \pm \sqrt{y^2 - 4xz}}{2x}$$

(30)

where, $y^2 - 4xz \geq 0$　(31)

If the inequality constraint equation (31) is violated then the power output of the generator are again reinitialized until the constraint Equation is satisfied including all other constraints of the problem concerned. If the Equation is still violated at later stage of the algorithm, the same procedure is repeated.

(II) Calculation of Power Output of Dependent Unit Violating the Capacity Constraints

For the population of strings, if the power generation of the dependent unit P_n evaluated in equation (30) exceeds the maximum limit, calculate the differential amount,

$$Difference = P_n - P_n^{\max} \tag{32}$$

$$Let \ E = \frac{Differnce}{n-1} \tag{33}$$

$$P_n = \begin{cases} P_n^{\min}, if \ P_n < P_n^{\min} \\ P_n^{\max} \ and \ P_i = P_i + E \ for \ i = 1, 2, ..., n-1, if \ P_n > P_n^{\max} \end{cases} \tag{34}$$

If for any of the generator capacity constraints equation (17) is violated, P_i is defined as follows.

$$P_i = \begin{cases} P_i^{\min}, if \ P_i \le P_i^{\min} \ for \ i = 1, 2, ..., n-1 \\ P_i^{\max}, if \ P_i \ge P_i^{\max} \ fori = 1, 2, ..., n-1 \end{cases} \tag{35}$$

(III) Handling of POZ Constraints (Yang, & Gandomi, 2012)

Let power output of ith generator satisfying the POZ constraints is given by

$$P_{i,j}^{lb} \le P_i \le P_{i,j}^{ub} \tag{36}$$

where, $P_{i,j}^{lb}$ and $P_{i,j}^{ub}$ are the lower bound and upper bound of the jth operating zone of the ith generator.

$$Evaluate \ P_{i,j}^{avg} = \left(\frac{P_{i,j}^{lb} + P_{i,j}^{ub}}{2} \right) \tag{37}$$

The power output P_i of the ith generator is defined as equation (38)

$$P_i = \begin{cases} P_{i,j}^{lb}, if\ P_{i,j}^{lb} \leq P_i \leq P_{i,j}^{avg} \\ P_{i,j}^{ub}, if\ P_{i,j}^{avg} \leq P_i \leq P_{i,j}^{ub} \end{cases} \tag{38}$$

6.3. Constraint Handling Technique in ELD Problem

The fitness of ELD problem is defined as follows:

$$Fit\_Fun = \sum_{i=1}^{n} f_i\left(P_i\right) + R\left\langle\left(g\left(x\right)\right)\right\rangle^2 \tag{39}$$

where, the objective function value f is taken as per equation (16). The penalty parameter R and bracket operator penalty function $\left\langle g\left(x\right)\right\rangle$ is defined as equation (40) and equation (41) respectively.

The penalty parameter $R^{(t)}$ for a particular generation t is proposed as follows.

$$R^{(t)} = 1.2^{\left\lfloor\frac{t}{22}\right\rfloor} \tag{40}$$

where, $\lfloor\cdot\rfloor$ indicates the floor function.

$$\left\langle g\left(x\right)\right\rangle = \begin{cases} 0, & if\ g\left(x\right) \geq 0 \\ \alpha, & if\ g\left(x\right) < 0 \end{cases} \tag{41}$$

It is worth here to note that each equality constraint in equation (39) is being equivalently expressed in two inequality terms with $\leq$ and $\geq$. For the constraint handling technique, an exterior penalty term has been used, where the bracket operator assigns a positive value to the infeasible points. The algorithm starts with a small initial value of $R^{(t)}$ and it increases step-wise with t. This way, the quality of the solution improves gradually by forcing the infeasible points towards the feasibility and finally approaches to a near optimal solution. The value of the penalty parameter in equation (40) is so fixed because it is suitable for the above constrained problem considered, which is experimentally verified.

6.4 Selection of Individuals in ELD Problem

The CGAC uses the tournament selection according to Deb's rule (2000), where two candidates in the population are compared by applying the following criteria.

1. Feasible solution is preferred over an infeasible solution.
2. Between two feasible solutions, the one having better objective function value is preferred.
3. Between two infeasible solutions, the one having smaller constraint violation is preferred.

6.5. Solution Methodology of the Proposed CGAC for the ELD Problem with Ramp Rate Limit and POZ Constraints

```
Algorithm 3: CGAC_Algo()
1.          Get the system data for the system
2.          Generate the power output of n-1 generators
```
$$P_1, P_2, \ldots, P_{n-1}$$
```
Satisfying the constraints equation (17-23)
3.          Handle the POZ constraints as equation (36-38).
4.          Calculate x, y, z from equation (27), equation (28),
and equation (29)
```
5.   Compute the power output of slack generator P_n from equation (30) satisfying the constraint defined as in equation (31)

6.   If the power output of dependent unit P_n violates equation (30)

Evaluate P_n and remaining power output of the generators by equation (32) -equation (35). Handle the POZ constraints as equation (36-38).

7.   Evaluate the Fitness function value of the ELD problem as equation (39)

8.   Evaluate the power loss P_L defined by equation (25).

9.   Apply Binary tournament selection operator as (Deb, 2000)

10.   Apply Crossover operator to get better strings from the existing strings.

11.   Apply Mutation operator.

   Compute the fitness function value and power loss as equation

(39) and equation   (25)
12.   Apply Elitism operator
13.   Chemo tactic loop:
     // Tumble and Move
(a) Initialize the search space as per equation (6)
(b) Repeat Step 2 to Step 8
(c) Update the position of the best string and best fitness
function value.
(d) Compute the Step sizes of Chemo tactic step as per equation
(5), equation (7)
(e) Compute   position of new search point as equation (8)
(f) Repeat Step 3 to Step 8
(g) Update the position of the best string and best fitness
function value
     // Swim loop:
(a) Modify the searching point in the Swim loop defined as per
equation (9)
(b) Repeat Step 3 to Step 8
(c) Update the position of the best string and best fitness
function value.
(d) Terminate the Swim loop if the maximum swim steps completed.
(e) Terminate the Chemo tactic loop if Chemo tactic steps
reached its upper limit.
14.   Repeat the process from Step 2 until the maximum
iteration is reached.

6.6. Result Discussion of Test Case

The test case includes the 15 generating units and the expected power demand is 2630MW. The system data can be found from (Chaturvedi, Pandit, & Srivastava, 2008; Gaing, 2003). It is solved considering all the operational constraints i.e. Quadratic cost function, Generator capacity constraint, Power balance constraints, Power loss, Ramp rate limits, Prohibited operating zones. For the above problem, 100 independent runs are performed by keeping the following basic parameters fixed. Population size = 40. Number of Bacteria initialized in Chemo tactic loop= 4. The Probability of cross over (P_c) = 0.9. Probability of mutation (P_m) = 0.001. Bit length $\left(l = 20\right)$. The stopping criteria is either a maximum of 500 generations is attained or no improvement is observed in the best objective function value in

Table 5. Best simulation of 15 unit systems with POZ constraints and ramp rate limits (Safari & Shayegi, 2011)

Unit power output	PSO	CPSO1	CPSO2	SOH_PSO	IPSO	CGAC
P_1	439.1162	450.05	450.02	455.00	455.00	454.9999
P_2	407.9727	454.04	454.06	380.00	380.00	380
P_3	119.6324	124.82	124.81	130.00	129.97	130
P_4	129.9925	124.82	124.81	130.00	130.00	130
P_5	151.0681	151.03	151.06	170.00	169.93	170
P_6	459.9978	460	460	459.96	459.88	460
P_7	425.5601	434.53	434.57	430.00	429.25	430
P_8	98.5699	148.41	148.46	117.53	60.43	76.0148875
P_9	113.4936	63.61	63.59	77.90	74.78	49.3533983
P_{10}	101.1142	101.13	101.12	119.54	158.02	159.972272
P_{11}	33.9116	28.656	28.655	54.50	80.00	80
P_{12}	79.9583	20.912	20.914	80.00	78.57	80
P_{13}	25.0042	25.001	25.002	25.00	25.00	25.00773494
P_{14}	41.414	54.418	54.414	17.86	15.00	15.00777308
P_{15}	35.614	20.625	20.624	15.00	15.00	20.0024973
Total power output	2662.4	2662.1	2662.1	2662.29	2660.8	2660.3585
Minimum cost($/h)	32858	32835	32834	32751.39	32709	32707.2428
P_{loss}	32.4306	32.1302	32.1303	32.28	30.858	30.358
Mean cost($/h)	33039	33021	33021	32878	32784.5	32710.0588

consecutive 200 generations. The Chemo tactic loop is initialized after 100 generations. Number of Chemo tactic steps= 40. Number of swim steps= 4.It can be visualized from the Table 4 that CGAC outperforms PSO, CPSO1, CPSO2, IPSO(Safari & Shayegi, 2011) and all other algorithms mentioned in the Table 5 in terms of minimum cost, mean cost and Power loss.

7. CONCLUSION

In this Chapter, a novel hybridization has been done inserting the Chemo tactic step at the end of the GA cycle which is named as CGA. The said algorithm has been applied on benchmark problems. Initially it is compared with Simple GA and next it is applied on GABF. It has been found from the result analysis that CGA successfully proved its efficiency over GA and GABF in terms of function value, CPU time and average number of generations. It has been further developed to handle constraints and the algorithm is named as CGAC. It has been applied on a real life constrained optimization problem i.e. Economic Load Dispatch problem. In the ELD problem it is solved taking the Quadratic cost function and power loss into account. Four operational constraints are considered in the above considered constrained problem and the problem is compared with other state of art algorithms. The designed algorithm is compared with PSO, CPSO1, CPSO2, and IPSO. It is found that it also supersedes all the algorithms with whom it is being compared. In future, the designed algorithm CGA will be further developed to handle multi-objective optimization problems. It will be applied on constrained real life problems viz. Central Time tabling problem and solving Sudoku puzzle.

REFERENCES

Bakward, K. M., Pattnaik, S. S., Sohi, B. S., Devi, S., Panigrahi, K. B., Das, S., & Lohokare, M. R. (2009). Hybrid Bacterial Foraging with parameter free PSO. *Proceedings of IEEE conference on Nature and Biologically Inspired Computing*, 1077-1081.

Beasley, D., Bull, D. R., & Martin, R. R. (1993). An overview of Genetic Algorithm: Part I-Fundamentals. *University Computing*, *15*(2), 58–69.

Bhattacharya, A., & Chattopadhyay, P. K. (2010). Hybrid Differential Evolution with Biogeography Based optimization for solution of Economic Load Dispatch. *IEEE Transactions on Power Systems*, *25*(4), 1955–1964. doi:10.1109/TPWRS.2010.2043270

Bukharov, O. E., & Bogolyubov, D. P. (2015). Development of a decision support system based on neural network and Genetic Algorithm. Expert System with Applications, 42, 6177-6183.

Chaturvedi, K. T., Pandit, M., & Srivastava, L. (2008). Self-organizing Hierarchical PSO for non -convex Economic Dispatch. *IEEE Transactions on Power Systems, 23*(3). doi:10.1109/TPWRS.2008.926455

Chen, T. C., Ksai, P. W., Chu, S. C., & Pan, J. S. (2007). A novel optimization approach: bacterial-GA foraging.*Proceedings of the Second International Conference on Innovative Computing, Information and Control*, 391–394.

Chen, Y., & Lin, W. (2009). An Improved Bacterial Foraging Optimization.*Proceedings of the IEEE International Conference on Robotics and Biomimetics*.

Ciornei, I., & Kyriakides, E. (2012). Hybrid Ant Colony-Genetic Algorithm (GAAPI) for Global Continuous Optimization. *Systems, Man and Cybernetics part B, IEEE Transactions, 42*(1), 234-245.

Costa, G. H. R., & Baldo, F. (2015). Generation of road maps from trajectories collected with Smartphone-A Method based on Genetic Algorithm. *Applied Soft Computing, 37*, 799-808.

Das, K. N. (2013). Hybrid Genetic Algorithm: An Optimization Tool. In Global Trends in Knowledge Representation and Computational Intelligence, (pp. 268-305). IGI Global.

Deb, K. (2000). An efficient constraint handling method for genetic algorithms. *Computer Methods in Applied Mechanics and Engineering, 186*(2-4), 311–338. doi:10.1016/S0045-7825(99)00389-8

Deep, K., & Das, K. N. (2007). Choice of selection and crossover on some Benchmark problems. *International Journal of Computer. Mathematical Sciences and Applications, 1*(1), 99–117.

Deep, K., & Das, K. N. (2008). Quadratic approximation based Hybrid Genetic Algorithm for Function Optimization. *Applied Mathematics and Computation, Elsevier, 203*(1), 86–98. doi:10.1016/j.amc.2008.04.021

Fa, M. X., & Ling, L. (2012). Bacterial Foraging algorithm based on gradient PSO algorithm.*Proceedings of Eighth International Conference*, 29-31.

Fan, S. K., Liang, Y. C., & Zahara, E. (2006). A genetic algorithm and a particle swarm optimizer hybridized with Nelder–Mead simplex search. *Computers & Industrial Engineering, 50*(4), 401–425. doi:10.1016/j.cie.2005.01.022

Fatma, A. O., & Mona, M. A. (2010). Genetic Algorithm for task scheduling problem, *J. Parallel Distrib. Comput, Elsevier, 70*, 13–22.

Gaing, Z. L. (2003). PSO to solving the Economic Dispatch considering the generator constraints. *IEEE Transactions on Power Systems, 18*(3). doi:10.1109/TPWRS.2003.814889

Goldbarg, M. C., Goldbarg, E. F. G., Menzes, M. S., & Luna, H. P. L. (2016). Quota Travelling Car rentor Problem: Model and Evolutionary Algorithm. *Information Sciences, 367-368*, 232–245. doi:10.1016/j.ins.2016.05.027

Goldberg, D. E. (1989). *Genetic Algorithms in Search, Optimization, and Machine Learning.* Addison Wesley.

Hashemi, S., Kiani, S., Noroozi, N., & Moghaddam, M. E. (2010). An Image Contrast enhancement method based on Genetic Algorithm. *Pattern Recognition Letters, 31*(13), 1816–1824. doi:10.1016/j.patrec.2009.12.006

Holland, J. H. (1975). *Adaptation in Natural and Artificial systems.* Ann Arbor, MI: The University of Michigan Press.

Hu, Y., Liu, K., Zhang, X., Su, L., Ngai, E. W. T., & Liu, M. (2015). Application of Evolutionary Computation for rule discovery in Stock Algorithmic trading: A Literature Review. *Applied Soft Computing, Elsevier, 36*, 534–551. doi:10.1016/j.asoc.2015.07.008

Hwang, S. F., & He, R. S. (2006). A hybrid real parameter genetic algorithm for function optimization. *Advanced Engineering Informatics, 20*(1), 7–21. doi:10.1016/j.aei.2005.09.001

Kao, Y. T., & Zahara, E. (2008). A hybrid genetic algorithm and PSO for multimodal functions. Applied Soft Computing, 8, 849-857.

Kim, D. H., Abraham, A., & Cho, J. H. (2007). A hybrid genetic algorithm and bacterial foraging approach for global optimization. *Information Sciences, 177*(18), 3918–3937. doi:10.1016/j.ins.2007.04.002

Liu, Q., & Xu, J. (2012). Traffic Signal Timing Optimization based on Differential Evolution Bacterial Foraging Algorithm. *Procedia: Social and Behavioral Sciences, 43*, 210–215. doi:10.1016/j.sbspro.2012.04.093

Michalewicz, Z. (1994). *Genetic Algorithms+ Data structures=Evolution program* (2nd ed.). Berlin: Springer-Verlag. doi:10.1007/978-3-662-07418-3

Niu, B., Fan, Y., Xiao, H., & Xue, B. (2012). Bacteria foraging based approach to Portfolio Optimization with liquidity risk. *Neuro Computing, 98*, 90–100.

Niu, B., Wang, H., Wang, J., & Tan, L. (2013). Multiobjective Bacterial foraging Optimization. *Neuro Computing, 116*, 336–345.

Panigrahi, B. K., & Pandi, V. R. (2009). Congestion Management using Adaptive foraging algorithm. *Energy Conversion & Management, 50*(5), 1202–1209. doi:10.1016/j.enconman.2009.01.029

Passino, K. (2002). Biomimicry of bacterial foraging for distributed optimization and control. *IEEE Control Systems Magazine, 22*(3), 52–67. doi:10.1109/MCS.2002.1004010

Pattanaik, S. S., Bakward, K. M., Devi, S., Panigrahi, B. K., & Das, S. (2010). Parallel Bacterial Foraging optimization. *Handbook of swarm intelligence Adaptation, Learning and optimization, 8*, 487-502.

Qu, B. Y., Liang, J. J., Wang, Z. Y., Chen, Q., & Suganthan, P. N. (2016). Novel Benchmark functions for Continuous Multimodal Optimization with Comparative results. *Swarm and Evolutionary Computation, Elsevier, 26*, 23–34. doi:10.1016/j.swevo.2015.07.003

Ray, P. K., & Subudhi, B. (2012). BFO optimized RLS algorithm for Power system harmonics Estimation. *Applied Soft Computing, 12*(8), 1965–1977. doi:10.1016/j.asoc.2012.03.008

Russo, M. (2016). A Distributed Neuro-genetic Programming Tool. *Swarm and Evolutionary Computation, 27*, 145–155. doi:10.1016/j.swevo.2015.10.009

Safari, A., & Shayeghi, H. (2011). Iteration PSO procedure for economic load dispatch with generator constraints. Expert Systems with Applications, 38, 6043-6048.

Shen, H., Zhu, Y., Zhou, X., Guo, H., & Chang, C. (2009). Bacterial foraging optimization algorithm with particle swarm optimization strategy for global numerical optimization. *Proceedings of the ACM/SIGEVO Summit on Genetic and Evolutionary Computation*, 497-504.

Singh, T. K., & Das, K. N. (2016). Behavioural Study of Drosophila Fruit Fly and its Modelling for Soft Computing Application. In Problem Solving and Uncertainty Modelling through Optimization and Soft Computing Applications, (pp. 32-84). IGI Global. doi:10.4018/978-1-4666-9885-7.ch003

Srinivas, M., & Patnaik, L. M. (1994). Genetic Algorithm: A Survey. *Computer, IEEE. Computers & Society, 27*(6), 17–26. doi:10.1109/2.294849

Tan, X., & Bhanu, B. (2006). Fingerprint Matching by genetic algorithms. *Pattern Recognition, Elsevier, 39*(3), 465–477. doi:10.1016/j.patcog.2005.09.005

Tripathy, B. K., & Acharjya, D. P. (2014a). *Global Trends in Intelligent Computing Research and Development*. IGI Global Publishers. Retrieved from www.igi-global.com

Tripathy, B. K., & Acharjya, D. P. (2014b). *Advances in Secure Computing, Internet Services, and Applications*. IGI Global Publishers. Retrieved from www.igi-global.com

Tripathy, M., & Mishra, S. (2007). Bacterial Foraging Based solution to optimize Both Real Power Loss and Voltage Stability Limit. *IEEE Transactions on Power Systems, 22*(1), 240–248. doi:10.1109/TPWRS.2006.887968

Tripathy, M., Mishra, S., Lai, L. L., & Zhang, Q. P. (2006).Transmission Loss Reduction based on FACTS and Bacterial Foraging Algorithm. *Proceedings of 9*[th] *International Conference* on *Parallel Problem Solving from Nature*, 222-231.

Wang, F., Yu, P. L. H., & Cheung, D. W. (2014). Combining technical trading rules using Particle Swarm Optimization. *Expert System with Applications, Elsevier, 41*(6), 3016–3026. doi:10.1016/j.eswa.2013.10.032

Wei, L., & Zhao, M. (2005). A niche hybrid genetic algorithm for global optimization of continuous multi modal functions. *Applied Mathematics and Computation, 160*(3), 649–661. doi:10.1016/j.amc.2003.11.023

Wolpert, D. H., & Macready, W. G. (1997). No free lunch Theorems for Optimization. *IEEE Transactions on Evolutionary Computation, 1*(1), 67–82. doi:10.1109/4235.585893

Wu, M. S., Jeng, J. H., & Hsieh, J. G. (2006). Schema Genetic Algorithm for fractal Image Compression. *Engineering Applications of Artificial Intelligence, Elsevier, 20*(4), 531–538. doi:10.1016/j.engappai.2006.08.005

Yang, X. S., Hosseini, S. S. S., & Gandomi, A. H. (2012). Firefly Algorithm for solving non-convex economic dispatch problems with valve loading effect. *Applied Soft Computing, Elsevier, 12*(3), 1180–1186. doi:10.1016/j.asoc.2011.09.017

Yuan, Q., Qian, F., & Du, W. (2010). A hybrid genetic algorithm with the Baldwin effect. *Information Sciences, Elsevier, 180*(5), 640–652. doi:10.1016/j.ins.2009.11.015

Yudong, Z., & Lenin, W. (2009). Stock Market Prediction of S&P 500 via combination of Improved BCO approach and BP Neural network. Expert Systems with Applications, 36, 8849-8854.

Zhang, G., & Lu, H. (2006). Hybrid real coded genetic algorithm with quasi simplex technique. *International Journal of Computer Science and Network Security*, 6(10), 246–255.

KEY TERMS AND DEFINITIONS

Bacterial Foraging Optimization: It is a Bio-inspired Computing technique used for solving Optimization problems.

Benchmark Functions: These are the standard problems which are being used by researchers for testing the efficiency of their designed/proposed techniques for both unconstrained and constrained optimization problems. These are readily available in the internet.

Chemo-Taxis: It is an important computational step in Bacterial Foraging optimization.

Economic Load Dispatch: Economic Load Dispatch is determination of the optimal combination of power generations by minimizing the total generation cost satisfying all generational constraints at the same time.

Hybridization: It is the process of designing of new efficient and robust algorithm by combining different types of Evolutionary algorithms.

Power Balance Constraint: It is an important constraint under which the objective function of the Economic load dispatch problem is minimized. This function describes that the total power generation is sum of the total load demand of the system and total transmission losses of the system.

Prohibited Operating Zones: In Prohibited operating zones, restrictions are imposed on generating units due to the limitation of machine components and instability concerns of the operation zones.

Ramp Rate Limit: The power generation in certain interval cannot exceed that of the previous generation by more than a certain amount which is called up ramp limit and also it will not be less than the previous interval by more than a certain amount which is defined as down ramp limit.

Chapter 10
Gene Expression Programming

Baddrud Zaman Laskar
NIT Silchar, India

Swanirbhar Majumder
NERIST, India

ABSTRACT

Gene expression programming (GEP) introduced by Candida Ferreira is a descendant of genetic algorithm (GA) and genetic programming (GP). It takes the advantage of both the optimization and search technique based on genetics and natural selection as GA and its programmatic Darwinian counterpart GP. It is gaining popularity because; it has to some extent eradicated the 'cons' of both while keeping in the 'pros'. It is still a new technique not much explored since its introduction in 2001. In this chapter both GA and GP is first discussed followed by the elaborate discussion of GEP. This is followed up by the discussion on research work done is different fields using GEP as a tool followed up by GEP architectures. Finally, here GEP has been used for detection of age from facial features as a soft computing based optimization problem using genetic operators.

1. INTRODUCTION

In 1950 and 1960 several scientists independently started studying evolutionary systems with this idea that it can be used as an optimization tools for engineers in future. Genetics is a biological process where a parent passes certain genes onto their children. Every child inherits genes from both of their biological parents and

DOI: 10.4018/978-1-5225-2375-8.ch010

Copyright ©2017, IGI Global. Copying or distributing in print or electronic forms without written permission of IGI Global is prohibited.

these genes inherit certain specific quality. Thus, genetics is study of heredity. Gene lies within a chromosome. This biological process leads to an idea of evolving a population of candidate solution to a given problem by the concepts of natural genetic variation and natural selection. Genetic algorithm was invented by John Holland and it was developed by his students and colleagues in the middle of 1960 and 1970. Holland's main focus is to design an algorithm to solve some unusual specific problem. Gradually he developed the ways in which natural adaptation can be imported into computer systems. Present day, a genetic algorithm (GA) is an optimization tool that mimics the process of natural selection, in the computer science field of artificial intelligence. Genetic programming (GP) is an extension of GA. GP began with an evolutionary algorithm, first used by Nilis Aall Barricelli, applied to evolutionary simulations in 1954. Tree-based genetic programming concept was first introduced by Nicheal L. Cramer but it is expanded by Koza (1992). Gene expression programming (GEP) was then first introduced by Ferreira (2001, 2002). It is related to both genetic algorithm and genetic programming. The chapter discuss in detail about GA, GP and how they lead to the development of genetic expression programming.

2. GENETIC ALGORITHM

Genetic algorithm is an optimization and search technique which is mainly based on the principles of genetics and natural selection. It is inspired by Darwin's theory of evolution. It starts with a set of solution (represented by chromosome) called initial population. Solution from one population is taken based on its fitness and is used to generate new population. The fitness function is defined over the genetic representation and measures the quality of represented solution. The fitness function is always dependent upon the problem specified. This gives a hope that new population will be far better than the old population. Thereby it can be concluded that GA can be a parallel mathematical algorithm that transforms a set of individual population with some fitness value into a whole new set of population with better fitness value associate with it. GA believes in the survival of the fittest. It is a search algorithm that mimics the natural process of evolution, where each individual can be an aspirant solution. Genetic algorithm is the larger class of evolutionary algorithm (EA), which generates optimized solutions for problems using techniques inspired by natural evolution, such as inheritance, mutation, selection, and crossover. GA allows a population composed of many individuals to evolve under specified selection rules to a state that maximizes the fitness. It can be applied in bioinformatics, phylogenetic, computational science, engineering, economics, chemistry, manufacturing, physics, mathematics, pharmacometrics, and other fields.

2.1 Methodology

In genetic algorithm, a population of candidate solutions to an optimization problem is evolved towards better solutions. Each candidate solution has a set of properties which can be mutated and altered. Traditionally, solutions are represented in terms of binary digits, as strings of 0's and 1's, but other encodings are also possible. The evolution usually starts from a population of randomly generated individuals and is an iterative process, where the population in each iteration is called a generation. In each generation, the fitness of every individual in the population is evaluated; the fitness is usually the value of the objective function in the optimization problem being solved. The relatively fitter individuals are stochastically selected from the current population, and each individual's genome is modified (recombined and possibly randomly mutated) to form a new generation. The new generations of candidate solutions are then used in the next iteration of the algorithm. Commonly, the algorithm terminates when either a maximum number of generations has been produced, or a satisfactory fitness level has been reached for the population. A typical genetic algorithm requires a genetic representation of the solution domain, and a fitness function to evaluate the fitness of the solution domain.

A standard representation of each candidate solution is as an array of bits. Arrays of other types and structures can also be used essentially the same way. The main property that makes these genetic representations convenient is that their parts are easily aligned due to their fixed size, which facilitates simple crossover operations. Variable length representations may also be used, but crossover implementation is more complex in such cases. Tree-like representations are explored in genetic programming and graph-form representations are explored in evolutionary programming; a mix of both, linear chromosomes and trees are explored in gene expression programming.

Once the genetic representations and the fitness functions are defined, a GA proceeds to initialize a population of solutions and try to improve it through repetitive application of the mutation, crossover, inversion and selection operators. The various steps in applying Genetic Algorithm for a problem are briefly discussed below.

1. **Initialization**: Initially many individual solutions are (usually) randomly generated to form an initial population. The population size depends on the nature of the problem, but typically contains several hundreds or thousands of possible solutions. Traditionally, the population is generated randomly, allowing the entire range of possible solutions (the search space). Occasionally, the solutions may be "seeded" in areas where optimal solutions are likely to be found.

2.   **Selection**: During each successive generation, a proportion of the existing population is selected to breed a new generation. Individual solutions are selected through a fitness-based process, where more fitter solutions (as measured by a fitness function) are typically more likely to be selected. Certain selection methods rate the fitness of each solution and preferentially select the best solutions. Other methods rate only a random sample of the population, as the former process may be very time-consuming.

The fitness function is defined over the genetic representation and measures the quality of the represented solution. The fitness function is always problem dependent. For instance, in the knapsack problem, one wants to maximize the total value of objects that can be put in a knapsack of some fixed capacity. A representation of a solution might be an array of bits, where each bit represents a different object, and the value of the bit (0 or 1) represents whether or not the object is in the knapsack. Not every such representation is valid, as the size of objects may exceed the capacity of the knapsack. The fitness of the solution is the sum of values of all objects in the knapsack if the representation is valid or 0 otherwise.

In some problems, it is hard or even impossible to define the fitness expression; in such cases, a simulation may be used to determine the fitness function value of a phenotype (e.g. computational fluid dynamics is used to determine the air resistance of a vehicle whose shape is encoded as the phenotype), or even interactive genetic algorithms are used.

3.   **Genetic Operators**: The next step is to generate a second generation population of solutions from the already selected solutions, through genetic operators such as crossover and mutation.

For each new solution to be produced, a pair of parent solutions is selected for breeding from the pool selected previously. By producing a child solution using the above methods of crossover and mutation, a new solution is created which typically shares many of the characteristics of its parents. New parents are selected for each new child, and the process continues until a new population of solutions of appropriate size is generated. Although reproduction methods that are based on the use of two parents are more biology inspired, some research suggests that more than two parents generate higher quality chromosomes. These processes ultimately result in the next generation population of chromosomes that are different from the initial generation. Generally the average fitness would have increased by this procedure for the population, since only the best organisms from the first generation are selected for breeding, along with a small proportion of less fit solutions, for reasons already mentioned above. Opinions vary over the importance of crossover versus mutation. There are many references in works of L. J. Fogel in 1998 and 2006, which support the importance of mutation-based search. Although crossover and mutation are considered as the main genetic operators, it is possible to use other operators such as regrouping, colonization-extinction, or migration in genetic algorithms. It is worth tuning parameters, such as the mutation probability, crossover probability and population size to find reasonable settings for the problem class being worked on. A very small mutation rate may lead to genetic drift. A recombination rate that is too high may lead to premature convergence of the genetic algorithm. A mutation rate that is too high may lead to loss of good solutions unless there is elitist selection. There are theoretical but not yet practical upper and lower bounds for these parameters that can guide in selection.

4. **Termination**: This generational process is repeated until a termination condition has been reached. Common terminating conditions are, if a solution is found that satisfies minimum criteria, or a fixed number of generations reached, or allocated budget (computation time/money) reached, or the highest ranking solution's fitness is reaching or has reached a plateau such that successive iterations no longer produce better results or manually inspected and terminated or all the above are satisfied.

2.2 Advantages and Disadvantages of Genetic Algorithm

The advantages of genetic algorithm are linearization of the problem is not needed, more probable models sampled more frequently than less probable ones and computation of partial derivatives is not needed.

The disadvantages of genetic algorithm are initially show fast convergence but improvement is progressively slower, convergence is lot more difficult in presence of lots of noises, and models with more parameters are computationally difficult to deal with.

2.3 Important Applications of GA

Some of the real world application of GA in GP is given below. These are automotive design, hardware evolves and biometric invention.

1. **Automotive Design**: Best engineering for faster, lighter and fuel efficient cars gene algorithm can give best combinations of materials and also aerodynamic shapes.
2. **Hardware Evolves**: GA computer model is used to design electronic circuit of new configurations from old one.
3. **Biometric Invention**: Since GA is use in biological evolution so it makes sense that it is used in invention also.

3. GENETIC PROGRAMMING

Genetic programming is an extension of GA proposed by Koza (1992), where each individual is a computer program not just raw data. Koza defines GP as a domain independent problem solving approach in which computer programs are evolved to solve, or approximately solve the problems based on the Darwinian principle of reproduction and survival of the fittest and analogs of naturally occurring genetic operations such as crossover and mutation. It has evolved to rectify some drawbacks of GA. There is no assurance that a genetic algorithm will find a global optimum, as it often happens that the populations have lots of subject. In real world problems such as structural optimization problem, one single function evaluation may take several hours to several days for simulation.

Genetic programming typically starts with a population of randomly generated computer programs, composed of the available programmatic ingredients. Genetic programming iteratively transforms a population of computer programs into a new generation of the population by applying analogs of naturally occurring genetic operations. These operations are applied to individual(s) selected from the population. The individuals are probabilistically selected to participate in the genetic operations based on their fitness. The fundamental elements of an individual are its genes, which come together to form a code. An individual's program is a tree like structure and as such there are two types of genes, functions $(+, -, *, /, \cdots)$ and terminals $(x, y, 1, 2, \cdots)$. Terminals in tree terminology are leaves, while functions are nodes with children. The function-children provide arguments for the functions. Assuming the genes have been chosen, the first step is to create random population. Once the random population has been created, the individuals needs to assess for the fitness. After passing all the individuals through the fitness test, the evolutionary process starts and the individuals in the new population are generated by some genetic operators. Figure 1 represents the block diagram of GP.

GP evolves computer programs, traditionally represented in memory as tree structures. Trees can be easily evaluated in a recursive manner. Every tree node has an operator function and every terminal node has an operand, making mathematical expressions easy to evolve and evaluate. Thus traditionally GP favors the use of programming languages that naturally embody tree structures. Non tree representations (Ting, 2005) has been suggested and successfully implemented, such as linear genetic programming, which suits the more traditional imperative languages. The commercial GP software disciples use automatic induction of binary machine code AIM to achieve better performance. μGP uses directed multi-graphs to generate programs that fully exploit the syntax of a given assembly language. Figure 2 represents as an example of a function represented as a tree structure.

Figure 1. Block diagram of GP

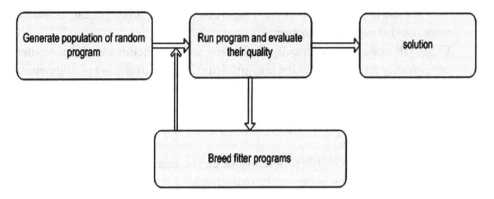

Figure 2. A function represented as a tree structure

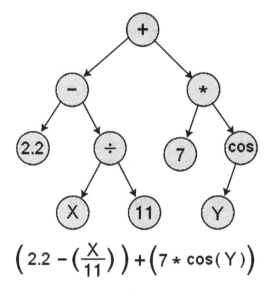

$$\left(2.2 - \left(\tfrac{X}{11}\right)\right) + \left(7 * \cos(Y)\right)$$

3.1 Advantages and Disadvantages of GP

The main advantages of genetic programming are discussed below.

1. Computer programs which are evolved by GP are of variable length, it does not have fixed length solution. It can find a solution up to hardware imitation.
2. It does not require as much as knowledge as GA. Normally, GA requires a lot of domain knowledge. Whereas, it is not necessarily required in GP to decide on a genotype representation and a genotype phenotype (genotype and phe-

notype words are used in genetics which represent organism's full hereditary information and actual observed properties such as development, behavior respectively) mapping function.

3. Using GP one can theoretically evolve any series of actions that a computer can possibly provide, provided one gives the GP algorithm a set of commands to choose, that can describe all possible actions.

Some of the disadvantages of genetic programming are as follows:

1. In GP, number of possible problems that can be constructed by the algorithm is extremely big. This is one of the reasons why one can think that it would be impossible to find programs that are good solutions to a given problem. But this problem is not as big as it seems to be, because there are also an enough number of ways to construct a solution. One can already construct a nearly infinite number of solutions by simply adding commands that do not have any influence on the result. However, this proves that it is very improbable that GP finds the best solution.

2. In GP algorithm it might take a very long time to find a good solution. Machine codes are usually fast but if someone uses high level statements then those must be compiled and they create very big program which makes them very slow.

3. A small variation might have huge effect on fitness or the quality of the solution. In GP it is normally more serious than GA.

3.2 Applications of Genetic Programming

The different applications of the genetic programming include function synthesis and symbolic regression, data mining and classification process, circuit designing (analog circuit), robotics (for optimizing robot control), creating security protocols, network and communication (sorting networks).

3.3 Comparison Between GA and GP

Output of the genetic programming is a computer program while the output of the genetic algorithm is a quantity. Genetic programming is highly influential and also powerful than genetic algorithms. Genetic programming works best for several types of problems. Suppose there is a no idle solution then in such cases genetic programming will attempt to find a solution to compromise and be the most efficient solution from the list of variables. Moreover, genetic programming is useful in finding solutions where variables are constantly changing.

4. GENE EXPRESSION PROGRAMMING

Gene expression programming (GEP) belongs to the family of evolutionary algorithms and is closely related to genetic algorithm and genetic programming. It evolves computer programs of different sizes and shapes encoded in linear chromosomes of fixed length. From the genetic programming, it inherited the parse trees of various sizes and shapes. Similarly, from genetic algorithm, it inherits the linear chromosome of fixed length. In GEP, the linear chromosome works as the genotype and the expression tree as phenotype, creating a genotype-phenotype system. The chromosomes are composed of multiple genes. Each gene is encoding a smaller sub program. Furthermore, the structural and functional organization of the linear chromosomes allows the unconstrained operation of important genetic operators such as mutation, transposition, and recombination.

First of all, both GAs and GP are simple replicator systems, with the latter considerably more complex than the former. This means that the entities these systems evolve go about their business doing what has to be done and when their time comes, they must reproduce their bodies to perpetuate their line. But reproducing bodies with modification might not be an easy task, especially if the bodies are complex structures like the parse trees that GP evolves. Indeed, the canonical GP technique is limited to the use of very conservative operators that change the trees in a way reminiscent of the grafting and pruning familiar to gardeners and farmers around the world. Firstly, in genotype-phenotype systems there are no restrictions concerning the type and number of modifications in the genome and therefore all the paths and crannies of the fitness landscape are accessible to meander through. Secondly, these systems are free to explore different levels of organization for instance, genes are expressed into proteins; proteins form ribosomes etc. Obviously these higher levels of complexity are completely inaccessible to simple replicator systems, for no matter how complex, they continue to be a single structure, forever incapable of becoming a part of a much more complex being.

Kangshun et al. (2008) had introduced the concept of auto design of digital circuit and optimization of the complex digital with a specific function in a feasible and effective way by using GEP. The new method of designing hardware is combined programmable logic devices with evolutionary algorithm. The k-map way is one of the popular traditional methods, but it meets trouble with the large scale ones to get optimized structure of the circuit. They proposed a new method to optimize the complex digital circuit and design a new fitness function based on GEP. Antonine (2006) derived the problem of traffic engineering (TE) to evaluate the performance of evolutionary algorithms when used as IP routing optimizers and assess the relevance of using GEP as a new fine tuning algorithm in destination and flow based TE. They compared the evolutionary algorithms when used in fine-tuning IGP routing with the objective of finding link weights that maximize a network bandwidth usage. Zhao, Zhou & Meifang (2010) had proposed indoor positioning model based on GEP and it made full use of GEP to dig up the hidden nonlinear relationship between the distance and the received signal strength.

Varrette & Muszynski (2012) has recently introduced cryptographic hash function in modern cryptography. It has many security applications. In their paper, the GEP hash search frame work was proposed. The objective was to build compression function with reasonably good properties by means of the gene expression programming heuristic which was an efficient alternative to the classical genetic programming (GP). Khattab, Abdelaziz, Mekhamer, Badr & Saadany (2012) had introduced GEP for the first time in literature to judge static security of power systems. The algorithm was formulated as a multi class classification problem using the one against all binarization method.

Omkar, Ramaswamy, Senthilnath, Bharath & Anuradha (2012) recently proposed GEP based fuzzy logic approach for multiclass crop classification using multispectral satellite images. This was aimed at utilizing the optimization capabilities of GEP for tuning the fuzzy membership functions. Aminuddin & Azamathulla (2012) had introduced development of GEP based functional relationship for sediment transport in tropical rivers. For their experiment they had modeled for the functional relationship for three rivers of Malaysia. Results of which suggested that the proposed GEP model was a robust total sediment load predictor. A functional relation had been developed using GEP with non-dimensional variables. The proposed GEP approach gave satisfactory results compared to existing predictors.

Fernando, Jose, & Ramos (2012) had introduced GEP in sensor characterization. They combined impedance spectroscopy, gene expression programming (GEP), and genetic algorithms to perform sensor characterization. Improvements on the application of GEP for impedance characterization were also presented. It has been shown that impedance spectroscopy could be used to characterize a sensor even when there was no knowledge of whatsoever the sensor's internal structure. GEP is a suitable tool to search for an appropriate equivalent circuit topology and GAs that are used to estimate the circuit component value. Wang, Zhang & Wang (2010) had introduced the research idea of neural network prediction based on GEP. They had taken 30 GEP-BP groups and the average forecast error was 0.03313. The same data when used by BP neural network gave the average prediction error as 0.03325. So their analysis showed that GEP-BP neural network had good prediction, high precision, and was better than the BP neural network. Weihong, Wei & Li (2010) had proposed fuzzy decision tree construction with gene expression programming. It had been used to evolve parsimonious decision tree with high accuracy comparable to C4.5. In that paper they proposed a GEP based decision tree technique with fuzzy attributes transformation strategy, the technique could significantly reduce the number of branches need to split the decision tree, thus improving the classification accuracy. There they described the details of fuzzification process of classification attributes and the member function results in two benchmark problems. This showed that the GEP method could find better generalized ability rules.

In GEP basically do classification, function finding, time series prediction and logic synthesis based problems can be dealt with. Some of the important, published work has been tabulated in the Tables 1, 2, 3 and 4.

The performance of basic GEP is highly dependent on the genetic operator's rate. Siwei, Zhihua, Dan, Yadong & Li, (2005) had presented a new algorithm called GEPSA that combined GEP and simulated annealing (SA). GEPSA actually decreases the dependence on genetic operator's rate without impairing the performance of GEP. Results suggest that GEPSA is more efficient, not only in terms of the accuracy of the best evolved models are better than basic GEP, but also in terms of the average fitness and average R-square. It was better than the basic GEP, when run on 100 independent times. Chen, Li, Wang, Yang & Zhu (2008) proposed a HDN-GEP model by which many complex high or super-high power polynomial functions in function finding could be solved easily and efficiently. Furthermore, the efficiency of evolution was improved drastically. Extensive Experiments demonstrated that HDN-GEP algorithm was effective in dealing with function finding for high or super high ranks. GEP had difficulty in finding the appropriate numeric constants for terminal nodes in the expression trees. Zhang, Zhou, Xiao &

Table 1. For classification

Researchers	No of samples	No of generations	Technique	No of chrom-osomes	Reduced error
Li et. al (2007)	100	300	DM tools with GEP	gene 3	1%-6% acc
Omkar et. al (2012)	n/a	1000	GEP based fuzzy logic	Chromosome 20	N/A
Wang et. al (2010)	2-5	N/A	GEP with fuzzy attribution	N/A	0.7%-2.852%
Alsulaiman et. al (2009)	1000	100000	GEP	Gene 3	N/A
Wu et. al (2008)	20	100	Improved GEP	N/A	43.3%-48.8%
Zhang et. al (2007)	21	1000	GEP	N/A	5.901x10-6
Duan et. al (2009)	200	500	HDGEP	N/A	1.63-9.61%
Zhang et. al (2009)	30	1000	GEP with PCA	Gene 4	0.5458%
Yu et. al (2012)	30	100	GEP	Gene 3	N/A

Table 2. In the field of function finding

Researchers	No of samples	No of generations	Technique	No of chromosomes	Reduced error
Ghani et. al (2012)	3	1000	GEP	Gene 2	N/A
Lin et. al (2010)	2	100	PGEP	Gene 7	40%
Chen et. al, (2008)	1	N/A	HDNGEP	Gene 1	1.8%
Siwei et. al (2005)	3	3897	GEPSA	Gene 6	8%
Yuan (2009)	3	5000	DFF-GEP	Gene 3	10%

Table 3. In the field of time series prediction

Researchers	No of samples	No of generation's	Technique	No of chromosomes	Reduced error
Bautu et. al (2005)	50	200	GEP	Gene 3	N/A
Zhang et. al (2011)	80	1000	GEP	Gene 4	>2.73%
Zhao et. al (2010)	100	2000	GEP	Gene 5	15-29%
Moghassem et. al (2011)	10-100	2000-8000	GEP	Gene 3, 4, 6, 10	0.02-5.14 Absolute

Table 4. In the field of logic synthesis

Researchers	No of samples	No of generation	Technique	No of chromosome	Reduced error
Li, Liang, Jheng & Wang (2008)	100	2000	GEP	N/A	N/A

Nelson (2007), had described an approach of constant generation using differential evolution (DE), a real-valued GA robust and efficient at parameter optimization. Experimental results on two symbolic regression problems showed that the approach significantly improved the performance of the GEP algorithm. Li, Chen, Wang, Ren & Xia (2012) had introduced an adaptive multi-phenotype GEP algorithm. They proposed a way to solve the problem of excessive evolutionary generations and massive time consuming. In the evolutionary process of AM-GEP, individuals changed the number of genes adaptively and the convergence rate was greatly improved with a new gene combination mechanism. AM-GEP took the advantage of the gene combination, not only improved the convergence rate, leading to the significant decrease in the running times, but also extended the expression space of chromosomes.

4.1 Architecture of GEP Programs

There are two main players in GEP: the chromosomes and the expression trees (ETs). Here the latter being the expression of the genetic information encoded in the former. As in nature, the process of information decoding is called translation. And this translation implies obviously a kind of code and a set of rules. The genetic code of GEP is very simple: a one-to-one relationship between the symbols of the genes and the nodes they represent in the trees. The rules are also very simple: they determine the spatial organization of nodes in the expression trees and the type of interaction between sub-ETs. Therefore, there are two languages in GEP: the language of genes and the language of expression trees. Due to the simple rules that determine the structure of ETs and their interactions, it is possible to infer immediately the expression tree given the sequence of a gene, and vice versa. This means that a very complex program can be chosen to be represented by its compact genome without losing in meaning. This unequivocal bilingual notation is called Karva language.

The structural organization of GEP genes is better understood in terms of open reading frames (ORFs). In biology, an ORF or coding sequence of a gene begins with the start codon, continues with the amino acid codons, and ends at a termination codon. However, a gene is more than the respective ORF, with sequences upstream of the start codon and sequences downstream of the stop codon. And although in GEP the start site is always the first position of a gene, the termination point does not always coincide with the last position of a gene. Consequently, it is common for GEP genes to have non-coding regions downstream of the termination point. These non-coding regions obviously do not interfere with expression but, nonetheless, they play a crucial role in evolution, for they alone allow the creation of valid programs no matter how profoundly their chromosomes are modified. Consider, for example, the algebraic expression in equation 1. It can also be represented as a diagram or an expression tree in Figure 3.

$$\sqrt{(a - b)(c + d)} \tag{1}$$

Here Q represents the square root function. This kind of diagrammatic representation is what is called the phenotype in Gene Expression Programming. And the genotype can be easily inferred from the phenotype as in the figure above is the straightforward reading of the expression tree from left to right and from top to bottom.

Figure 3. Expression tree and the genotype can be easily inferred from the phenotype

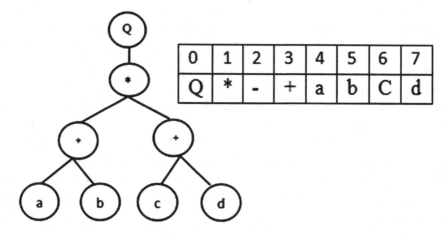

0	1	2	3	4	5	6	7
Q	*	-	+	a	b	C	d

4.1 K-Expressions and Genes

The k-expressions of gene expression programming correspond to the region of genes that gets expressed. This means that there might be sequences in the genes that are not expressed, which is indeed true for most genes. The reason for these non coding regions is to provide a buffer of terminals so that all *k*-expressions encoded in GEP genes correspond always to valid programs or expressions. The genes of gene expression programming are therefore composed of two different domains – a head and a tail – each with different properties and functions. The head is used mainly to encode the functions and variables chosen to solve the problem at hand, whereas the tail, while also used to encode the variables, provides essentially a reservoir of terminals to ensure that all programs are error-free. For GEP genes the length of the tail is given by the formula in equation (2).

$$t = h\left(n_{\text{max}} - 1\right) + 1 \tag{2}$$

Here h is the heads length and n_{max} is maximum arity. For example, for a gene created using the set of functions $F = \{Q, +, -, *, /\}$ and the set of terminals $T = \{a, b\}$, $n_{\text{max}} = 2$. If a head length of 15 is chosen, then $t = 15\,(2 - 1) + 1 = 16$, which gives a gene length g of $15 + 16 = 31$. The randomly generated string in Figure 4 is an example of one such gene.

In this case, it only uses 8 of the 31 elements that constitute the gene. Each gene codes for a sub ET and sub ETs interact with one another forming a more complex multi subunit ET. It is not hard to see that, despite of their fixed length, each gene

Figure 4. Randomly generated string and its expression tree

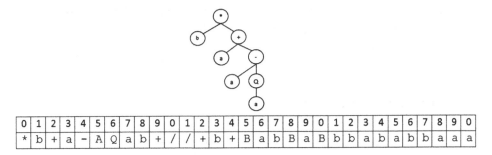

0	1	2	3	4	5	6	7	8	9	0	1	2	3	4	5	6	7	8	9	0	1	2	3	4	5	6	7	8	9	0
*	b	+	a	–	A	Q	a	b	+	/	/	+	b	+	B	a	b	B	a	B	b	b	a	b	a	b	b	a	a	a

has the potential to code for expression trees of different sizes and shapes, with the simplest form, composed of only one node (when the first element of a gene is a terminal) and the largest form, composed of as many nodes as there are elements in the gene (when all the elements in the head are functions with maximum arity). It is also not hard to see that it is trivial to implement all kinds of genetic modification (mutation, inversion, insertion, recombination, and so on) with the guarantee that all resulting offspring encode correct, error-free programs.

4.2 The Basic Gene Expression Algorithm

Once the initial random population has been created the process of evolution can be used to find individuals that model the data better. The fundamental steps of the basic gene expression algorithm are as under.

1. Select function set
2. Select terminal set
3. Load dataset for fitness evaluation
4. Create chromosomes of initial population randomly
5. For each program in population
    a) Express chromosome
    b) Execute program
    c) Evaluate fitness
6. Verify stop condition;
7. Select programs;
8. Replicate selected programs to form the next population;
9. Modify chromosomes using genetic operators;
10. Go to step 5

The first four steps prepare all the ingredients that are needed for the iterative loop of the algorithm (steps 5 through 10). Of these preparative steps, the crucial one is the creation of the initial population, which is created randomly using the elements of the function and terminal sets. Figure 5 represents a flowchart of gene expression programming.

4.3 Important Features of GEP

The important functions of GEP are (*i*) many fitness functions can be chosen, (*ii*) algebraic simplification of the combined function can be done automatically, (*iii*) automatic generation of 16 different language's source code including C, MATLAB, VHDL, etc. (*iv*) relative importance of the predictor values can be computed, (*v*) random and fixed constant.

Figure 5. Flowchart of GEP

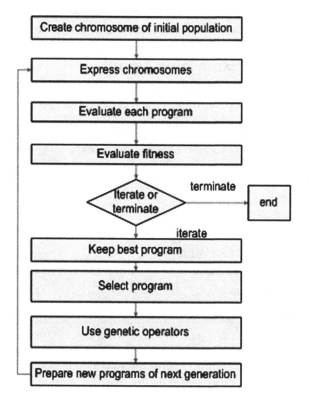

4.4 Applications of GEP

Here the exact applications of GEP tool is problem solving. How the basic gene expression algorithm can be used to solve complex problems from very different fields is mainly discussed here. Some of the open source libraries for GEP tool are GEP4J (GEP for Java Project), PyGEP (Gene Expression Programming for Python) and jGEP (Java GEP toolkit). Another most popular GEP tool is GeneXpro. GeneXpro tool is a flexible modeling tool designed for function finding, classification, time series prediction, and logic synthesis. Once the raw data of relevant format is loaded the model as per the problem is generated. Indeed, all models evolved by gene expression programming can be immediately converted into virtually any programming language (Ada, C, C++, C#, Fortran, Java, Java Script, Matlab, Pascal, Perl, PHP, Python, Visual Basic, VB.Net, Verilog, and VHDL) through the use of grammars, including the universal representation of parse trees. These trees can then be used to grasp immediately the mathematical intricacies of the evolved models and therefore are ideal for extracting knowledge from data. The evolved models or code files can be used in their respective interactive development environment or IDE. These are used to create software for prediction of unknown behavior, classification of unclassified samples, futuristic forecasting based on past samples, parsimonious circuit designing and so on. Thereby creating sophisticated software applications as well as even aid for hardware applications.

This algorithm has the power to extract knowledge from noisy data, not only by mining a noisy computer-generated dataset but also by mining complex real world data. Also it provides the flexibility of choosing different approaches to achieve the goal. There can be numerous ways of solving a particular problem. Here two examples are discussed. They are the work implemented by the authors and their associates. The first one is a three class prediction of the medicinal plant data which can be tackled using two different approaches is also discussed (Pathak, Pathak, Shaw & Majumder, 2014). The goal is to classify three different types of plants based on four measurements: sepal length, sepal width, petal length and petal width. The first consisting of the conventional way of partitioning the data in to three separate datasets so that three different models are created and afterwards combined to make final prediction; and the second consisting of a three-genic system evolving three different models at the same time, in which each model is responsible for classifying a certain type of plant. Here the plant data or biological data is first interpreted, then segregated and classified using GEP. Then the system model generated by the GEP 'karva' is converted to VHDL module. Finally RTL synthesis is done in Xilinx as in Figure 6 (Pathak, Pathak, Shaw & Majumder, 2014).

The second example is outcome of research study done by Baddrud, Sunil & Majumder, 2013) where they estimate age of a human being in four age groups 0-17,

Figure 6. Process of taxonomy of biological data using GEP

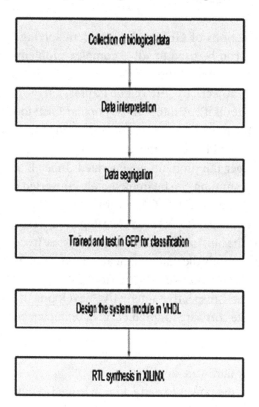

18-34, 35-50 and 51-69.In this the first consisting of the conventional way of partitioning the whole data in three separate dataset so that three different models are created and afterwards combined to make the final classification; and the second consisting of a four genic system evolving four different models at the same time, in which each model is responsible for classification of a certain age group. The algorithm used for this is as shown in Figure 7 (Baddrud, Sunil & Majumder, 2013) and the four class classification via 3 models of GEP is shown in Figure 8.

The second approach is very appealing and GEP system with multiple outputs (GEP-MO) is indeed very efficient at solving relatively complex problems of this kind. But for really complex problems (problems with more than 10 different classes and/or more than 50 attributes),the first approach although more time consuming, is a better choice as it is much more flexible in terms of both the structure and the composition of each sub model. In that paper we follow the first approach, the conventional one. Because the numbers of attributes were 68 and they are highly nonlinear.

Figure 7. Proposed Algorithm for GEP based age estimation using facial features

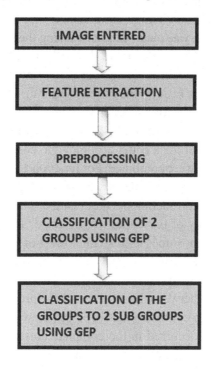

Figure 8. Classification of four age groups using 3 GEP system models

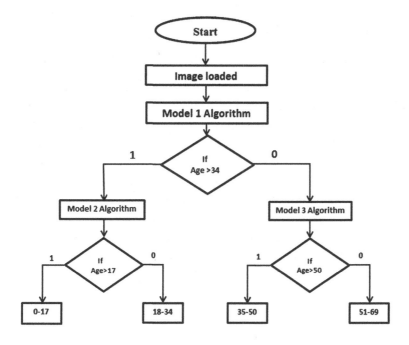

In this study, the numbers of chromosomes have been varied and different results were obtained at different numbers of chromosomes for each of the three models. The tabulated result which was obtained after varying the number of chromosomes is shown below in Table 5. Here the table shows the best fitness and accuracy for each of the three functions at different number of chromosomes. The best fitness is out of 1000 and the result is better if the fitness is near to 1000. Accuracy shows the percentage of correct classification for each function. The number of chromosomes have been increasingly changed from 20-42. At 26 chromosomes the best accuracy i.e., 80% was obtained. But for a better accuracy the best functions were selected from each of the three and were combined. For function 1, the best result is obtained at 22 chromosomes, for function 2, the best result is obtained at 26 chromosomes, but interestingly in the third function the best result has been obtained at 20, 22, 34 and 36 chromosomes. Any of these four was selected. The program size depends upon the number of chromosomes used so the lowest of the lot was decided upon. The result obtained by combining the above mentioned best three functions can be shown through confusion matrix.

The confusion matrix between the response of the program and required output is taken for the analysis. A confusion matrix plot is shown in Figure 9 which shows different types of errors occurred in the complete classification model. Thus on choosing the best of three models much better accuracy is achieved compared to the classification at any fixed number of chromosomes.

In classification problems where the output (the dependent variable) is often binary, it is important to set criteria to convert predicted values (usually real valued numbers) in to zero or one. This is the 0/1 rounding threshold R that converts the output of an individual program in to 1 if the output is equal to or greater than R, or in to 0 otherwise.

Several studies show that not all the attributes integrate the model evolved by GEP, which indicates that they are apparently irrelevant to the decision at hand. In fact, of the many attributes, only some of them are used in the extremely accurate models. This is indeed a good example of how gene expression programming can be successfully used for extracting knowledge from huge databases and designing good predictive models. For those who are not very good in programming the gene expressions GeneXproTools is an ideal tool. This is because it can be used to make extrapolations or predictions once the automated model of GEP is created by it. This automated model is normally created by the GeneXproTools based on the number of chromosomes as defined by the user of the default number (if not provided by the user) once the raw data is provided.

Figure 9. Confusion matrix obtained using the three best functions in GEP

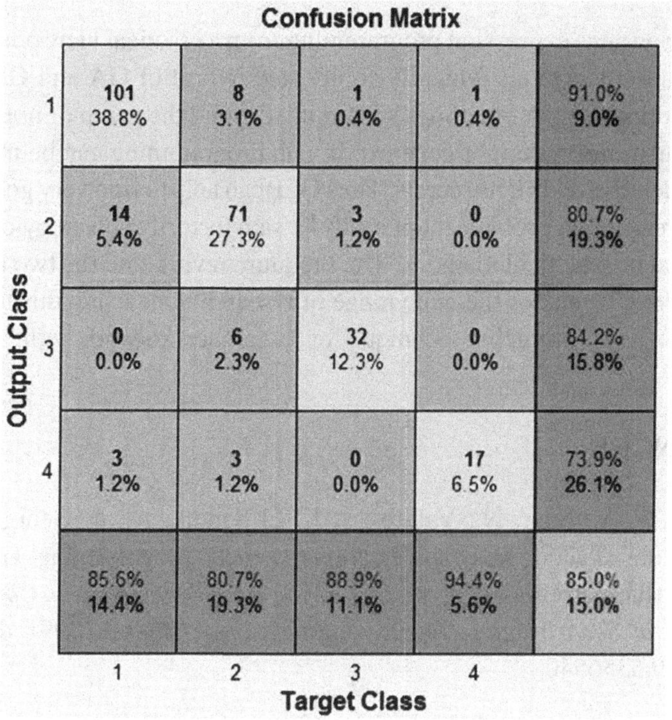

Table 5. GEP function accuracy results

No. of chromosomes	Best Fitness (out of 1000)			Accuracy (%)			Overall Accuracy (%)
	Fun1	Fun2	Fun3	Fun1	Fun2	Fun3	
20	685.86	675	1000	83.85	86.41	100	72.69
22	811.33	656.01	1000	93.46	84.95	100	73.46
24	614.43	732.47	918.2	84.62	89.81	96.30	73.08
26	745.62	786.25	972.2	88.46	93.21	98.15	80.00
28	705.92	672.68	944.4	89.23	85.92	98.15	75.00
30	652.32	613.40	833.3	86.15	83.50	94.44	70.38
32	622.80	618.55	888.8	84.23	83.01	96.30	78.85
34	607.61	695.87	1000	83.85	87.38	100	71.54
36	690.90	690.37	1000	85.38	87.38	100	73.46
38	738.00	636.59	944.4	88.85	83.98	98.15	74.23
40	632.01	673.53	972.2	79.62	86.41	98.15	66.54
42	655.91	671.13	918.2	86.54	85.92	96.30	73.46

5. CONCLUSION

This chapter on gene expression programming from a practical view point discusses the optimization technique which is an updated hybrid of GA and GP. Although natural evolution seems sometimes something beyond the grasp of normal people, the simple artificial system of gene expression programming can be minutely dissected in order to reveal all its secrets. Thus GEP can help to find very good solutions to difficult real-world problems, not easily or satisfactorily solved by conventional mathematical or statistical methods. The literature review and the two applications briefly referred, discusses the wide range of research done using this tool, thereby introducing a new optimizing technique for researchers to work with.

REFERENCES

Alsulaiman, F. A., Sakr, N., Vald'es, J. J., El Saddik, A., & Georganas, N. D. (2009). Feature selection and classification in genetic programming: application to haptic-based biometric data. *Proceedings of the IEEE Symposium on Computational Intelligence in Security and Defense Applications (CISDA 2009)*. doi:10.1109/CISDA.2009.5356540

Ashutosh, Laskar, Kumar, & Majumder. (2013). Gene Expression Programming Based Age Estimation Using Facial Features. *IEEE Second International Conference on Image Information Processing (ICIIP-2013)*. doi:10.1109/ICIIP.2013.6707631

Bagula, A. B. (2006). *Traffic Engineering Next Generation IP Networks using Gene Expression Programming*. IEEE.

Bautu, Bautu, & Luchian. (2005). *A GEP based approach for solving fredholm first kind integral equations*. IEEE.

Chen, Li, Wang, Yang, & Zhu. (2008). HDN-GEP a novel gene expression programming with high density node. *Proceedings IEEE*.

Ding & Yuan. (2009). A compression algorithm for multi-streams based on GEP. *Proceeding to 2009 Third International Conference on Genetic and Evolutionary Computing*. DOI doi:10.1109/WGEC.2009.26

Duan, L., Tang, C., Tang, L., Zuo, J., & Zhang, T. (2009). An effective microarray data classifier based on gene expression programming. *Proceeding of fifth International Conference on Natural Computation*. doi:10.1109/ICNC.2009.267

Ferreira, C. (2001). Gene Expression Programming: A New Adaptive Algorithm for Solving Problems. *Complex Systems, 13*(2), 87–129.

Ferreira, C. (2002). Gene Expression Programming: Mathematical Modeling by an Artificial Intelligence. Angra do Heroismo.

Ghani & Azamathulla. (2012). *Development of GEP-based functional relationship for sediment transport in tropical rivers.* Springer-Verlag London.

Hongbin, W., Liyi, Z., & Huakui, W. (2010). The research of neural network prediction based on GEP. *Proceedings of second international workshop on educational technology and computer science.* doi:10.1109/ETCS.2010.16

Janeiro, Santos, & Ramos. (2012). *Gene Expression Programming in Sensor Characterization: Numerical Results and Experimental Validation.* IEEE.

Khattab, Abdelaziz, Mekhamer, Badr, & EI-Saadany. (2012). *Gene Expression Programming for Security Assessment of Power Systems.* IEEE.

Koza, J. R. (1992). *Genetic Programming: On the Programming of Computers by Means of Natural Selection.* MIT Press.

Li, K., Liang, J., Jheng, W., & Wang, F. (2008). *A new method of evolving digital circuit based on Gene Expression Programming.* IEEE.

Li, Q., Chen, C., Wang, W., Ren, C., & Xia, S. (2012). An adaptive multi-phenotype GEP algorithm. *Proceedings of 8th International Conference on Natural Computation (ICNC 2012).*

Li, Q., Wang, W., Han, S., & Li, J. (2007). Evolving classifier ensemble with gene expression programming. *Proceedings of third International Conference on Natural Computation.* doi:10.1109/ICNC.2007.362

Lin, Y.-S., & Liang, X.-T. (2010). Gene expression programming with parallel hybrid model. *Proceedings of the Ninth International Conference on Machine Learning and Cybernetics.* doi:10.1109/ICMLC.2010.5580717

Moghassem & Fallahpour. (2011). *Processing parameters optimization of draw frame for rotor spun yarn strength using gene expression programming (GEP) Fibers and Polymers.* DOI 10.1007/s12221-011-0970

Omkar, S. N., Nikhil Ramaswamy, J., Senthilnath, Bharath, S., & Anuradha, N.S. (2012). Gene Expression Programming- Fuzzy Logic method for crop type classification. IEEE.

Pathak, B. J., Pathak, K. J., Shaw, A. K., & Majumder, S. (2014). GEP based Classification of Biological Data. *Proceedings of National Conference on Emerging Global Trends in Engineering & Technology (EGTET)*.

Siwei, Zhihua, Dan, Yadong, & Qu. (2005). Gene expression programming based on simulated annealing. *Proceedings IEEE*.

Ting, C.-K. (2005). On the Mean Convergence Time of Multi-parent Genetic Algorithms Without Selection. Advances in Artificial Life, 403–412. doi:10.1007/11553090_41

Varrette, Muszynski, & Bouvry. (2013). *Hash Function generation by means of Gene expression programming*. DOI:10.2478/v10065-012-0027-x

Weihong, W., Wei, R., & Qu, L. (2010). *Fuzzy decision tree construction with Gene Expression Programming*. IEEE. doi:10.1109/ISKE.2010.5680877

Wu, Y., Chun-nian, Z., Zhang-can, H., & Zong-yue, W. (2008). An improved gene expression programming(GEP) algorithm based on classification. *Proceeding of 3rd International Conference on Innovative Computing Information and Control (ICICIC'08)*. doi:10.1109/ICICIC.2008.145

Yu, J., & Qian, J. (2012). Students creativity modeling with gene expression programming. In *Proceeding of International Conference on Computer Science and Electronics Engineering*. IEEE.

Zhang, D., Huang, Y., Zhi, J., & Zhang, D. (2009). Discovery of mineralization predication classification rules by using gene expression programming based on PCA. *Proceeding of Fifth International Conference on Natural Computation*. doi:10.1109/ICNC.2009.367

Zhang, D., Zhang, J., Cheng, R., & Zhang, W. (2011). A combination forecasting method based on GEP. *Proceeding of 2011 Fourth International Conference on Business Intelligence and Financial Engineering*. DOI doi:10.1109/BIFE.2011.1

Zhang, Q., Zhou, C., Xiao, W., & Nelson, P. C. (2007). Improving gene expression programming performance by using differential evolution. *Proceeding of Sixth International Conference on Machine Learning and Applications*. doi:10.1109/ICMLA.2007.62

Zhao, Y., Zhou, H., & Li, M. (2010). *Gene Expression Programming Model for Determining Location in Wireless LANs*. IEEE. doi:10.1109/WICOM.2010.5601087

Chapter 11
Bio–Inspired Techniques in Rehabilitation Engineering for Control of Assistive Devices

Geethanjali Purushothaman
VIT University, India

ABSTRACT

The intelligent control of assistive devices is possible from bio-signals or gestures to find the user's intention. The goal of the user intention recognition system is to develop computational methods for decoding the acquired bio-signal data. One of the methods of accomplishing the objective will be using the pattern recognition system. The study of higher level control of assistive device using various data processing techniques with bio-inspired techniques is in progress. The knowledge of bio-inspired computation is essential for the neophytes to develop algorithms for identification of intention from bioelectric signals. Most literatures, demonstrates the application using signals and not much definite study describes the various bio-inspiring computation involved to develop the control of assistive devices in real-time. Therefore, this chapter presents a brief survey of the various bio-inspiring techniques used in interfacing devices for identification of information from the user intends.

DOI: 10.4018/978-1-5225-2375-8.ch011

Copyright ©2017, IGI Global. Copying or distributing in print or electronic forms without written permission of IGI Global is prohibited.

1. INTRODUCTION

Pattern recognition is a method of identifying the input information into particular category or class from various classes. Various researches have been carried out in improving control of intelligent assistive devices in the various stages of pattern recognition techniques, namely data preprocessing, feature extraction, feature selection/reduction, classification along with the development of control strategy of electric motor. In pattern recognition, the data usually considered as the raw measurements or raw values taken from the subjects to be classified. A simple block diagram of pattern recognition based control of assistive devices is shown in Figure 1.

The term feature in pattern recognition, refer to the result of the transformations applied to the raw data in order to transform them into another domain or space using time domain/ frequency domain/ time-frequency domain technique. Although, many features can be extracted from raw data for decoding intention and not all of them possesses discriminant capabilities. Some of the extracted features could cause confusion and degrade the classifier. Further, smaller the dimension of the feature vector, lesser the computation time and memory requirements. Therefore, choice of features or reduction of features is essential. Feature dimension reduction provides a method to decide whether it is necessary to include more features that would significantly contribute to the performance of the classifier. It is not a trivial to select the best set of features or the best transformation. The features must be selected or transformed based on the given problem. For the feature selection, some neural networks, population based bio-inspired techniques can be used. The features selection process involves choice of subset of extracted features in feature space by starting with all/without features or subset consisting of random features from the feature space. Feature selection process in the context of assistive devices will be reviewed later in this chapter. The Fourier transform and time-frequency transom yield coefficients of larger dimension and few of its coefficients carry the useful information to obtain the good classification performance. In literature, researchers applied feature reduction using linear or nonlinear projection of features to transform high dimensional feature space to lower dimensional feature space. A very popular method of feature reduction is principal component analysis (PCA) in which the features are projected to lower dimensional space to visualize the underlying class

Figure 1. Block diagram of pattern recognition based control of assistive device

by linear projection. There are other many feature reduction approaches like linear discriminant analysis (LDA), fuzzy discriminant analysis (FDA), self-organizing feature map (SOFM), kernel-based FDA, etc. are discussed in literatures.

The feature selection aims to cut the dimensionality by eliminating irrelevant and redundant features, thus considering a subset of features that characterize the best discrimination of patterns. Since, it is difficult to find the discriminant features and selection algorithm using population based technique, use evaluation function to find the features of good discriminating capability. Feature selection would ease the problem of over fitting and reduces the classifier computation time. The existing feature selection techniques in the literature are divided as filters and wrappers according to their dependency on the classification algorithms. Typically, feature selection techniques could be useful in supervised or unsupervised learning algorithms. The filter approach is independent of classification algorithm and uses statistical properties to identify the relevant features. Due to this capability, filter approach is computationally preferred than the wrapper approach. However, it has disadvantage of local optimal solution due to its single iteration. The wrapper approach is based on a classification algorithm need more computation time, but more accurate than the filter approach. The hybrid approach combines the advantages of the filter and wrapper.

Feature selection based on a search strategy is necessary to explore the feature space. However, an exhaustive search from the feature space is computationally difficult, starting from an empty/full feature set for the entire/no feature set with all possible combinations to decide the relevance features. This exhaustive search takes $2n$ possible combination and computationally very expensive. Therefore, heuristic or population based search techniques have been employed.

Various search algorithms that differ in their optimality and computational cost have been utilized by the researchers to search the solution space. Bio-inspired computation algorithms have been successfully applied to the feature selection approach using wrapper approach. The bio-inspired computation algorithm has been an active research area in various disciplines such as image processing, signal processing, electrical drives, power system, data mining, rehabilitation engineering, load forecasting, curve fitting, etc. due to their capability maximize or minimize the objective function. These computation algorithms are stochastic techniques and found to be computationally efficient than the deterministic approaches. The various bio-inspired computational techniques are population-based search techniques include Evolutionary Programming (EP), Evolutionary Strategy, (ES) Genetic Algorithm (GA), Particle Swarm Optimization (PSO), etc. to find the optimal solution. The bio-inspired technique, neural network (NN) is useful in identification of the category from the input feature. These bio-inspired algorithm find potential application, not only in feature selection, feature classification and also in the development of control of assistive devices.

The bio-inspired computation in rehabilitation engineering is useful at two different control levels, i.e. feature selection, classification for high level and identification of parameters of the drive, development of controller for the drive at a low level to do the desired movement control in assistive devices.

This chapter aims to cover various bio-inspired computation approaches in the context of dimensionality reduction, classification, parameter identification, controller in rehabilitation engineering are discussed in detail. Most literatures, demonstrates the application of EEG signals, EMG signals, EOG signals, speech signals, etc. and not much definite study describes the various bio-inspiring computation involved in the development of assistive devices in various stages in real-time. This chapter covers the applications of bio-inspired algorithm in various perspectives. This chapter describes various bio-inspired techniques and algorithm widely considered in assistive device control. Subsequently, the application of the approaches in assistive devices is discussed (Barrero, Grisales, Rosas, Sanchez & Leon, 2001; Guo, Yang, Chen, Wang & Li, 2006; Jung, Kim, Lee, Chung & Eom, 2007; Shuman, 2009; Yazama, Mistukura, Fukumi & Akamatsu, 2003).

2. BIO-INSPIRED TECHNIQUES

The biologically inspired (or bio-inspired) paradigms have ability to solve complex problems to simple problems with little or without the knowledge of the system. Bio-inspired algorithms conceive a natural phenomenon through adaptation possesses the speed, robust capabilities for solving computationally complex optimization, controller and decision-making problems in a number of fields. The neural computing had been formulated in late 1960's and the concept of evolutionary computation had been proposed in early 1970's. Most applications of neural network (NN) have been in control engineering and decision making application. The evolutionary computation techniques have been in optimization of drive parameter and feature selection to the classifier. The techniques are briefly discussed in the following subsection (Chong & Sundaraj, 2009; Kelly, Parker, Scott, 1990; Markou & Singh, 2003, Smith, Nanda & Brown, 2009).

2.1 Artificial Neural Network

Researchers are inspired by the human brain and its capability of solving control problems, decision making problems, etc. The human brain, consists of densely interconnected neurons and forming the synapses between the interconnection. Each neuron is composed of cell body a processing element, input units called dendrites and an output is transferred via axon. The information is transferred from one neuron to another neuron, when the electric potential due to release of ions from the synaptic junction, reaches a threshold called an action potential. The network receives input data from the sensory system and process the input to perform a complex task.

An artificial neural network also consists of a computing element which receives input signals. Each input has an associated weight to express the strength or importance of the signals which are analogous to synapse in biological brain. The weights are adapted through the learning process. The computing element transforms the weighted sum of input using the transfer function/activation function to a specific output. An artificial representation of a neuron with three inputs $[P_1, P_2, P_3]$ and an output is shown in Figure. 2. The inputs are connected with weights $[W_1, W_2, W_3]$.

The output of the neuron is given as $f(P_1 W_1 + P_2 W_2 + P_3 W_3)$. The weights are calculated using supervised learning rule or unsupervised learning rule. In supervised learning, weights are calculated during the training phase using input and output pattern, whereas in unsupervised learning, the prior output is unknown for the training input. During training the neural network maps the input to output to perform optimization, clustering. Supervised training is suitable for solving complex pattern recognition problems (Ma, Kumar & Pah, 2001; Matsumura, Mitsukura, Fukumi & Akamatsu, 2002; Tsuji, Fukuda, Kaneko & Koji, 2000; Zhao, Xie, Jiang, Cai, Liu & Hirzinger, 2005).

There are many activation functions to transform the input to the output. The widely used activations function is unipolar binary, bipolar binary, logarithmic sigmoidal activation function, tan sigmoidal activation, linear function. The activation functions are functions of weighted sum of input X, the mathematical model of the widely used activation function is given below.

Figure 2. Structure of three input neuron

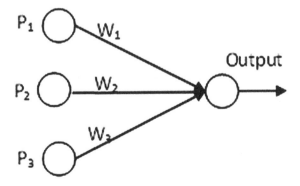

$$\text{Unipolar binary} = \begin{cases} 1; & X > 0 \\ 0; & X < 0 \end{cases} \quad (1)$$

$$\text{Bipolar binary} = \begin{cases} 1; & X > 0 \\ -1; & X < 0 \end{cases} \quad (2)$$

$$\text{Logarithmic Sigmoid} = \frac{1}{1 + e^{-X}} \quad (3)$$

$$\text{Tan sigmoid} = \frac{1 - e^{-X}}{1 + e^{-X}} \quad (4)$$

Linear $y = X$

$$\text{Unipolar binary} = \begin{cases} 1; & X > 0 \\ 0; & X < 0 \end{cases} \cdot \text{Bipolar binary} = \begin{cases} 1; & X > 0 \\ -1; & X < 0 \end{cases}$$

Iliterature, different types of ANN architecture are available such as the single layer perceptron, multilayer perceptron, Hopfield network, Hamming network, Kohenen's self organizing maps, and so on. Each type of ANN exhibits different properties due to the connection between neurons, i.e. architecture, activation function, and learning algorithm to adjust the weights. The number of input and output neurons depends upon the application to be solved. The architecture of ANN, learning algorithm for adjusting weights is chosen depending upon the nature of the problem. From all these types of ANNs, in this chapter a widely used multilayer perceptron and self-organizing feature map are discussed in this chapter (Huynh & Dunnigan, 2010; Del & Park, 1994; Guo, Yu, Zhen, Liu, Zhang & Zhang, 2009; Tsenov, Zeghbib, Palis, Shoylev & Mladenov, 2006).

2.2 Multilayer Perceptron

A single layer perceptron network has a layer of neurons with connected weights and suitable to solve only linearly separable problems. The multiayer perceptron (MLP) is a feedforward, neural network to overcome the limitation of the single layer perceptron network, consists of hidden layer between input and output layer of neurons. The number of hidden layers and units of hidden layers varies with the complexity of the problem. A structure of three layered network with input, hidden and an output layer is shown in Figure. 3 (Huang, Liu, Liu, W & Wong, 2003; Kennedy & Eberhart, 1995;.

Figure 3. Multilayer feedforward neural network

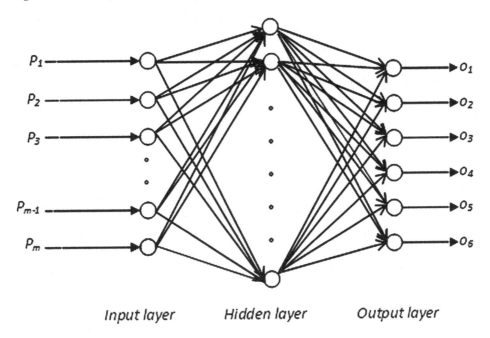

Input layer   Hidden layer   Output layer

The neurons in the input layers and does not process and accept inputs, neurons in hidden layer perform computation and output layer for accepting the signal of output. There are different learning algorithms and the widely used approach is the back-propagation algorithm. The MLP is trained with a set of training input and output patterns. The training starts with the initialization of random weights and calculating the output signal for every stage based on the activation function considered. The neural network output is compared with the actual output to find the mismatch and adjust the error in backward. If the network output is satisfying the criterion, then the network is said to be trained and the performance of the network is tested with the untrained input pattern. If the network output is within the criterion, the MLP is said to be trained. There is a parameter called momentum constant, used to accelerate/decelerate the speed of learning in MLP. The response of the MLP in the classification task is commonly calculated using the confusion matrix. The off-diagonal elements of the confusion matrix indicates, the number of times a pattern belonging to the class i, was misclassified as class j. The diagonal of confusion matrix corresponds to an accuracy of classification. Since each class pattern may be confused with another class pattern. Therefore, the sum on each row and column may be different from 100%. The generalization capability of the neural network, is checked using cross-validation process Chong & Sundaraj, 2009; Kelly, Parker & Scott, 1990; Ma, Kumar & Pah, 2001).

The objective of cross-validation is to determine the weights that maximize the accuracy of prediction. The k fold cross validation is carried out by dividing the training pattern U into k equal parts, i.e., $U_i = i; i = 1, 2, \cdots, k$. In the ith fold of the cross validation, the set U_i is used for testing and the remaining $(k-1)$ sets are used for training the neural network. After all k folds of cross validation, over the k folds, the weights of highest predication accuracy is chosen (Del & Park, 1994; Markou & Singh, 2003).

2.3 Kohonen Self-Organizing Maps

A Kohonen self-organizing map (KSOM), (Kohonen, 1995) is an unsupervised neural network used for clustering input patterns. In addition to clustering, the network reduces the size input vector by mapping into lower dimension map. This network is commonly known as self-organizing map (SOM), find application in signal processing, image processing, decision making, etc. The SOM is a feed forward network consists of input layer and D dimensional computational or output layer. The dimension D could be one or two. The neurons in computational layer are defined with topological neigbours based on neigbouring function. The neighboring neurons are defined based on Gaussian function or distance based function varying in number from dozen to thousands. Every neuron in computational layers is connected to input neuron with weights. The structure of 1-D, SOM is shown in Figure. 4.

Figure 4. 1-D SOM Structure

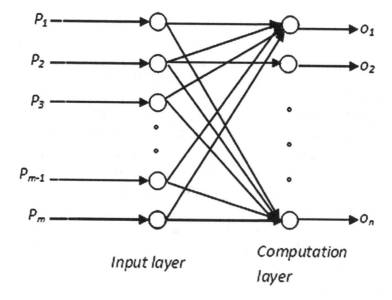

Input layer

Computation layer

The unsupervised training for clustering starts with input data without class labels for good representation of the training data set as possible. The unsupervised network weight is updated based on competitive learning. During training, the network weights are initialized from the initial random weight values and distance between input vector and weight vectors are calculated. The winner as well as neighbouring neurons weights is updated during the training. The training continues until the clustering of training vector stabilizes by repeated exposing of input. However, SOM is not widely used for clustering of input in control of assistive device.

SOM is preferred to reduce the dimension of feature vectors. The number of feature weight elements is equal to the input feature vector in the feature space. In case of feature selection, SOM is trained similar to clustering. The weight vector with large value of weight preserves the information and those features are considered for further processing. Therefore, dimension of the feature is reduced from original dimension to lower dimension without losing much information (Kennedy & Eberhart, 1995; Khushaba, Al-Ani & Al-Jumaily, 2007).

2.4 Fuzzy Clustering

The fuzzy approach for transition of fuzzy sets consisting of classes of objects is gradual and not binary 0 or 1. This is the convenient form for representation of uncertain data. The information is represented using linguistic variables like slight, small, large etc. The degree of transition depends on level of uncertainty. The objective function for clustering in P with sum of square error is given below where $C = (c_1, c_2, \cdots, c_i)$ denotes center of cluster for weighting exponent of membership V is the $c-$ partition of P. The fuzzy clustering may be adapted for classification of extracted features in the stage of classification for the purpose of assistive device control (Khushaba, Al-Jumaily & Al-Ani, 2009; Yazama, Mitsukura, Fukumi & Fukumi, 2004).

$$J = \sum_j \sum_k v_{jk} \| p_k - c_i \|^2 \tag{6}$$

3. POPULATION BASED BIO-INSPIRED TECHNIQUES

The success of the intelligent assistive devices is measured by its performance, like safety, flexibility, speed, uncertainty in environment/user condition, etc. and cost. Further, the developed intelligent control systems should be robust and operate devices without delay that could be perceived by the user in real-time application.

The multifunction control of pattern recognition based intelligent devices is limited due to copious data from a number of sensors and or due to extraction of features using frequency and time-frequency techniques. A copious amount of data and or features leads to increased computation cost and time-delay in operating the assistive devices. Among several factors, the performance of classification is characterized by the features which represent the particular category/class of patterns and hence, the performance of the assistive device at an intelligent/high level control in case of pattern recognition based systems. This in turn necessitates the application of dimension reduction techniques, namely feature selection and feature reduction in pattern recognition techniques to reduce the input data to the classifier. The dimension reduction techniques may improve the classification task by eliminating the redundant and irrelevant spurious data leading to reduced time and computational burden. The estimation of motor parameters is vital in developing the controller for assistive devices. The poor estimation of parameters of motors may leads to poor design of controller and leads to instability.

In order to alleviate the problem of computation burden and parameter identification in case of assistive devices, population based bio-inspired search techniques are proposed in the literature developed from nature motivation. The advantage of these techniques over other techniques is that knowledge of the system or problem is not required and can be solved to reach the global optimum solution. Typically, the nature inspired algorithms may be based on biological behaviour of organisms bat, firefly, swarm etc. or based on physics/chemistry such as gravitation, central force, river formation, etc. These algorithms are studied to improve the performance of the system or solve the problem under study. Although there are plenty of nature inspired algorithms have been developed such as evolutionary algorithms (EA), particle swarm optimization (PSO), ant colony optimization (ACO), Bats algorithm, gravitational search algorithm, etc. In this chapter, starting with evolutionary algorithms and other widely used optimization techniques in feature selection process and motor parameter estimation has been discussed (Back, 1996; Beyer & Schwefel, 2002; Dorigo & Caro, 1999; Khushaba, Al-Ani & Al-Jumaily, 2007; Kohonen, 1995; Udomsuk, Areerak, Areerak & Srikaew, 2010; Yang, 2010).

The evolutionary algorithms are inspired from biological process based on mutation, fitness, social interaction and reproduction. Search techniques based on components of evolutionary framework include genetic algorithm (GA), evolutionary strategy (ES), evolutionary programming (EP) and genetic programming (GP) (Back, 1996; Dupuis, Ghribi & Kaddouri, 2004; Holland, 1973; Zalzala & Chaiyaratana, 2000). These algorithms differ in technical representation for example representation of candidate solution. But these algorithms utilize previous history, memory updates to mimic biological evolution and interaction. The next section discusses the brief description of these different evolutionary algorithms.

3.1 Genetic Algorithm

The genetic algorithm (GA) is introduced by Holland (Holland, 1973) using binary string representation. The evolution starts from a random generation of population of individuals. The next generation individual are stochastically selected (e.g., roulette wheel selection) based on fitness value. The selected pairs of current generation produce offspring using genetic operators crossover and mutation. During crossover, m number of points is chosen at random and exchange between the parents. In mutation, the binary 1 is converted to 0 and vice-versa at one or more occurrences in random. The new population of individual is then used in the next iteration of the algorithm and the process terminates with the maximum number of iterations has been reached or desired fitness value is reached. In GA the solution is characterized as strings.

In GA-based feature subset selection, each of the individual is represented by presence and absence of features with 1 or 0. A binary string of length equal to the number of features is considered for feature selection process. The bit 1 is to represent the selection of feature and 0 for dropping of feature in an individual representation. Each individual in the population is feature subset. The initial population size is set to random value with randomly generated individuals.

3.2 Evolutionary Strategy

Evolution strategy was invented in early 1960. In evolution strategy (ES), the population is represented as real-valued numbers. Similar to GA, random population of individual is generated (Beyer & Schwefel, 2002). Offspring are generated from the parents with high fitness value using recombination. The offspring undergo mutation and replace the parent only if fitness value of offspring is greater than the parent. The iterative process terminates when the termination criteria is met. There are different types of evolution strategies in considering the parents for next generation.

3.3 Particle Swarm Optimization

Particle swarm optimization (PSO) is a stochastic, population-based computation technique inspired from the behaviour of bird flocks, fish school (Kennedy & Eberhart, 1995). Similar to evolutionary algorithm, a population of individuals (or particles) is initialized for a given problem in PSO. Each particle represents a point in multidimensional space. The population of these particles is referred as swarm. The PSO iterative program begins with random initialization of size of the swarm as well as the particle value in the swarm. Further, the boundaries of variables in particle are also necessarily to be specified with the minimum and maximum value of each variable. Each particle is evaluated with fitness function at every iteration to direct the velocity of the particle and hence the position in multidimensional search space. The particles moves in the search space until the termination condition is reached.

The algorithm begins with the random initialization of particles, size of the swarm, position with zero velocity. The fitness function is evaluated and the particle's best position (pb) or the local best (lb), and the globally the best position (gb) is updated. In the solution space, the particles local solution and or global position is updated based on the current particle performance. Further, the velocity and position of the particle is updated using the equation (7) and (8).

$$u_i^{k+1} = a^k u_i^k + c_1 \ ran1_i^k (pb_i^k - x_i^k) + c_2 \ ran2_i^k (gb_i^k - x_i^k) \tag{7}$$

$$x_i^{k+1} = x_i^k + v_i^{k+1} \Delta t \tag{8}$$

Where, v_i^k is the velocity of the particle at k^{th} iteration; pb_i^k is the best position of the particle i in the search space at k^{th} iteration; gb_i^k is the best position of the particle i in the search space at k^{th} iteration; x_i^k is the position of the particle at k^{th} iteration; c_1 and c_2 are the coefficients for cognitive and social behaviour, $ran1_i^k$ and $ran2_i^k$ generation of random number in the interval $\{0, 1\}$; $\Delta t = 1$.

The PSO algorithm steps are given below

1. Initialize particles population, position and maximum number of iterations.
2. Evaluate the fitness function
3. Selection of best position of particle from all particles is referred as global best and from personal position of same particle is local best.
4. Update the position and velocity of the particle.
5. Repeat steps 2-4 until termination is reached

During feature selection task, the swarm is feature subset candidate. The selection of feature is based on presence or absence of bit 1 in a string from the value of fitness function. The equations (7) and (8) to be modified due to use of binary number in the particle position. The fitness value is estimation of accuracy in classification problem with the feature subset.

3.4 Ant Colony Optimization

Ant colony optimization (ACO) is another population based optimization technique introduced by Marco Dorigo and his colleague, in early 1990 (Dorigo & Caro 1999) from the inspiration of cooperative work of ant colonies. Since the introduction of algorithm, a lot of modified algorithms have been proposed to improve the solution to the problem. Typically, ants find their shortest path between food and its destination using the chemical substance called pheromone, left in trails while ants are moving. Ants are modeled as agents in optimization problem and solution are pheromone model. The concentration of pheromone guides the ants to select the path. The paths with less pheromone concentration are not the optimal path and path with higher level of concentration are considered as optimal path due to frequent traversal of ants. In case of feature selection process, features represent nodes in the path. The algorithm begins with the random initialization of number of ants and with the selection probability for the nodes as 1. The ants begin with solution from the randomly selected nodes. The selection measure for next node is influenced by evaluation probability of selection using equation (9).

$$P_i^k = \frac{(\tau_i)^\beta (v_i)^\alpha}{\sum_{j \notin N^k} (\tau_j)^\beta (v_j)^\alpha} \tag{9}$$

Where, τ_i is the level of pheromone, v_i is the heuristic indication of selection of feature i, N^k is the neighbouring nodes of kth ant, α and β parameters associated with pheromone trail and heuristic information to control the movement of ant. At the end iteration, when all ants completed the transverse movement, the strength of pheromone is updated using equation (10).

$$\tau_i = \rho \tau_i + \sum_{k=1}^{n} \Delta \tau_i^k \tag{10}$$

Where n the number of ants is, ρ is the parameter for pheromone evaporation between 0 and 1. The algorithm steps are as follows

1. Initialize ants population, intensity of pheromone, parameters associated with pheromone trail and heuristic information and number of iterations.
2. Randomly assign nodes to the plant

3. Evaluate the movement of ant from food to destination
4. Update for globally best ant and locally best ant.
5. Update pheromone level
6. Repeat steps 3-5 until maximum iteration or termination condition is met.

3.5 Bat Algorithm

Bat algorithm is one of the recent heuristics algorithms derived from the biological behaviour of a natural system (Yang, 2010). Yang has introduced the algorithm from the inspiration of bats' echo locative behaviour. Bats are capable of tracking the food/prey using the following three rules as given by Yang (Yang, 2010). All bats use echolocation to sense distance, and they also know the difference between food or prey and background barriers in some magical way. A bat b_i flies randomly with velocity v_i at position x_i with a fixed frequency f_{min}, varying wavelength λ and loudness A_0 to search for prey. They can automatically adjust the wavelength of their emitted pulses and adjust the rate of pulse emission $r \in [0,1]$, depending on the proximity of their target. Although the loudness can vary in many ways, assume that the loudness varies from a large (positive) A_0 to a minimum constant value A_{min}.

The following steps present the Bat algorithm in finding the optimal solution for the given objective function.

1. Initialize ants population, pulse frequency, pulse rates and the loudness and number of iterations.
2. Evaluate the solution for bat using the equation (11) to (13) to update the velocity and its position.

$$f_i = f_{min} + (f_{min} - f_{max})\beta \tag{11}$$

$$v_i^j(t) = v_i^j(t-1) + [\tilde{x}^j - x_i^j(t-1)]\,f_i \tag{12}$$

$$x_i^j(t) = x_i^j(t-1) + v_i^j(t) \tag{13}$$

Where, f_i is the pulse frequency to control the movement of bats, v_i is the velocity at position x_i, $x_i^j(t)$ is the decision value of ith bat at time t for the jth variable, $\tilde{x}^j$ is the global best for the jth variable, β is a random number.

3. If $rand > pulse\ rate_i$ then find global best and local best solution.

4. If $rand < A_i$ and $f\left(x_i\right) < f(\widehat{x})$. $f\left(x_i\right) < f(\widehat{x})$ en accept the new solution. Increase *pulse rate_i* and reduce A_i .

5. Repeat steps 2-4 for all the bats and rank them to find the best solution

6. Repeat steps 3-5 until maximum iteration or termination condition is met.

In addition to above mentioned bio-inspired algorithms, there are various optimization algorithms such as Wolf search algorithm, Firefly algorithm, Monkey search algorithm, Glowworm swarm optimization, Cat swarm, Bees swarm optimization, etc. are discussed in the literature. However, the selection of appropriate algorithm for feature selection, classification which improves the accuracy of identification is a challenging task. (Huynh & Dunnigan, 2010; Kennedy & Eberhart, 1995; Khushaba, Al-Ani & Al-Jumaily, 2007)

4. BIO-INSPIRED ALGORITHM IN REHABILITATION ENGINEERING

The bio-inspired techniques find application in pattern recognition for selection of subset of features from the feature space, classification of features in pattern recognition and estimation of motor parameters for development of accurate control in assistive devices. Pattern recognition (classification), maps the feature vectors into specific classes of motion. Many literatures highlight the success of neural networks (NN) and its ability to learn the distinction among different conditions in pattern recognition. The advantage of the neural network is, its ability to learn linear and non-linear relationships directly from data being modelled. Various type of neural network has been used to identify the information contained in the signals in developing real-time pattern recognition-based myoelectric control (Du, Lin, Shyu & Chen, 2010; Hudgins, Parker & Scott, 1993; Ito, Tsukamoto & Kondo, 2008; Khushaba & Al-Jumaily, 2007a; Sebelius, Eriksson, Holmberg, Levinsson, Lundborg, Danielsen, Schouenborg, Balkenius, Laurell & Montelius, 2005; Tenore, Ramos, Fahmy, Acharya, Etienne-cummings & Thakor, 2009; Wang, Wang, Li, Jiang & Jin, 2005; Wojtczak, Amaral, Dias, Wolczowski & Kurzynski, 2009).

Kelly et al (1990) used Hopfield neural network to calculate time-series parameter and perceptron network to classify the MES signals. In this myoelectric signal features are classified using two layer perceptron. The transfer function of hidden and output units is given below.

$$F(\alpha) = \frac{1}{(1 + e^{-(\alpha - \theta)})} \tag{14}$$

Where, $\alpha = \Sigma_{k=1}^{n} P_k W_k$ and θ is the threshold.

Hudgins et al (1993), Tenore & Ramos (2007), Tsenov et al (2006) used a multi-layer perceptron (MLP) neural network to classify time-domain features. Wang et al (2005) applied back-propagation neural network (BPNN) with AR coefficients for classification. Zhao et al (2005) applied Levenberg-Marquardt based neural network with parametric AR model and integral of EMG to control five-fingered prosthetic hand. Tsuji et al (2000) proposed a NN that combines a common BPNN with recurrent neural filter to classify from time-series of EMG signals, rather than features. Barrero et al (2001) discriminated EMG signals for externally controlled upper extremity prosthesis using artificial neural network (ANN).

Del and Park (1994) extracted myoelectric signal features through Fourier analysis and clustered using Fuzzy C-Means (FCM) algorithm. The EMG data have been interpreted using fuzzy clustering approach. The feature space is clustered into 9 classes with FCM technique. Three membership functions have been used to perform clustering. Data obtained by this unsupervised learning technique are then presented to MLP type NN. Khushaba et al (2009) used evolutionary fuzzy discriminant technique for feature reduction in myoelectic control.

Jung et al (2007) proposed linear vector quantisation (LVQ) neural network to classify spectral estimates from fourth order AR parameters of EMG signals obtained using Yule-Walker method. Guo et al (2006) used wavelet packet transform features of EMG signals to LVQ neural network. Ito et al (2008) proposed a multiple NN to determine the movement intended by an amputee from EMG signals. Ma et al (2001) used NN to classify EMG signals resulting from the dynamic muscle contraction. Guo et al (2009) used Levenberg-Marquardt algorithm to advance the training speed and accuracy compared to back-propagation algorithm for pattern recognition of human motion from AR coefficients. Matsumura et al (2002) used NN to FFT spectra of EMG signals for recognition hand motion. Shuman (2009) performed classification using ANN, random forest (RF), one nearest-neighbour (1NN), decision tree with Boosting (DT/B), support vector machine (SVM) and decision tree (DT) and found that ANN with 6 internal nodes and 30 forest for RF resulted in the highest accuracy. Wojtczak et al (2009) proposed an NN identification system using features based on time and energy histograms. Markou and Singh (2003) discussed various neural network based approaches for the purpose of identification of unknown data or signal.

Smith et al (2009) studied the applicability of time delayed neural network (TDNN) to track movement of the shoulder and elbow joints. Huang et al (2003) discriminated eight kinds of prehensile postures using cascaded architecture of neural networks with feature map (CANFM) and obtained higher discrimination rate compared to k-nearest neighbour (kNN), fuzzy kNN, and BPNN. Sebelius et al (2005) applied a modified SOFM composed of a combination of a Kohonen network with conscience mechanism algorithm for EMG classification and found results are superior in performance than MLP. Chong and Sundaraj (2009) investigated that BPNN is well performed for fast weak and fast strong muscle activities and probabilistic neural network (PNN) is well performed for slow weak and slow strong muscle activities. Xizhi (2008) shown that EMG pattern recognized using radial basis function (RBF) neural network is higher than BPNN. Zalzala and Chaiyaratana (2000) used hybrid radial basis function multilayer perceptron (RBF-MLP) network for classification. Yuan et al (2008) used BPNN to classify feature vector extracted from recurrence plots and recurrence quantification analysis (RQA). Yazama et al (2004) used NN to classify the EMG signals using multidimensional directed information (MDI) for wrist motions. Du et al (2010) recognised EMG signal patterns using grey relational analysis (GRA) and shown better performance than multi-layer neural network based classifier.

Due to the multi-channel approach used for acquisition of signals, the extracted feature vector dimension can become large. Also, wavelet transform generates many coefficients to represent time-scale features. Thus dimensionality reduction can be achieved using either feature selection (FS) or feature projection (FP) methods. Feature selection requires a search strategy that selects a candidate subset and an objective function that evaluates these candidates.

Yazama et al (2003) selected features using GA. The FFT have been used for the extraction of frequency distribution information from four channel EMG data. The purpose of GA is the selection of frequency band to perform classification using NN classifier. The frequency corresponding to a code 1 us utilized and 0 has been ignored. Oskoei and Hu (2006) presented feature subset selection, to find an optimal subset of myoelectric features using GA as a search strategy. In this features subset selection Davies-Bouldin index, Fishers linear discriminant index, and linear discriminant analysis (LDA) has been used as objective functions. The time frequency domain features have been used for feature subset selection. Huang et al (2003) demonstrated reduction of feature space by Kohonen's self-organizing map. Khushaba and Al-Jumaily (2007a) selected features using particle swarm optimisation (PSO) and Khushaba et al (2007) developed a mixture of PSO and the concept of mutual information (MI) for selection of features. Researchers have used bio-inspired optimization techniques in different motor parameter estimation (Dupuis et al 2004; Udomsuk et al 2010; Huynh & Dunnigan, 2010).

5. FUTURE RESEARCH DIRECTIONS

Researchers are attempting to address several significant problems, like response time, computational burden etc. with the bio-inspired techniques in pattern recognition. Researchers can attempt on feature selection and classification algorithms that significantly improve the performance of assistive devices.

Further, few researchers have shown that bio-inspired algorithms have important role in selection of channels/number of electrodes in brain computer interface for the development of communication and control assistance. Similarly, in EMG based assistive devices bio-inspired based optimization techniques may be used for the choice of number of channels, eliminating number of sensors used for degree of control. Recently researchers are using bio-inspired techniques in various electrical motor parameter identification for the purposed of development of controller, fault diagnosis, etc. The appropriate identification of motor parameter enables to actuate the assistive devices with appropriate control strategy. Techniques such as, rough set classification, rough set on fuzzy approximation space, rough set on fuzzy approximation and rough set on fuzzyapproximation and Bayesian classification, rough set with ANN etc. may be attempted to identify the discriminating capability with the bio-electric signals.

6. CONCLUSION

The processing of bioelectric signals is a challenging and heart of pattern recognition based assistive device control. The objective is achieved through the successive processing of input bioelectric signals in several combinations of intermediate stages, before the decision making/output stage. The various stages such as digital filtering, preprocessing, extraction of relevant information in the form of features, identification of the relevance of channel (channel selection)/ extracted features (feature selection), feature reduction and interpretation of the information through a classification algorithm may be included to translate the human intention in the bioelectric signals. The number of intermediate signals processing stages depends on the real-time factors such as computational complexity, time, memory, etc. Several combinations of signal processing stages and techniques have been developed and a wide application of bio-inspired techniques in rehabilitation engineering is due to the fact that big amount of data and usually introduces a time delay in continuous control. The second limitation, besides the time delay, is the computational burden in processing the features extracted from large number of data. To reduce the computational burden, researchers used bio-inspired based feature selection techniques. The performance of the classification is also depends on the classifier. The bio-inspired techniques have the ability to learn from training and are used as classifier due to generalisation capability on unseen data like neural network. The identification of motor parameters in developing the controller and controller parameters, are other bio-inspired optimization research areas.

REFERENCES

Back, T. (1996). *Evolutionary Algorithms in Theory and Practice*. New York: Oxford University Press.

Barrero, V., Grisales, E. V., Rosas, F., Sanchez, C., & Leon, J. (2001). Design and implementation of an intelligent interface for myoelectric controlled prosthesis. In *Proceedings of the 23rd Annual International Conference of the IEEE*. Istanbul, Turkey: IEEE.

Beyer, H. G., & Schwefel, H. P. (2002). Evolution strategies. *Natural Computing*, *1*(1), 3–52. doi:10.1023/A:1015059928466

Chong, Y. L., & Sundaraj, K. (2009). A study of back-propagation and radial basis neural network on EMG signal classification. In *Proceedings of Mechatronics and its Applications, 2009. ISMA '09.6th International Symposium*. Sharjah: IEEE.

Del, B. A., & Park, D. C. (1994). Myoelectric signal recognition using fuzzy clustering and artificial neural networks in real time. In *Proceedings of Neural Networks 1994, IEEE World Congress on Computational Intelligence*. Orlando, FL: IEEE.

Dorigo, M., & Caro, G. D. (1999). Ant Colony Optimization: A New Meta-heuristic. Proceedings of Evolutionary Computation, 1999. CEC 99.

Du, Y.-C., Lin, C.-H., Shyu, L.-Y., & Chen, T. (2010). Portable hand motion classifier for multi-channel surface electromyography recognition using grey relational analysis. *Journal Expert Systems with Applications*, *37*(6), 4283–4291. doi:10.1016/j.eswa.2009.11.072

Dupuis, A., Ghribi, M., & Kaddouri, A. (2004). Multi-objective genetic estimation of DC motor parameters and load torque. In *Proceedings of Industrial Technology, 2004. IEEE ICIT '04*. IEEE.

Guo, X., Yang, P., Chen, L., Wang, X., & Li, L. (2006). Study of the control mechanism of robot-prosthesis based-on the EMG processed. In *Proceedings of 6th World Congress on Intelligent Control and Automation* (pp. 9490-9493), Dalian, China: IEEE.

Guo, X., Yu, H., Zhen, G., Liu, Y., Zhang, Y., & Zhang, Y. (2009). Artificial intelligent based human motion pattern recognition and prediction for the surface electromyographic signals. In *Proceedings of Information Technology and Computer Science, 2009. ITCS 2009*. IEEE. doi:10.1109/ITCS.2009.65

Holland, J. H. (1973). Genetic algorithms and the optimal allocation of trials. *SIAM Journal on Computing*, 2(2), 88–105. doi:10.1137/0202009

Huang, H.-P., Liu, Y.-H., Liu, L.-W., & Wong, C.-S. (2003). EMG classification for prehensile postures using cascaded architecture of neural networks with self-organizing maps. *2006 6th World Congress on Intelligent Control and Automation*. Taipei, Taiwan: IEEE.

Hudgins, B., Parker, P., & Scott, R. N. (1993). A new strategy for multifunction myoelectric control. *IEEE Transactions on Bio-Medical Engineering*, 40(1), 82–94. doi:10.1109/10.204774 PMID:8468080

Huynh, D. C., & Dunnigan, M. W. (2010). Parameter estimation of an induction machine using advanced particle swarm optimization algorithms. *IET Electric Power Applications*, 4(9), 748–760. doi:10.1049/iet-epa.2009.0296

Ito, K., Tsukamoto, M., & Kondo, T. (2008). Discrimination of intended movements based on nonstationary EMG for a prosthetic hand control. In *Proceedings of Communications, Control and Signal Processing, 2008. ISCCSP 2008*. St. Julians, Malta: IEEE.

Jung, K. K., Kim, J. W., Lee, H. K., Chung, S. B., & Eom, K. H. (2007). EMG pattern classification using spectral estimation and neural network. In *Proceedings SICE, 2007 Annual Conference*. Takamatsu, Japan: IEEE.

Kelly, M. F., Parker, P. A., & Scott, R. N. (1990). The application of neural networks to myoelectric signal analysis: A preliminary study. *IEEE Transactions on Bio-Medical Engineering*, 37(3), 221–230. doi:10.1109/10.52324 PMID:2328997

Kennedy, J., & Eberhart, R. C. (1995). Particle swarm optimization. In *Proceedings of the IEEE International Conference on Neural Networks*. Piscataway, NJ: IEEE. doi:10.1109/ICNN.1995.488968

Khushaba, R. N., Al-Ani, A., & Al-Jumaily, A. (2007). Swarm intelligence based dimensionality reduction for myoelectric control. In *Proceedings ofIntelligent Sensors, Sensor Networks and Information, 2007. ISSNIP 2007*. Melbourne, QLD, Australia: IEEE. doi:10.1109/ISSNIP.2007.4496907

Khushaba, R. N., & Al-Jumaily, A. (2007a). Channel and feature selection in multifunction myoelectric control. In *Proceedings of2007 29th Annual International Conference ofthe IEEE Engineering in Medicine and Biology Society*. Lyon, France: IEEE. doi:10.1109/IEMBS.2007.4353509

Khushaba, R. N., Al-Jumaily, A., & Al-Ani, A. (2009). Evolutionary fuzzy discriminant analysis feature projection technique in myoelectric control. *Pattern Recognition Letters*, *30*(7), 699–707. doi:10.1016/j.patrec.2009.02.004

Kohonen, T. (1995). *Self-Organizing Maps*. Berlin: Springer. doi:10.1007/978-3-642-97610-0

Ma, N., Kumar, D. K., & Pah, N. (2001). Classification of hand direction using multi-channel electromyography by neural network. In *Proceedings ofIntelligent Information Systems Conference, The Seventh Australian and New Zealand 2001*. Perth, Western Australia: IEEE.

Markou, M., & Singh, S. (2003). Novelty detection: a review-part 2: neural network based approaches. *Journal of Signal Processing*, *83*(12), 2499–2521. doi:10.1016/j.sigpro.2003.07.019

Matsumura, Y., Mitsukura, Y., Fukumi, M., & Akamatsu, N. (2002). Recognition of EMG signal patterns by neural networks. In *Proceedings of Neural Information Processing, 2002. ICONIP '02*. Singapore, Singapore: IEEE. doi:10.1109/ICONIP.2002.1198158

Sebelius, F., Eriksson, L., Holmberg, H., Levinsson, A., Lundborg, G., Danielsen, N., & Montelius, L. et al. (2005). Classification of motor commands using a modified self-organising feature map. *Journal of Medical Engineering and Physics*, *27*(5), 403–413. doi:10.1016/j.medengphy.2004.09.008 PMID:15863349

Shuman, G. (2009). Using forearm electromyograms to classify hand gestures. Proceedings of Bioinformatics and Biomedicine, 2009, BIBM '09.

Smith, A., Nanda, P., & Brown, E. E. (2009). Development of a myoelectric control scheme based on a time delayed neural network. In *Proceedings of2009 Annual International Conference of the IEEE Engineering in Medicine and Biology Society*. Minneapolis, MN: IEEE. doi:10.1109/IEMBS.2009.5332846

Tenore, F. V. G., Ramos, A., Fahmy, A., Acharya, S., Etienne-cummings, R., & Thakor, N. T. (2009). Decoding of individuated finger movements using surface electromyography. *IEEE Transactions on Bio-Medical Engineering*, *56*(5), 1427–1434. doi:10.1109/TBME.2008.2005485 PMID:19473933

Tsenov, G., Zeghbib, A. H., Palis, F., Shoylev, N., & Mladenov, V. (2006). Neural networks for online classification of hand and finger movements using surface EMG signals. In *Proceedings of 2006 8th Seminar on Neural Network Applications in Electrical Engineering*. Belgrade, Serbia: IEEE.

Tsuji, T., Fukuda, O., Kaneko, M., & Koji, I. (2000). Pattern classification of time-series EMG signals using neural networks. *International Journal of Adaptive Control and Signal Processing*, *14*(8), 829–848. doi:10.1002/1099-1115(200012)14:8<829::AID-ACS623>3.0.CO;2-L

Udomsuk, S., Areerak, K.-L., Areerak, K.-N., & Srikaew, A. (2010). Parameters identification of separately excited dc motor using adaptive tabu search technique. In *Proceedings of Advances in Energy Engineering (ICAEE)*. IEEE. doi:10.1109/ICAEE.2010.5557618

Wang, J. Z., Wang, R. C., Li, F., Jiang, M. W., & Jin, D. W. (2005). EMG signal classification for myoelectric teleoperating a dexterous robot hand. In *Proceedings of 2005 IEEE Engineering in Medicine and Biology 27th Annual Conference*. Shanghai, China: IEEE. doi:10.1109/IEMBS.2005.1615841

Wojtczak, P., Amaral, T. G., Dias, O. P., Wolczowski, A., & Kurzynski, M. (2009). Hand movement recognition based on biosignal analysis. *Journal of Engineering Applications of Artificial Intelligence*, *22*(4-5), 608–615. doi:10.1016/j.engappai.2008.12.004

Yang, X. S. (2010). *A New Metaheuristic Bat-Inspired Algorithm*. Springer Berlin.

Yazama, Y., Mistukura, Y., Fukumi, M., & Akamatsu, N. (2003). Feature analysis for the EMG signals based on the class distance. In *Proceedings of Computational Intelligence in Robotics and Automation, 2003*. Kobe, Japan: IEEE. doi:10.1109/CIRA.2003.1222292

Yazama, Y., Mitsukura, Y., Fukumi, M., & Fukumi, N. (2004). Analysis and recognition of wrist motions by using multidimensional directed information and EMG signal. In *Proceedings of Fuzzy Information, 2004. Processing NAFIPS '04. IEEE Annual Meeting of the*. Banff, Alberta: IEEE.

Zalzala, A. M. S., & Chaiyaratana, N. (2000). Myoelectric signal classification using evolutionary hybrid RBF-MLP networks. In *Proceedings of Evolutionary Computation*. La Jolla, CA: IEEE. doi:10.1109/CEC.2000.870365

Zhao, Xie, Jiang, Cai, Liu, & Hirzinger. (2005). Levenberg-Marquardt based neural network control for a five-fingered prosthetic hand. In *Proceedings of the 2005 IEEE International Conference on Robotics and Automation*. Barcelona, Spain: IEEE.

KEY TERMS AND DEFINITIONS

Classification: Identification of a category/class from the input feature vector.

Electroencephalogram (EEG): A record of the electrical activity of the brain.

Electromyogram (EMG): A record of the electrical activity of the muscle.

Feature Extraction: The process of defining meaningful and efficient information from the raw data.

Feature Reduction: The process of reducing number of extracted features to optimal numbers to identify a category/class of data using transformation.

Feature Selection: The process of selection of existing features to identify the class of data.

Neural Network: A computing system made up of a number of simple, highly interconnected processing elements which process information by their dynamic state response to external inputs.

Neuromuscular Disorder: A disorder that affects the muscles and or nerves.

Pattern Recognition: The process of identification of category/class of the pattern from the raw data.

Prosthetic Hand: An artificial hand that replaces the missing hand.

Chapter 12
Bioinspired Algorithms in Solving Three-Dimensional Protein Structure Prediction Problems

Raghunath Satpathy
MITS Engineering College, India

ABSTRACT

Proteins play a vital molecular role in all living organisms. Experimentally, it is difficult to predict the protein structure, however alternatively theoretical prediction method holds good for it. The 3D structure prediction of proteins is very much important in biology and this leads to the discovery of different useful drugs, enzymes, and currently this is considered as an important research domain. The prediction of proteins is related to identification of its tertiary structure. From the computational point of view, different models (protein representations) have been developed along with certain efficient optimization methods to predict the protein structure. The bio-inspired computation is used mostly for optimization process during solving protein structure. These algorithms now a days has received great interests and attention in the literature. This chapter aim basically for discussing the key features of recently developed five different types of bio-inspired computational algorithms, applied in protein structure prediction problems.

DOI: 10.4018/978-1-5225-2375-8.ch012

Copyright ©2017, IGI Global. Copying or distributing in print or electronic forms without written permission of IGI Global is prohibited.

1. INTRODUCTION

Proteins belong to one of the major classes of macromolecules that are ubiquitously present in the living systems. These molecules are often envisaged as the molecular machines of life because they carry out many types of functions starting from catalysis, transport, regulation movement, transport, signaling, immunity and structure determination. Due to the versatility of the proteins, it is important to study their role area in molecular and cell biology. As the number of completely sequenced genomes grows, we are faced with the important but daunting task of assigning a function to proteins encoded by newly sequenced genomes (Habeck et al., 2005). A protein, is a polymer of amino acids can adopt different conformations and the most stable state is achieved by minimization of energy is known as native state (Lee et al., 2007; Whisstock et al., 2003). Amongst the 20 different naturally occurring amino acids, any two can join in a series by forming the peptide bond (C=O ---NH linkage), that remains in a plane. Figure 1 represents the peptic bond in between two amino acids, planar feature has been shown in dotted green lines, R1 and R2 corresponds to the functional group of two amino acids.

Figure 1. Peptide bond in between two amino acids

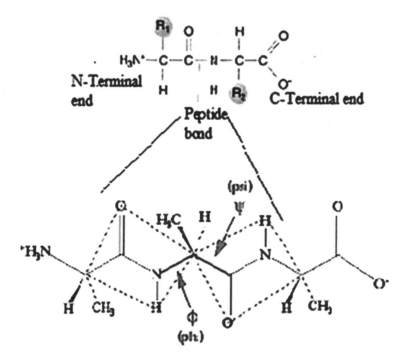

The primary structure consists of amino acids when present in an aqueous environment will spontaneously adopt local (secondary) and non-local (tertiary) structures while some require the presence of factors like molecular chaperones. This observation generates the hypothesis that the native state is determined by the primary sequence of amino acids. During its assembly, the amino acids present in the protein are organized in a regular local structural mostly stabilized by the hydrogen bonds. The examples of such structural entities are alpha-helices (Branson, 1951) and beta-strands (Pauling & Corey, 1951). The local arrangements of a polypeptide chain are collectively called secondary structure or two-dimensional structure. Later the assembly in the in the three-dimensional space is called tertiary structure of protein. The three-dimensional structure is usually stabilized by several non-local interactions, hydrophobic interaction, disulfide bonds and salt bridges etc. Finally, in some cases, two or more polypeptide chains, called as protein subunits can undergo assembly to form larger complexes that are regarded as the quaternary structure (Marqusee & Baldwin, 1987). It is a keen observation that during the protein folding process transition to the native state the amino acid sequences proceeds on roughly through the same intermediate states. The folding process involves several regular secondary and super secondary structural features (Oas et al., 1988), particularly α-helices and β-sheets, and afterward of tertiary ones. However, the formation of quaternary structure usually involves the assembly of already assembled subunits. The planar arrangement of the peptide bonds is most important as it helps to determine a specific overall 3D structure of a specific polypeptide protein chain (Weiss et al., 1998). The planar arrangement of atoms in the peptide bond is assumed to be rigid and the rotation of different bonds can be given as dihedral angles, ϕ (N-Cα) and ψ (Cα-C)that provide flexibility in rotation about 180 degrees around the atom connecting axis.

Currently, based on experimentation three methods for prediction of the protein structure is available such as *X*-ray crystallography, nuclear magnetic resonance (NMR) spectroscopy and electron microscopy (EM). The basic technique involves in the *X*-ray crystallography, is the purified protein is crystallized by crystallization methods and after this, the protein crystal is subjected to an X-ray beam. The electrons present in the protein scatter the X-rays and the pattern generated is used to calculate an electron density map further by modeling the amino acids in the protein are fitted to give a 3D structure (McPherson, 2004). In case of NMR spectroscopy technique, the solution of the purified protein is placed under the influence of a strong magnetic field and then exposed to radio waves (Marion, 2013). The resonance that are observed in a spectrum enable the determination of which atom nuclei are close to each other and there by analyzing the atom bond conformation followed by 3D structure determination. The EM is also used for structure prediction of large macromolecular complexes, which are determined by exposing the molecule to a beam of electrons to obtain a 3D image (Kuhlbrandt, 2013; Callaway, 2015). One advantage of the EM method is that this can produce good quality models quickly.

2. CURRENT CHALLENGES OF PROTEIN 3D STRUCTURE PREDICTION

Determination of protein 3D structure from a linear amino acid sequence is known as Protein structure prediction (PSP) problem (Bowie, Luthy & Eisenberg, 1991). PSP methods deal with the 3D arrangement of amino acids in the space. The total number of arrangement corresponds to the different possible protein structures which may be astronomically large (Zwanzig, Szabo, & Bagchi, 1992). Therefore, this is considered as one of the most interesting and highly challenging problems, both in the biological and computational point of view. The current challenges exist in experimental mode of determination of the three-dimensional (3D) structure of a protein, as it is very difficult, time taking as well as costly (Marks et al., 2011). Therefore theoretical methods are utilized and considered as an alternative for the prediction of the protein structure. Prediction of an accurate 3-dimensional (3D) protein structures have an important contribution in computational biology point of view because the functions of a protein aredirectly related to its 3D structure rather than to its amino acid sequence.

Using several algorithms to solve the above problems of the protein represents a good alternative (Al-Akwaa 2014). In general, during the design of a suitable search algorithm for protein 3D structure prediction is made by taking account of all possible combinations of the parameters like dihedral and torsion angles, steric hindrance among functional groups of amino acids, the shape and size of the atoms and their positioning, degree of freedom of atoms, search space as shown in Figure 2 (Gibrat, Garnier & Robson, 1987). Because the protein structure prediction is a fundamental problem in biology that is helpful to open the door to explore the complex mechanism exists behind several bio-molecular functions. The solving of the protein structure prediction problem is applicable in several fields of biotechnology as well as health care. For example, in the field of human health care it can be applied for the prediction of the suitable drug targets that ultimately lead to treatment of diseases. In biotechnology point of view the application is directly related to production of large-scale enzymatic processes. Correct three-dimensional structure prediction also leads to the classification of the proteins or enzymes into a particular category also further lead to study about its phylogeny (Venkatesan et al.,2010; Nishant, Sathish, & VVL, 2011). Currently, many computational algorithms inspired by biological processes are becoming more popular for solving the protein folding problems. The

Figure 2. Rough demonstration of method of 3D structure prediction of protein

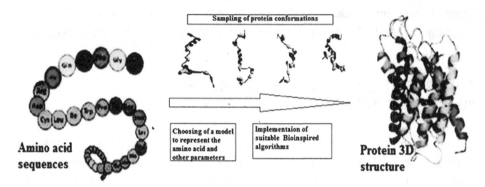

natural process is predominantly used to derive the sources of ideas for the model development in several artificial systems. These bio-inspired algorithms are derived based on the analogy of natural evolution methods and biological activities. The algorithms are usually random search methods and utilize some heuristic way to find the search towards an optimal solution. The bio-inspired methods are having several unique features and advantages in comparison to the existing optimization methods (Irback & Sandelin, 1998; Irback et al., 1997).

2.1 Protein Structure Prediction

The protein structure prediction by computational modelling method have several simplified models. These are proposed to interpret the local interaction among amino acids. As it is known that the local interactions might be important for the local structure of the chains and subsequently gives rise to a compact defined native 3Dstructure (Zhang et al.,2010). One of the model is known as HP model that is frequently used to solve the PSP problem. This model basically classifies the 20 standard amino acids into only two classes as hydrophobic amino acid is represented by (H) and polar amino acid is represented by (P) based on their affinity to water. The folding of amino acid sequences is best represented in a lattice structure as shown in Figure 3 in which dark spheres are hydrophobic monomers and light spheres are polar residues.

The lattice may be the bi-dimensional model known as 2D HP or may be cubic lattice known as a three-dimensional model (3D) HP. In these models, each amino acid occupies a part of one lattice site, connected to its chain neighbours. After such type of arrangement of all the amino acids, this forms a shape that is considered as the conformation (3D structure) of the protein. The example for a protein conformation under the 3D HP model is shown in Figure 3. In the HP model, the energy of

Figure 3. Diagram representing HP model

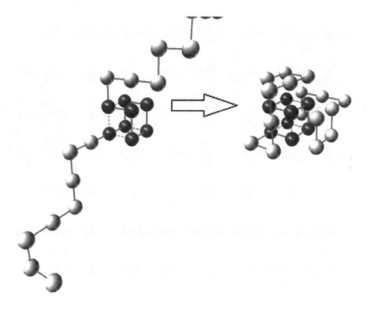

a conformation can be modelled by computing the number of topological contacts and interactions between neighbours Hydrophobic (H) amino acids. In this way, the HP model presentation formulates as the hydrophobic interaction are mostly responsible in attaining 3D protein structures. Currently, another similar model is known as AB off-lattice model is being widely applied to 3D protein structure prediction and many other improved models have been proposed based on the original model. In this AB off-lattice model, two types of monomers are taken into consideration. The hydrophobic and hydrophilic monomers are represented by A and B respectively is shown in Figure 4 in which A is shown as black and B is shown as white sphere. Unlike HP model, the AB off-lattice model, include both sequence dependent interaction as well as the independent and that finally forms a hydrophobic core, subsequently folding results 3D structure of the protein.

In case of off-lattice AB model, the amino acid monomers are modelled as they are linked by therigid unit bond length to form a linear un-oriented polymer in the space. After a structural model is adopted, an important technique in theoretical PSP is to develop the appropriate optimization techniques to search for the best conformation of a protein based on the assumed structure model (Stillinger, Head-Gordon, & Hirshfel, (1993, 1995)). As per the computational complexity is concerned, the protein structure prediction (PSP) is considered as an NP-hard problem, hence difficult to solve by using any simple modelling method. In order to sort out this issue, many heuristic approaches have been developed by researchers in the form

Figure 4. Representation of AB off lattice model

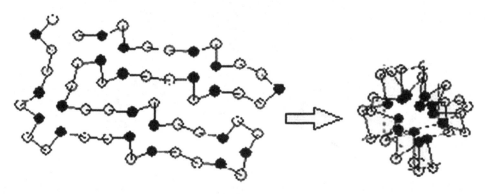

of algorithms to solve the global optimization problem. There are essentially five approaches are frequently used to model the PSP problems: molecular dynamics (Levitt, 1983), Monte Carlo methods (Covell, 1992), statistical mechanical models (Alm & Baker, 1999; Munoz & Eaton, 1999) probabilistic road map-based (Apaydin et al., 2002), and lattice models (Lau & Dill, 1992; Amato, Dill & Song, 2003). The first two techniques are preliminarily used to study characteristics of folding pathways under different conditions. The second two techniques are useful tools for studying the protein folding landscape, and the final technique, is relevant to the fundamental theoretical approaches (Dill et al., 1995). The major technical challenge exists in this approach is to search for the most stable structure of the different conformation of the protein in a huge search space. Moreover, the general mode of theoretical modeling procedure of PSP can be given in the following four steps.

Step 1: Suitable Model Representation: A model must be chosen with a desired level of accuracy to represent the protein structure is the first and foremost approach towards the PSP problem. This also represents the protein structure is required in the problem space. Basically two categories of representation are there; first category is the all-atom model, where the protein structures are represented by lists of 3D atomic coordinates of a protein) and simplified models (this model is further classified into lattice models and off-lattice models) as explained above.

Step 2: Define an Energy Function: The energy function must be defined in order to effectively discriminate native states from non-native states of the protein. For example, in case of HP model it is based on the principle that the hydrophobic force of interaction is responsible for the protein folding process.

Step 3: Design of an Efficient Algorithm: This is an important part of the PSP to compute and find minimal energy conformations of the amino acids in a protein.

Step 4: Defining Optimization Function: This step is crucial and decisive for the algorithm and the specific functions are used to search the conformational space to obtain the correct conformation with the lowest free energy. Specifically, in the case of the protein structure prediction, the number of possible conformations for chains of amino acids is very large as explained above. Therefore the application of a bio inspired algorithm holds good for solving this. Several studies using these algorithms have been proposed, among these we find the use of bee colony optimization (Mahmood, Mahmuddin & Mahmood, 2012), immune algorithms (Bennett et al., 2008), tabu search algorithms (Zhang & Cheng, 2009), ant colony optimization (Daniel & Zomaya, 2006), particle swarm optimization (PSO) (Mansour, Kanj & Khachfe, 2012) has been used extensively in the literature. These algorithms work by considering the computational complexity to find the suitable configuration of the amino acid chain in the space, having the minimum energy.

3. BIOINSPIRED ALGORITHMS IN PSP PROBLEM

This section illustrates the implementation of bio-inspired algorithms in PSP problem. The chapter discusses bee colony optimization, immune algorithm, particle swarm optimization, ant colony optimization algorithm, tabu search in the context of PSP problem.

3.1 Bee Colony Optimization

The Bee Colony Optimization (BCO) method is meta-heuristic optimization method and has been classified within the *Bio-Inspired Algorithms*. The bee based optimization considers many features of bees such as dancing of bee, foraging and following nature of bees etc. are used in the modeling purpose. It is based on the fact that how the bees collects nectar naturally by help of their nest mate bee. In case of BCO, the artificial bees are used to solve complex optimization problem. These artificial bees during the searching process moves locally by causing forward and backward pass iteratively. The minimum number of iteration in which best solution is obtained is determined (Ozturk, Hancer, & Karaboga, 2015).The pseudo code of the BCO based method could be described in the following 10 steps.

Algorithm

1. Initialization: an empty result is assigned to every bee
2. For every bee the forward pass starts

    a.   Counter for constructive moves in the forward pass

    b.   Evaluate all possible moves

    c.   According to evaluation, choose one move

3.   All bees are back to the hive; (starts the backward pass)

4.   Evaluate objective function value for each bee;

5.   Every bee decides randomly

6.   For every follower, choose a new solution

7.   If solutions are not completed Go to step 2

8.   Evaluate all solutions and find the best one

9.   Find the best solution found as Output.

This method of optimization is frequently practiced by many researchers to solve PSP. Bahamish *et. al* (2008) proposed the backbone and side chain protein information for calculation of the protein's free energy conformations. The BCO algorithm starts with an initial randomly number of the food source which is the protein conformations. Then the conformations are computed by using the specific energy functions. The lowest free energy conformation numbers were chosen by the onlooker bees as the number of best conformations is equal to the number of the onlooker bees. After that, a new type of dihedral angle rotation method is applied to generate the new conformations from the previous conformations. This method works on the basis of choosing the lowest energies of conformations that were generated in the previous stage of the process and by regenerating a new Phi and Psi angles. So a huge number of the energy based conformations are needs to be searched in order to identify the lowest energy conformation lead to the prediction of the native state of a protein. Similarly Bahamish *et al.* (2009) also described about a new artificial Bee Colony algorithm to improve the protein conformation search algorithm. This is implemented by using ECEPP/2 force fields for the energy calculation purpose of the protein, derived due to the changing the torsion angles of the amino acids. Also, they used a random change method to change the angles. This approach usually focuses on the effect of changing the angles to others (Bahamish, Abdullah, & Salam, (2008, 2009)). The bee based system is typically an improved version of the genetic algorithm that having the advantage for the improved local searches (Yuce et al., 2013; Wang, Pan, & Jiao; 2000).

3.2 Immune Algorithm

Immune algorithm (IA) is one of the optimization algorithm based on the analogy of the biological immune system to solve the optimization problem. The IA model employs two types of parameters viz. antigens (Ag) and B cells. The immune system inhuman protects the body by defending against the entrance of harmful microorganisms and infections. It is capable of recognizing foreign pathogens (antigens) by some cells known as B-cells. Each antigen is having a specific physical feature (shape) which is recognized by the B-cell surface receptors. The B-cells synthesizes protein molecules, known as antibodies that act like detectors to find out antigens. If a B-cell is efficient to recognize the antigen, it may undergo proliferation, the process is known as clonal selection (Rodin et al., 2004; Forsdyke, 1995). The inefficient clones are subjected to somatic permutations that result in daughter clones having different antibodies from the parent. Clonal selection ensures that, only efficient B-cells (i.e., with high affinity to the antigen) can be cloned to represent the next generation (Hofmeyr, 2001). However, clones with low affinity with antigen do not divide and will be discarded. Therefore, the clonal selection process enables the animal body to have sufficient numbers of antigen-specific B cells to build up an effective immune response.

Algorithm

Input: S = set of problems
Output: M = set of memory detectors capable of figure out the solution
1. Create an initial random set of antibodies, N
2. For all problem sets in S do
3. Determine the affinity with each antibody in N
4. Generate a subset of the antibodies in N with the highest affinity (specific clones).
5. Mutate the clones belongs to the set N, and place a copy of the highest affinity antibodies in N into the memory set, M
6. Replace the lowest affinity antibodies in N with new randomly generated antibodies

The antigen in this model is the hydrophobic model of the given protein, that is a sequence, contains the number of amino acids in the protein. The B cell population represents a set of candidate solutions in the current energy conformations at each generation. The B cell is represented as a set of directions, which corresponds to a relative direction with respect to the previous direction. In this manner an overall sequence of length of the protein can be obtained that enables the particular 3-D conformation which is suitable for computing the energy value. At each generation, there is a B cell population of size. The initial population of B- cell is randomly generated. After this, there exist two main functions within the algorithm viz. evaluation of the fitness function value of each B cell (corresponds to the energy associated with the protein conformation) and the termination condition (where, it returns true if a optimized 3D structure is obtained in a maximum number of fitness function) (Cutello etal.,2007). Not only hydrophobic model, there are also several common features are used to represent protein as Cartisian coordinates of all atoms, internal coordinate and the distance geometry etc. during implementing this algorithm (Eberhart and Kennedy, 1995).

3.3 Particle Swarm Optimization

Particle swarm optimization (PSO) is a technique that optimizes a solution by iteratively improvement. Basically, the PSO method optimizes a complex problem, when there is a population of candidate solutions. The candidate solution is known as *dubbed* particles, and moving these particles around in the search space by using a simple mathematical formulation with respect to the position and velocity of the particle. Then each movement of the particle is influenced by its best known position locally further follow up to the best known positions in the search-space and subsequently updated as a better positions found by other particles. This phenomenon is actually used for the movement of the swarm toward the best optimized solution. By the application of a fitness function by user, the best position of each particle is computed based on the best fitness value. Then, for the new updated positions and the velocities of the particles the fitness evaluations are calculated. The concept of particle swarm optimization method was introduced by Kennedy and to study social behavior (Eberhart & Kennedy, 1995; Nashat, Fatima & Hassan, 2012). The pseudo code for the above algorithm is given below.

Algorithm

Begin

1. Initialize particle
2. For each particle
    a. calculate fitness value
    b. if the fitness value is better than the best fitness value (best) in history
    c. set current value as the new best
    d. choose the particle with the best fitness value of all the particles as the best
3. For each particle
    a. Calculate particle velocity according equation
    b. Update particle position according equation
    c. While maximum iterations or minimum error criteria is not attained

Nashat Mansour et al. (2012) presented a particle swarm optimization (PSO) based algorithm for predicting protein structures in a 3D hydrophobic polar model. In this case the proposed algorithm performs better than previous algorithms by finding the best conformation (lower energy structures) from an energy evaluation method (Khakzad, Karami, & Arab, 2015; Kanj et al. 2009). Recently, one of the best efforts to accelerate PSP is the application of parallel processing architecture, such graphical processing unit (GPU), which is used to reduce the time frame to solve the different topologies of PSO algorithms. The output result belongs to abinitio structure prediction methods, based on the dihedral angles and calculates the energy-levels to find and predict the best pair of angle that gives the minimum free energy (Kondov, & Berlich, 2011).. By considering the 3D HP model, starting from a small set of potential solutions, the PSO algorithm has observed to be very much efficient to explore the search space of candidate solutions, thereby returns 3D protein structures with minimal energy. By employing an all-atom force field the efficiency of the standard PSO algorithm, has been demonstrated in this paper (Chu & Zomaya, 2006).

3.4 Ant Colony Optimization

The ant colony optimization algorithm (ACO) method is a probabilistic mode of technique for solving computational problems which are used to finding best paths through the graphs (Salami, 2009). This method is inspired by random movement of ants upon finding food return to their colony while laying down pheromone trails. If other ants find such a path, then they stop the random traveling, but follow the trail to find the food. As time goes on, the pheromone starts to evaporate, hence reducing its attractive power. The time period that is taken by an ant to travel along the path and back is directly proportional to the pheromones evaporation (reducing pheromone density). So in a short path is frequently adopted by the ants that provide the higher pheromone density rather than the longer ones. A condition whenever there is no evaporation of pheromones then, the paths chosen by the first ants can be considered as attractive to the previous one that follows. Therefore, whenever from the ant colony, one ant finds a shortest path to specific a food source and other ants are more likely to follow that particular path. The idea the ant colony algorithm is to mimic this behaviour with ants moving around the graph that represents the problem to be solved. The components of the algorithm contribute to its performance and that is affected by the implementation of heuristic function and selectivity of pheromone updating (Dorigo & Blum, 2005). The pseudocode can be shown as below.

Algorithm

Begin

1.   Initialize parameters
2.   Initialize the array heuristically
3.   Initialize the pheromone matrix
4.   While the stopping conditions not satisfied with the movement
5.   build solutions
6.   Apply Local Search
7.   Update Pheromone
8.   View best solution

Stefka Fidanova & Ivan Lirkov (2008) develop an ant algorithm for 3D HP model protein folding based structure prediction with the aim to study about more realistic behavior of protein folding. Similarly, Alena Shmygelska et al. (2005), investigated a new algorithm, dubbed ACO-HPPFP-3, and are based on very simple structure components, to predict the best known energy conformations. The Hydrophobic-Hydrophilic (HP) method is most frequently used due to its simplicity to solve the problem by using ACO (Shmygelska & Hoos, 2005).

3.5 Tabu Search Algorithm

Tabu search (TS) is a local meta-heuristic searching procedure efficiently used to solve the mathematical optimization process (Dorigo & Stützle, 2003).The classical local searches take a potential solution to a problem and then it check its next immediate neighbours for finding an improved form of the solution. But local search methods problem is generally encountered that it may stuck in the suboptimal regions, where actually many solutions are equally fit. However, tabu search maximises the output of the local search by changing its basic rule. The pseudo code can be given in following steps.

Algorithm

1.   Set initial states
2.   Perform tabu search (apply minima condition)
3.   Whether many solutions have been produced (if no)
4.   Restart diversification
5.   If enough restarts has been applied

In this case three categories of memory structures are used in computation as described by Glover (1986). These are short-term memory concepts of a list of solutions and considers for a potential solution, then intermediate-term requires the set of rules to bias the search towards the potential solution in search space and finally long-term type in which change of rules occurs that basically search the drive the search into new regions. Sometimes these three types of memories can be overlapped in practice. In order to overcome the global searches in GA, tabu search has been implemented within the crossover and mutation operators in GAs to improve the local search capability (Glover, 1990). Lin et al. (2014) described about a local adjusted tabu search algorithm for prediction of protein 3D structure. The binary encoding for the residues has been done in 3D off lattice model, followed by the implementation of the optimization method. The result accuracy was obtained as good in comparison to the other meta-heuristic methods (Zhang et al., 2010; Lin, & Zhang, 2014).

4. FUTURE RESEARCH DIRECTIONS

In general, the limitation of all the bio-inspired algorithms crucially by the two issues (Yang et al., 2013). One is premature convergence results which is either due to lack of accuracy of the final solution or that do not satisfy the optimal solution. Another is slow convergence that corresponds to the solution quality does not improve sufficiently quickly. Despite of the limitations the list of the bio-inspired algorithms is expanding rapidly under the name clever algorithms due to their efficiency. These algorithms are also capable of hybridization with a large number of other optimization process resulting novel algorithms. Many of these efficient novel hybridized algorithms are being developed and many are yet to come in future. Bio-inspired computation has become an emerging and popular part of computer science is implemented to solve the most complex protein structure prediction. Most of these bio-inspired algorithms based computation can be very broad in nature (Fister et al.,2013; Adamatzky et al., 2012; Cui et al., 2014). Implementation of the current bio-inspired algorithms in protein structure prediction research should be improved as protein structure prediction from its sequence information in the following area.

1. **Complexity:** As the PSP is a complex, nonlinear and a multimodal event occurs under stringent constraints, so algorithms should be designed to address the issue.
2. **Computationally Expensive Methods:** In case of PSP, the large-scale astronomical conformations of the folded amino acids to be searched and analyzed

so, developments in this area is essential to speed up the computational prediction strategy.

3. **Novel Model Presentation:** For modeling purpose (protein presentation) there is a need to establish a new model systems apart from the established one, so as to effective application of the different types of bio-inspired algorithms is needed to draw a solid conclusion.

5. CONCLUSION

Protein structure prediction (PSP) approach having a wide range of important applications ranges from design and development of drugs to the prediction of disease. Being a complex phenomena, the protein structure prediction problem solving theoretically is associated with two most important issues; the first one is consideration of a structural model of a protein, thereby defining the parameters and the second one is the development and application of a suitable optimization method to choose the right native 3D conformation. Many optimization algorithms, that are inspired from the nature and natural behavior of animals has been developed and implemented with proper structural model. This combinatorial mode of study has uncovered the efficiency feature of these optimization algorithms that has lead to the development of several improved strategies to solve the PSP. The five types of bio-inspired algorithm we discussed, are used to predict the protein 3D structure have shown their efficiency when utilized in a hybridized form. The hybrid algorithm has the advantages from both the conventional algorithms in terms of capability of searching multiple search points, using flexible memory functions, avoiding global searching and also making less computational complexity.

REFERENCES

Adamatzky, A. (2012). Slime mould computes planar shapes. *International Journal of Bio-inspired Computation*, *4*(3), 149–154. doi:10.1504/IJBIC.2012.047239

Al-Akwaa, F. M., Elhetari, H., Al Naggar, N., & Al-Rumaima, M. A. (2014). Comparison of the 3D Protein Structure Prediction Algorithms. *International Journal of Engineering Research and Applications*, *4*(2), 462–467.

Al Salami, N. M. (2009). Ant colony optimization algorithm. *UbiCC Journal*, *4*(3), 823–826.

Alm, E., & Baker, D. (1999). Prediction of protein-folding mechanisms from free-energy landscapes derived from native structures. *Proceedings of the National Academy of Sciences of the United States of America, 96*(20), 11305–11310. doi:10.1073/pnas.96.20.11305 PMID:10500172

Amato, N. M., Dill, K. A., & Song, G. (2003). Using motion planning to map protein folding landscapes and analyze folding kinetics of known native structures. *Journal of Computational Biology, 10*(3-4), 239–255. doi:10.1089/10665270360688002 PMID:12935327

Apaydin, M. S., Brutlag, D. L., Guestrin, C., Hsu, D., Latombe, J. C., & Varma, C. (2003). Stochastic roadmap simulation: An efficient representation and algorithm for analyzing molecular motion. *Journal of Computational Biology, 10*(3-4), 257–281. doi:10.1089/10665270360688011 PMID:12935328

Bahamish, H. A. A., Abdullah, R., & Salam, R. A. (2008, May). Protein conformational search using bees algorithm. In *2008 Second Asia International Conference on Modelling &# x00026; Simulation (AMS)* (pp. 911-916). IEEE. doi:10.1109/AMS.2008.65

Bahamish, H. A. A., Abdullah, R., & Salam, R. A. (2009, May). Protein tertiary structure prediction using artificial bee colony algorithm. In *2009 Third Asia International Conference on Modelling & Simulation* (pp. 258-263). IEEE. doi:10.1109/AMS.2009.47

Bennett, A. J., Johnston, R. L., Turpin, E., & He, J. Q. (2008). Analysis of an immune algorithm for protein structure prediction. *Informatica, 32*(3), 245–251.

Bowie, J. U., Luthy, R., & Eisenberg, D. (1991). A method to identify protein sequences that fold into a known three-dimensional structure. *Science, 253*(5016), 164–170. doi:10.1126/science.1853201 PMID:1853201

Branson, L. P. B. C. H. (1951). Two hydrogen-bonded helical configuration of the polypeptide chain. *Proceedings of the National Academy of Sciences of the United States of America, 37*, 205–211. doi:10.1073/pnas.37.4.205 PMID:14816373

Callaway, E. (2015). The revolution will not be crystallized: A new method sweeps through structural biology. *Nature, 525*(7568), 172–174. doi:10.1038/525172a PMID:26354465

Chu, D., & Zomaya, A. (2006). Parallel ant colony optimization for 3D protein structure prediction using the HP lattice model. In *Parallel Evolutionary Computations* (pp. 177–198). Springer Berlin Heidelberg. doi:10.1007/3-540-32839-4_9

Covell, D. G. (1992). Folding protein α-carbon chains into compact forms by monte carlo methods. Proteins. *Structure, Function, and Bioinformatics, 14*(3), 409–420. doi:10.1002/prot.340140310

Cui, Z., Alex, R., Akerkar, R., & Yang, X. S. (2014). Recent advances on bioinspired computation. *The Scientific World Journal.* doi:10.1155/2014/934890

Cutello, V., Nicosia, G., Pavone, M., & Timmis, J. (2007). An immune algorithm for protein structure prediction on lattice models. *IEEE Transactions on Evolutionary Computation, 11*(1), 101–117. doi:10.1109/TEVC.2006.880328

Dill, K. A., Bromberg, S., Yue, K., Fiebig, K. M., Yee, D. P., Thomas, P. D., & Chan, H. S. (1995). Principles of protein folding--a perspective from simple exact models. *Protein Science, 4*(4), 561-602.

Dorigo, M., & Blum, C. (2005). Ant colony optimization theory: A survey. *Theoretical Computer Science, 344*(2), 243–278. doi:10.1016/j.tcs.2005.05.020

Dorigo, M., & Stützle, T. (2003). The ant colony optimization metaheuristic: Algorithms, applications, and advances. In Handbook of metaheuristics (pp. 250-285). Springer US.

Eberhart, R. C., & Kennedy, J. (1995, October). A new optimizer using particle swarm theory. In *Proceedings of the sixth international symposium on micro machine and human science* (Vol. 1, pp. 39-43). doi:10.1109/MHS.1995.494215

Fidanova, S., & Lirkov, I. (2008, October). Ant colony system approach for protein folding. In *Computer Science and Information Technology, 2008. IMCSIT 2008. International Multiconference on* (pp. 887-891). IEEE. doi:10.1109/IMCSIT.2008.4747347

Fister, I., Yang, X. S., & Brest, J. (2013). A comprehensive review of firefly algorithms. *Swarm and Evolutionary Computation, 13*, 34–46. doi:10.1016/j.swevo.2013.06.001

Forsdyke, D. R. (1995). The origins of the clonal selection theory of immunity. *The FASEB Journal, 9*, 164–166. PMID:7781918

Gibrat, J. F., Garnier, J., & Robson, B. (1987). Further developments of protein secondary structure prediction using information theory: New parameters and consideration of residue pairs. *Journal of Molecular Biology, 198*(3), 425–443. doi:10.1016/0022-2836(87)90292-0 PMID:3430614

Glover, F. (1986). Future paths for integer programming and links to artificial intelligence. *Computers & Operations Research, 13*(5), 533–549. doi:10.1016/0305-0548(86)90048-1

Glover, F. (1990). Tabu search: A tutorial. *Interfaces*, *20*(4), 74–94. doi:10.1287/inte.20.4.74

Habeck, M., Rieping, W., & Nilges, M. (2005). Bayesian estimation of Karplus parameters and torsion angles from three-bond scalar couplings constants. *Journal of Magnetic Resonance (San Diego, Calif.)*, *177*(1), 160–165. doi:10.1016/j.jmr.2005.06.016 PMID:16085438

Hofmeyr, S. A. (2001). An interpretative introduction to the immune system. *Design principles for the immune system and other distributed autonomous systems*, *3*, 28-36.

Irbäck, A., Peterson, C., Potthast, F., & Sommelius, O. (1997). Local interactions and protein folding: A three-dimensional off-lattice approach. *The Journal of Chemical Physics*, *107*(1), 273–282. doi:10.1063/1.474357

Irbäck, A., & Sandelin, E. (1998). Local interactions and protein folding: A model study on the square and triangular lattices. *The Journal of Chemical Physics*, *108*(5), 2245–2250. doi:10.1063/1.475605

Kanj, F., Mansour, N., Khachfe, H., & Abu-Khzam, F. (2009, May). Protein structure prediction in the 3D HP model. In *2009 IEEE/ACS International Conference on Computer Systems and Applications* (pp. 732-736). IEEE. doi:10.1109/AICCSA.2009.5069408

Kennedy, J. (2011). Particle swarm optimization. In Encyclopedia of machine learning (pp. 760-766). Springer US.

Khakzad, H., Karami, Y., & Arab, S. S. (2015). *Accelerating Protein Structure Prediction using Particle Swarm Optimization on GPU*. https://doi.org/10.1101/022434

Kondov, I., & Berlich, R. (2011, June). Protein structure prediction using particle swarm optimization and a distributed parallel approach. In *Proceedings of the 3rd workshop on Biologically inspired algorithms for distributed systems* (pp. 35-42). ACM. doi:10.1145/1998570.1998579

Kuhlbrandt, W. (2013). Introduction to electron crystallography. *Methods in Molecular Biology (Clifton, N.J.)*, *955*, 1–16. doi:10.1007/978-1-62703-176-9_1 PMID:23132052

Lau, K. F., & Dill, K. A. (1989). A lattice statistical mechanics model of the conformational and sequence spaces of proteins. *Macromolecules*, *22*(10), 3986–3997. doi:10.1021/ma00200a030

Lee, D., Redfern, O., & Orengo, C. (2007). Predicting protein function from sequence and structure. *Nature Reviews. Molecular Cell Biology*, 8(12), 995–1005. doi:10.1038/nrm2281 PMID:18037900

Levitt, M. (1983). Protein folding by restrained energy minimization and molecular dynamics. *Journal of Molecular Biology*, 170(3), 723–764. doi:10.1016/S0022-2836(83)80129-6 PMID:6195346

Lin, X., & Zhang, X. (2014). Protein structure prediction with local adjust tabu search algorithm. *BMC Bioinformatics*, 15(15). doi:10.1186/1471-2105-15-S15-S1 PMID:25474708

Mahmood, Z. N., Mahmuddin, M., & Mahmood, M. N. (2012). Protein tertiary structure prediction based on main chain angle using a hybrid bees colony optimization algorithm. International Journal of Modern Physics, 9, 143-156. doi:10.1142/S201019451200520X

Mansour, N., Kanj, F., & Khachfe, H. (2012). Particle swarm optimization approach for protein structure prediction in the 3D HP model. *Interdisciplinary Sciences: Computational Life Sciences*, 4(3), 190–200. PMID:23292692

Marion, D. (2013). An introduction to biological NMR spectroscopy. *Molecular & Cellular Proteomics: MCP*, 12(11), 3006–3025. doi:10.1074/mcp.O113.030239 PMID:23831612

Marks, D. S., Colwell, L. J., Sheridan, R., Hopf, T. A., Pagnani, A., Zecchina, R., & Sander, C. (2011). Protein 3D structure computed from evolutionary sequence variation. *PLoS ONE*, 6(12), e28766. doi:10.1371/journal.pone.0028766 PMID:22163331

Marqusee, S., & Baldwin, R. L. (1987). Helix stabilization by Glu-... Lys+ salt bridges in short peptides of de novo design. *Proceedings of the National Academy of Sciences of the United States of America*, 84(24), 8898–8902. doi:10.1073/pnas.84.24.8898 PMID:3122208

McPherson, A. (2004). Introduction to protein crystallization. *Methods (San Diego, Calif.)*, 34(3), 254–265. doi:10.1016/j.ymeth.2004.03.019 PMID:15325645

Muñoz, V., & Eaton, W. A. (1999). A simple model for calculating the kinetics of protein folding from three-dimensional structures. *Proceedings of the National Academy of Sciences of the United States of America*, 96(20), 11311–11316. doi:10.1073/pnas.96.20.11311 PMID:10500173

Nishant, T., & Sathish Kumar, D., & Vvl, P. K. A. (2011). Computational Methods for Protein Structure Prediction and Its Application in Drug Design. *J Proteomics Bioinform, 1*. doi:10.4172/jpb.R1-002

Oas, T. G., & Kim, P. S. (1988). A peptide model of a protein folding intermediate. *Nature, 336*(6194), 42–48. doi:10.1038/336042a0 PMID:3185721

Ozturk, C., Hancer, E., & Karaboga, D. (2015). A novel binary artificial bee colony algorithm based on genetic operators. *Information Sciences, 297*, 154–170. doi:10.1016/j.ins.2014.10.060

Pauling, L., & Corey, R. B. (1951). Configurations of polypeptide chains with favored orientations around single bonds two new pleated sheets. *Proceedings of the National Academy of Sciences of the United States of America, 37*(11), 729–740. doi:10.1073/pnas.37.11.729 PMID:16578412

Rodin, V., Benzinou, A., Guillaud, A., Ballet, P., Harrouet, F., Tisseau, J., & Le Bihan, J. (2004). An immune oriented multi-agent system for biological image processing. *Pattern Recognition, 37*(4), 631–645. doi:10.1016/j.patcog.2003.09.014

Shmygelska, A., & Hoos, H. H. (2005). An ant colony optimisation algorithm for the 2D and 3D hydrophobic polar protein folding problem. *BMC Bioinformatics, 6*(1), 1. doi:10.1186/1471-2105-6-30 PMID:15710037

Shmygelska, A., & Hoos, H. H. (2005). An ant colony optimisation algorithm for the 2D and 3D hydrophobic polar protein folding problem. *BMC Bioinformatics, 6*(1), 30. doi:10.1186/1471-2105-6-30 PMID:15710037

Stillinger, F. H., & Head-Gordon, T. (1995). Collective aspects of protein folding illustrated by a toy model. *Physical Review E: Statistical Physics, Plasmas, Fluids, and Related Interdisciplinary Topics, 52*(3), 2872–2877. doi:10.1103/PhysRevE.52.2872 PMID:9963733

Stillinger, F. H., Head-Gordon, T., & Hirshfeld, C. L. (1993). Toy model for protein folding. *Physical Review E: Statistical Physics, Plasmas, Fluids, and Related Interdisciplinary Topics, 48*(2), 1469–1477. doi:10.1103/PhysRevE.48.1469 PMID:9960736

Venkatesan, A., Gopal, J., Candavelou, M., Gollapalli, S., & Karthikeyan, K. (2013). Computational approach for protein structure prediction. *Healthcare Informatics Research, 19*(2), 137-147.

Wang, L., Pan, J., & Jiao, L. (2000). The immune algorithm. *Tien Tzu Hsueh Pao, 28*(7), 74–78.

Weiss, M. S., Jabs, A., & Hilgenfeld, R. (1998). Peptide bonds revisited. *Nature Structural & Molecular Biology*, 5(8), 676–676. doi:10.1038/1368 PMID:9699627

Whisstock, J. C., & Lesk, A. M. (2003). Predictions of protein function from protein sequence and structure. *Quarterly Reviews of Biophysics*, 36(03), 307–340. doi:10.1017/S0033583503003901 PMID:15029827

Yang, X. S., Cui, Z., Xiao, R., Gandomi, A. H., & Karamanoglu, M. (Eds.). (2013). *Swarm intelligence and bio-inspired computation: theory and applications.* Newnes. doi:10.1016/B978-0-12-405163-8.00001-6

Yuce, B., Packianather, M. S., Mastrocinque, E., Pham, D. T., & Lambiase, A. (2013). Honey bees inspired optimization method: The Bees Algorithm. *Insects*, 4(4), 646–662. doi:10.3390/insects4040646 PMID:26462528

Zhang, X., Wang, T., Luo, H., Yang, J. Y., Deng, Y., Tang, J., & Yang, M. Q. (2010). 3D Protein structure prediction with genetic tabu search algorithm. *BMC Systems Biology*, 4(1). doi:10.1186/1752-0509-4-S1-S6 PMID:20522256

Zhang, X. L., & Cheng, W. (2009). Protein 3D structure prediction based on improved tabu search. *Computer Engineering*, 4, 13. doi: 10.1186/1752-0509-4-S1-S6

Zwanzig, R., Szabo, A., & Bagchi, B. (1992). Levinthals paradox. *Proceedings of the National Academy of Sciences of the United States of America*, 89(1), 20–22. doi:10.1073/pnas.89.1.20 PMID:1729690

KEY TERMS AND DEFINITIONS

Amino Acids: Amino acidsare important bio-organic compounds containing amine (-nh2) and carboxylic acid (-cooh) functional group, which are polymerised to form proteins.

Bioinspired Algorithms: These are biologically inspired computing a category of optimization methods derived from the biological behavior from different organisms.

HP Model: Hydrophobic polar (HP) protein is a simplified model used to study the protein folding process in space by observing the hydrophobic interactions between amino acids.

Off Lattice Model: Lattice protein models is an efficient computer model for proteins, used to investigate protein folding.

Optimization Method: Selection of a best element from some set of available alternative based on some sort of criteria used mostly in mathematics and computer science research.

Protein Structure Prediction: Protein structure prediction is the prediction of the three-dimensional structure of a protein from its amino acid sequence.

Three Dimensional Structures: Protein structure is the bio-molecular structure of a protein molecule. Proteins are polymers specifically polypeptides formed from sequences of monomer amino acids.

Compilation of References

Abbott, R. (2005). Challenges for Bio-inspired Computing. In *Proceedings of The BioGEC workshop* (pp. 12-22). New York. ACM.

Abdul Nazeer, , & Sebastian, , & Kumar. (2013). A Novel harmony search-K means hybrid algorithm for clustering gene expression data. *Bioinformatics (Oxford, England)*, *9*(2), 84–88. PMID:23390351

Abrams, M., Allison, D., Kafura, D., Ribbens, C., Rosson, M. B., Shaffer, C., & Watson, L. (1998). PSE research at Verginia Tech: An Overview. Technical Report: TR-98-21. Virginia Polytechnic Institute & State University.

Abuobieda, A., Salim, N., Binwahlan, M. S., & Osman, A. H. (2013, August). Differential evolution cluster-based text summarization methods. In *Computing, Electrical and Electronics Engineering (ICCEEE), 2013 International Conference on* (pp. 244-248). IEEE. doi:10.1109/ICCEEE.2013.6633941

Acharjya, D. P., & Kauser, A. P. (2015). Swarm Intelligence in Solving Bio-Inspired Computing Problems: Reviews, Perspectives, and Challenges. In Handbook of Research on Swarm Intelligence in Engineering (pp. 74-98). IGI Global.

Acharjya, D. P. (2014). Rough set on two universal sets and knowledge representation. In B. Issac & N. Israr (Eds.), *Case Studies in Intelligent Computing* (pp. 79–108). CRC Press. doi:10.1201/b17333-6

Acharjya, D. P., & Ezhilarasi, L. (2011). A knowledge mining model for ranking institutions using rough computing with ordering rules and formal concept analysis. *International Journal of Computer Science Issues*, *8*(2), 417–425.

Acharjya, D. P., & Kauser Ahmed, P. (2015). Swarm Intelligence in Solving Bio-Inspired Computing Problems – Reviews, Perspectives, and Challenges. In S. Bhattacharyya & P. Dutta (Eds.), *Swarm Intelligence in Engineering* (pp. 74–98). IGI Global Publishers.

Acharjya, D. P., Roy, D., & Rahaman, M. A. (2012). Prediction of Missing Associations using Rough Computing and Bayesian Classification. *International Journal of Intelligent Systems and Applications*, *4*(11), 1–13. doi:10.5815/ijisa.2012.11.01

Compilation of References

Adamatzky, A. (2012). Slime mould computes planar shapes. *International Journal of Bio-inspired Computation*, *4*(3), 149–154. doi:10.1504/IJBIC.2012.047239

Ahmed, N. S. S., & Acharjya, D. P. (2015). Detection of denial of service attack in wireless network using dominance based rough set. *International Journal of Advanced Computer Science and Applications*, *6*(12), 267–278.

Ahuja, M. S., & Dr, J. S. B. (2014). Varnica Web Crawler: Extracting the Web Data. *International Journal of Computer Trends and Technology*, *13*(3).

Al Salami, N. M. (2009). Ant colony optimization algorithm. *UbiCC Journal*, *4*(3), 823–826.

Al-Akwaa, F. M., Elhetari, H., Al Naggar, N., & Al-Rumaima, M. A. (2014). Comparison of the 3D Protein Structure Prediction Algorithms. *International Journal of Engineering Research and Applications*, *4*(2), 462–467.

Al-Betar, M. A., Khader, A. T., & Nadi, F. (2010b). Selection mechanisms in memory consideration for examination timetabling with harmony search. *12th Annual Conference on Genetic and Evolutionary Computation*, 1203-1210.

Al-Betar, M., Khader, A., & Liao, I. (2010a). A harmony search with multi-pitch adjusting rate for the university course timetabling. In Z. W. Geem (Ed.), *Recent Advances in Harmony Search Algorithm* (pp. 147–161). Springer. doi:10.1007/978-3-642-04317-8_13

Alguliev, R. M., & Aliguliyev, R. M. (2005, September). Effective summarization method of text documents. In *Web Intelligence, 2005. Proceedings. The 2005 IEEE/WIC/ACM International Conference on* (pp. 264-271). IEEE. doi:10.1109/WI.2005.57

Alguliev, R. M., Aliguliyev, R. M., & Hajirahimova, M. S. (2012). GenDocSum+MCLR: Generic document summarization based on maximum coverage and less redundancy. *Expert Systems with Applications*, *39*(16), 12460–12473. doi:10.1016/j.eswa.2012.04.067

Alguliev, R. M., Aliguliyev, R. M., Hajirahimova, M. S., & Mehdiyev, C. A. (2011). MCMR: Maximum coverage and minimum redundant text summarization model. *Expert Systems with Applications*, *38*(12), 14514–14522. doi:10.1016/j.eswa.2011.05.033

Alguliev, R. M., Aliguliyev, R. M., & Isazade, N. R. (2012). DESAMC+ DocSum: Differential evolution with self-adaptive mutation and crossover parameters for multi-document summarization. *Knowledge-Based Systems*, *36*, 21–38. doi:10.1016/j.knosys.2012.05.017

Alguliev, R. M., Aliguliyev, R. M., & Isazade, N. R. (2013). Multiple documents summarization based on evolutionary optimization algorithm. *Expert Systems with Applications*, *40*(5), 1675–1689. doi:10.1016/j.eswa.2012.09.014

Alguliev, R. M., Aliguliyev, R. M., & Mehdiyev, C. A. (2011). An optimization model and DPSO-EDA for document summarization. *International Journal of Information Technology and Computer Science*, *3*(5), 59–68. doi:10.5815/ijitcs.2011.05.08

Alguliev, R. M., Aliguliyev, R. M., & Mehdiyev, C. A. (2011). Sentence selection for generic document summarization using an adaptive differential evolution algorithm. *Swarm and Evolutionary Computation, 1*(4), 213–222. doi:10.1016/j.swevo.2011.06.006

Alguliev, R., & Aliguliyev, R. (2009). Evolutionary algorithm for extractive text summarization. *Intelligent Information Management, 1*(02), 128–138. doi:10.4236/iim.2009.12019

Alia, O. M., Mandava, R., & Aziz, M. E. (2010). A hybrid harmony search algorithm to mri brain segmentation. *The 9th IEEE International Conference on Cognitive Informatics,* 712-719.

Alia, O. M., Mandava, R., Ramachandram, D., & Aziz, M. E. (2009a). A novel image segmentation algorithm based on harmony fuzzy search algorithm.*International Conference of Soft Computing and Pattern Recognition,* 335-340. doi:10.1109/SoCPaR.2009.73

Alia, O. M., Mandava, R., Ramachandram, D., & Aziz, M. E. (2009b). Dynamic fuzzy clustering using harmony search with application to image segmentation.*International Symposium on Signal Processing and Information Technology,* 538-543. doi:10.1109/ISSPIT.2009.5407590

Aliguliyev, R. M. (2009). A new sentence similarity measure and sentence based extractive technique for automatic text summarization. *Expert Systems with Applications, 36*(4), 7764–7772. doi:10.1016/j.eswa.2008.11.022

Alizadeh, A. A., Eisen, M. B., Davis, R. E., Ma, C., Lossos, I. S., Rosenwald, A., & Staudt, L. M. et al. (2000). Distinct types of diffuse large B-cell lymphoma identified by gene expression profiling. *Nature, 403*(6769), 503–511. doi:10.1038/35000501 PMID:10676951

Alm, E., & Baker, D. (1999). Prediction of protein-folding mechanisms from free-energy landscapes derived from native structures. *Proceedings of the National Academy of Sciences of the United States of America, 96*(20), 11305–11310. doi:10.1073/pnas.96.20.11305 PMID:10500172

Alon, U., Barkai, N., Notterman, D. A., Gish, K., Ybarra, S., Mack, D., & Levine, A. J. (1999). Broad patterns of gene expression revealed by clustering analysis of tumor and normal colon tissues probed by oligonucleotide arrays. *Proceedings of the National Academy of Sciences of the United States of America, 96*(12), 6745–6750. doi:10.1073/pnas.96.12.6745 PMID:10359783

Alsafasfeh, Q., Abdel-Qader, I., & Harb, A. (2010). Symmetrical pattern and PCA based framework for fault detection and classification in power systems. In *Proceedings of International Conference on Electro / Information Technology (EIT)* (pp. 1-5). doi:10.1109/EIT.2010.5612179

Alsulaiman, F. A., Sakr, N., Vald'es, J. J., El Saddik, A., & Georganas, N. D. (2009). Feature selection and classification in genetic programming: application to haptic-based biometric data. *Proceedings of the IEEE Symposium on Computational Intelligence in Security and Defense Applications (CISDA 2009).* doi:10.1109/CISDA.2009.5356540

Amadek & Trnkova. (1990). *Automata and Algebras in Categories.* Dordrecht: Kluwer Academic Publishers.

Compilation of References

Amato, N. M., Dill, K. A., & Song, G. (2003). Using motion planning to map protein folding landscapes and analyze folding kinetics of known native structures. *Journal of Computational Biology*, *10*(3-4), 239–255. doi:10.1089/10665270360688002 PMID:12935327

Amaya, I., Cruz, J., & Correa, R. (2015). Harmony search algorithm: A variant with self-regulated fretwidth. *Applied Mathematics and Computation*, *266*, 1127–1152. doi:10.1016/j.amc.2015.06.040

Amiri, B., Hossain, L., & Mosavi, S. E. (2010) Application of Harmony Search Algorithm on Clustering.*Proceedings of World Congress on Engineering and Computer Science*, 1, 20-22.

André, B., Harmen, S., & Michael, S. (2002). Fitness function design to improve evolutionary structural testing. *Proceedings of the genetic and evolutionary computation conference*, 1329-1336.

Anitha, A., & Acharjya, D. P. (2015). Neural network and rough set hybrid scheme for prediction of missing associations. *International Journal of Bioinformatics Research and Applications*, *11*(6), 503–524. doi:10.1504/IJBRA.2015.073237 PMID:26642360

Anuradha, J., & Tripathy, B. K. (2011). *Improved Intelligent Dynamic Swarm PSO Algorithm and Rough Set for feature Selection, Obcom 2011 conference*. VIT, Vellore.

Apaydin, M. S., Brutlag, D. L., Guestrin, C., Hsu, D., Latombe, J. C., & Varma, C. (2003). Stochastic roadmap simulation: An efficient representation and algorithm for analyzing molecular motion. *Journal of Computational Biology*, *10*(3-4), 257–281. doi:10.1089/10665270360688011 PMID:12935328

Arunkumar, C., & Ramakrishnan, S. (2014). *Binary Classification of cancer microarray gene expression data using Extreme Learning Machines*. Paper presented at the 2014 IEEE International Conference on Computational Intelligence and Computing Research(ICCIC).

Arunkumar, C., & Ramakrishnan, S. (2015). *Hybrid Feature Selection using correlation coefficient and particle swarm optimization on microarray gene expression data: Innovations in Bioinspired computing and applications*. Paper presented at the 6th International Conference in Bioinspired computing and Applications, Advances in Intelligent Systems and Computing.

Asgari, H., Masoumi, B., & Sheijani, O. S. (2014, February). Automatic text summarization based on multi-agent particle swarm optimization. In *Intelligent Systems (ICIS), 2014 Iranian Conference on* (pp. 1-5). IEEE. doi:10.1109/IranianCIS.2014.6802592

Ashrafi, S. M., & Dariane, A. B. (2011). A novel and effective algorithm for numerical optimization: melody search algorithm.*International Conference on Hybrid Intelligent Systems*, 109-114.

Ashrafi, S. M., & Dariane, A. B. (2013). Performance evaluation of an improved harmony search algorithm for numerical optimization: Melody search (MS). *Engineering Applications of Artificial Intelligence*, *26*(4), 1301–1321. doi:10.1016/j.engappai.2012.08.005

Ashutosh, Laskar, Kumar, & Majumder. (2013). Gene Expression Programming Based Age Estimation Using Facial Features. *IEEE Second International Conference on Image Information Processing (ICIIP-2013)*. doi:10.1109/ICIIP.2013.6707631

Atmar, W. (1994). Notes on the Simulation of Evolution. *IEEE Transactions on Neural Networks*, *5*(1), 130–147. doi:10.1109/72.265967 PMID:18267786

Ayvaz, M. T., Kayhan, A. H., Ceylan, H., & Gurarslan, G. (2009). Hybridizing the harmony search algorithm with a spreadsheet solver for solving continuous engineering optimization problems. *Engineering Optimization*, *41*(12), 1119–1144. doi:10.1080/03052150902926835

Babaoglu, İ., Fındık, O., Ülker, E., & Aygül, N. (2012). A novel hybrid classification method with particle swarm optimization and k-nearest neighbor algorithm for diagnosis of coronary artery disease using exercise stress test data. *International Journal of Innovative Computing, Information and Control, 8*(5), 3467-3475.

Back, T. (1996). *Evolutionary Algorithms in Theory and Practice*. New York: Oxford University Press.

Bagula, A. B. (2006). *Traffic Engineering Next Generation IP Networks using Gene Expression Programming*. IEEE.

Bahamish, H. A. A., Abdullah, R., & Salam, R. A. (2008, May). Protein conformational search using bees algorithm. In *2008 Second Asia International Conference on Modelling &# x00026; Simulation (AMS)* (pp. 911-916). IEEE. doi:10.1109/AMS.2008.65

Bahamish, H. A. A., Abdullah, R., & Salam, R. A. (2009, May). Protein tertiary structure prediction using artificial bee colony algorithm. In *2009 Third Asia International Conference on Modelling & Simulation* (pp. 258-263). IEEE. doi:10.1109/AMS.2009.47

Bakward, K. M., Pattnaik, S. S., Sohi, B. S., Devi, S., Panigrahi, K. B., Das, S., & Lohokare, M. R. (2009). Hybrid Bacterial Foraging with parameter free PSO. *Proceedings of IEEE conference on Nature and Biologically Inspired Computing*, 1077-1081.

Bandyopadhyay, S., Mukhopadhyay, A., & Maulik, U. (2007). An improved algorithm for clustering gene expression data. *Bioinformatics (Oxford, England)*, *23*(21), 2859–2865. doi:10.1093/bioinformatics/btm418 PMID:17720981

Barabasi, A., & Albert, R. (1999). Emergence of scaling in random networks. *Science*, *286*(509). PMID:10521342

Barrero, V., Grisales, E. V., Rosas, F., Sanchez, C., & Leon, J. (2001). Design and implementation of an intelligent interface for myoelectric controlled prosthesis. In *Proceedings of the 23rd Annual International Conference of the IEEE*. Istanbul, Turkey: IEEE.

Baumgartner, R., Flesca, S., & Gottlob, G. (2001), Visual Web information extraction with Lixto. *Proceedings of the 27th International Conference on Very Large Data Bases (VLDB'01)*, 119-128.

Bautu, Bautu, & Luchian. (2005). *A GEP based approach for solving fredholm first kind integral equations*. IEEE.

Compilation of References

Bazghandi, M., Tabrizi, G. T., Jahan, M. V., & Mashahd, I. (2012). Extractive Summarization Of Farsi Documents Based On PSO Clustering. *International Journal of Computer Science Issues*, *9*(4), 329–332.

Beasley, D., Bull, D. R., & Martin, R. R. (1993). An overview of Genetic Algorithm: Part I-Fundamentals. *University Computing*, *15*(2), 58–69.

Benjamin, S. C., Johnson, N. F., & Hui, P. M. (1996). Cellular automata models of traffic ow along a highway containing a junction. *Journal of Physics. A, Mathematical and General*, *29*(12), 3119–3127. doi:10.1088/0305-4470/29/12/018

Bennett, A. J., Johnston, R. L., Turpin, E., & He, J. Q. (2008). Analysis of an immune algorithm for protein structure prediction. *Informatica*, *32*(3), 245–251.

Berndt, D. J., Fisher, J., Johnson, L., Pinglikar, J., & Watkins, A. (2003). Breeding Software Test Cases with Genetic Algorithms. *Proceedings of the Thirty-Sixth Hawaii International Conference on System Sciences,* 1-10. doi:10.1109/HICSS.2003.1174917

Berndt, D. J., & Watkins, A. (2004). Investigating the Performance of Genetic Algorithm-Based Software Test Case Generation. *Proceedings of the Eighth IEEE International Symposium on High Assurance Systems Engineering*, 261-262. doi:10.1109/HASE.2004.1281750

Berry, M. J. A., & Linoff, G. (1996). *Data Mining Techniques for Marketing, Sales and Customer Support*. John Wiley & Sons, Inc.

Beyer, H. G., & Schwefel, H. P. (2002). Evolution strategies. *Natural Computing*, *1*(1), 3–52. doi:10.1023/A:1015059928466

Bezdek, J. C. (1981). *Pattern Recognition with Fuzzy Objective Function Algorithms*. New York: Plenum Press. doi:10.1007/978-1-4757-0450-1

Bhagya Shree, S. R., & Sheshadri, H. S. (2014). *An initial investigation in the diagnosis of Alzheimer's disease using various classification techniques*. Paper presented at the 2014 IEEE International Conference on Computational Intelligence and Computing Research (ICCIC). doi:10.1109/ICCIC.2014.7238300

Bhattacharya, A., & Chattopadhyay, P. K. (2010). Hybrid Differential Evolution with Biogeography Based optimization for solution of Economic Load Dispatch. *IEEE Transactions on Power Systems*, *25*(4), 1955–1964. doi:10.1109/TPWRS.2010.2043270

Binitha, S., & Sathya, S. S. (2012). A survey of bio inspired optimization algorithms. *International Journal of Soft Computing and Engineering*, *2*(2), 137–151.

Binwahlan, M. S., Salim, N., & Suanmali, L. (2009, April). Swarm based text summarization. In *Computer Science and Information Technology-Spring Conference, 2009. IACSITSC'09. International Association of* (pp. 145-150). IEEE. doi:10.1109/IACSIT-SC.2009.61

Bonabeau, E., Dorigo, M., & Theraulaz, G. (1999). *Swarm Intelligence: From Natural to Artificial System*. New York: Oxford University Press.

Bowie, J. U., Luthy, R., & Eisenberg, D. (1991). A method to identify protein sequences that fold into a known three-dimensional structure. *Science, 253*(5016), 164–170. doi:10.1126/science.1853201 PMID:1853201

Braga, G., Cattaneo, G., Flocchini, P., & Vogliotti, C. Q. (1995). Pattern growth in elementary cellular automata. *Theoretical Computer Science, 145*(1-2), 1–26.

Branson, L. P. B. C. H. (1951). Two hydrogen-bonded helical configuration of the polypeptide chain. *Proceedings of the National Academy of Sciences of the United States of America, 37*, 205–211. doi:10.1073/pnas.37.4.205 PMID:14816373

Breiman, L. (1996). Bagging Predictors. *Journal of Machine Learning, 24*(2), 123–140. doi:10.1007/BF00058655

Broder, A. Z., Kumar, S. R., Maghoul, F., Raghavan, P., Rajagopalan, S., Stata, R., & Wiener, J. L. et al. (2000). Graph structure in the web.*Proc. Of WWW Conf.*

Brownlee, J. (2005). *On Biologically Inspired Computation a.k.a. The Field* (PhD Thesis). Swinburne University of Technology.

Bryan, J. (2004). Problems in gene clustering based on gene expression data. *Journal of Multivariate Analysis, 90*(1), 44–66. doi:10.1016/j.jmva.2004.02.011

Bukharov, O. E., & Bogolyubov, D. P. (2015). Development of a decision support system based on neural network and Genetic Algorithm. Expert System with Applications, 42, 6177-6183.

Califf, M. E., & Mooney, R. J. (1999). Relational learning of pattern-match rules for information extraction.*Proceedings of the Sixteenth National Conference on Artificial Intelligence (AAAI-99)*, 487-493.

Callaway, E. (2015). The revolution will not be crystallized: A new method sweeps through structural biology. *Nature, 525*(7568), 172–174. doi:10.1038/525172a PMID:26354465

Chakrabarti, S., van den Berg, M., & Dom, B. (1999). Distributed hypertext resource discovery through examples. *Proc. Of 25th Int.Conf. on Very Large Data Bases*, 375–386.

Chakrabarti, S., van den Berg, M., & Dom, B. (1999). Focused crawling: A new approach to topic-specific web resource discovery. . doi:10.1016/S1389-1286(99)00052-3

Chakraborty, P., Roy, G. G., Das, S., Jain, D., & Abraham, A. (2009). An improved harmony search algorithm with differential mutation operator. *Fundamenta Informaticae, 95*(4), 401–426.

Chakraborty, P., Roy, G. G., Das, S., Jain, D., & Abraham, A. (2009). An Improved Harmony Search Algorithm with Differential Mutation Operator.*Fundamenta Informaticae, 95*(4), 401–426.

Chakraborty, P., Saxena, P. C., & Katti, C. P. (2011). Fifty Years of Automata Simultion: A Review. *ACM Inroads, 2*(4), 59–70. doi:10.1145/2038876.2038893

Compilation of References

Chaturvedi, K. T., Pandit, M., & Srivastava, L. (2008). Self-organizing Hierarchical PSO for non -convex Economic Dispatch. *IEEE Transactions on Power Systems, 23*(3). doi:10.1109/TPWRS.2008.926455

Chen, Li, Wang, Yang, & Zhu. (2008). HDN-GEP a novel gene expression programming with high density node. *Proceedings IEEE*.

Chen, T. C., Ksai, P. W., Chu, S. C., & Pan, J. S. (2007). A novel optimization approach: bacterial-GA foraging.*Proceedings of the Second International Conference on Innovative Computing, Information and Control*, 391–394.

Chen, Y., & Lin, W. (2009). An Improved Bacterial Foraging Optimization.*Proceedings of the IEEE International Conference on Robotics and Biomimetics*.

Cho & Garcia-Molina. (2002). *Parallel Crawlers*. ACM.

Cho, J., & Garcia-Molina, H. (2000). Synchronizing a database to improve freshness.*Proc. of the ACM SIGMOD Int. Conf. on Management of Data*, 117–128.

Cho, J., & Garcia-Molina, H. (2000). The evolution of the web and implications for an incremental crawler.*Proc. of 26th Int. Conf. on Very Large Data Bases*, 117–128.

Cho, J., Garcia-Molina, H., & Page, L. (1998). Efficient crawling through URL ordering.*Proc. of WWW Conf.*

Chong, Y. L., & Sundaraj, K. (2009). A study of back-propagation and radial basis neural network on EMG signal classification. In *Proceedings of Mechatronics and its Applications, 2009. ISMA '09.6th International Symposium*. Sharjah: IEEE.

Chowdhury, D., Santen, L., & Schadschneider, A. (2000). Statistical Physics of Vehicular Traffic and Some Related Systems. *Physics Reports, 329*(4–6), 199–329. doi:10.1016/S0370-1573(99)00117-9

Chuang, Wu, & Yang. (2008). *Hybrid feature selection method using gene expression data*. Paper presented at the IEEE Conference on Soft Computing in Industrial Applications.

Chu, D., & Zomaya, A. (2006). Parallel ant colony optimization for 3D protein structure prediction using the HP lattice model. In *Parallel Evolutionary Computations* (pp. 177–198). Springer Berlin Heidelberg. doi:10.1007/3-540-32839-4_9

Ciornei, I., & Kyriakides, E. (2012). Hybrid Ant Colony-Genetic Algorithm (GAAPI) for Global Continuous Optimization. *Systems, Man and Cybernetics part B, IEEE Transactions, 42*(1), 234-245.

Contreras, J., Amaya, I. A., & Correa, R. (2014). An improved variant of the conventional harmony search algorithm.*Applied Mathematics and Computation, 227*(4), 821–830. doi:10.1016/j.amc.2013.11.050

Costa, G. H. R., & Baldo, F. (2015). Generation of road maps from trajectories collected with Smartphone-A Method based on Genetic Algorithm. *Applied Soft Computing, 37*, 799-808.

Covell, D. G. (1992). Folding protein α-carbon chains into compact forms by monte carlo methods. Proteins. *Structure, Function, and Bioinformatics, 14*(3), 409–420. doi:10.1002/prot.340140310

Cremer, M., & Ludwig, J. (1986). A Fast Simulation Model for Traffic Flow on the Basis of Boolean Operations. *Mathematics and Computers in Simulation, 28*(4), 297–303. doi:10.1016/0378-4754(86)90051-0

Crescenzi, V., Mecca, G., & Merialdo, P. (2001). Roadrunner: Towards automatic data extraction from large web sites.*Proceedings of the 27th International Conference on Very Large Data Bases (VLDB'01)*, 109-118.

Cui, Z., Alex, R., Akerkar, R., & Yang, X. S. (2014). Recent advances on bioinspired computation. *The Scientific World Journal.* doi:10.1155/2014/934890

Culik, K. II, & Yu, S. (1988). Undecidability of Cellular Automata classification schemes. *Complex Systems, 2*(2), 177–190.

Cutello, V., Nicosia, G., Pavone, M., & Timmis, J. (2007). An immune algorithm for protein structure prediction on lattice models. *IEEE Transactions on Evolutionary Computation, 11*(1), 101–117. doi:10.1109/TEVC.2006.880328

Dai, X., Yuan, X., & Zhang, Z. (2015). A self-adaptive multi-objective harmony search algorithm based on harmony memory variance. *Applied Soft Computing, 35*, 541–557. doi:10.1016/j.asoc.2015.06.027

Dalstein, T., & Kulicke, B. (1995). Neural network approach to fault classification for high speed protective relaying. *IEEE Transactions on Power Delivery, 10*(2), 1002–1011. doi:10.1109/61.400828

Das, K. N. (2013). Hybrid Genetic Algorithm: An Optimization Tool. In Global Trends in Knowledge Representation and Computational Intelligence, (pp. 268-305). IGI Global.

Das, B., & Reddy, J. V. (2005). Fuzzy-logic-based fault classification scheme for digital distance protection. *IEEE Transactions on Power Delivery, 20*(2), 609–616. doi:10.1109/TPWRD.2004.834294

Dash, P. K., Pradhan, A. K., & Panda, G. (2000). A novel fuzzy neural network based distance relaying scheme. *IEEE Transactions on Power Delivery, 15*(3), 902–907. doi:10.1109/61.871350

Das, T. K., & Acharjya, D. P. (2014). A decision making model using soft set and rough set on fuzzy approximation spaces. *International Journal of Intelligent Systems Technologies and Applications, 13*(3), 170–186. doi:10.1504/IJISTA.2014.065172

Davidson, S. B., Overton, C., Tannen, V., & Wong, L. (1997). Biokleisli: A Digital Library for Biomedical Researchers. *International Journal on Digital Libraries, 1*(1), 36–53.

Compilation of References

Davies, D. L., & Bouldin, D. W. (1979). A cluster separation measure. *IEEE Transactions on Pattern Analysis and Machine Intelligence*, *1*(4), 224–227. doi:10.1109/TPAMI.1979.4766909 PMID:21868852

De Castro, P. A. D., de França, O. F., Ferreira, H. M., & Von Zuben, F. J. (2007). Applying Bi-clustering to Perform Collaborative Filtering. *Proceedings of the Seventh International Conference on Intelligent Systems Design and Applications*. 421-426.

de Souto, M. C. P., Costa, I. G., de Araujo, D. S. A., Ludermir, T. B., & Schliep, A. (2008). Clustering Cancer Gene Expression Data: A Comparative Study. *BMC Bioinformatics*, *9*(1), 497. doi:10.1186/1471-2105-9-497 PMID:19038021

De Souza Gomes, A., Costa, M. A., de Faria, T. G. A., & Caminhas, W. M. (2013). Detection and classification of faults in power transmission lines using functional analysis and computational intelligence. *IEEE Transactions on Power Delivery*, *28*(3), 1402–1413. doi:10.1109/TPWRD.2013.2251752

Deb, K. (2000). An efficient constraint handling method for genetic algorithms. *Computer Methods in Applied Mechanics and Engineering*, *186*(2-4), 311–338. doi:10.1016/S0045-7825(99)00389-8

Deep, K., & Das, K. N. (2007). Choice of selection and crossover on some Benchmark problems. *International Journal of Computer. Mathematical Sciences and Applications*, *1*(1), 99–117.

Deep, K., & Das, K. N. (2008). Quadratic approximation based Hybrid Genetic Algorithm for Function Optimization. *Applied Mathematics and Computation, Elsevier*, *203*(1), 86–98. doi:10.1016/j.amc.2008.04.021

Degertekin, S. (2008). Optimal design of steel frames using harmony search algorithm. *Structural and Multidisciplinary Optimization*, *36*(4), 393–401. doi:10.1007/s00158-007-0177-4

Del, B. A., & Park, D. C. (1994). Myoelectric signal recognition using fuzzy clustering and artificial neural networks in real time. In *Proceedings of Neural Networks 1994, IEEE World Congress on Computational Intelligence*. Orlando, FL: IEEE.

Di Caro, G., Ducatelle, F., & Gambardella, L. M. (2005). An adaptive nature-inspired algorithm for routing in mobile ad hoc networks. *European Transactions on Telecommunications*, *16*(5), 443–455. doi:10.1002/ett.1062

Dietterich, T. G. (2000). Ensemble Methods in Machine Learning. In *First International Workshop on Multiple Classifier Systems*. Springer Verlag. doi:10.1007/3-540-45014-9_1

Diligenti, M., Coetzee, F., Lawrence, S., Giles, C., & Gori, M. (2000). Focused crawling using context graphs. *Proc. of 26th Int. Conf. on Very Large Data Bases*.

Dill, K. A., Bromberg, S., Yue, K., Fiebig, K. M., Yee, D. P., Thomas, P. D., & Chan, H. S. (1995). Principles of protein folding--a perspective from simple exact models. *Protein Science*, *4*(4), 561-602.

Ding & Yuan. (2009). A compression algorithm for multi-streams based on GEP. *Proceeding to 2009 Third International Conference on Genetic and Evolutionary Computing.* DOI doi:10.1109/WGEC.2009.26

Doraisamy, Sulaiman, Udzir, & Norowi. (2008). Artificial Immune Recognition System with Nonlinear Resource Allocation Method and Application to Traditional Malay Music Genre Classification. Lecture Notes in Computer Science: Vol. 5132. Artificial Immune Systems (pp. 132-141). Berlin: Springer.

Dorigo, M., & Caro, G. D. (1999). Ant Colony Optimization: A New Meta-heuristic. Proceedings of Evolutionary Computation, 1999. CEC 99.

Dorigo, M., & Stützle, T. (2003). The ant colony optimization metaheuristic: Algorithms, applications, and advances. In Handbook of metaheuristics (pp. 250-285). Springer US.

Dorigo, M., & Blum, C. (2005). Ant colony optimization theory: A survey. *Theoretical Computer Science, 344*(2), 243–278. doi:10.1016/j.tcs.2005.05.020

Dorigo, M., Maniezzo, V., & Colorni, A. (1991). *Positive feedback as a search strategy.* Milan, Italy: Technical Report, InDipartimento di Elettronica, Politecnico di Milano.

Dorigo, M., Maniezzo, V., & Colorni, A. (1996). Ant system: Optimization by a colony of cooperating agents. *IEEE Transactions on Systems, Man, and Cybernetics, 26*(1), 29–41. doi:10.1109/3477.484436 PMID:18263004

Dorigo, M., & Stützle, T. (2000). *Ant Colony Optimization.* Cambridge, MA: MIT Press.

Duan, L., Tang, C., Tang, L., Zuo, J., & Zhang, T. (2009). An effective microarray data classifier based on gene expression programming. *Proceeding of fifth International Conference on Natural Computation.* doi:10.1109/ICNC.2009.267

Duda, R. O., Hart, P. E., & Stork, D. G. (2001). *Pattern classification.* New York: John Wiley and Sons.

Dunn, J. C. (1973). A Fuzzy Relative of the ISODATA Process and its Use in Detecting Compact Well-Separated Clusters. *Journal Cybernetics, 3*(3), 32–57. doi:10.1080/01969727308546046

Dupuis, A., Ghribi, M., & Kaddouri, A. (2004). Multi-objective genetic estimation of DC motor parameters and load torque. In *Proceedings of Industrial Technology, 2004. IEEE ICIT '04.* IEEE.

Du, Y.-C., Lin, C.-H., Shyu, L.-Y., & Chen, T. (2010). Portable hand motion classifier for multi-channel surface electromyography recognition using grey relational analysis. *Journal Expert Systems with Applications, 37*(6), 4283–4291. doi:10.1016/j.eswa.2009.11.072

Eberhart, R. C., & Kennedy, J. (1995, October). A new optimizer using particle swarm theory. In *Proceedings of the sixth international symposium on micro machine and human science* (Vol. 1, pp. 39-43). doi:10.1109/MHS.1995.494215

Compilation of References

Eisen, M. B., Spellman, P. T., Brown, P. O., & Botstein, D. (1998). Cluster Analysis and Display of Genome-Wide Expression Patterns. *Proceedings of the National Academy of Sciences of the United States of America*, *95*(25), 14863–14868. doi:10.1073/pnas.95.25.14863 PMID:9843981

Embley, D. W., Campbell, D. M., Jiang, Y. S., Liddle, S. W., Lonsdale, D. W., Ng, Y.-K., & Smith, R. D. (1999). Conceptual-model-based data extraction from multiple-record Web pages. *Data & Knowledge Engineering*, *31*(3), 227–251. doi:10.1016/S0169-023X(99)00027-0

Embley, D., Jiang, S., & Ng, Y.-K. (1999). Record-boundary discovery in Web documents. *Proceedings of the 1999 ACM SIGMOD International Conference on Management of Data*, 467-478. doi:10.1145/304182.304223

Enayatifar, R., Yousefi, M., Abdullah, A. H., & Darus, A. N. (2013). LAHS: A novel harmony search algorithm based on learning automata. *Numerical Simulation*, *18*(12), 3481–3497. doi:10.1016/j.cnsns.2013.04.028

Fa, M. X., & Ling, L. (2012). Bacterial Foraging algorithm based on gradient PSO algorithm. *Proceedings of Eighth International Conference*, 29-31.

Fan, S. K., Liang, Y. C., & Zahara, E. (2006). A genetic algorithm and a particle swarm optimizer hybridized with Nelder–Mead simplex search. *Computers & Industrial Engineering*, *50*(4), 401–425. doi:10.1016/j.cie.2005.01.022

Fatma, A. O., & Mona, M. A. (2010). Genetic Algorithm for task scheduling problem, *J. Parallel Distrib. Comput, Elsevier*, *70*, 13–22.

Fattah, M. A., & Ren, F. (2009). GA, MR, FFNN, PNN and GMM based models for automatic text summarization. *Computer Speech & Language*, *23*(1), 126–144. doi:10.1016/j.csl.2008.04.002

Ferreira, C. (2002). Gene Expression Programming: Mathematical Modeling by an Artificial Intelligence. Angra do Heroismo.

Ferreira, C. (2001). Gene Expression Programming: A New Adaptive Algorithm for Solving Problems. *Complex Systems*, *13*(2), 87–129.

Ferrero, A., Sangiovanni, S., & Zappitelli, E. (1994, April). A fuzzy-set approach to fault-type identification in digital relaying. In *Proceedings of Transmission and Distribution Conference, IEEE Power Engineering Society* (pp. 269-275). IEEE. doi:10.1109/TDC.1994.328391

Fesanghary, M., Mahdavi, M., Minary-Jolandan, M., & Alizade, Y., (2008). Hybridizing harmony search algorithm with sequential quadratic programming for engineering optimization problems. *Computer Methods in Applied Mechanics and Engineering*, *197*(33-40), 3080-3091.

Fidanova, S., & Lirkov, I. (2008, October). Ant colony system approach for protein folding. In *Computer Science and Information Technology, 2008. IMCSIT 2008. International Multiconference on* (pp. 887-891). IEEE. doi:10.1109/IMCSIT.2008.4747347

Fister, I., Jr., Yang, X. S., Fister, I., Brest, J., & Fister, D. (2013). *A brief review of nature inspired algorithms for optimization*. arXiv preprint, arXiv:1307.4186

Fister, I., Yang, X. S., & Brest, J. (2013). A comprehensive review of firefly algorithms. *Swarm and Evolutionary Computation, 13,* 34–46. doi:10.1016/j.swevo.2013.06.001

Floreano & Mattiussi. (2008). *Bio-Inspired Artificial Intelligence- Theories, Methods, and Technologies.* The MIT Press.

Forsati, R., Mahdavi, M., Kangavari, M., & Safarkhani, B. (2008). Web page clustering using harmony search optimization.*Canadian Conference on Electrical and Computer Engineering,* 1601-1604. doi:10.1109/CCECE.2008.4564812

Forsdyke, D. R. (1995). The origins of the clonal selection theory of immunity. *The FASEB Journal, 9,* 164–166. PMID:7781918

Freitag, D. (1998). Information extraction from HTML: Application of a general machine learning approach. In *Proceedings Fourteenth National Conference on Artificial Intelligence (AAAI-1998) / the Tenth Innovative Applications of Artificial Intelligence Conference,* 517-523.

Freund, Y., & Schapire, R. E. (1996). Experiments with a new boosting algorithm. In *Proceedings Thirteenth International Conference on Machine Learning.* Morgan Kaufman.

Fukui, M., & Ishibashi, Y. (1996). Traffic Flow in 1D Cellular Automaton Model Including Cars Moving with High Speed. *Journal of the Physical Society of Japan, 65*(6), 1868–1870. doi:10.1143/JPSJ.65.1868

Fu, L., He, Z., & Bo, Z. (2009, March). Novel approach to fault classification in EHV transmission line based on multi-information measurements of fault transients. In *Proceedings ofAsia-Pacific Power and Energy Engineering Conference* (pp. 1-4). doi:10.1109/APPEEC.2009.4918524

Gaing, Z. L. (2003). PSO to solving the Economic Dispatch considering the generator constraints. *IEEE Transactions on Power Systems, 18*(3). doi:10.1109/TPWRS.2003.814889

Gaizauskas, R., Demetriou, G., Artymiuk, P. J., & Willett, P. (2003). Protein structures and information extraction from biological texts: The PASTA system. *Bioinformatics (Oxford, England), 19*(1), 135–143. doi:10.1093/bioinformatics/19.1.135 PMID:12499303

Gallopoulos, E., Houstis, E., & Rice, J. R. (1994). Computer as thinker/doer: Problem-solving environments for computational science. *IEEE Computational Science & Engineering, 1*(2), 11–23. doi:10.1109/99.326669

Gao, X. Z., Wang, X., & Ovaska, S. J. (2008). Modified harmony search methods for uni-modal and multi-modal optimization.*8th International Conference on Hybrid Intelligent Systems,* 65-72. doi:10.1109/HIS.2008.20

Gao, X. Z., Wang, X., & Ovaska, S. J. (2009). Uni-modal and multi-modal optimization using modified harmony search methods. *International Journal of Innovative Computing, Information, & Control, 5*(10), 2985–2996.

Compilation of References

García, O. C., de Moya Anegón, F., & Zarco, C. (2000). A GA-P algorithm to automatically formulate extended Boolean queries for a fuzzy information retrieval system. *Mathware & Soft Computing, 7*(2), 309–322.

Garis & Brain. (1996), ATR's Bbillion Neuron Artificial Brain Project: A Three Year Progress Report. *Proceedings of the International Conference on Evolutionary Computation*, 886-891.

Geem, Z. W. (2006). Improved harmony search from ensemble of music players. In B. Gabrys, R. J. Howlet, & L. C. Jain (Eds.), Knowledge-Based Intelligent Information and Engineering Systems (pp. 86-93). Bournemouth, UK: Springer. doi:10.1007/11892960_11

Geem, Z. W., Tseng, C. L., & Park, Y. (2005). Harmony search for generalized orienteering problem: best touring in china. In L. Wang, K. Chen, & Y. S. Ong (Eds.), Advances in Natural Computation (pp. 741-750). Changsha: Springer. doi:10.1007/11539902_91

Geem, Z. W. (2009). Particle-swarm harmony search for water network design. *Engineering Optimization, 41*(4), 297–311. doi:10.1080/03052150802449227

Geem, Z. W., Kim, G. H., & Loganathan, G. V. (2001). A new heuristic optimization algorithm: Harmony search. *Simulation, 76*(2), 60–68. doi:10.1177/003754970107600201

Gershenson & Rosenblueth. (2009). Modeling self-organizing traffic lights with elementary cellular automata. *Complex Systems, 19*(4), 305-322.

Ghani & Azamathulla. (2012). *Development of GEP-based functional relationship for sediment transport in tropical rivers*. Springer-Verlag London.

Gholamrezazadeh, S., Salehi, M. A., & Gholamzadeh, B. (2009). A Comprehensive Survey on Text Summarization Systems. *Proceedings of CSA*, 1–6. doi:10.1109/CSA.2009.5404226

Gibrat, J. F., Garnier, J., & Robson, B. (1987). Further developments of protein secondary structure prediction using information theory: New parameters and consideration of residue pairs. *Journal of Molecular Biology, 198*(3), 425–443. doi:10.1016/0022-2836(87)90292-0 PMID:3430614

Girgis, A. A., & Johns, M. B. (1989). A hybrid expert system for faulted section identification, fault type classification and selection of fault location algorithms. *IEEE Transactions on Power Delivery, 4*(2), 978–985. doi:10.1109/61.25578

Glover, F. (1977). Heuristic for integer using surrogate constraint. *Decision Sciences, 8*(1), 156–166. doi:10.1111/j.1540-5915.1977.tb01074.x

Glover, F. (1986). Future paths for integer programming and links to artificial intelligence. *Computers & Operations Research, 13*(5), 533–549. doi:10.1016/0305-0548(86)90048-1

Glover, F. (1990). Tabu search: A tutorial. *Interfaces, 20*(4), 74–94. doi:10.1287/inte.20.4.74

Golberg, D. E. (1989). *Genetic algorithms in search, optimization, and machine learning*. Reading, MA: Addison Wesley.

Goldbarg, M. C., Goldbarg, E. F. G., Menzes, M. S., & Luna, H. P. L. (2016). Quota Travelling Car rentor Problem: Model and Evolutionary Algorithm. *Information Sciences, 367-368*, 232–245. doi:10.1016/j.ins.2016.05.027

Goldberg, D. E. (1989). *Genetic Algorithms in Search, Optimization, and Machine Learning*. Addison Wesley.

Goldberg, D. E. (1989). Genetic Algorithms. In *Search, Optimization & Machine Learning*. Addison Wesley.

Golub, T. R., Slonim, D. K., Tamayo, P., Huard, C., Gaasenbeek, M., Mesirov, J. P., & Lander, E. S. et al. (1999). Molecular classification of cancer: Class discovery and class prediction by gene expression monitoring. *Science, 286*(5439), 531–537. doi:10.1126/science.286.5439.531 PMID:10521349

Golze, U. (1976). Differences between 1- and 2-dimensional cell spaces. In Automata, Languages. Development. North-Holland Publishing Co.

Gordon, M. D. (1988). Probabilistic and genetic algorithms for document retrieval. *Communications of the ACM, 31*(10), 1208–1218. doi:10.1145/63039.63044

Govindarajan, M., & Chandrasekaran, R. M. (2011). Intrusion detection using neural based hybrid classification methods. *Computer Networks, 55*(8), 1662–1671. doi:10.1016/j.comnet.2010.12.008

Gowda Asha, K., Jayaram, M.A., & Manjunath, A.S. (2011). Feature Subset Selection using Cascaded GA & CFS: A Filter Approach in Supervised Learning. *International Journal of Computer Applications, 23*(2).

Guillen, D., Paternina, M. R. A., Zamora, A., Ramirez, J. M., & Idarraga, G. (2015). Detection and classification of faults in transmission lines using the maximum wavelet singular value and Euclidean norm. *IET Generation. Transmission & Distribution, 9*(15), 2294–2302. doi:10.1049/iet-gtd.2014.1064

Guo, X., Yang, P., Chen, L., Wang, X., & Li, L. (2006). Study of the control mechanism of robot-prosthesis based-on the EMG processed. In *Proceedings of 6th World Congress on Intelligent Control and Automation* (pp. 9490-9493), Dalian, China: IEEE.

Guo, X., Yu, H., Zhen, G., Liu, Y., Zhang, Y., & Zhang, Y. (2009). Artificial intelligent based human motion pattern recognition and prediction for the surface electromyographic signals. In *Proceedings of Information Technology and Computer Science, 2009. ITCS 2009*. IEEE. doi:10.1109/ITCS.2009.65

Gupta. (2011). *Search Engines and Web Crawler: Part I*. Dept. of Computer Science & Engg., I.I.T. Kharagpur.

H'el`ene. (2003). *An Introduction to Cellular Automata*. IRIF.

Compilation of References

Habeck, M., Rieping, W., & Nilges, M. (2005). Bayesian estimation of Karplus parameters and torsion angles from three-bond scalar couplings constants. *Journal of Magnetic Resonance (San Diego, Calif.), 177*(1), 160–165. doi:10.1016/j.jmr.2005.06.016 PMID:16085438

Hahn, U., & Mani, I. (2000). The challenges of automatic summarization. *IEEE Computer, 33*(11), 29–36. doi:10.1109/2.881692

Hall, M. A., & Smith, L. A. (1997). Feature subset selection: a correlation based filter approach. *University of Waikato Research-Computing and Mathematical Sciences Papers,* (pp. 855-858). Berlin: Springer.

Hall. (1999). *Correlation-based Feature Selection for Machine Learning.* University of Waikato.

Hall, F. L., Allen, B. L., & Gunter, M. A. (1986). Empirical Analysis of Freeway Flow-Density Relationships. *Transportation Research Part A, General, 20*(3), 197–210. doi:10.1016/0191-2607(86)90094-4

Hasancebi, O., Erdal, F., & Saka, M. P. (2009). An adaptive harmony search method for structural optimization. *Journal of Structural Engineering, 136*(4), 419–431. doi:10.1061/(ASCE)ST.1943-541X.0000128

Hashemi, S., Kiani, S., Noroozi, N., & Moghaddam, M. E. (2010). An Image Contrast enhancement method based on Genetic Algorithm. *Pattern Recognition Letters, 31*(13), 1816–1824. doi:10.1016/j.patrec.2009.12.006

Hassan, B. H. F., Doush, I. A., Maghayreh, E. I. A., Alkhateeb, F., & Hamdan, M. (2014). Hybridizing harmony search algorithm with different mutation operators for continuous problems. *Applied Mathematics and Computation, 232,* 1166–1182. doi:10.1016/j.amc.2013.12.139

Hassan, R., Cohanim, B., De Weck, O., & Venter, G. (2005, April). A comparison of particle swarm optimization and the genetic algorithm. In *Proceedings of the 1st AIAA multidisciplinary design optimization specialist conference* (pp. 1-13). doi:10.2514/6.2005-1897

He, Y. X., Liu, D. X., Ji, D. H., Yang, H., & Teng, C. (2006, August). Msbga: A multi-document summarization system based on genetic algorithm. In *Machine Learning and Cybernetics, 2006 International Conference on* (pp. 2659-2664). IEEE. doi:10.1109/ICMLC.2006.258921

Henzinger, M. R., Heydon, A., Mitzenmacher, M., & Najork, M. (1999), Measuring index quality using random walks on the web. *Proc. of the 8th Int. World Wide Web Conference (WWW8),* 213–225. doi:10.1016/S1389-1286(99)00016-X

Henzinger, M. R., Heydon, A., Mitzenmacher, M., & Najork, M. (2000), On near-uniform URL sampling. *Proc. of the 9th Int. World Wide Web Conference.*

He, Y., & Hui, S. C. (2009). Exploring ant-based algorithms for gene expression data analysis. *Artificial Intelligence in Medicine, 47*(2), 105–119. doi:10.1016/j.artmed.2009.03.004 PMID:19376690

He, Z., Lin, S., Deng, Y., Li, X., & Qian, Q. (2014). A rough membership neural network approach for fault classification in transmission lines. *International Journal of Electrical Power & Energy Systems, 61*, 429–439. doi:10.1016/j.ijepes.2014.03.027

Hofmeyr, S. A. (2001). An interpretative introduction to the immune system. *Design principles for the immune system and other distributed autonomous systems, 3*, 28-36.

Holland, J. H. (1973). Genetic algorithms and the optimal allocation of trials. *SIAM Journal on Computing, 2*(2), 88–105. doi:10.1137/0202009

Holland, J. H. (1975). *Adaptation in Natural and Artificial systems.* Ann Arbor, MI: The University of Michigan Press.

Holland, J. H. (1975). *Adaptation in natural and artificial systems.* Ann Arbor, MI: University of Michigan Press.

Holland, J. H. (1975). *Adaptation in natural and artificial systems: an introductory analysis with applications to biology, control, and artificial intelligence.* U Michigan Press.

Hongbin, W., Liyi, Z., & Huakui, W. (2010). The research of neural network prediction based on GEP. *Proceedings of second international workshop on educational technology and computer science.* doi:10.1109/ETCS.2010.16

Houstis, E., Gallopoulos, E., Bramley, J., & Rice, J. R. (1997). Problem-solving environments for computational science. *IEEE Computational Science & Engineering, 4*(3), 18–21. doi:10.1109/MCSE.1997.615427

Hovy, E., & Lin, C. Y. (1998, October). Automated text summarization and the SUMMARIST system. In *Proceedings of a workshop on held at Baltimore* (pp. 197-214). Association for Computational Linguistics. Automated Text Summarization And The Summarist System, TIPSTER III Final Report (SUMMAC).

Huang, H.-P., Liu, Y.-H., Liu, L.-W., & Wong, C.-S. (2003). EMG classification for prehensile postures using cascaded architecture of neural networks with self-organizing maps. *2006 6th World Congress on Intelligent Control and Automation.* Taipei, Taiwan: IEEE.

Huang, K. (1987). Statistical Mechanics (2nd ed.). New York: Wiley.

Huang, J.-H., He, R.-H., Yi, L.-Z., Xie, H.-L., Cao, D., & Liang, Y.-Z. (2013). Exploring the relationship between 5'AMP-activated protein kinase and markers related to type 2 diabetes mellitus. *Talanta, 110*, 1–7. doi:10.1016/j.talanta.2013.03.039 PMID:23618167

Hudgins, B., Parker, P., & Scott, R. N. (1993). A new strategy for multifunction myoelectric control. *IEEE Transactions on Bio-Medical Engineering, 40*(1), 82–94. doi:10.1109/10.204774 PMID:8468080

Hu, Y., Liu, K., Zhang, X., Su, L., Ngai, E. W. T., & Liu, M. (2015). Application of Evolutionary Computation for rule discovery in Stock Algorithmic trading: A Literature Review. *Applied Soft Computing, Elsevier, 36*, 534–551. doi:10.1016/j.asoc.2015.07.008

Compilation of References

Huynh, D. C., & Dunnigan, M. W. (2010). Parameter estimation of an induction machine using advanced particle swarm optimization algorithms. *IET Electric Power Applications*, *4*(9), 748–760. doi:10.1049/iet-epa.2009.0296

Hwang, S. F., & He, R. S. (2006). A hybrid real parameter genetic algorithm for function optimization. *Advanced Engineering Informatics*, *20*(1), 7–21. doi:10.1016/j.aei.2005.09.001

Irbäck, A., Peterson, C., Potthast, F., & Sommelius, O. (1997). Local interactions and protein folding: A three-dimensional off-lattice approach. *The Journal of Chemical Physics*, *107*(1), 273–282. doi:10.1063/1.474357

Irbäck, A., & Sandelin, E. (1998). Local interactions and protein folding: A model study on the square and triangular lattices. *The Journal of Chemical Physics*, *108*(5), 2245–2250. doi:10.1063/1.475605

Ito, K., Tsukamoto, M., & Kondo, T. (2008). Discrimination of intended movements based on nonstationary EMG for a prosthetic hand control. In *Proceedings of Communications, Control and Signal Processing, 2008. ISCCSP 2008*. St. Julians, Malta: IEEE.

Izakian, H., & Abraham, A. (2011). Fuzzy C-means and fuzzy Swarm for fuzzy clustering problem. *Expert Systems with Applications*, *38*(3), 1835–1838. doi:10.1016/j.eswa.2010.07.112

Jamehbozorg, A., & Shahrtash, S. M. (2010). A decision tree-based method for fault classification in double-circuit transmission lines. *IEEE Transactions on Power Delivery*, *25*(4), 2184–2189. doi:10.1109/TPWRD.2010.2050911

Janeiro, Santos, & Ramos. (2012). *Gene Expression Programming in Sensor Characterization: Numerical Results and Experimental Validation*. IEEE.

Jang, W. S., Kang, H. I., & Lee, B. H. (2008). Hybrid simplex-harmony search method for optimization problems. *IEEE Congress on Evolutionary Computation*, 4157-4164. doi:10.1109/CEC.2008.4631365

Jiang, J. A., Chen, C. S., Fan, P. L., Liu, C. W., & Chang, R. S. (2002). A composite index to adaptively perform fault detection, classification, and direction discrimination for transmission lines. In *Proceedings of Power Engineering Society Winter Meeting, IEEE* (Vol. 2, pp. 912-917). IEEE.

Jiang, D., Tang, C., & Zhang, A. (2004). Cluster Analysis for Gene Expression Data: A Survey. *IEEE Transactions on Data and Knowledge Engineering*, *16*(11), 1370–1386. doi:10.1109/TKDE.2004.68

Jiang, J. A., Chen, C. S., & Liu, C. W. (2003). A new protection scheme for fault detection, direction discrimination, classification, and location in transmission lines. *IEEE Transactions on Power Delivery*, *18*(1), 34–42. doi:10.1109/TPWRD.2002.803726

Ji, G., Yang, Z., & You, W. (2011). PLS-Based Gene Selection and Identification of Tumor-Specific Genes. *IEEE Transactions on Systems, Man and Cybernetics. Part C, Applications and Reviews*, *41*(6), 830–841. doi:10.1109/TSMCC.2010.2078503

Joaquim, F. (2011). A Weighted Principal Component Analysis and Its Application to Gene Expression Data. *IEEE/ACM Transactions on Computational Biology and Bioinformatics*, 8(1), 246–252. doi:10.1109/TCBB.2009.61 PMID:21071812

Jones, B. F., Sthamer, H., & Eyres, D. E. (1996). Automatic structural testing using genetic algorithms. *Software Engineering Journal*, 11(September), 299–306. doi:10.1049/sej.1996.0040

Jung, K. K., Kim, J. W., Lee, H. K., Chung, S. B., & Eom, K. H. (2007). EMG pattern classification using spectral estimation and neural network. In *Proceedings SICE,2007 Annual Conference*. Takamatsu, Japan: IEEE.

Jung, C. K., Kim, K. H., Lee, J. B., & Klöckl, B. (2007). Wavelet and neuro-fuzzy based fault location for combined transmission systems. *International Journal of Electrical Power & Energy Systems*, 29(6), 445–454. doi:10.1016/j.ijepes.2006.11.003

Kahle, B. (1997). Archiving the internet. *Scientific American*.

Kai, N., & Michael, S. (1992). A Cellular Automaton Model for Freeway Traffic. *Journal de Physique. I*, 2(12), 2221–2229. doi:10.1051/jp1:1992277

Kaneko, K. (Ed.). (1993). *Theory and Applications of Coupled Map Lattices*. Wiley.

Kanj, F., Mansour, N., Khachfe, H., & Abu-Khzam, F. (2009, May). Protein structure prediction in the 3D HP model. In *2009 IEEE/ACS International Conference on Computer Systems and Applications* (pp. 732-736). IEEE. doi:10.1109/AICCSA.2009.5069408

Kao, Y. T., & Zahara, E. (2008). A hybrid genetic algorithm and PSO for multimodal functions. Applied Soft Computing, 8, 849-857.

Karaboga, D. (2005). *An idea based on honey bee swarm for numerical optimization*. Technical Report-TR06. Available at http://mf.erciyes.edu.tr/abc/pub/tr06_2005.pdf

Karaboga, D., & Akay, B. (2009). A comparative study of artificial bee colony algorithm. *Applied Mathematics and Computation*, 214(1), 108–132. doi:10.1016/j.amc.2009.03.090

Karaboga, D., Ozturk, C., Karaboga, N., & Gorkemli, B. (2012). Artificial bee colony programming for symbolic regression. *Information Sciences*, 209, 1–15. doi:10.1016/j.ins.2012.05.002

Karwa, S., & Chatterjee, N. (2014, December). Discrete Differential Evolution for Text Summarization. In *Information Technology (ICIT), 2014 International Conference on* (pp. 129-133). IEEE. doi:10.1109/ICIT.2014.28

Kattan, A., Abdullah, R., & Salam, R. A. (2010). Harmony search based supervised training of artificial neural network.*International Conference on Intelligent Systems, Modeling and Simulation*, 105-110. doi:10.1109/ISMS.2010.31

Kaveh, A., & Talatahari, S. (2009). Particle swarm optimizer, ant colony strategy and harmony search scheme hybridized for optimization of truss structures. *Computers & Structures*, 87(5-6), 267–283. doi:10.1016/j.compstruc.2009.01.003

Compilation of References

Kelly, M. F., Parker, P. A., & Scott, R. N. (1990). The application of neural networks to myoelectric signal analysis: A preliminary study. *IEEE Transactions on Bio-Medical Engineering, 37*(3), 221–230. doi:10.1109/10.52324 PMID:2328997

Kennedy, J. (2011). Particle swarm optimization. In Encyclopedia of machine learning (pp. 760-766). Springer US.

Kennedy, J., & Eberhart, R. C. (1995). Particle swarm optimization.*Proceeding of IEEE International Conference on Neural Networks*, 1942-1948. doi:10.1109/ICNN.1995.488968

Kennedy, J., Eberhart, R. C., & Shi, Y. (2001). *Swarm Intelligence (book)*. San Francisco, CA: Morgan Kaufmann.

Kerr, G., Ruskin, H. J., Crane, M., & Doolan, P. (2008). Techniques for Clustering Gene Expression data. *Computers in Biology and Medicine, 36*(3), 283–293. doi:10.1016/j.compbiomed.2007.11.001 PMID:18061589

Khakzad, H., Karami, Y., & Arab, S. S. (2015). *Accelerating Protein Structure Prediction using Particle Swarm Optimization on GPU.* https://doi.org/10.1101/022434

Khalili, M., Kharrat, R., Salahshoor, K., & Haghighat-Sefat, M. (2014). Global dynamic harmony search algorithm: GDHS. *Applied Mathematics and Computation, 228*, 195–219. doi:10.1016/j.amc.2013.11.058

Khattab, Abdelaziz, Mekhamer, Badr, & EI-Saadany. (2012). *Gene Expression Programming for Security Assessment of Power Systems.* IEEE.

Khushaba, R. N., Al-Ani, A., & Al-Jumaily, A. (2007). Swarm intelligence based dimensionality reduction for myoelectric control. In *Proceedings of Intelligent Sensors, Sensor Networks and Information, 2007. ISSNIP 2007.* Melbourne, QLD, Australia: IEEE. doi:10.1109/ISSNIP.2007.4496907

Khushaba, R. N., & Al-Jumaily, A. (2007a). Channel and feature selection in multifunction myoelectric control. In *Proceedings of 2007 29th Annual International Conference of the IEEE Engineering in Medicine and Biology Society.* Lyon, France: IEEE. doi:10.1109/IEMBS.2007.4353509

Khushaba, R. N., Al-Jumaily, A., & Al-Ani, A. (2009). Evolutionary fuzzy discriminant analysis feature projection technique in myoelectric control. *Pattern Recognition Letters, 30*(7), 699–707. doi:10.1016/j.patrec.2009.02.004

Kim, D. H., Abraham, A., & Cho, J. H. (2007). A hybrid genetic algorithm and bacterial foraging approach for global optimization. *Information Sciences, 177*(18), 3918–3937. doi:10.1016/j.ins.2007.04.002

Kinghorn, B. P., & Shepherd, R. K. (1999).Mate selection for the tactical implementation of breeding programs.*AAABG Conference Proceedings*, 13, 130-133.

Kirkpatrick, S., Gelatt, C. D., & Vecchi, M. P. (1983). Optimization by simulated annealing. *Science, 220*(4598), 671–680. doi:10.1126/science.220.4598.671 PMID:17813860

Kleinberg, J. (1998), Authoritative sources in a hyperlinked environment.*9th ACM-SIAM Symposium on Discrete Algorithms.*

Kogilavani, A., & Balasubramanie, P. (2010, December). Clustering based optimal summary generation using genetic algorithm. In *Communication and Computational Intelligence (INCOCCI), 2010 International Conference on* (pp. 324-329). IEEE.

Kohonen, T. (1995). *Self-Organizing Maps.* Berlin: Springer. doi:10.1007/978-3-642-97610-0

Kondov, I., & Berlich, R. (2011, June). Protein structure prediction using particle swarm optimization and a distributed parallel approach. In *Proceedings of the 3rd workshop on Biologically inspired algorithms for distributed systems* (pp. 35-42). ACM. doi:10.1145/1998570.1998579

Korel, B. (1990). Automated software test data generation. *IEEE Transactions on Software Engineering, 16*(8), 870–879. doi:10.1109/32.57624

Koza, J. R. (1992). *Genetic Programming: On the Programming of Computers by Means of Natural Selection.* MIT Press.

Krauthammer, M., Rzhetsky, A., Morozov, P., & Friedman, C. (2000). Using BLAST for identifying gene and protein names in journal articles. *Gene, 259*(1-2), 245–252. doi:10.1016/S0378-1119(00)00431-5 PMID:11163982

K, S., Subba Reddy, V., & B.Rananavare, L. (2011, February28). PCA Analysis of Few Parameters Role in Software Development. *International Journal of Computers and Applications, 14*(6), 15–20. doi:10.5120/1889-2506

Kuhlbrandt, W. (2013). Introduction to electron crystallography. *Methods in Molecular Biology (Clifton, N.J.), 955*, 1–16. doi:10.1007/978-1-62703-176-9_1 PMID:23132052

Kumar, A. P., & Valsala, P. (2013). Feature Selection for high Dimensional DNA Microarray data using hybrid approaches. *Bioinformation, 9*(16), 824–828. doi:10.6026/97320630009824 PMID:24143053

Kumaravel, A., & Aarthi, A. (2013). Malware Classification based on Clustering and classification. *International Journal of Advanced Research in Computer Science and Software Engineering, 3*(5), 121–123.

Kumar, G., & Kumar, K. (2012). The Use of Artificial-Intelligence-Based Ensembles for Intrusion Detection: A Review. *Applied Computational Intelligence and Soft Computing, 2012*, 1–20. doi:10.1155/2012/850160

Kumar, P., Jamil, M., & Thomas, M. S. (1999, December). Fuzzy approach to fault classification for transmission line protection. In *Proceedings of the IEEE Region 10 Conference* (Vol. 2, pp. 1046-1050). IEEE. doi:10.1109/TENCON.1999.818602

Lau, K. F., & Dill, K. A. (1989). A lattice statistical mechanics model of the conformational and sequence spaces of proteins. *Macromolecules, 22*(10), 3986–3997. doi:10.1021/ma00200a030

Compilation of References

Layeb, A. (2013). A hybrid quantum inspired harmony search algorithm for 01 optimization problems. *Journal of Computational and Applied Mathematics*, *253*, 14–25. doi:10.1016/j.cam.2013.04.004

Lazar, C., Taminau, J., Meganck, S., Steenhoff, D., Coletta, A., Molter, C., & Nowe, A. et al. (2012). A Survey on Filter Techniques for Feature Selection in Gene Expression Microarray Analysis. *IEEE/ACM Transactions on Computational Biology and Bioinformatics*, *9*(4), 1106–1119. doi:10.1109/TCBB.2012.33 PMID:22350210

Lee, D., Redfern, O., & Orengo, C. (2007). Predicting protein function from sequence and structure. *Nature Reviews. Molecular Cell Biology*, *8*(12), 995–1005. doi:10.1038/nrm2281 PMID:18037900

Lee, K. S., Geem, Z. W., Lee, S. H., & Bae, K. W. (2005). The harmony search heuristic algorithm for discrete structure optimization. *Engineering Optimization*, *37*(7), 663–684. doi:10.1080/03052150500211895

Lee, K. Y., & El-Sharkawi, M. A. (Eds.). (2008). *Modern heuristic optimization techniques*. Hoboken, NJ: John Wiley & Sons. doi:10.1002/9780470225868

Lee, Y. C., & Zomaya, A. Y. (2009). Fusion of clonal selection algorithm and harmony search method in optimization of fuzzy classification systems.*IEEE International Symposium on Parallel and Distributed Processing*, 1-8.

Leon, F., Lisa, C., & Curteanu, S. (2010). Prediction of the Liquid-Crystalline Property Using Different Classification Methods. *International Journal of Molecular Crystals and Liquid Crystals*, *518*(1), 129–148. doi:10.1080/15421400903574391

Leung, Y. (2010). A Multiple-Filter-Multiple-Wrapper Approach to Gene Selection and Microarray Data Classification. *IEEE/ACM Transactions on Computational Biology and Bioinformatics*, *7*(1), 108–117. doi:10.1109/TCBB.2008.46 PMID:20150673

Levitt, M. (1983). Protein folding by restrained energy minimization and molecular dynamics. *Journal of Molecular Biology*, *170*(3), 723–764. doi:10.1016/S0022-2836(83)80129-6 PMID:6195346

Li, Q., Wang, W., Han, S., & Li, J. (2007). Evolving classifier ensemble with gene expression programming. *Proceedings of third International Conference on Natural Computation*. doi:10.1109/ICNC.2007.362

Li, K., Liang, J., Jheng, W., & Wang, F. (2008). *A new method of evolving digital circuit based on Gene Expression Programming*. IEEE.

Li, M. (2003). Improving Reliability of Gene Selection From Microarray Functional Genomics Data. *IEEE Transactions on Information Technology in Biomedicine*, *7*(3), 191–196. doi:10.1109/TITB.2003.816558 PMID:14518732

Li, M. J., Ng, M. K., Cheung, Y. M., & Huang, J. Z. (2008). Agglomerative fuzzy k-means clustering algorithm with selection of number of clusters. *IEEE Transactions on Knowledge and Data Engineering*, *20*(11), 1519–1534. doi:10.1109/TKDE.2008.88

Lin, C. Y., & Hovy, E. (1997). Identify Topic by Position. In *Proc. 5th Conference on Applied Natural Language Processing*(pp.283-290). doi:10.3115/974557.974599

Lin, J. C., & Yeh, P. L. (2000). Using Genetic Algorithms for Test Case Generation in Path Testing.*Proceedings of the 9th Asian Test Symposium (ATS'00)*.

Lin, X., & Zhang, X. (2014). Protein structure prediction with local adjust tabu search algorithm. *BMC Bioinformatics*, *15*(15). doi:10.1186/1471-2105-15-S15-S1 PMID:25474708

Lin, Y.-S., & Liang, X.-T. (2010). Gene expression programming with parallel hybrid model. *Proceedings of the Ninth International Conference on Machine Learning and Cybernetics.* doi:10.1109/ICMLC.2010.5580717

Li, Q., Chen, C., Wang, W., Ren, C., & Xia, S. (2012). An adaptive multi-phenotype GEP algorithm. *Proceedings of 8th International Conference on Natural Computation (ICNC 2012)*.

Li, Q., Mitianoudis, N., & Stathaki, T. (2007). Spatial kernel k-harmonic means clustering for multispectral image segmentation. *Image Process IET*, *1*(2), 156–167. doi:10.1049/iet-ipr:20050320

Liu, Yu, & Meng. (2002). Personalized web search by mapping user queries to categories. *CIKM'02*.

Liu, Q., & Xu, J. (2012). Traffic Signal Timing Optimization based on Differential Evolution Bacterial Foraging Algorithm. *Procedia: Social and Behavioral Sciences*, *43*, 210–215. doi:10.1016/j.sbspro.2012.04.093

Liu, S. (2012). Combined Rule Extraction and Feature Elimination in Supervised Classification. *IEEE Transactions on Nanobioscience*, *11*(3), 228–236. doi:10.1109/TNB.2012.2213264 PMID:22987128

Li, X. L., Shao, Z. J., & Qian, J. X. (2002). Optimization method based on autonomous animates: Fish-swarm algorithm. *System Engineering Theory and Practice*, *22*(11), 32–38.

López-Pujalte, C., Guerrero-Bote, V. P., & de Moya-Anegón, F. (2003). Order-based fitness functions for genetic algorithms applied to relevance feedback. *Journal of the American Society for Information Science and Technology*, *54*(2), 152–160. doi:10.1002/asi.10179

Lu, Y., Lu, S., Fotouhi, F., Deng, Y., & Brown, S. (2004). Fast genetic K-means algorithm and its application in gene expression data analysis. *Proceedings of the ACM Symposium on Applied Computing (SAC)*.

Lumer, E., & Faieta, B. (1994) Diversity and adaptation in populations of clustering ants. *Proceedings of the 3rd International Conference on Simulation of Adaptive Behaviour: From Animals to Animats*, *3*, 501–508.

Ma, N., Kumar, D. K., & Pah, N. (2001). Classification of hand direction using multi-channel electromyography by neural network. In *Proceedings ofIntelligent Information Systems Conference, The Seventh Australian and New Zealand 2001*. Perth, Western Australia: IEEE.

Compilation of References

Mahamedi, B. (2011, November). A novel setting-free method for fault classification and faulty phase selection by using a pilot scheme. In *Proceedings of 2nd International Conference on Electric Power and Energy Conversion Systems (EPECS)* (pp. 1-6). IEEE. doi:10.1109/EPECS.2011.6126835

Mahanty, R. N., & Gupta, P. D. (2007). A fuzzy logic based fault classification approach using current samples only. *Electric Power Systems Research*, *77*(5), 501–507. doi:10.1016/j.epsr.2006.04.009

Mahdavi, M., Chehreghani, M. H., Abolhassani, H., & Forsati, R. (2008). Novel meta-heuristic algorithms for clustering web documents. *Applied Mathematics and Computation*, *201*(1-2), 441–451. doi:10.1016/j.amc.2007.12.058

Mahdavi, M., Fesanghary, M., & Damangir, E. (2007). An improved harmony search algorithm for solving optimization problems. *Applied Mathematics and Computation*, *188*(2), 1567–1579. doi:10.1016/j.amc.2006.11.033

Maheri, M. R., & Narimani, M. M. (2014). An enhanced harmony search algorithm for optimum design of side sway steel frames. *Computers & Structures*, *136*(4), 78–89. doi:10.1016/j.compstruc.2014.02.001

Mahmood, Z. N., Mahmuddin, M., & Mahmood, M. N. (2012). Protein tertiary structure prediction based on main chain angle using a hybrid bees colony optimization algorithm. International Journal of Modern Physics, 9, 143-156. doi:10.1142/S201019451200520X

Maji, P. (2012). Mutual Information-Based Supervised Attribute Clustering for Microarray Sample Classification. *IEEE Transactions on Knowledge and Data Engineering*, *24*(1), 127–140. doi:10.1109/TKDE.2010.210

Malaki, M., Pourbagheri, J. A., & Abolhassani, H. (2008). *A combinatory approach to fuzzy clustering with harmony search and its applications to space shuttle data*. SCIS & ISIS.

Malathi, V., & Marimuthu, N. S. (2008, November). Multi-class support vector machine approach for fault classification in power transmission line. In *Proceedings of IEEE International Conference on Sustainable Energy Technologies* (pp. 67-71). IEEE. doi:10.1109/ICSET.2008.4746974

Malhotra. (2013). *Web Crawler And It's Concepts*. Academic Press.

Mallipeddi, R., Suganthan, P. N., Pan, Q. K., & Tasgetiren, M. F. (2011). Differential evolution algorithm with ensemble of parameters and mutation strategies. *Applied Soft Computing*, *11*(2), 1679–1696. doi:10.1016/j.asoc.2010.04.024

Mani, I., & Maybury, M. T. (Eds.). (1999). *Advances in automatic text summarization* (Vol. 293). Cambridge, MA: MIT press.

Manne, & Fatima. (2011). A Novel Approach for Text Categorization of Unorganized data based with Information Extraction. *International Journal on Computer Science and Engineering*, *3*(7), 2846–2854.

Manning, C. D., Raghavan, P., & Schtze, H. (2009). *An Introduction to Information Retrieval.* Cambridge University Press.

Mansour, N., Kanj, F., & Khachfe, H. (2012). Particle swarm optimization approach for protein structure prediction in the 3D HP model. *Interdisciplinary Sciences: Computational Life Sciences, 4*(3), 190–200. PMID:23292692

Marc Lane, S. (1971). *Categories for the working Mathematician* (2nd ed.). Springer Publication. doi:10.1007/978-1-4612-9839-7

Marion, D. (2013). An introduction to biological NMR spectroscopy. *Molecular & Cellular Proteomics: MCP, 12*(11), 3006–3025. doi:10.1074/mcp.O113.030239 PMID:23831612

Markou, M., & Singh, S. (2003). Novelty detection: a review-part 2: neural network based approaches. *Journal of Signal Processing, 83*(12), 2499–2521. doi:10.1016/j.sigpro.2003.07.019

Markov & Larose. (2007). *Data mining the web.* Wiley Interscience.

Marks, D. S., Colwell, L. J., Sheridan, R., Hopf, T. A., Pagnani, A., Zecchina, R., & Sander, C. (2011). Protein 3D structure computed from evolutionary sequence variation. *PLoS ONE, 6*(12), e28766. doi:10.1371/journal.pone.0028766 PMID:22163331

Marqusee, S., & Baldwin, R. L. (1987). Helix stabilization by Glu-... Lys+ salt bridges in short peptides of de novo design. *Proceedings of the National Academy of Sciences of the United States of America, 84*(24), 8898–8902. doi:10.1073/pnas.84.24.8898 PMID:3122208

Martinez-Glez, V., Franco-Hernandez, C., & Rey, J. A. (2008). Microarray gene expression profiling in meningiomas and schwannomas. *Current Medicinal Chemistry, 15*(8), 826–833. doi:10.2174/092986708783955527 PMID:18393851

Martin-Valdivia, M. T., Diaz-Galiano, M. C., Montejo-Raez, A., & Urena-Lopez, L. A. (2008). Using information gain to improve multi-modal information retrieval systems. *Information Processing & Management, 44*(3), 1146–1158. doi:10.1016/j.ipm.2007.09.014

Massinaei, M., Sedaghati, M. R., Rezvani, R., & Mohammadzadeh, A. A. (2014). Using Data Mining to Assess and Model the Metallurgical Efficiency of a Copper Concentrator. *International Journal of Chemical Engineering Communications, 201*(10), 1314–1326. doi:10.1080/00986445.2013.808997

Mathur, P., & Aditya, P. (2008). *Foundation of Software Testing* (1st ed.). Pearson Education.

Matsumura, Y., Mitsukura, Y., Fukumi, M., & Akamatsu, N. (2002). Recognition of EMG signal patterns by neural networks. In *Proceedings of Neural Information Processing, 2002. ICONIP '02.* Singapore, Singapore: IEEE. doi:10.1109/ICONIP.2002.1198158

Maulik, U., Mukhopadhyay, A., & Bandyopadhyay, S. (2009). Combining pareto-optimal clusters using supervised learning for identifying coexpressed genes. *BMC Bioinformatics, 10*(27). PMID:19154590

Compilation of References

McPherson, A. (2004). Introduction to protein crystallization. *Methods (San Diego, Calif.), 34*(3), 254–265. doi:10.1016/j.ymeth.2004.03.019 PMID:15325645

McQueen, J. (1967) Some methods for classification and analysis of multivariate observations. *Proceedings of the Fifth Berkeley Symp. Math. Statistics and Probability, 1*, 281–297.

Medigue, C., Viari, A., Henaut, A., & Danchin, A. (1992). Colibri: A Functional Database for the Escherichia coli Genome. *Microbiology and Molecular Biology Reviews, 57*(3), 623–654.

Megahed, A. I., Moussa, A. M., & Bayoumy, A. E. (2006). Usage of wavelet transform in the protection of series-compensated transmission lines. *IEEE Transactions on Power Delivery, 21*(3), 1213–1221. doi:10.1109/TPWRD.2006.876981

Mendoza, M., Bonilla, S., Noguera, C., Cobos, C., & León, E. (2014). Extractive single-document summarization based on genetic operators and guided local search. *Expert Systems with Applications, 41*(9), 4158–4169. doi:10.1016/j.eswa.2013.12.042

Michalewicz, T., & Fogel, D. B. (2000). *How to solve it: modern heuristics.* Heidelberg, Germany: Springer-Verlag. doi:10.1007/978-3-662-04131-4

Michalewicz, Z. (1994). *Genetic Algorithms+ Data structures=Evolution program* (2nd ed.). Berlin: Springer-Verlag. doi:10.1007/978-3-662-07418-3

Mitra, A., Paul, S., Panda, S., & Padhi, P. (2016). A Study on the representation of the various models for Dynamic Social Networks. *Procedia Computer Science, 79*, 624–631. doi:10.1016/j. procs.2016.03.079

Mitra, S., Banka, H., & Pedrycz, W. (2006). Rough Fuzzy Colloborative Clustering. *IEEE Transactions on Systems, Man, and Cybernetics, 36*(4), 795–805. doi:10.1109/TSMCB.2005.863371 PMID:16903365

Moeinzadeh, H., Asgarian, E., Zanjani, M., Rezaee, A., & Seidi, M. (2009). Combination of harmony search and linear discriminate analysis to improve classification. *Third Asia International Conference on Modeling & Simulation*, 131-135. doi:10.1109/AMS.2009.125

Moghassem & Fallahpour. (2011). *Processing parameters optimization of draw frame for rotor spun yarn strength using gene expression programming (GEP) Fibers and Polymers.* DOI 10.1007/s12221-011-0970

Moravej, Z., Pazoki, M., & Khederzadeh, M. (2015). New pattern-recognition method for fault analysis in transmission line with UPFC. *IEEE Transactions on Power Delivery, 30*(3), 1231–1242. doi:10.1109/TPWRD.2014.2365674

Morita, K., & Imai, K. (1996). Self-reproduction in a reversible cellular space. *Theoretical Computer Science, 168*(2), 337–366. doi:10.1016/S0304-3975(96)00083-7

Mukhopadhyay, A., Roy, A., Das, S., & Abraham, A. (2008). Population-variant and explorative power of harmony search: An analysis. *Third International Conference on Digital Information Management.*

Mukras, R., Wiratunga, N., Lothian, R., Chakraborti, S., & Harper, D. (2007). Information gain feature selection for ordinal text classification using probability re-distribution. *Proceedings of IJCAI Textlink Workshop*, 1-10.

Muñoz, V., & Eaton, W. A. (1999). A simple model for calculating the kinetics of protein folding from three-dimensional structures. *Proceedings of the National Academy of Sciences of the United States of America, 96*(20), 11311–11316. doi:10.1073/pnas.96.20.11311 PMID:10500173

Nadi, F., Khader, A. T., & Al-Betar, M. A. (2010). Adaptive genetic algorithm using harmony search. *12th Annual Conference on Genetic and Evolutionary Computation*, 819-820.

Nagel, K. (1996). Particle hopping models and traffic ow theory. *Physical Review E: Statistical Physics, Plasmas, Fluids, and Related Interdisciplinary Topics, 53*(5), 4655–4672. doi:10.1103/PhysRevE.53.4655 PMID:9964794

Nandhini, K., & Balasundaram, S. R. (2014). Extracting easy to understand summary using differential evolution algorithm. *Swarm and Evolutionary Computation, 16*, 19–27. doi:10.1016/j.swevo.2013.12.004

Nashat, M., & Miran, S. (2004). Data Generation for Path Testing. *Software Quality Journal, 12*(2), 121–136. doi:10.1023/B:SQJO.0000024059.72478.4e

Neshat, M., Yazdi, S. F., Yazdani, D., & Sargolzaei, M. (2012). A New Cooperative Algorithm Based on PSO and K-Means for Data Clustering. *J. of Computer Science, 8*(2), 188–194. doi:10.3844/jcssp.2012.188.194

Nishant, T., & Sathish Kumar, D., & Vvl, P. K. A. (2011). Computational Methods for Protein Structure Prediction and Its Application in Drug Design. *J Proteomics Bioinform, 1*. doi:10.4172/jpb.R1-002

Niu, B., Fan, Y., Xiao, H., & Xue, B. (2012). Bacteria foraging based approach to Portfolio Optimization with liquidity risk. *Neuro Computing, 98*, 90–100.

Niu, B., Wang, H., Wang, J., & Tan, L. (2013). Multiobjective Bacterial foraging Optimization. *Neuro Computing, 116*, 336–345.

Nizar Banu, P. K., & Andrews, S. (2014). Harmony Search PSO Clustering for Tumor and Cancer Gene Expression Dataset. *International Journal of Swarm Intelligence Research, 5*(3), 1–22. doi:10.4018/ijsir.2014070101

Nizar Banu, P. K., & Andrews, S. (2015a). Gene Clustering Using Metaheuristic Optimization Algorithms. *International Journal of Applied Metaheuristic Computing, 6*(4), 14–38. doi:10.4018/IJAMC.2015100102

Nizar Banu, P. K., & Andrews, S. (2015b). Evaluation of Fitness Functions for Swarm Clustering Applied to Gene Expression Data. Smart. *Innovation Systems and Technologies., 33*, 571–581. doi:10.1007/978-81-322-2202-6_52

Compilation of References

Oas, T. G., & Kim, P. S. (1988). A peptide model of a protein folding intermediate. *Nature, 336*(6194), 42–48. doi:10.1038/336042a0 PMID:3185721

Olston & Najork. (2010). Web Crawling, Foundations and Trend sRF. *Information Retrieval, 4*(3), 75–246. DOI: 10.1561/1500000017

Omkar, S. N., Nikhil Ramaswamy, J., Senthilnath, Bharath, S., & Anuradha, N.S. (2012). Gene Expression Programming- Fuzzy Logic method for crop type classification. IEEE.

Omran, M. G. H., Mahdavi, M., & Damangir, E. (2008). Global best harmony search. *Applied Mathematics and Computation, 198*(2), 643–656. doi:10.1016/j.amc.2007.09.004

Ozturk, C., Hancer, E., & Karaboga, D. (2015). A novel binary artificial bee colony algorithm based on genetic operators. *Information Sciences, 297*, 154–170. doi:10.1016/j.ins.2014.10.060

Packard, N., & Wolfram, S. (1985). Two-dimensional cellular automata. *Journal of Statistical Physics, 30*(5-6), 901–942. doi:10.1007/BF01010423

Pal, N. R., & Bezdek, J. C. (1995). On cluster validity for the fuzzy c-means model. *IEEE Transactions on Fuzzy Systems, 3*(3), 370–379. doi:10.1109/91.413225

Pang, W., Wang, K., Zhou, C., & Dong, L. (2004) Fuzzy Discrete Particle Swarm Optimization for Solving Traveling Salesman Problem. *Proceedings of the Fourth International Conference on Computer and Information Technology*, 796–800. doi:10.1109/CIT.2004.1357292

Panigrahi, B. K., & Pandi, V. R. (2009). Congestion Management using Adaptive foraging algorithm. *Energy Conversion & Management, 50*(5), 1202–1209. doi:10.1016/j.enconman.2009.01.029

Pan, Q. K., Suganthan, P. N., Liang, J. J., & Tasgetiren, M. F. (2010b). A local-best harmony search algorithm with dynamic sub-populations. *Engineering Optimization, 42*(2), 101–117. doi:10.1080/03052150903104366

Pan, Q. K., Suganthan, P. N., Tasgetiren, M. F., & Liang, J. J. (2010a). A self-adaptive global best harmony search algorithm for continuous optimization problems. *Applied Mathematics and Computation, 216*(3), 830–848. doi:10.1016/j.amc.2010.01.088

Pan, S., Morris, T., & Adhikari, U. (2015). Classification of disturbances and cyber-attacks in power systems using heterogeneous time-synchronized data. *IEEE Transactions on Industrial Informatics, 11*(3), 650–662. doi:10.1109/TII.2015.2420951

Passino, K. M. (2002). Biomimicry of bacterial foraging for distributed optimization and control. *IEEE Control Systems, 22*(3), 52–67. doi:10.1109/MCS.2002.1004010

Pathak, B. J., Pathak, K. J., Shaw, A. K., & Majumder, S. (2014). GEP based Classification of Biological Data. *Proceedings of National Conference on Emerging Global Trends in Engineering & Technology (EGTET)*.

Pattanaik, S. S., Bakward, K. M., Devi, S., Panigrahi, B. K., & Das, S. (2010). Parallel Bacterial Foraging optimization. *Handbook of swarm intelligence Adaptation, Learning and optimization, 8,* 487-502.

Pattekari, & Parveen. (2012). Prediction system for heart disease using Naïve Bayes. *International Journal of Advanced Computer and Mathematical Sciences, 3*(3), 290–294.

Pauling, L., & Corey, R. B. (1951). Configurations of polypeptide chains with favored orientations around single bonds two new pleated sheets. *Proceedings of the National Academy of Sciences of the United States of America, 37*(11), 729–740. doi:10.1073/pnas.37.11.729 PMID:16578412

Pérez, F. E., Orduna, E., & Guidi, G. (2011). Adaptive wavelets applied to fault classification on transmission lines. *IET generation, transmission & distribution, 5*(7), 694-702.

Perez-Diez, Morgun, & Shulzhenko. (2007). Microarrays for Cancer Diagnosis and Classification. *Advances in Experimental Medicine and Biology,* 74–85.

Petrovic, G., & Cojbasic, Z. (2011) Comparison of Clustering Methods for Failure Data Analysis: A Real Life Application.*Proceedings of International Scientific Conference on Industrial Systems,*14-16.

Prasad, A., & Edward, J. B. (2016). Application of wavelet technique for fault classification in transmission systems. *Procedia Computer Science, 92,* 78–83. doi:10.1016/j.procs.2016.07.326

Prasad, A., Edward, J. B., Roy, C. S., Divyansh, G., & Kumar, A. (2015). Classification of faults in power transmission lines using fuzzy-logic technique. *Indian Journal of Science and Technology, 8*(30), 1–6. doi:10.17485/ijst/2015/v8i1/77065

Prasad, C. D., & Prasad, D. J. V. (2014, January). Fault detection and phase selection using Euclidean distance based function for transmission line protection. In *Proceedings of International Conference on Advances in Electrical Engineering* (pp. 1-4). IEEE. doi:10.1109/ICAEE.2014.6838516

Preston, K.J., Du, M.J.B., Levialdi, S., Norgen, P., & Toriwaki, J. (1979). Basics of Cellular Logic with Some Applications in Medical Image Processing. *Proc. IEEE,* (67), 826-857.

Price, K. V. S., & Rainer, M. (1997). Differential evolution - A simple evolution strategy for fast optimization. Dr. Dobb's Journal, 22, 18-24.

Price, V. K., Storn, M. R., & Lampinen, A. J. (2005). Differential evolution: A practical approach to global optimization. Springer-Verlag.

Qinghua, L., Shida, Y., & Youlin, R. (2006). A hybrid algorithm for optimizing multi-modal functions. *Wuhan University Journal of Natural Sciences, 11*(3), 551–554. doi:10.1007/BF02836663

Qu, B. Y., Liang, J. J., Wang, Z. Y., Chen, Q., & Suganthan, P. N. (2016). Novel Benchmark functions for Continuous Multimodal Optimization with Comparative results. *Swarm and Evolutionary Computation, Elsevier, 26,* 23–34. doi:10.1016/j.swevo.2015.07.003

Compilation of References

Raghavan, S., & Garcia-Molina, H. (2001). Crawling the hidden web.*Proceedings of the 27th International Conference on Very Large Data Bases (VLDB'01)*, 129-138.

Rahideh, A., Gitizadeh, M., & Mohammadi, S. (2013). A fault location technique for transmission lines using phasor measurements. *International Journal of Engineering and Advanced Technology*, *3*(1), 241–248.

Rana, S., Jasola, S., & Kumar, R. (2010). A hybrid sequential approach for data clustering using K-Means and particle swarm optimization algorithm. *International Journal of Engineering Science and Technology*, *2*(6), 67–176.

Rashedi, E., Nezamabadi-pour, H., & Saryazdi, S. (2009). GSA: A Gravitational Search Algorithm. *Information Sciences*, *179*(13), 2232–2248. doi:10.1016/j.ins.2009.03.004

Rautray, R., & Balabantaray, R. C. (2015). Comparative Study of DE and PSO over Document Summarization. In *Intelligent Computing, Communication and Devices* (pp. 371–377). Springer India. doi:10.1007/978-81-322-2012-1_38

Rautray, R., Balabantaray, R. C., & Bhardwaj, A. (2015). Document Summarization Using Sentence Features. *International Journal of Information Retrieval Research*, *5*(1), 36–47. doi:10.4018/IJIRR.2015010103

Ray, P., Panigrahi, B. K., & Senroy, N. (2012, December). Extreme learning machine based fault classification in a series compensated transmission line. In *Proceedings ofIEEE International Conference on Power Electronics, Drives and Energy Systems* (pp. 1-6). IEEE. doi:10.1109/PEDES.2012.6484297

Ray, P. K., & Subudhi, B. (2012). BFO optimized RLS algorithm for Power system harmonics Estimation. *Applied Soft Computing*, *12*(8), 1965–1977. doi:10.1016/j.asoc.2012.03.008

Razi, K., Hagh, M. T., & Ahrabian, G. (2007, December). High accurate fault classification of power transmission lines using fuzzy logic. In *Proceedings of International Power Engineering Conference* (pp. 42-46). IEEE.

Reddy, J. M., & Kumar, N. D. (2012). Computational algorithms inspired by biological processes and evolution. *Current Science (Bangalore)*, *103*(4), 370–380.

Reddy, M. J., & Mohanta, D. K. (2007). A wavelet-fuzzy combined approach for classification and location of transmission line faults. *International Journal of Electrical Power & Energy Systems*, *29*(9), 669–678. doi:10.1016/j.ijepes.2007.05.001

Rennie, J., & McCallum, A. (1999), Using reinforcement learning to spider the web efficiently. *Proc. of the Int. Conf. on Machine Learning (ICML)*.

Rodin, V., Benzinou, A., Guillaud, A., Ballet, P., Harrouet, F., Tisseau, J., & Le Bihan, J. (2004). An immune oriented multi-agent system for biological image processing. *Pattern Recognition*, *37*(4), 631–645. doi:10.1016/j.patcog.2003.09.014

Ruiz, H. S., Zhang, X., & Coombs, T. A. (2015). Resistive-type superconducting fault current limiters: Concepts, materials, and numerical modeling. *IEEE Transactions on Applied Superconductivity, 25*(3), 1–5. doi:10.1109/TASC.2014.2387115

Russo, M. (2016). A Distributed Neuro-genetic Programming Tool. *Swarm and Evolutionary Computation, 27,* 145–155. doi:10.1016/j.swevo.2015.10.009

Safari, A., & Shayeghi, H. (2011). Iteration PSO procedure for economic load dispatch with generator constraints. Expert Systems with Applications, 38, 6043-6048.

Saha, M. M., Rosolowski, E., Izykowski, J., Pierz, P., Balcerek, P., & Fulczyk, M. (2010a, March). An efficient method for faulty phase selection in transmission lines. In *Proceedings of 10th IET International Conference on Developments in Power System Protection. Managing the Change,* (pp. 1-5). IET. doi:10.1049/cp.2010.0320

Saha, M. M., Rosolowski, E., Izykowski, J., Pierz, P., Balcerek, P., & Fulczyk, M. (2010b). A novel fault classification technique for high speed protective relaying of transmission lines. In *Proceedings of the Modern Electric Power Systems (MEPS),International Symposium* (pp. 1-6). IEEE.

Saka, M. P., & Hasancebi, O. (2009). Adaptive harmony search algorithm for design code optimization of steel structure. *Harmony Search Algorithms for Structural Design Optimization, 239,* 79–120. doi:10.1007/978-3-642-03450-3_3

Samantaray, S. R. (2009). Decision tree-based fault zone identification and fault classification in flexible AC transmissions-based transmission line. *IET generation, transmission & distribution, 3*(5), 425-436.

Samantaray, S. R. (2013). A systematic fuzzy rule based approach for fault classification in transmission lines. *Applied Soft Computing, 13*(2), 928–938. doi:10.1016/j.asoc.2012.09.010

Santos-Coelho, L. D., & De-Andrade-Bernert, D. L. (2009). An improve harmony search algorithm for synchronization of discrete-time chaotic systems. *Chaos, Solitons, and Fractals, 41*(5), 2526–2532. doi:10.1016/j.chaos.2008.09.028

Sanyog Choudhary, N., Yadav, H., & Jain, A. (2015). Enhanced Techniques for Filtering of Wall Messages over Online Social Networks (OSN) User Profiles. *International Journal of Wireless and Microwave Technologies, 5*(4), 47–61. doi:10.5815/ijwmt.2015.04.05

Sarmah, , & Bhattacharyya. (2010). An Effective Technique for Clustering Incremental Gene Expression data. *International Journal of Computer Science Issues, 7*(3), 31–41.

Schiff, J. L. (2008). *Cellular Automata.* Wiley.

Schoonderwoerd, R., Holland, O., Bruten, J., & Rothkrantz, L. (1996). Ant-based load balancing in telecommunications networks. *Adaptive Behavior, 5*(2), 169–207. doi:10.1177/105971239700500203

Compilation of References

Sebelius, F., Eriksson, L., Holmberg, H., Levinsson, A., Lundborg, G., Danielsen, N., & Montelius, L. et al. (2005). Classification of motor commands using a modified self-organising feature map. *Journal of Medical Engineering and Physics, 27*(5), 403–413. doi:10.1016/j.medengphy.2004.09.008 PMID:15863349

Seyedtabaii, S. (2012). Improvement in the performance of neural network-based power transmission line fault classifiers. *IET generation, transmission & distribution, 6*(8), 731-737.

Shahrtash, S. M., & Jamehbozorg, A. (2008, April). A decision tree based method for fault classification in transmission lines. In *Proceedings of IEEE/PES Transmission and Distribution Conference and Exposition* (pp. 1-5). IEEE. doi:10.1109/TDC.2008.4517258

Shakhnarovish, G., Darrell, T., & Indyk, P. (2005). *Nearest-Neighbor Methods in Learning and Vision*. MIT Press.

Shapiro, G. P., & Tamayo, P. (2003). Microarray Data Mining: Facing the Challenges. *SIGKDD Explorations, 5*(2), 1–5. doi:10.1145/980972.980974

Shareghi, E., & Hassanabadi, L. S. (2008). Text summarization with harmony search algorithm-based sentence extraction. In *Proceedings of the 5th international conference on soft computing as transdisciplinary science and technology* (pp. 226–231). Cergy-Pontoise, France: ACM. doi:10.1145/1456223.1456272

Sharma, S. (2008). *Web-Crawling Approaches in Search Engines, Report*. Patiala: Thapar University.

Shen, H., Zhu, Y., Zhou, X., Guo, H., & Chang, C. (2009). Bacterial foraging optimization algorithm with particle swarm optimization strategy for global numerical optimization. *Proceedings of the ACM/SIGEVO Summit on Genetic and Evolutionary Computation*, 497-504.

Shilpi, Shweta, & Parul. (2011). A Reminiscent Study of Nature Inspired Computation. *International Journal of Advances in Engineering & Technology*, 117-125.

Shivaie, M., & Ameli, M.-T. (2016). Strategic multiyear transmission expansion planning under severe uncertainties by a combination of melody search algorithm and Powell heuristic method. *Energy, 115*, 338–352. doi:10.1016/j.energy.2016.08.100

Shivaie, M., Salemnia, A., & Ameli, M.-T. (2013a). Optimal multi-objective placement and sizing of passive and active power filters by a fuzzy-improved harmony search algorithm. *International Transaction on Electrical Energy System, 25*(3), 520–546. doi:10.1002/etep.1863

Shivaie, M., Salemnia, A., & Ameli, M.-T. (2014). A multi-objective approach to optimal placement and sizing of multiple active power filters using a music-inspired algorithm. *Applied Soft Computing, 22*, 189–204. doi:10.1016/j.asoc.2014.05.011

Shivaie, M., Salemnia, A., & Sheikh-El-Eslami, M. K. (2013b). Multi-objective transmission expansion planning based on reliability and market considering phase shifter transformers by fuzzy-genetic algorithm. *International Transaction on Electrical Energy System, 23*(8), 1468–1489. doi:10.1002/etep.1672

Shi, Y., & Eberhart, R. C. (1998) A modified particle swarm optimizer.*Proceedings of the IEEE International Conference on Evolutionary Computation*, 69–73.

Shmygelska, A., & Hoos, H. H. (2005). An ant colony optimisation algorithm for the 2D and 3D hydrophobic polar protein folding problem. *BMC Bioinformatics*, *6*(1), 1. doi:10.1186/1471-2105-6-30 PMID:15710037

Shuman, G. (2009). Using forearm electromyograms to classify hand gestures. Proceedings of Bioinformatics and Biomedicine, 2009, BIBM '09.

Silva, K. M., Souza, B. A., & Brito, N. S. D. (2006). Fault detection and classification in transmission lines based on wavelet transform and ANN. *IEEE Transactions on Power Delivery*, *21*(4), 2058–2063. doi:10.1109/TPWRD.2006.876659

Singh, T. K., & Das, K. N. (2016). Behavioural Study of Drosophila Fruit Fly and its Modelling for Soft Computing Application. In Problem Solving and Uncertainty Modelling through Optimization and Soft Computing Applications, (pp. 32-84). IGI Global. doi:10.4018/978-1-4666-9885-7.ch003

Singh, M., Panigrahi, B. K., & Maheshwari, R. P. (2011, March). Transmission line fault detection and classification. In *Proceedings of International Conference on Emerging Trends in Electrical and Computer Technology*(pp. 15-22). IEEE. doi:10.1109/ICETECT.2011.5760084

Sipper, M., & Tomassini, M. (1999). Computation in Artificially Evolved Non-Uniform Cellular Automata. *Theoretical Computer Science*, *217*(1), 81–98. doi:10.1016/S0304-3975(98)00151-0

Siwei, Zhihua, Dan, Yadong, & Qu. (2005). Gene expression programming based on simulated annealing. *Proceedings IEEE.*

Smith, A., Nanda, P., & Brown, E. E. (2009). Development of a myoelectric control scheme based on a time delayed neural network. In *Proceedings of2009 Annual International Conference of the IEEE Engineering in Medicine and Biology Society*. Minneapolis, MN: IEEE. doi:10.1109/IEMBS.2009.5332846

Sone, Y. (2002). *Kinetic theory and fluid dynamics. Birkhauser.* Springer. doi:10.1007/978-1-4612-0061-1

Song, Q. (2013). A Fast Clustering-Based Feature Subset Selection Algorithm for High-Dimensional Data. *IEEE Transactions on Knowledge and Data Engineering*, *25*(1), 1–14. doi:10.1109/TKDE.2011.181

Song, Y. H., Johns, A. T., Xuan, Q. Y., & Liu, J. Y. (1997, March). Genetic algorithm based neural networks applied to fault classification for EHV transmission lines with a UPFC. In *Proceedings of Sixth International Conference on Developments in Power System Protection* (pp. 278-281). IET. doi:10.1049/cp:19970081

Compilation of References

Spellman, P. T., Sherlock, G., Zhang, M. Q., Iyer, V. R., Anders, K., Eisen, M. B., & Futcher, B. et al. (1998). Comprehensive Identification of cell cycle-regulated genes of the Yeast Saccharomyces Cerevisiae by Microarray Hybridization. *Molecular Biology of the Cell, 9*(12), 3273–3297. doi:10.1091/mbc.9.12.3273 PMID:9843569

Spezzano, G., & Talis, D. (1999). Programming Cellular Automata Algorithms on Parallel Computers. *Future Generation Computer Systems, 16*(2-3), 203–216. doi:10.1016/S0167-739X(99)00047-3

Srinivas, M., & Patnaik, L. M. (1994). Genetic Algorithm: A Survey. *Computer, IEEE. Computers & Society, 27*(6), 17–26. doi:10.1109/2.294849

Srivastava. (2008). *Generation of test data using Meta heuristic approach. In IEEE TENCON* (pp. 1–6). IEEE.

Stephen, W. (1983). Statistical Mechanics of Cellular Automata. *Reviews of Modern Physics, 55*(3), 601–644. doi:10.1103/RevModPhys.55.601

Stillinger, F. H., & Head-Gordon, T. (1995). Collective aspects of protein folding illustrated by a toy model. *Physical Review E: Statistical Physics, Plasmas, Fluids, and Related Interdisciplinary Topics, 52*(3), 2872–2877. doi:10.1103/PhysRevE.52.2872 PMID:9963733

Stillinger, F. H., Head-Gordon, T., & Hirshfeld, C. L. (1993). Toy model for protein folding. *Physical Review E: Statistical Physics, Plasmas, Fluids, and Related Interdisciplinary Topics, 48*(2), 1469–1477. doi:10.1103/PhysRevE.48.1469 PMID:9960736

Storn, R., & Price, K. (1997). Differential evolution–a simple and efficient heuristic for global optimization over continuous spaces. *Journal of Global Optimization, 11*(4), 341–359. doi:10.1023/A:1008202821328

Sujatha, M., & Kumar, M. V. (2011). On-line monitoring and analysis of faults in transmission and distribution lines using GSM. *Journal of Theoretical and Applied Information Technology, 33*(2), 258–265.

Sutner, K. (1989). A note on the Culik-Yu classes. *Complex Systems, 3*(1), 107–115.

Sutner, K. (1990). Classifying circular cellular automata. *Physica D. Nonlinear Phenomena, 45*(1-3), 1–3, 386–395. doi:10.1016/0167-2789(90)90196-V

Taherinejad, N. (2009). Highly reliable harmony search algorithm.*European Conference on Circuit Theory and Design*, 818-822. doi:10.1109/ECCTD.2009.5275109

Tan, X., & Bhanu, B. (2006). Fingerprint Matching by genetic algorithms. *Pattern Recognition, Elsevier, 39*(3), 465–477. doi:10.1016/j.patcog.2005.09.005

Tarca, L., Romero, R., & Draghici, S. (2006). Analysis of microarray experiments of gene expression profiling. *American Journal of Obstetrics and Gynecology, 195*(2), 373–388. doi:10.1016/j.ajog.2006.07.001 PMID:16890548

Tenore, F. V. G., Ramos, A., Fahmy, A., Acharya, S., Etienne-cummings, R., & Thakor, N. T. (2009). Decoding of individuated finger movements using surface electromyography. *IEEE Transactions on Bio-Medical Engineering, 56*(5), 1427–1434. doi:10.1109/TBME.2008.2005485 PMID:19473933

Ting, C.-K. (2005). On the Mean Convergence Time of Multi-parent Genetic Algorithms Without Selection. Advances in Artificial Life, 403–412. doi:10.1007/11553090_41

Tjaden, & Cohen, J. (2006). A Survey of computational methods used in microarray data interpretation. *Applied Mycology and Biotechnology, Bioinformatics, 6*, 7-18.

Toffoli, T., & Margolus, N. (1987). *Cellular Automata machines: A new environment for modelling*. The MIT Press.

Tripathi, P., Sharma, A., Pillai, G. N., & Gupta, I. (2011). Accurate fault classification and section identification scheme in TCSC compensated transmission line using SVM. *World Academy of Science. Engineering and Technology, 60*, 1599–1605.

Tripathy, B. K., & Acharjya, D. P. (2014a). *Global Trends in Intelligent Computing Research and Development*. IGI Global Publishers. Retrieved from www.igi-global.com

Tripathy, B. K., & Acharjya, D. P. (2014b). *Advances in Secure Computing, Internet Services, and Applications*. IGI Global Publishers. Retrieved from www.igi-global.com

Tripathy, M., Mishra, S., Lai, L. L., & Zhang, Q. P. (2006).Transmission Loss Reduction based on FACTS and Bacterial Foraging Algorithm. *Proceedings of 9th International Conference on Parallel Problem Solving from Nature*, 222-231.

Tripathy, B. K., & Acharjya, D. P. (2010). Knowledge mining using ordering rules and rough sets on fuzzy approximation spaces. *International Journal of Advances in Science and Technology, 1*(3), 41–50.

Tripathy, B. K., & Acharjya, D. P. (2013). Approximation of classification and measures of uncertainty in rough set on two universal sets. *International Journal of Advanced Science and Technology, 40*, 77–90.

Tripathy, M., & Mishra, S. (2007). Bacterial Foraging Based solution to optimize Both Real Power Loss and Voltage Stability Limit. *IEEE Transactions on Power Systems, 22*(1), 240–248. doi:10.1109/TPWRS.2006.887968

Tsalides, P. (1990). Cellular Automata based Built-in Self Test Structures for VLSI Systems. *Electronics Letters, 26*(17), 1350–1352. doi:10.1049/el:19900869

Tsenov, G., Zeghbib, A. H., Palis, F., Shoylev, N., & Mladenov, V. (2006). Neural networks for online classification of hand and finger movements using surface EMG signals. In *Proceedings of 2006 8th Seminar on Neural Network Applications in Electrical Engineering*. Belgrade, Serbia: IEEE.

Compilation of References

Tsuji, T., Fukuda, O., Kaneko, M., & Koji, I. (2000). Pattern classification of time-series EMG signals using neural networks. *International Journal of Adaptive Control and Signal Processing, 14*(8), 829–848. doi:10.1002/1099-1115(200012)14:8<829::AID-ACS623>3.0.CO;2-L

Turgut, O. E., Turgut, M. S., & Coban, M. T. (2014). Design and economic investigation of shell and tube heat exchangers using improved intelligent tuned harmony search algorithm. *Ain Shams Engineering Journal, 5*(4), 1215–1231. doi:10.1016/j.asej.2014.05.007

Tzionas, P., Tsalides, P., & Thanailakis, A. (1992). Design and VLSI Implementation of a Pattern Classifier Using Pseudo-2D Cellular Automata. *IEEE Proceedings Part G, 139*(6), 661-668.

Udomsuk, S., Areerak, K.-L., Areerak, K.-N., & Srikaew, A. (2010). Parameters identification of separately excited dc motor using adaptive tabu search technique. In *Proceedings of Advances in Energy Engineering (ICAEE)*. IEEE. doi:10.1109/ICAEE.2010.5557618

Ullas, M. (2008). *Bio Inspired Computing*. Cochin, India: Seminar Report School of Engineering Cochin University of Science & Technology.

Upendar, J., Gupta, C. P., & Singh, G. K. (2008, December). Discrete wavelet transform and genetic algorithm based fault classification of transmission systems.*Proceedings ofNational Power Systems Conference*, 323-328.

Valsan, S. P., & Swarup, K. S. (2009). High-speed fault classification in power lines: Theory and FPGA-based implementation. *IEEE Transactions on Industrial Electronics, 56*(5), 1793–1800. doi:10.1109/TIE.2008.2011055

Varrette, Muszynski, & Bouvry. (2013). *Hash Function generation by means of Gene expression programming*. DOI:10.2478/v10065-012-0027-x

Vasilic, S., & Kezunovic, M. (2005). Fuzzy ART neural network algorithm for classifying the power system faults. *IEEE Transactions on Power Delivery, 20*(2), 1306–1314. doi:10.1109/TPWRD.2004.834676

Velur, R., Arun, B., & Satanik, P. (2008). Efficient Software Test Case Generation Using Genetic Algorithm Based Graph Theory. *First International Conference on Emerging Trends in Engineering and Technology, ICETET '08*, (pp. 298-303). IEEE.

Venkatesan, A., Gopal, J., Candavelou, M., Gollapalli, S., & Karthikeyan, K. (2013). Computational approach for protein structure prediction.*Healthcare Informatics Research, 19*(2), 137-147.

von Neumann. (1958). The General and Logical theory of Automata. In L.A. Jeffress (Ed.), *Cerebral Mechanisms in Behaviour – The Hixon Symposium*. John Wiley & Sons.

von Neumann, J. (1966). *Theory of Self-Reproducing Automata*. University of Illinois Press.

Wafaa, O., Badr, A., & Hegazy, A. E.-F. (2013). Hybrid Ant-Based Clustering Algorithm with Cluster Analysis Techniques. *Journal of Computer Science, 9*(6), 780–793. doi:10.3844/jcssp.2013.780.793

Waleed, J., Jun, H. D., Abbas, T., Hameed, S., & Hatem, H. (2014). A Survey of Digital Image Watermarking Optimization based on Nature Inspired Algorithms NIAs. *International Journal of Security and Its Applications*, *8*(6), 315–334. doi:10.14257/ijsia.2014.8.6.28

Walker, D. W., Li, M., Rana, O. F., Shields, M. S., & Huang, Y. (2000). The software architecture of a distributed problem solving environment. *Concurrency (Chichester, England)*, *12*(15), 1445–1480. doi:10.1002/1096-9128(20001225)12:15<1455::AID-CPE538>3.0.CO;2-#

Wang, Z., & Zhao, P. (2009, August). Fault location recognition in transmission lines based on support vector machines. In *Proceedings of 2nd IEEE International Conference on Computer Science and Information Technology* (pp. 401-404). IEEE.

Wang, C. M., & Huang, Y. F. (2010). Self-adaptive harmony search algorithm for optimization. *Expert Systems with Applications*, *37*(4), 2826–2837. doi:10.1016/j.eswa.2009.09.008

Wang, F., Yu, P. L. H., & Cheung, D. W. (2014). Combining technical trading rules using Particle Swarm Optimization. *Expert System with Applications, Elsevier*, *41*(6), 3016–3026. doi:10.1016/j.eswa.2013.10.032

Wang, H., & Keerthipala, W. W. L. (1998). Fuzzy-neuro approach to fault classification for transmission line protection. *IEEE Transactions on Power Delivery*, *13*(4), 1093–1104. doi:10.1109/61.714467

Wang, J. Z., Wang, R. C., Li, F., Jiang, M. W., & Jin, D. W. (2005). EMG signal classification for myoelectric teleoperating a dexterous robot hand. In *Proceedings of 2005 IEEE Engineering in Medicine and Biology 27th Annual Conference*. Shanghai, China: IEEE. doi:10.1109/IEMBS.2005.1615841

Wang, L., Pan, J., & Jiao, L. (2000). The immune algorithm. *Tien Tzu Hsueh Pao*, *28*(7), 74–78.

Wang, X., Gao, X. Z., & Ovaska, S. J. (2009). Fusion of clonal selection algorithm and harmony search method in optimization of fuzzy classification systems. *International Journal of Bio-inspired Computation*, *1*(1), 80–88. doi:10.1504/IJBIC.2009.022776

Wang, X., Gao, X. Z., & Zenger, K. (2015). The Overview of Harmony Search. In *An Introduction to Harmony Search Optimization Method* (pp. 5–11). Springer International Publishing.

Wegener, J., Baresel, A., & Sthamer, H. (2002). Suitability of Evolutionary Algorithms for Evolutionary Testing. *Proceedings of the 26th Annual International Computer Software and Applications Conference*. doi:10.1109/CMPSAC.2002.1044566

Wei, F., Li, W., & Liu, S. (2010). IRANK: A rank-learn-combine framework for unsupervised ensemble ranking. *Journal of the American Society for Information Science and Technology*, *61*(6), 1232–1243.

Weihong, W., Wei, R., & Qu, L. (2010). *Fuzzy decision tree construction with Gene Expression Programming*. IEEE. doi:10.1109/ISKE.2010.5680877

Compilation of References

Wei, L., & Zhao, M. (2005). A niche hybrid genetic algorithm for global optimization of continuous multi modal functions. _Applied Mathematics and Computation, 160_(3), 649–661. doi:10.1016/j.amc.2003.11.023

Weiss, M. S., Jabs, A., & Hilgenfeld, R. (1998). Peptide bonds revisited. _Nature Structural & Molecular Biology, 5_(8), 676–676. doi:10.1038/1368 PMID:9699627

Wen, X., & Fuhrman, S. (1998). Large-scale temporal gene expression mapping of central nervous system development. Proc. Natl. Acad. Sci. USA, Neurobiology, 95(1), 334-339.

Whisstock, J. C., & Lesk, A. M. (2003). Predictions of protein function from protein sequence and structure. _Quarterly Reviews of Biophysics, 36_(03), 307–340. doi:10.1017/S0033583503003901 PMID:15029827

Wojtczak, P., Amaral, T. G., Dias, O. P., Wolczowski, A., & Kurzynski, M. (2009). Hand movement recognition based on biosignal analysis. _Journal of Engineering Applications of Artificial Intelligence, 22_(4-5), 608–615. doi:10.1016/j.engappai.2008.12.004

Wolfram, S. (1984). Universality and complexity in cellular automata. _Physica D. Nonlinear Phenomena, 10_(1-2), 1–35. doi:10.1016/0167-2789(84)90245-8

Wolfram, S. (1986). _Theory and Applications of Cellular Automata_. Singapore: World Scientific.

Wolpert, D. H., & Macready, W. G. (1997). No free lunch Theorems for Optimization. _IEEE Transactions on Evolutionary Computation, 1_(1), 67–82. doi:10.1109/4235.585893

Wongthanavasu, S., & Sadananda, R. (2000). _Pixel-level Edge Detection Using a Cellular Automata-Based Model. In Advances in Intelligent Systems: Theory and Applications_ (Vol. 59, pp. 343–351). IOS Press.

Wu, B., Zheng, Y., Liu, S., & Shi, Z. (2002). CSIM: a document clustering algorithm based on swarm intelligence. _Proceedings of the 2002 congress on Evolutionary Computation_, 477–482.

Wu, M. S., Jeng, J. H., & Hsieh, J. G. (2006). Schema Genetic Algorithm for fractal Image Compression. _Engineering Applications of Artificial Intelligence, Elsevier, 20_(4), 531–538. doi:10.1016/j.engappai.2006.08.005

Wu, Y., Chun-nian, Z., Zhang-can, H., & Zong-yue, W. (2008). An improved gene expression programming(GEP) algorithm based on classification. _Proceeding of 3rd International Conference on Innovative Computing Information and Control (ICICIC'08)_. doi:10.1109/ICICIC.2008.145

Xiang, W., An, M., Li, Y., He, R., & Zhang, J. (2014). An improved global-best harmony search algorithm for faster optimization. _Expert Systems with Applications, 41_(13), 5788–5803. doi:10.1016/j.eswa.2014.03.016

Xie, X. L., & Beni, G. (1991). A Validity Measure for fuzzy Clustering. _IEEE Transactions on Pattern Analysis and Machine Intelligence, 13_(8), 841–847. doi:10.1109/34.85677

Xiong, X., & Tan. (2004). Similarity-Driven Cluster Merging Method for Unsupervised Fuzzy Clustering.*Proceedings of the 20th Conference in Uncertainty in Artificial Intelligence*, 611-627.

Yadav, P., Kumar, R., Panda, S. K., & Chang, C. S. (2012). An intelligent tuned harmony search algorithm for optimization. *Information Science, 196*, 47–72. doi:10.1016/j.ins.2011.12.035

Yan, S. Y. (1998). An Introduction to Formal Languages and Machine Computation. Singapore: World Scientific Publishing Co. Pte.

Yang, Chuang, & Yang. (2010). IG-GA: A Hybrid Filter/Wrapper Method for Feature Selection of Microarray Data. *Journal of Medical and Biological Engineering, 30*(1), 23–28.

Yang, Chuang, Ke, & Yang. (2008). A Hybrid Feature Selection Method for Microarray Classification. *International Journal of Computer Science, 35*(3), 285-290.

Yang, Chuang, Li, & Yang. (2008). Information gain with chaotic genetic algorithm for gene selection and classification problem. *IEEE International Conference on Systems, Man and Cybernetics*, 1128-1123.

Yang, C.-S., Chuang, L.-Y., Ho, C.-H., & Yang, C.-H. (2008). Microarray Data Feature Selection Using Hybrid GA-IBPSO. *Trends in Intelligent Systems and Computer Engineering, Lecture Notes in Electrical Engineering, 6*, 243–253. doi:10.1007/978-0-387-74935-8_18

Yang, X. S. (2009). Firefly algorithm for multimodal optimization. *Stochastic Algorithm: Foundations and Applications, 5792*, 169–178. doi:10.1007/978-3-642-04944-6_14

Yang, X. S. (2010). *A New Metaheuristic Bat-Inspired Algorithm*. Springer Berlin.

Yang, X. S. (2010). A new metaheuristic bat-inspired algorithm. *Nature Inspired Cooperative Strategies for Optimization, 284*, 65–74. doi:10.1007/978-3-642-12538-6_6

Yang, X. S., Cui, Z., Xiao, R., Gandomi, A. H., & Karamanoglu, M. (Eds.). (2013). *Swarm intelligence and bio-inspired computation: theory and applications*. Newnes. doi:10.1016/B978-0-12-405163-8.00001-6

Yang, X. S., & Deb, S. (2009). Cuckoo search via levy flights.*World Congress on Nature & Biologically Inspired Computing*, 210-214. doi:10.1109/NABIC.2009.5393690

Yang, X. S., Hosseini, S. S. S., & Gandomi, A. H. (2012). Firefly Algorithm for solving nonconvex economic dispatch problems with valve loading effect. *Applied Soft Computing, Elsevier, 12*(3), 1180–1186. doi:10.1016/j.asoc.2011.09.017

Yang, X.-S., & Deb, S. (2010). Engineering optimization by cuckoo search. *International Journal of Mathematical Modelling and Numerical Optimization, 1*(4), 330–343. doi:10.1504/IJMMNO.2010.035430

Yazama, Y., Mitsukura, Y., Fukumi, M., & Fukumi, N. (2004). Analysis and recognition of wrist motions by using multidimensional directed information and EMG signal. In *Proceedings of Fuzzy Information, 2004. Processing NAFIPS '04. IEEE Annual Meeting of the*. Banff, Alberta: IEEE.

Compilation of References

Yazama, Y., Mistukura, Y., Fukumi, M., & Akamatsu, N. (2003). Feature analysis for the EMG signals based on the class distance. In *Proceedings of Computational Intelligence in Robotics and Automation, 2003*. Kobe, Japan: IEEE. doi:10.1109/CIRA.2003.1222292

Yildiz, A. R. (2008). Hybrid taguchi-harmony search algorithm for solving engineering optimization problems. *Journal of Industrial Engineering: Theory. Applications and Practice, 15*(3), 286–293.

Yildiz, A. R., & Ozturk, F. (2010). Hybrid taguchi-harmony search approach for shape optimization. In Z. W. Geem (Ed.), *Recent Advances In Harmony Search Algorithm* (pp. 89–98). Springer. doi:10.1007/978-3-642-04317-8_8

Youssef, O. A. (2004a). A novel fuzzy-logic-based phase selection technique for power system relaying. *Electric Power Systems Research, 68*(3), 175–184. doi:10.1016/j.epsr.2003.06.006

Youssef, O. A. (2004b). Combined fuzzy-logic wavelet-based fault classification technique for power system relaying. *IEEE Transactions on Power Delivery, 19*(2), 582–589. doi:10.1109/TPWRD.2004.826386

Youssef, O. A. (2009, March). An optimised fault classification technique based on Support-Vector-Machines. In *Proceedings of Power Systems Conference and Exposition, IEEE/PES* (pp. 1-8). doi:10.1109/PSCE.2009.4839949

Yu, J., & Qian, J. (2012). Students creativity modeling with gene expression programming. In *Proceeding of International Conference on Computer Science and Electronics Engineering*. IEEE.

Yuan, Q., Qian, F., & Du, W. (2010). A hybrid genetic algorithm with the Baldwin effect. *Information Sciences, Elsevier, 180*(5), 640–652. doi:10.1016/j.ins.2009.11.015

Yuan, X., Zhao, J., Yang, Y., & Wang, Y. (2014). Hybrid parallel chaos optimization algorithm with harmony search algorithm. *Applied Soft Computing, 17*, 12–22. doi:10.1016/j.asoc.2013.12.016

Yuce, B., Packianather, M. S., Mastrocinque, E., Pham, D. T., & Lambiase, A. (2013). Honey bees inspired optimization method: The Bees Algorithm. *Insects, 4*(4), 646–662. doi:10.3390/insects4040646 PMID:26462528

Yudong, Z., & Lenin, W. (2009). Stock Market Prediction of S&P 500 via combination of Improved BCO approach and BP Neural network. Expert Systems with Applications, 36, 8849-8854.

Zalzala, A. M. S., & Chaiyaratana, N. (2000). Myoelectric signal classification using evolutionary hybrid RBF-MLP networks. In *Proceedings of Evolutionary Computation*. La Jolla, CA: IEEE. doi:10.1109/CEC.2000.870365

Zhang, B., Pan, Q. K., Zhang, X. L., & Duan, P. Y. (2015). An effective hybrid harmony search-based algorithm for solving multidimensional knapsack problems. *Applied Soft Computing, 29*, 288–297. doi:10.1016/j.asoc.2015.01.022

Zhang, D., Huang, Y., Zhi, J., & Zhang, D. (2009). Discovery of mineralization predication classification rules by using gene expression programming based on PCA. *Proceeding of Fifth International Conference on Natural Computation*. doi:10.1109/ICNC.2009.367

Zhang, D., Zhang, J., Cheng, R., & Zhang, W. (2011). A combination forecasting method based on GEP. *Proceeding of 2011 Fourth International Conference on Business Intelligence and Financial Engineering*. DOI doi:10.1109/BIFE.2011.1

Zhang, G., & Lu, H. (2006). Hybrid real coded genetic algorithm with quasi simplex technique. *International Journal of Computer Science and Network Security, 6*(10), 246–255.

Zhang, Q., Zhou, C., Xiao, W., & Nelson, P. C. (2007). Improving gene expression programming performance by using differential evolution. *Proceeding of Sixth International Conference on Machine Learning and Applications*. doi:10.1109/ICMLA.2007.62

Zhang, S. Y. (2001). A Brief Introduction to Complex Systems and Complexity Science. *Journal of Qingdao University, 16*(4), 25–28.

Zhang, X., Wang, T., Luo, H., Yang, J. Y., Deng, Y., Tang, J., & Yang, M. Q. (2010). 3D Protein structure prediction with genetic tabu search algorithm. *BMC Systems Biology, 4*(1). doi:10.1186/1752-0509-4-S1-S6 PMID:20522256

Zhao, Xie, Jiang, Cai, Liu, & Hirzinger. (2005). Levenberg-Marquardt based neural network control for a five-fingered prosthetic hand. In *Proceedings of the 2005 IEEE International Conference on Robotics and Automation*. Barcelona, Spain: IEEE.

Zhao, F., Liu, Y., Zhang, C., & Wang, J. (2015). A self-adaptive harmony PSO search algorithm and its performance analysis. *Expert Systems with Applications, 42*(21), 7436–7455. doi:10.1016/j.eswa.2015.05.035

Zhao, X., & Tang, J. (2010, March). Query-focused Summarization Based on Genetic Algorithm. In *2010 International Conference on Measuring Technology and Mechatronics Automation* (pp. 968-971). IEEE. doi:10.1109/ICMTMA.2010.429

Zhao, Y., Zhou, H., & Li, M. (2010). *Gene Expression Programming Model for Determining Location in Wireless LANs*. IEEE. doi:10.1109/WICOM.2010.5601087

Zipf, G. K. (1949). *Human Behaviour and the Principle of Least Effort: an Introduction to Human Ecology*. Addison-Wesley.

Zou, D., Gao, L., Wu, J., & Li, S. (2010). Novel global harmony search algorithm for unconstrained problems. *Neurocomputing, 37*(16-18), 3308–3318. doi:10.1016/j.neucom.2010.07.010

Zwanzig, R., Szabo, A., & Bagchi, B. (1992). Levinthals paradox. *Proceedings of the National Academy of Sciences of the United States of America, 89*(1), 20–22. doi:10.1073/pnas.89.1.20 PMID:1729690

About the Contributors

D. P. Acharjya received his PhD in computer science from Berhampur University, India. Currently he is working as a Professor in the School of Computing Science and Engineering, VIT University, Vellore, India. He has authored many national and international journal papers, book chapters, and five books to his credit. Additionally he has edited four books to his credit. He is reviewer of many international journals such as Fuzzy Sets and Systems, Knowledge Based Systems, and Applied Soft Computing. He has been awarded with Gold Medal from NIT, Rourkela; Eminent Academician Award from Khallikote Sanskrutika Parisad, Berhampur, Odisha; and Outstanding Educator and Scholar Award from National Foundation for Entrepreneurship Development, Coimbatore; The Best Citizens of India Award from the International Publishing House, New Delhi. Dr. Acharjya is actively associated with many professional bodies like CSI, ISTE, IMS, AMTI, ISIAM, OITS, IACSIT, CSTA, IEEE and IAENG. He was founder secretary of OITS Rourkela chapter. His current research interests include rough sets, formal concept analysis, knowledge representation, data mining, granular computing, bio-inspired computing, and business intelligence.

Anirban Mitra is presently associated with VITAM, Berhampur as Associate Professor and Head in the Department of Computer Science & Engineering. He has authored around 40 national and international journal/conference papers and few book chapters to his credit. He is in technical review committee of near about 8 reputed conferences and journals. Now, he is handling Industrial projects as a honorary consultant and also associated with a funded research project at I.I.T. Kharagpur. He has 08 years plus of regular experience which also includes teaching- as visiting faculty at Khallikote Govt. (Auto.) College and Berhampur University, academic guide, research and handling administrative responsibilities like as a regular Examiner for UG and PG courses. His present research field are Rough sets, Knowledge Representation, Social Network, Data Mining and Graph Mining.

* * *

Rakesh Chandra Balabantaray is currently working as Associate Professor in the Department of Computer Science & Engineering, and Dean (Academics) at IIIT Bhubaneswar, Odisha, India. He did his Masters in Computer Science in the year 2001 and Ph.D. in Computer Science in the year 2008 from Utkal University, Odisha, India. He was born in the year 1978. He has more than eighty publications in various reputed journals and conferences. His major area of research is Artificial Intelligence, Natural Language Processing & Information Retrieval.

P. K. Nizar Banu is faculty from Department of Computer Applications, B. S. Abdur Rahman University, Chennai, India. She received M. Sc., and M. Phil., degrees in Computer Science from Periyar University, Salem, Tamil Nadu, India. Also she received M.C.A degree from the Same University. She is a University Rank Holder in M. Sc., and University Gold Medalist in M. Phil. Her research interests include Rough Sets, Fuzzy Systems, Web Mining, and Image Processing. She has published several research papers in the areas like Web Usage Mining, Rough Sets, Clustering Gene expression patterns and feature selection in reputed International Journals and Conferences.

J. Belwin Edward was born in 1977. He received his B.E., Degree in electrical engineering from Manonmaniam Sundaranar University, Tamilnadu, India in 1999. M.E. degree in Power Systems from Annamalai University, Tamilnadu, India in 2002 and PhD from Anna University, Chennai in 2013. He has more than 14 years of experience in teaching and research. His major scientific interest is focused on Power system optimization and protection, optimal location of FACTS and DG devices, Renewable Energy Systems.

Avagaddi Prasad was born in India in 1989. He received B.Tech degree from JNTU Kakinada, Andhra pradesh in 2011 and M.Tech degree from GITAM University, Andhra Pradesh in 2013. He is currently a PhD candidate in School of Electrical Engineering, VIT University, Tamil Nadu, India. His research interests are power system protection, fault analysis, power quality and soft computing techniques.

Arunkumar Chinnaswamy received his M.Tech in Computer Science and Engineering from Vellore Institute of Technology University, Tamilnadu, India in 2006 and his B.E in Computer Science and Engineering from Bharathiar University, Tamilnadu, India. He is currently working as an Assistant Professor in the Department of Computer Science and Engineering, Amrita University, Tamilnadu, India. He is responsible for starting "Institution of Electronics and Telecommunication Engineers"(IETE) student forums in all engineering colleges and polytechnics in Tamilnadu under the jurisdiction of IETE Coimbatore center which expands its wings to more than 12 districts in Tamilnadu. He has also inaugurated student forums and delivered technical and non-technical lectures in more than 50 engineering colleges in Tamilnadu.He also assisted the Amrita University in conducting a one day tutorial in the area of Network Security in association with Symantec Corporation at IIT Madras during May 2010 as a part of IFIP-Networking 2010.He is also appointed as the Organizing Secretary for the International Conference on Distributed Computing and Networking 2014 which is one of the top 10 conferences in the world to be hosted at Amrita in 2014. He is an institutional member of Computer Society of India, Coimbatore chapter and also a member of IETE and Machine Intelligence Research Labs, USA. He has published more than 15 papers in leading national and international conferences and journals. He is in the reviewer board of International Journal of Fuzzy Systems (Springer), Computer Methods and Programs in Biomedicine (Elsevier) and Knowledge Based Systems (Elsevier).

Kedar Nath Das is currently working as an Assistant Professor at National Institute of Technology, Silchar, Assam, INDIA in the Department of Mathematics since 2010. He has awarded with Ph. D. Degree from the Indian Institute of Technology, Roorkee, India in 2008. During Ph.D. he was awarded with MHRD Scholarship from Govt. of India. He has around 45 publications in refereed International journals and International conferences. Dr Das has 4 books/book chapters to his credit. He has organized one International Conference in 2014 and 3 STTPs/Workshops too at NIT Silchar. His research focuses on designing efficient hybrid evolutionary algorithms to solve real life problems in Science and Engineering. Apart from this, he has also guided 3 PhD scholars and now 2 are ongoing.

Mohammad Kiani-Moghaddam was born and raised in Junqan, Shahr-e Kord, Iran, in 1986. He received the B.Sc. degree with first class honors in Electrical Engineering from the Islamic Azad University of Najafabad (IAUN), Isfahan, Iran, and the M.Sc. degree with first class honors in Electrical Engineering from the Shahid Beheshti University (SBU), Tehran, Iran. His research interests include power quality, smart electrical grid applications, operations & planning of power systems, as well as artificial intelligence and optimization theory.

Baddrud Laskar did his B.Tech. fron Dept of ECE NERIST, presently he is pursuing MTech from NIT Silchar. This chapter is part of his B. Tech. thesis under the supervision of Professor Majumder. His research interest includes gene expression programming, evolutionary computing, and optimization.

Brojo Kishore Mishra is an Associate Professor in the Department of IT and Institutional IQAC Coordinator, C. V. Raman College of Engineering (Autonomous),

Bhubaneswar, Odisha, India. He is the Regional Student Coordinator (2016-17), CSI Region – IV, India. Also he is the IEEE Day 2016 Ambassador for IEEE Kolkata Section. He has received his Ph. D. (Computer Science) from Berhampur University in 2012 and has supervised more than 08 M. Tech. thesis and currently guiding 04 Ph.D research scholars in the area of Data Mining, Opinion Mining, Soft Computing and Security. Dr. Mishra has published more than 25 research papers in international journals and conference proceedings and 3 invited book chapters. He serves as Guest Editor in IJKDB, IJSE, IJACR, and IJRSDA special issue journals and an editorial board member of many international journals. He is associated with a CSI funded research project as a Principal Investigator. He was the Regional Convener of CSI YITP 2015-16, CSI State Student Coordinator (2015-16), Jury Coordination Committee Member of All IEEE Young Engineers' Humanitarian Challenge (AIYEHUM 2015) project competition, organized by IEEE Region 10 (Asia pacific) and IEEE Day 2015 Ambassador for IEEE Kolkata section.

Rajashree Mishra currently working as Assistant Professor in Depart of Mathematics, School of Applied Sciences, KIIT University, Bhubaneswar, Odisha. Prior to that she was working as Assistant Professor in Mathematics in VITAM College of Engineering, Vishakhapatnam, Andhrapradesh. She received her Ph. D Degree from KIIT University in 2014 and completed M.Sc Degree in Mathematics in the year 1999 from Utkal University, Bhubaneswar. Her areas of research interest are Evolutionary Computing which specifically includes (Genetic Algorithm and Bacterial Foraging Optimization), Fuzzy probabilistic Programming, and Multi-objective non linear optimization. She is having publications in reputed journals. She has presented research papers and participated in many National and International Conference of repute. She is also the Reviewer to International Conferences like: 4th international conference on Soft Computing for Problem solving (SocProS-2014) and 5th international conference on Soft Computing for Problem solving (SocProS-2015).

Sushruta Mishra has completed his M.Tech degree from IIIT Bhubaneswar. Currently he is working as an Assistant Professor in the departtment of Computer Science and Engineering of C. V. Raman College of Engineering, Bhubaneswar. He is also contnuing his Ph.D(CSE) in KIIT University.

Subrata Paul is currently working as Assistant Professor in the VIGNAN Institute of Technology and Management, Berhampur (Odisha). He had completed his B.E(CSE) from VTU – Belgaum, Karnataka in 2010 and M.Tech(CS) from Berhampur University in the year 2013. His research area includes Social Network Analysis, Computational Intelligence and Cloud Computing. He had several publications at national and international levels, both in journals and conferences including papers in IEEE and Elsevier conference. He had an experience of nearly 4.5 years in teaching undergraduate courses and 1 year in handling post graduate classes. He usually teaches papers like Compiler Design, Formal Languages and Automata Theory, Software Engineering, Computer Network, Artificial Intelligence and Programming in C Language.

Geethanjali Purushothaman received her B.E. degree in Electrical and Electronics Engineering from University of Madras, Tamilnadu, India in 2001. She obtained M. Tech in Electrical Drives and Control from Pondicherry Engineering College, Puducherry, India in 2004. She received her Ph. D degree from VIT University, Vellore, India in 2012. Her Ph.D thesis has been nominated for "Best Thesis" by Indian National Academy of Engineering (INAE). She received grants from the Department of Science and Technology (DST), Government of India. She also received Fulbright-Nehru Academic and Professional Excellence Fellowship for 2014-15. Her research interests include bio-signal and image processing, pattern recognition, development of assistive devices, biomechanics and application of renewable energy in assistive devices.

Rasmita Rautray received her B.Tech degree from Utkal University, India in 2003 and M.Tech degree in 2006 from the same University. She is currently working as Asst. Professor in the Department of Computer Science and Engineering at Institute of Technical Education and Research(I.T.E.R.), Siksha O' Anusandhan University. She is having a teaching experience of more than 10 years . Her major research Interests includes Information Retrieval.

K. Ravi was born in 1972. He received his B.E., Degree in electrical engineering from University of Madras, Chennai, India in 1993. M.E. degree in Power Systems from Annamalai University, India in 2001 and PhD from Anna University, Chennai in 2012. He has more than 21 years of experience in teaching, research and industry. His major scientific interest is focused on optimal location of FACTS devices, Reactive power control and modelling and simulation of power system dynamics including intelligent system applications.

Andrews Samraj is from the faculty of computing of Mahendra Engineering College. He obtained his Ph.D., in Information Technology from Multimedia University, Malaysia, and his Post Doctorate from World Scientific Engineering Association and Helnic naval academy, Greece. His research interests include Bio-Medical Engineering, Robotics, Cybernetics, and Bio-Metrics. He has organized many workshops on wearable technologies worldwide. He has been involved in various advanced research projects in wearable and cyborg technologies.

Raghunath Satpathy received his M.Sc in Botany from Berhampur University science, India; (Post M.Sc) Advanced P.G Diploma in Bioinformatics from University of Hyderabad and M. Tech. degree in Biotechnology from VIT University, Vellore India. He has submitted the thesis for the degree for the doctor of philosophy in Biotechnology of Sambalpur University, Odisha India. Currently he is working as an Assistant professor in M.I.T.S Engineering College Odisha, India. He is having more than 8 years of experiences in both teaching and research. He has authored many national and international journal papers and five book chapters to his credit. In addition to this Mr. Satpathy is associated with many professional bodies like ISRD, APCBEES, SCIEI, SABT, OBA. His current research interests include computational analysis of protein structure, data mining, biological database and analytical tool development.

Mojtaba Shivaie was born and raised in Semnan, Iran, in 1986. He received the B.Sc. degree with first class honors in Electrical Engineering from the Semnan University, Semnan, Iran, in 2008. He also received the M.Sc. degree with first class honors and Ph.D. degree with first class honors, both in Electrical Engineering, from the Shahid Beheshti University, A.C., Tehran, Iran, in 2010 and 2015, respectively. His research activities mostly concentrate on studying power systems planning, competitive electricity markets analysis, power systems reliability, smart electrical grids applications, and optimization methodologies.

Ramakrishnan Srinivasan received the B.E. degree in Electronics and Communication Engineering in 1998 from the Bharathidasan University, Trichy, and the M.E. degree in Communication Systems in 2000 from the Madurai Kamaraj University, Madurai. He received his PhD degree in Information and Communication Engineering from Anna University, Chennai in 2007. He has 14 years of teaching experience and 1 year industry experience. He is a Professor and the Head of the Department of Information Technology, Dr. Mahalingam College of Engineering and Technology, Pollachi, India. Dr. Ramakrishnan is a Reviewer of 23 International Journals such as IEEE Transactions on Image Processing, IET Journals(Formally IEE), ACM Computing Reviews, Elsevier Science, International Journal of Vibration and Control, IET Generation, Transmission & Distribution, etc. He is in the editorial board of 7 International Journals. He is a Guest Editor of special issues in 3 International Journals including Telecommunication Systems Journal of Springer. He has published 109 papers in international, national journals and conference proceedings. Dr. S. Ramakrishnan has published a book on Wireless Sensor Networks for CRC Press, USA and two Books on Speech Processing for InTech Publisher, Croatia and a book Computational Techniques for Lambert Academic Publishing, Germany. He has also reviewed 3 books for McGraw Hill International Edition and 10 books for ACM Computing Reviews. He was the convenor of IT board in Anna University of Technology- Coimbatore Board of Studies(BoS). He is guiding 10 PhD research scholars. His biography has been included in Marquis Whos's Who in the World 2012 & 2016 edition. His areas of research include digital image processing, soft computing, human-computer interaction, wireless sensor network and cognitive radio.

Hrudaya Kumar Tripathy has completed his Ph.D in Computer Science from Berhampur University & M.Tech (CSE) from Indian Institute of Technology, Guwahati. He is having 15 years of teaching & research experience. Currently he is working as an Associate Professor in the School of Computer Engineering, KIIT University, Bhubaneswar.

Index

3D structure 316, 318-321, 325, 329-330, 334, 336

A

ACO 2, 5, 123, 136, 144, 160, 302, 305, 327-328
Amino Acids 317-325, 329, 336-337
artificial bee Colony optimization 150
Assistive Device 293-294, 296, 301-302, 310

B

Bacterial Foraging Optimization 2, 230, 237, 239, 264, 266, 268
bagging 41, 48, 51, 222-223, 225
Benchmark Functions 125, 230, 245, 248-249, 266, 268
Bioinspired Algorithms 316, 323, 336
Bio Inspired Computing 150, 153, 180
Bio-signals 293

C

Cellular Automata 204, 207, 210-214, 216, 218-228
Chemo-Taxis 230, 232, 237, 268
Classification 36-37, 39, 41-45, 47-50, 53, 64, 67-70, 94-95, 124, 146-147, 153, 157, 174-176, 178-179, 181-184, 186-189, 191-194, 196-203, 212, 222-225, 276, 278-279, 285-288, 290-296, 299, 301-302, 304, 307-315, 319
Computational biology 68, 93, 112, 319, 331

computational complexity 139, 310, 316, 321, 323, 330
Cuckoo Search 2, 39, 123, 125, 129-132, 140, 142, 144, 149

D

Decision stump 41, 51
Differential Evolution 71, 73, 78-79, 88-89, 91-92, 150, 157, 164-165, 180, 263, 265, 280, 292

E

Economic Load Dispatch 249-251, 263, 266, 268
Electroencephalogram (EEG) 315
Electromyogram (EMG) 315
Estimation 182, 186, 191, 193, 237, 266, 287, 290, 293, 302, 304, 307, 310-312, 333
Evolutionary Algorithms 74, 135, 150, 154, 180, 222, 231-232, 268, 277, 302, 311

F

Fault 158, 181-203, 310
Fault Classification 181-184, 186-189, 191-194, 196-203
Fault Detection 181, 198-199, 201-202
Feature Extraction 294, 315
Feature Reduction 294-295, 302, 308, 310, 315

Feature Selection 41-46, 53-56, 64, 67-70, 119, 173, 290, 293-296, 301-305, 307, 309-311, 313, 315

Formal Languages 228

Fuzzy PSO 123, 134-135, 144

G

Gene Clustering 123, 145, 147

Gene Expression Programming (GEP) 269-270, 277-278, 291

Genetic Algorithm (GA) 2, 37, 70-71, 73-75, 84, 90-92, 126, 167-169, 171, 173, 180, 186-188, 202-203, 230, 232, 234, 241-243, 249, 263-271, 273-274, 276-277, 295, 302-303, 324

Genetic Operators 91, 269, 272-274, 277, 283, 303, 335

Genetic Programming (GP) 269-270, 278, 302

Genetic Search 44, 150, 157, 164, 171, 235

H

Harmonic search 71, 73, 86, 88

Harmony memory 1, 4, 34, 86-87, 132-133

Harmony Search 1, 3-4, 7, 33-40, 89-90, 92, 123-124, 132-133, 140, 144-145, 147

harmony search algorithm 1, 3-4, 7, 33-40, 89, 145

homogeneous music players 1, 11, 15, 17, 22

HP Model 320-322, 327-328, 333-334, 336

Hybridization 42, 148, 184, 232, 241-242, 263, 268, 329

I

Image processing 204, 219, 221, 227, 295, 300, 335

improvisation 1, 4, 6-13, 15-18, 20-25, 32, 86

information extraction 69, 93, 113-116, 119-120, 204

Information gain (IG) 41, 45

Information processing 69, 204, 290, 313

inhomogeneous music players 16, 23, 33

intelligent systems 34-36, 67, 70, 89, 93, 145, 198, 228

J

J48 41, 49

L

low energy conformation 316

M

melody search algorithm 1, 4, 8, 34, 38

N

naive bayes 41, 47-48, 174

Neural Network 36, 184, 188, 198-199, 203, 264, 267, 278, 291, 295-300, 307-309, 311-315

Neuromuscular Disorder 315

O

Off Lattice Model 322, 329, 336

optimal solution 33, 78, 127, 153, 155-156, 160, 188, 231, 233, 241-242, 245, 259, 295, 306, 320, 329

Optimization Method 37, 92, 127, 156, 323, 326, 329-330, 336

P

Particle swarm optimization 2, 36, 67, 71, 73, 80, 84, 89-90, 124, 126-127, 134, 147, 150, 160, 173, 178-179, 231, 249, 266-267, 295, 302-303, 312, 323, 326-327, 333-334

Pattern Recognition 33, 145, 265, 267, 293-294, 297, 302, 307-308, 310, 312-313, 315, 335

Pearsons coefficient 41

player memory 4, 22-24

Power Balance Constraint 249, 254, 268

Power System 181-183, 191, 193, 195-
196, 198, 201-203, 237, 266, 295
Prohibited Operating Zones 249, 256, 261,
268
Prosthetic Hand 308, 312, 315
Protective Relaying 198, 201
Protein Structure Prediction 316, 319-321,
323, 329-337

R

Ramp Rate Limit 249-250, 256, 260, 268
random forest 41, 48-50, 308

S

Serial processing 204
Soft Computing 33-34, 38-40, 67-68, 89-
92, 160, 183, 202, 264-267, 269
Soft Computing Techniques 183

Swarm Intelligence 2, 4, 73, 88, 118, 136,
147-148, 150, 153-154, 157-159, 177-
179, 232, 266, 313, 336
Symphony orchestra search algorithm 1,
6, 11, 32

T

Three Dimensional Structures 337
Transmission Line Protection 200-201,
203
Transmission System 181, 191, 193, 198

W

web crawler 93-94, 97-98, 100-103, 109,
116, 118-120

Purchase Print + Free E-Book or E-Book Only*

Purchase a print book through the IGI Global Online Bookstore and receive the e-book for free or purchase the e-book only! Shipping fees apply.

www.igi-global.com

Recommended Reference Books

ISBN: 978-1-4666-7456-1
© 2015; 2,072 pp.
List Price: $1,880

ISBN: 978-1-4666-5864-6
© 2014; 570 pp.
List Price: $276

ISBN: 978-1-4666-5198-2
© 2014; 398 pp.
List Price: $164

ISBN: 978-1-4666-4679-7
© 2014; 387 pp.
List Price: $140

ISBN: 978-1-4666-6567-5
© 2015; 461 pp.
List Price: $160

ISBN: 978-1-4666-6493-7
© 2015; 643 pp.
List Price: $180

*IGI Global now offers the exclusive opportunity to receive a free e-book with the purchase of the publication in print, or purchase any e-book publication only. You choose the format that best suits your needs. This offer is only valid on purchases made directly through IGI Global's Online Bookstore and not intended for use by book distributors or wholesalers. Shipping fees will be applied for hardcover purchases during checkout if this option is selected.

Should a new edition of any given publication become available, access will not be extended on the new edition and will only be available for the purchased publication. If a new edition becomes available, you will not lose access, but you would no longer receive new content for that publication (i.e. updates). The free e-book is only available to single institutions that purchase printed publications through IGI Global. Sharing the free e-book is prohibited and will result in the termination of e-access.

Publishing Information Science and Technology Research Since 1988

www.igi-global.com   ✉ Sign up at www.igi-global.com/newsletters   f facebook.com/igiglobal   t twitter.com/igiglobal

Stay Current on the Latest Emerging Research Developments

Become an IGI Global Reviewer for Authored Book Projects

Premier Reference Source

Solutions for High-Touch Communications in a High-Tech World

Premier Reference Source

Advanced Research on Biologically Inspired Cognitive Architectures

Premier Reference Source

Workforce Development Theory and Practice in the Mental Health Sector

Premier Reference Source

Resource Management and Efficiency in Cloud Computing Environments

The overall success of an authored book project is dependent on quality and timely reviews.

In this competitive age of scholarly publishing, constructive and timely feedback significantly decreases the turnaround time of manuscripts from submission to acceptance, allowing the publication and discovery of progressive research at a much more expeditious rate. Several IGI Global authored book projects are currently seeking highly qualified experts in the field to fill vacancies on their respective editorial review boards:

Applications may be sent to:
development@igi-global.com

Applicants must have a doctorate (or an equivalent degree) as well as publishing and reviewing experience. Reviewers are asked to write reviews in a timely, collegial, and constructive manner. All reviewers will begin their role on an ad-hoc basis for a period of one year, and upon successful completion of this term can be considered for full editorial review board status, with the potential for a subsequent promotion to Associate Editor.

If you have a colleague that may be interested in this opportunity, we encourage you to share this information with them.

www.igi-global.com

InfoSci®-Books

A Database for Progressive Information Science and Technology Research

Maximize Your Library's Book Collection!

Invest in IGI Global's InfoSci®-Books database and gain access to hundreds of reference books at a fraction of their individual list price.

The InfoSci®-Books database offers unlimited simultaneous users the ability to precisely return search results through more than 75,000 full-text chapters from nearly 3,400 reference books in the following academic research areas:

Business & Management Information Science & Technology • Computer Science & Information Technology
Educational Science & Technology • Engineering Science & Technology • Environmental Science & Technology
Government Science & Technology • Library Information Science & Technology • Media & Communication Science & Technology
Medical, Healthcare & Life Science & Technology • Security & Forensic Science & Technology • Social Sciences & Online Behavior

Peer-Reviewed Content:
- Cutting-edge research
- No embargoes
- Scholarly and professional
- Interdisciplinary

Award-Winning Platform:
- Unlimited simultaneous users
- Full-text in XML and PDF
- Advanced search engine
- No DRM

Librarian-Friendly:
- Free MARC records
- Discovery services
- COUNTER4/SUSHI compliant
- Training available

To find out more or request a free trial, visit:
www.igi-global.com/eresources

IGI Global
Proudly Partners with

---

eContent Pro specializes in the following areas:

Academic Copy Editing
Our expert copy editors will conduct a full copy editing procedure on your manuscript and will also address your preferred reference style to make sure your paper meets the standards of the style of your choice.

Expert Translation
Our expert translators will work to ensure a clear cut and accurate translation of your document, ensuring that your research is flawlessly communicated to your audience.

Professional Proofreading
Our editors will conduct a comprehensive assessment of your content and address all shortcomings of the paper in terms of grammar, language structures, spelling, and formatting.

IGI Global Authors, Save 10% on eContent Pro's Services!
Scan the QR Code to Receive Your 10% Discount

The 10% discount is applied directly to your eContent Pro shopping cart when placing an order through IGI Global's referral link. Use the QR code to access this referral link. eContent Pro has the right to end or modify any promotion at any time.

Email: customerservice@econtentpro.com

econtentpro.com

Become an IRMA Member

Members of the **Information Resources Management Association (IRMA)** understand the importance of community within their field of study. The Information Resources Management Association is an ideal venue through which professionals, students, and academicians can convene and share the latest industry innovations and scholarly research that is changing the field of information science and technology. Become a member today and enjoy the benefits of membership as well as the opportunity to collaborate and network with fellow experts in the field.

IRMA Membership Benefits:

- **One FREE Journal Subscription**
- **30% Off Additional Journal Subscriptions**
- **20% Off Book Purchases**
- Updates on the latest events and research on Information Resources Management through the IRMA-L listserv.
- Updates on new open access and downloadable content added to Research IRM.
- A copy of the Information Technology Management Newsletter twice a year.
- A certificate of membership.

IRMA Membership $195

Scan code or visit **irma-international.org** and begin by selecting your free journal subscription.

Membership is good for one full year.

Encyclopedia of Information Science and Technology, Third Edition (10 Vols.)

Mehdi Khosrow-Pour, D.B.A. (Information Resources Management Association, USA)
ISBN: 978-1-4666-5888-2; **EISBN:** 978-1-4666-5889-9; © 2015; 10,384 pages.

The **Encyclopedia of Information Science and Technology, Third Edition** is a 10-volume compilation of authoritative, previously unpublished research-based articles contributed by thousands of researchers and experts from all over the world. This discipline-defining encyclopedia will serve research needs in numerous fields that are affected by the rapid pace and substantial impact of technological change. With an emphasis on modern issues and the presentation of potential opportunities, prospective solutions, and future directions in the field, it is a relevant and essential addition to any academic library's reference collection.

Take An Extra

30% Off[1]

[1] 30% discount offer cannot be combined with any other discount and is only valid on purchases made directly through IGI Global's Online Bookstore (www.igi-global.com/books), not intended for use by distributors or wholesalers. Offer expires December 31, 2016.

Free Lifetime E-Access with Print Purchase

Take 30% Off Retail Price:

Hardcover with Free E-Access:[2] **$2,765**
~~List Price: $3,950~~

E-Access with Free Hardcover:[2] **$2,765**
~~List Price: $3,950~~

E-Subscription Price:

One (1) Year E-Subscription: $1,288
~~List Price: $1,840~~

Two (2) Year E-Subscription: $2,177
~~List Price: $3,110~~

Recommend this Title to Your Institution's Library: www.igi-global.com/books

[2] IGI Global now offers the exclusive opportunity to receive free lifetime e-access with the purchase of the publication in print, or purchase any e-access publication and receive a free print copy of the publication. You choose the format that best suits your needs. This offer is only valid on purchases made directly through IGI Global's Online Bookstore and not intended for use by book distributors or wholesalers. Shipping fees will be applied for hardcover purchases during checkout if this option is selected.

The lifetime of a publication refers to its status as the current edition. Should a new edition of any given publication become available, access will not be extended on the new edition and will only be available for the purchased publication. If a new edition becomes available, you will not lose access, but you would no longer receive new content for that publication (i.e. updates). Free Lifetime E-Access is only available to single institutions that purchase printed publications through IGI Global. Sharing the Free Lifetime E-Access is prohibited and will result in the termination of e-access.

www.igi-global.com/infosci-ondemand

InfoSci®-OnDemand

Continuously updated with new material on a weekly basis, InfoSci®-OnDemand offers the ability to search through thousands of quality full-text research papers. Users can narrow each search by identifying key topic areas of interest, then display a complete listing of relevant papers, and purchase materials specific to their research needs.

Comprehensive Service

- Over 81,600+ journal articles, book chapters, and case studies.
- All content is downloadable in PDF format and can be stored locally for future use.

No Subscription Fees

- One time fee of $37.50 per PDF download.

Instant Access

- Receive a download link immediately after order completion!

Database Platform Features:

- Comprehensive Pay-Per-View Service
- Written by Prominent International Experts/Scholars
- Precise Search and Retrieval
- Updated With New Material on a Weekly Basis
- Immediate Access to Full-Text PDFs
- No Subscription Needed
- Purchased Research Can Be Stored Locally for Future Use

"It really provides an excellent entry into the research literature of the field. It presents a manageable number of highly relevant sources on topics of interest to a wide range of researchers. The sources are scholarly, but also accessible to 'practitioners'."

– Lisa Stimatz, MLS, University of North Carolina at Chapel Hill, USA

"It is an excellent and well designed database which will facilitate research, publication and teaching. It is a very very useful tool to have."

– George Ditsa, PhD, University of Wollongong, Australia

"I have accessed the database and find it to be a valuable tool to the IT/IS community. I found valuable articles meeting my search criteria 95% of the time."

– Lynda Louis, Xavier University of Louisiana, USA

Recommended for use by researchers who wish to immediately download PDFs of individual chapters or articles.

www.igi-global.com/e-resources/infosci-ondemand

IGI GLOBAL
DISSEMINATOR of KNOWLEDGE
www.igi-global.com

Printed in the United States
By Bookmasters